TUDOR ENGLAND A
C000285903

Themes in Focus
Published titles

Jonathan Barry and Christopher Brooks
THE MIDDLING SORT OF PEOPLE: Culture, Society
and Politics in England, 1550–1800

Patrick Collinson and John Craig
THE REFORMATION IN ENGLISH TOWNS, 1500–1640

Moira Donald and Tim Rees
REINTERPRETING REVOLUTION IN TWENTIETH-CENTURY EUROPE

Susan Doran and Glenn Richardson
TUDOR ENGLAND AND ITS NEIGHBOURS

Christopher Durston and Jacqueline Eales
THE CULTURE OF ENGLISH PURITANISM, 1560–1700

Paul Griffiths, Adam Fox and Steve Hindle
THE EXPERIENCE OF AUTHORITY IN EARLY-
MODERN ENGLAND

Tim Harris
THE POLITICS OF THE EXCLUDED, *c.* 1500–1850
POPULAR CULTURE IN ENGLAND, *c.* 1500–1850

Roy Porter and Marie Mulvey Roberts
PLEASURE IN THE EIGHTEENTH CENTURY

D. Power and N. Standen
FRONTIERS IN QUESTION: EURASIAN BORDERLANDS,
700–1700

R.W. Scribner and Trevor Johnson
POPULAR RELIGION IN GERMANY AND
CENTRAL EUROPE, 1400–1800

Themes in Focus Series

Series Standing Order

ISBN 0–333–71707–4 hardcover
ISBN 0–333–69353–1 paperback
(outside North America only)

You can receive future titles in this series as they are published by placing a standing
order. Please contact your bookseller or, in case of difficulty, write to us at the address
below with your name and address, the title of the series and the ISBN quoted above.

Customer Services Department, Macmillan Distribution Ltd
Houndmills, Basingstoke, Hampshire RG21 6XS, England

Tudor England and its Neighbours

Edited by

Susan Doran
and
Glenn Richardson

palgrave
macmillan

First published 2005 by
PALGRAVE MACMILLAN
Houndmills, Basingstoke, Hampshire RG21 6XS and
175 Fifth Avenue, New York, N.Y. 10010
Companies and representatives throughout the world.

PALGRAVE MACMILLAN is the global academic imprint of the Palgrave
Macmillan division of St. Martin's Press, LLC and of Palgrave Macmillan Ltd.
Macmillan® is a registered trademark in the United States, United Kingdom
and other countries. Palgrave is a registered trademark in the European
Union and other countries.

ISBN 0–333–94611–1 hardback
ISBN 0–333–94610–3 paperback

This book is printed on paper suitable for recycling and made from fully
managed and sustained forest sources.

A catalogue record for this book is available from the British Library.

Library of Congress Cataloging-in-Publication Data

Tudor England and its neighbours / edited by Susan Doran and Glenn
Richardson.
p. cm. — (Themes in focus)
Includes bibliographical references and index.
ISBN 0–333–94611–1 — ISBN 0–333–94610–3 (pbk.)
1. Great Britain – History – Tudors, 1485–1603. 2. Great Britain –
Foreign relations – 1485–1603. 3. England – Civilization – 16th century.
4. Tudor, House of. I. Title: Tudor England and its neighbors. II. Doran,
Susan. III. Richardson, Glenn. IV. Themes in focus (Palgrave Macmillan
(Firm))

DA315.T754 2004
942.05—dc22   2004056540

10 9 8 7 6 5 4 3 2 1
14 13 12 11 10 09 08 07 06 05

Printed in China.

For Alan and Jane

CONTENTS

CONVENTIONS AND ABBREVIATIONS

CONVENTIONS

The spelling of quotations in the text have been modernised but original spellings are used in the notes. The English form of foreign names and places are used whenever they exist. Unless stated otherwise, place of publication of books is London.

ABBREVIATIONS

AE	Archives du Ministère des Affaires Etrangères, Paris
AN	Archives Nationales de France, Paris
BL	British Library, London
BIHR	*Bulletin of the Institute of Historical Research*
Bod. L	Bodleian Library, Oxford
CSP. Dom.	Robert Lemon and M. A. E. Green (eds), *Calendar of State Papers Domestic* (6 vols, London, 1856–72)
CSPF Eliz.	Joseph Stevenson *et al.* (eds), *Calendar of State Papers, Foreign Series Elizabeth* (23 vols, 1853–1950)
CSP Milan	A. B. Hinds (ed.), *Calendar of State Papers and Manuscripts ... in the Archives ... of Milan* (1 vol., 1912)
CSP. Scot.	Jos. Bain *et al.* (eds), *Calendar of State Papers Relating to Scotland and Mary, Queen of Scots* (13 vols, 1898–1969)
CSP. Sp.	G. A. Bergenroth *et al.* (eds), *Calendar of Letters, Despatches, and State Papers Relating to Negotiations between England and Spain Preserved in the Archives at Simancas and Elsewhere,* (15 vols, 1862–1954)
CSPV	R. Brown *et al.* (eds), *Calendar of State Papers and Manuscripts Relating to English Affairs, Existing in the Archives and Collections of Venice etc.* (38 vols, 1864–1940)

DNB   *The Dictionary of National Biography*
EHR   *The English Historical Review*
Hall   Edward Hall, *The Union of the Two Noble and Illustre Famelies of York and Lancastre*, edited by Charles Whibley (2 vols, 1904)
HJ   *The Historical Journal*
HMC   Historical Manuscripts Commission Reports
LP   J. S. Brewer, J. Gairdner and R.H. Brodie (eds), *Letters and Papers, Foreign and Domestic of the Reign of Henry VIII* (21 vols in 33 parts, 1862–1910)
PRO   Public Record Office
Rymer   T. Rymer (ed.), *Foedera, Conventions, Litterae, et Cujuscumque Generis Acta Publica Inter Reges Angliae et Alios Imperatores, Reges, Pontifices, Principes vel Communitates etc.* (20 vols, 1727–35)
SP   State Papers
STC   *A Short Title Catalogue of Books ... 1475–1640* by A. W. Pollard, G. R. Redgrave *et al.* (1946)
St. P.   *State Papers of Henry VIII* (11 vols, 1830–52)

NOTES ON CONTRIBUTORS

Pauline Croft is Professor of History at Royal Holloway University of London. She has published widely on British History in the sixteenth and seventeenth centuries. Her recent publications include *King James* (Palgrave 2003) and *Patronage Culture & Power: The Early Cecils 1550–1612* (Yale 2002).

John M. Currin holds a PhD in history from the University of Minnesota and has published several articles on the foreign policy of Henry VII. Currently he is Director of Fact-checking and Research in the White House Office of Presidential Speechwriting.

Susan Doran is a Lecturer in Early-Modern History at Christ Church, Oxford. She has written many books and articles on both Elizabeth I and Tudor foreign policy. Her most recent works include *England and Europe in the Sixteenth Century* (Palgrave 1999) and *The Myth of Elizabeth I* (Palgrave 2003) co-edited with Thomas Freeman.

Paul E. J. Hammer is the author of *The Polarisation of Elizabethan Politics: the Political Career of Robert Devereux, 2nd Earl of Essex, 1585–1597* (1999) and *Elizabeth's Wars: War, Government and Society in Tudor England, 1544–1604* (2003), as well as numerous articles. He currently teaches at the University of St Andrew's.

Rory McEntegart is the Registrar/Director of Academic Affairs at the American College Dublin, Ireland. He is the author of *Henry VIII, The League of Schmalkalden, and the English Reformation* (Woodbridge 2002)

David Potter is Reader in French History at the University of Kent. He is the author of *War and Government in the French Provinces: Picardy 1470–1560* (1993); *A History of France 1460–1560: The Emergence of a Nation*

State (1995); *The French Wars of Religion* (1997); *Un homme de guerre au temps de la renaissance: la vie et les lettres d'Oudart du Biez* (2001); *France in the Later Middle Ages, 1200–1500* (2003) as well as numerous articles on the French nobility, politics and diplomacy in the Renaissance period.

Glenn Richardson is Senior Lecturer in History at St Mary's College Strawberry Hill, University of Surrey. He is the author of *Renaissance Monarchy, The Reigns of Henry VIII, Francis I and Charles V* (Hodder Arnold 2002) and has written a number of articles on different aspects of Anglo-French relations in the early-Tudor period.

David J. B. Trim is Lecturer in History at Newbold College and Honorary Research Fellow at the University of Reading. He is the author of many articles on early-modern European history and the editor of *The Chivalric Ethos and the Development of Military Professionalism* (Brill 2003) and *Cross, Crown and Community: Religion, Government and Culture in Early-Modern England* (Peter Lang 2004).

1

INTRODUCTION – TUDOR MONARCHS AND THEIR NEIGHBOURS

Glenn Richardson and Susan Doran

This book is about how the political leaders of Tudor England related to their counterparts in Europe, and how the rulers of neighbouring countries related to them. It covers a period that has acquired something of a mythic status in the history of English foreign policy. Thanks to the work of historians in the late-nineteenth and early-twentieth centuries, Tudor monarchs (especially Henry VIII and Elizabeth) have traditionally been held responsible for setting down the fundamental principles of 'modern' English foreign policy and for building up England's maritime strength, which became the basis of Britain's rise as a world power. Thus, it was claimed, Henry VIII was driven by a form of British nationalism to seek the union of England, Scotland, Ireland and Wales under his kingship; and both Henry VIII and Elizabeth actively tried to effect a 'balance of power' in Europe in order to prevent any one state dominating the Continent and threatening England's independence. Of even greater importance Henry VIII, building on the work of his father, was said to have founded the royal navy, while Elizabeth's sea-captains developed its technological edge, evolved aggressive maritime policies, defeated the imposing Spanish Armada, and took the first steps towards acquiring an overseas empire.[1]

This late nineteenth-century paradigm remained influential well into the middle of the twentieth century, and has not entirely disappeared even now. R. B. Wernham's *Before the Armada*, printed in 1966 and sadly not updated thereafter, contained much that was new, but his overarching theme was 'the development of an English foreign policy' along these lines. Under the Tudors, Wernham explained, England 'felt her way towards an insular policy based upon sea power and regarding herself as an island "off" rather than "of" Europe – the foreign policy that was to be characteristic of modern England until the growth of air power'.[2] Like his late-nineteenth century predecessors, Wernham detected in the Tudor period the conscious evolution of a set of foreign-policy principles and practices which were to become the basis of Britain's later relationship with European powers: in particular, the maintenance of a 'balance of power' on the Continent and a sense of an imperial destiny in the wider world.

Although some historians absorbed Wernham's approach within the interpretative frameworks of their own particular accounts of the Tudor period,[3] most historians today sniff out the 'Whig history' in such views, and are suspicious of grand patterns which explain England's relations with its neighbours in this (and probably any other) period of history.[4] They emphasise, instead, the continuities between the outlook of late-medieval kings and early-Tudor monarchs, and the *ad hoc* nature of political decision-making.[5] Indeed, Wernham himself subsequently published two volumes on foreign relations in the post-Armada period, which tried to avoid the central problem of his earlier work.[6] In *After the Armada*, for example, he described Elizabethan foreign policy as 'the story of day-to-day pressures of events and circumstances', and devoted his attention to 'the continental and military side of the Elizabethan war with Spain' rather than the naval engagements which had dominated earlier histories.[7]

As shall be seen, the chapters in this volume reflect this modern trend. The contributors implicitly question whether or not the Tudor monarchs even had a 'foreign policy' in the modern sense, since there is little evidence that they engaged in long-term strategic thinking beyond maintaining a number of general aims (like defence) common to all monarchs, and not particular to themselves. Like his contemporaries, Henry VIII's main aim was to make himself count among European princes while his younger daughter was not alone in determining that, so far as possible, her relations with foreign princes would not undermine or threaten her religious settlement and her personal authority at home. At different times in their reigns, neither of these monarchs knew precisely how these goals were to be achieved in practice although they and their advisors certainly knew that craft, guile, military strength, display and even simple bombast would be necessary for England to hold its own in the turbulent arena of Europe. Of 'policie', in its original sense, they were well aware but as John Currin, Pauline Croft and Susan Doran in particular show, the emphasis in foreign relations was more often on crisis-management than on shaping long-term principles of diplomatic conduct.

Besides Wernham, the most significant historian writing during the middle years of the last century was Garrett Mattingly, whose *Catherine of Aragon* (1950) and *Renaissance Diplomacy* (1955) were landmark studies of the workings of international relations in the late-fifteenth and early-sixteenth centuries.[8] Amongst his many insights, Mattingly recognised that they were profoundly dynastic, rather than nationalistic, in nature. The fact that this now seems obvious is a testament to the force of his arguments about the need to cast off nineteenth-century preoccupations with nationalism as the driving force in the diplomacy of the Renaissance. Mattingly, moreover, saw in late fifteenth-century Italy the birth of a 'new' or 'Renaissance' diplomacy in which trained resident diplomats, armed with formal instructions and received according to strict protocols, took over as intermediaries between states from the occasional ambassadors of an earlier, more rough and ready, age.[9] His work stimulated new research into the English diplomatic corps which has thrown great light on the workings of international relations.[10] David Potter's chapter (Chapter 5) in this collection makes another important contribution to our understanding in this area.

Finally, Wallace B. MacCaffrey deserves mention as one of the giants who has worked on England's relations with Europe. Between 1969 and 1992 MacCaffrey completed three important studies of the Elizabethan regime, all of which contained an in-depth narrative of its foreign relations. These volumes provided an excellent coverage of events and the decisions taken by Elizabeth's government, mainly as revealed in the State Papers.[11]

Wernham, Mattingly and MacCaffrey were all fully aware that foreign policy was always formulated in a domestic context and subject to a wide range of political, economic and social influences. The complexity of foreign policy formulation, however, has been lost in some popular biographies and textbooks, where it appears that relations with other nations were largely isolated from the aspirations, anxieties and even some of the more important institutions of the Tudor state such as the council and the court. The contributors to this volume recognise their debt to Wernham, Mattingly and MacCaffrey, but seek to extend their narrative and go beyond their interpretations. The contributors argue strongly that foreign relations should be treated holistically as part of a complex interplay with commerce, religion, the ideology of monarchy and domestic politics. The conduct of Tudor 'diplomacy' may well have been confined to a small group of people around the monarch but the formation of policy towards other states usually involved much larger groups of people than has often been apparent. Different pressure groups and interested parties – ambassadors, merchants, theologians and preachers – voiced their opinions about how the Crown should deal with the international situation, both privately and publicly. The chapter by David Potter takes on board the opinions and influence of mid-Tudor ambassadors and politicians, while that of Pauline Croft (Chapter 7) examines the interests of Elizabethan merchants.

The contributors to this volume also open up new areas of discussion in the light of recent developments in other branches of Tudor historiography. The origins of the English Reformation and its impact on political and social life have been extensively reappraised in the last two decades. Hitherto, however, except in the reign of Elizabeth, religious debate as a factor in determining foreign policy has rarely been discussed in any detail.[12] Here it is a major theme in the chapters by Rory McEntergart, David Potter, Pauline Croft and David Trim, but it is important to note that not all authors reach the same conclusion about the significance of religion in decision-making. Other contributors, meantime, address the question of how far religious attitudes had an impact upon the events with which they deal, while Glenn Richardson also proposes that Henry VIII's good relationship with Francis in the early 1530s helped propel the English king into schism.

Similarly, developments over the last 20 years in the history of early-modern mentalities are here brought to bear on the question of England's foreign relations. Consequently, types of evidence previously considered only marginally relevant or immaterial to foreign policy are also given greater weight. This includes evidence of the personal interactions between sovereigns themselves and their representatives. Richardson and Doran in particular demonstrate that the rituals of diplomatic intercourse, the terms of address used by sovereigns to each other, the exchange of gifts and the treatment of ambassadors were not, as they have usually been described, merely the 'window dressing' of Mattingly's 'new' diplomacy. Instead, they should be seen as products of the chivalric ethos to which sixteenth-century princes, including female ones, habitually subscribed and, as such, important aspects of monarchs' self-presentation to their friends and rivals in the international community. In an age of 'personal monarchy' relations between sovereigns could, at times, militate against strategic factors with positive, or negative, consequences for a kingdom's security and standing in the world.

As well as introducing evidence not usually considered by earlier generations, this volume demonstrates that fresh material is still coming to light. Stephen Alford's recent study of the 1560s has already shown how a greater emphasis on using manuscript sources and a new appreciation of the importance of drafts and corrections in such sources, can yield new insights not afforded to enquiries more heavily reliant upon edited, printed, primary sources such as the *Calendars of State Papers*.[13] Examining the originals of royal council working papers and minutes, diplomatic letters, instructions to ambassadors and their reports home, demonstrates not only the true complexity of foreign policy formulation but also the value assumptions made by the nineteenth-century compilers of the State Papers in the National Archives. Much of the material which they excised from the printed volumes as irrelevant or trivial actually reveals a good deal about the thought processes and priorities of the rulers of Tudor England and their advisors. Research in private family archives and on other sources not used in compiling the State Papers has also produced new evidence which challenges the accepted accounts of England's foreign relations.

These chapters also present evidence drawn directly from original documents in English and foreign archives. Much of the latter material, which illuminates attitudes to England in other countries, has never before been transcribed, much less translated into English. Even where it has, the translations have often been partial and potentially misleading. The work of McEntegart is particularly noteworthy in this respect as it brings to a new readership a wealth of material contained in German and Scandinavian archives and demonstrates that while Tudor foreign relations were conducted almost exclusively with Europe, they extended well beyond the westernmost regions of the Continent.

The chapters in this volume are ordered chronologically. As they have been arranged according to the conventional periodisation but with different themes and approaches, the fact that there is a little overlap between some of them in their opening sections may be advantageous for the reader in offering different perspectives on events. The chapters are of two types. John Currin, Glenn Richardson, David Potter and Pauline Croft offer broadly re-interpretive accounts of Tudor international relations over longer time spans. Each presents original archival research synthesised with familiar published material and raises questions about the accepted narratives of the period with which it deals. Rory McEntegart, David Trim, Susan Doran and Paul Hammer offer more detailed studies of shorter periods or particular themes in foreign policy. Their approach is also re-interpretive, using new material in specific contexts to challenge the orthodoxies of their subject. All contributors are interested in high-lighting the events and ideas which are of key importance in better appre-ciating the making and meaning of Tudor foreign relations.

We begin with Henry VII, the first Tudor monarch, who is convention-ally described as having little interest in foreign relations and no stomach for a fight. John Currin finds a very different Henry; one who cared greatly about his international prestige, but was also very careful to avoid damaging his position in Europe through unnecessary war. Thus, although he was conscious of the Plantagenet patrimony to which he had become heir as king of England, he was also well aware that wars were expensive and of his own relative poverty. These considerations did not, however, make him passive about asserting his honour as a European prince. Currin explains that rather than withdrawing from the uncer-tainties of an immensely complex international situation, Henry sought to increase the value of his alliance to European monarchs by settling disharmony at home and then using England's revived military potential to his own strategic and financial advantage.

Henry rebuilt the Anglo-Burgundian alliance in relations with Maximilian and his son Philip the Handsome, while taking such advan-tage as he could of endemic quarrels between France and the duchy of Brittany during the reign of Charles VIII. By 1489, he had also forged an alliance with the Most Catholic Kings of Spain. After 1492, Henry VII maintained peaceful but ambivalent relations with Charles VIII and his successor Louis XII, on the basis of his receiving a sizeable annual French pension, yet he never completely ruled out war if circumstances demanded it. Without jeopardising this Anglo-French accord, Henry actively supported such efforts at Italian diplomatic unity as were made in the face of French hostilities towards the kingdom of Naples and the duchy of Milan. At the same time, he kept his relations with James IV of Scotland reasonably peaceful, if not always very friendly. Henry's politic dealings with European princes established patterns which lasted for half a century. Henry VII is too often hidden in the shadow cast by his aggres-sive and ebullient son Henry VIII, who did indeed kick over the traces in many ways during his first six years as king. Yet on closer inspection it is clear that in relations with Europe, as in much else, Henry VII was the shrewder king and he led where his son would eventually follow.

The chapters dealing with Henry VIII concentrate on his relations with France and with the German Protestants. Chapters 3 and 4 argue that although historians' traditional concerns with strategic advantages, the protection and enhancement of trade, and the defence of England are properly part of any understanding of Henry's foreign relations, they are only part. Both chapters present evidence of how the personality of the king and the sixteenth-century ideology of monarchy which shaped it, profoundly influenced the conduct of his international relations. They highlight the great personal interest Henry took in his relations with foreign rulers and show how encounters with them or their representatives bore not only upon his foreign policy, but also upon his sense of his role as monarch of England, particularly in the context of the Reformation.

Glenn Richardson's chapter (Chapter 3) argues that throughout his reign, Henry VIII's principal personal desire was for international renown. This ambition was focused primarily on winning territory in France or, if that proved impracticable, then at least commanding the respect of the French king, either through 'wars of magnificence' or through 'magnificent peace'. The latter was orchestrated by Cardinal Wolsey in 1514, 1518 and 1527 and is often described as having died with him. Richardson argues that in fact the model of magnificent peace-making was followed explicitly by Henry himself in 1532. Richardson also demonstrates that maintaining peace with France was Henry's only realistic platform for action in Europe after the break with Rome, even though Anglo-French relations during the 1530s were always difficult. It was only in the mid-1540s when he had sufficient money and again had restored passably good relations with the Emperor Charles V, that the innately conservative Henry could vent his frustrations with Francis I in another war and compel the French king once more to acknowledge his military and political strength.

Henry's dealings with the princes of the Protestant League of Schmalkalden are considered by Rory McEntegart (Chapter 4) to have been prompted as much by the king's genuine interest in their religious ideas as by any desire to find friends and allies against the emperor. In 1533 and 1538 Henry sought 'conference and conversation' with members of the League, not simply as the by-play in the main diplomatic game between England, France and the Empire but because he wanted to understand their experiences of codifying religious beliefs and implementing changes to religious practice. Henry's hope was that once an understanding between them had been reached, alliances might follow but he always remained somewhat sceptical about their prospects. Not so others, whose more evangelical agendas at first ran parallel with, and then outran, the king's. Cromwell's efforts to forge an alliance with the League were finally hamstrung not by the king's indifference to their theology, as has been the traditional view, but precisely because he took it so seriously. As the League's ambassadors in England made clear in 1538, in order to obtain its support Henry would have to accept the League's theology as a whole. Henry worked solidly for a month on his response to the ambassadors' proposals (itself evidence against the conventional view that he was merely toying with them), copiously annotating the working papers of the seven-man committee set up to discuss the League's theology. In the end Henry would not concur with their beliefs and negotiations collapsed leaving Cromwell to try to revive a Protestant alliance with Cleves with disastrous consequence for all concerned, chiefly himself.

In reviewing the period from the accession of Edward VI to the end of the first decade of Elizabeth's reign David Potter, in Chapter 5, highlights changes in England's diplomacy and foreign relations. He points out that as a result of the youth of Edward and the gender of Mary, there could be no revival of Henry VIII's 'chamber diplomacy', and he reveals how the shift in religious orthodoxies during these years influenced the choice of ambassadors and even the extent of England's diplomatic network on the Continent. For the same reasons, foreign affairs also became the subject of wider discussion than would ever have been possible under Henry VIII. The absence of a strong, male, monarch, Potter argues, 'prompted a more complex and dispassionate analysis of international affairs', while an increased emphasis on defining and defending England's various religious 'settlements' between 1547 and 1559 allowed, and perhaps even provoked, an increased willingness among royal councillors to debate the best course in foreign policy. This willingness also extended beyond the confines of court and council; shaping public opinion – using mainly proclamations and sympathetic tracts – became increasingly important from the 1540s onwards. As Potter demonstrates by reference to these writings, it was during the period from the late 1540s to the early 1560s that, alongside strategic and personal factors, the defence of 'true religion' became an important theme in debates, official and unofficial, about England's international relations.

David Trim in Chapter 6 takes up many of the same themes in his analysis of Elizabeth's interventions in Scotland, France and the Netherlands between 1558 and 1585. He contests directly the traditional view of Elizabeth as purely *politique* in her dealings with the sovereigns of Northern Europe. Trim argues that rather than being reluctant in principle to support Protestants abroad, Elizabeth and her ministers maintained two consistent objectives: to aid fellow believers in securing liberty of conscience and to build up an alliance that could deter Catholic powers from oppressing the Reformed. The modest success of their initial military initiatives confirmed the view, first articulated in the early 1550s, that England really was in no position to tackle Spain or France directly. So between 1567 and 1585 a policy of covert but active support was followed until that support became more and more exposed and Philip II decided to take a decisive step to end it. Throughout her reign, Trim argues, religious motivations were at the forefront in policy making as Elizabeth intervened in a range of ways to try to secure or support friendly and godly regimes wherever she could.

Trim's argument is not fully embraced by Pauline Croft, who in Chapter 7 strongly criticises the tendency of many historians to see war between Catholic Spain and Protestant England as an inevitable conflict between religious irreconcilables, slowly but steadily escalating almost from the moment of Elizabeth's accession. Croft argues that there is no evidence for this assumption. As she observes, William Cecil thought the world 'marvellously changed' in 1589 precisely because he experienced the war in which England was then engaged as a sudden and unwelcome reversal of its traditional friendship with Iberian monarchs. Philip II probably felt the same, even as he gave orders to assemble the Grand Armada of 1588. His strong personal belief and sense of obligation to defend Catholicism were vital aspects of his kingship but these were inseparable from his sense of obligation to defend the patrimony handed to him by his father. So intertwined were these motivations that Philip felt he did one by doing the other yet his father had counselled that friendship with England was helpful in achieving these ambitions. Moreover, the alliance with England was only one of a vast range of considerations in governing Philip's empire. Croft argues that British (and some Spanish) historians have exaggerated the importance of England to Philip. As his father surely knew, the fact that there were tensions and frictions in relations with the English monarch did not negate the value of the alliance. The tensions were heightened in the 1570s by English privateering but even this did not stop a renewal of the alliance under the treaty of Bristol of 1574 with beneficial consequences for English trade in Iberia and beyond. Any 'drift' to war only began in 1585 with Philip's embargo on Dutch, Hanseatic and English ships in Spain. The English victory over the Armada the following year defeated a unique Spanish attempt to invade England. The naval campaigns of 1596, 1597 and that launched by the young Philip III in 1601 were not, contrary to the established view, reprises of the 1588 invasion but much smaller enterprises designed to restore Spanish honour by harassing English shipping, raiding harbours or aiding the Irish rebels but none of them came to anything.

It was not Elizabeth but her successor James I who restored peace with Spain. The relationship between these two monarchs is explored by Susan Doran in Chapter 8. The conventional view of this relationship is that it was almost the converse of that between Elizabeth and Philip II. Whereas with the king of Spain Elizabeth is said to have had good relations initially and then a steady decline, those with the king of Scots were very difficult until the signing of the treaty of Berwick in 1586. Virtually overnight, this agreement ended centuries of hostility between the two kingdoms and brought them into a relative harmony based on mutual self- interest. Doran finds a rather less cosy and more complex relationship. Elizabeth and James did co-operate but mutual hostility and suspicion continued between them over Scotland's military potential and Elizabeth's often patronising attitude to her Scottish cousin. Their formal and informal relations during the 1590s were characterised by the use of highly calibrated language, by gift exchanges, by the use of resident ambassadors and special embassies (often of close personal servants alongside aristocratic representatives), and by a constant preoccupation with defending their honour as princes. Accusations of supporting rebels and recusants were felt keenly on both sides of the border as is demonstrated by the most notorious of such cases, that of the earl of Bothwell. These interchanges were used by both sides to signal approval, annoyance or a willingness to be reconciled. James had the greater skill, and perhaps the greatest need, to read these signals correctly. Thus equipped, the two sovereigns could express their aggression in circumstances where outright hostility would have been dangerous for both sides. Surprising as it may be, Elizabeth's relations with her 'loving and affectionate' cousin James recall nothing so much as those between her father and his 'good brother and friend', Francis I of France during the 1530s and constitute further evidence of the importance of royal personality and personal interaction in early-modern diplomacy.

Paul Hammer's study of the military and political career of Robert Devereux, second earl of Essex, which concludes this collection, gives a final illustration of a number of the general themes discussed in the volume. The role of Essex in debating foreign policy and as a military commander has been somewhat obscured, due largely to the reliance of traditional accounts on the State Papers, which themselves reflect the priorities of William and Robert Cecil, the two main rivals of Essex in the royal council. These papers tend either to write Essex out or to depict him as headstrong, irrational and needlessly aggressive and most historians have followed suit. Hammer discusses Essex, not as a melodramatic tragic-hero or pantomime villain, but as a man of considerable intelligence and sophistication who tried to serve his own interests by serving the queen's as he saw best.

His advocacy of an alliance with Henry IV of France, the protection and advancement of Protestantism on the continent, and war against Spain by land and sea are shown to be less quixotic than is usually supposed and born of Devereux's aristocratic mentality and his conviction that England should play a leading role in Europe, or 'Christendom' as he knew it. His network of personal connections across Europe served Elizabeth's interests, but the failure of his personal efforts and those others he supported to curb the power of Spain led to increased frustration and polarisation within and beyond the Privy Council in the late 1590s. His military command in Ireland exacerbated the situation and led to his exclusion from the council and his ill-fated insurrection against Elizabeth. Having cast Essex as a warmonger, the peace party in the council then struggled to provide the settlement with Spain to which he was apparently such an obstacle and it was left to Elizabeth's successor to bring the war to an end.

This collection of essays does not claim to offer a comprehensive account of Tudor foreign relations. Significant gaps remain, such as coverage of England's relations with Ireland and with Scotland under Henry VIII and in the mid-Tudor period. In part this is because several monographs and significant articles covering aspects of these topics have been published relatively recently.[14] More work also needs to be done on England's relations with Scandinavia, with the Baltic states and with the Holy Roman Empire as a whole. A more thorough exploration of the Tudors' relations with the Italian states, especially Venice and Mantua, is long overdue and would hopefully yield some interesting insights into English attitudes towards the politics of the Italian peninsular. Further research on the subject of foreign relations as public discourse under the Tudors could significantly increase our knowledge of the awareness of other countries, or lack of it, among the English political elite and among the people generally. It must also be hoped that the publication of the *Oxford Dictionary of National Biography* will be helpful in building up a clearer picture of exactly who were England's ambassadors abroad and serve as a useful starting point for a more thorough study of them, their networks, and their role in the public discourse of England's foreign relations.

The aim of this collection of essays on Tudor foreign policy is not to set aside recent accounts of how England saw itself in relation to the rest of Europe in the sixteenth century. Rather, the editors and contributors hope to rekindle interest and to open some new areas of debate and discussion on the subject. They want to test some of the old assumptions about what drove England's relations with the rest of Europe, and to propose some alternative suggestions about how best to interpret the evidence as it exists at the start of the twenty-first century. Ideally these essays will stimulate further research and writing after a fairly long fallow period in significant scholarly publication on the subject.

The authors of these essays hope that the collection will stimulate a better awareness among teachers and students alike of the very great importance attached to foreign relations by all Tudor monarchs, their leading advisors and to the political nation beyond the confines of the royal court and council. Perhaps some of the more hoary old clichés about Tudor foreign policy can at last be laid aside in favour of a more complicated and, we hope, more interesting account of the Tudor monarchs' relationships with their neighbours.

NOTES

1. Montagu Burrows, *The History of the Foreign Policy of Great Britain* (1895); J. R. Seeley, *The Growth of British Policy* (2 vols, Cambridge, 1987); A. F. Pollard, *Henry VIII* (1902, 1925).
2. R. B. Wernham, *Before the Armada: The Growth of English Foreign Policy 1485–1588* (1966), p. 11.
3. For example, P. S. Crowson, *Tudor Foreign Policy* (1973) and D. M. Loades, *The Tudor Navy* (Aldershot, 1992).
4. See, for example, S. Doran, *England and Europe* (1999); S. Adams, 'England and the World under the Tudors, 1485–1603' in J. Morrill (ed.), *The Oxford Illustrated History of Tudor and Stuart Britain* (Oxford,1996), pp. 397–415; D. Potter, 'Foreign Policy' in D. MacCulloch (ed.), *The Reign of Henry VIII: Politics, Policy and Piety* (1995), pp. 106–7.
5. For continuities see, for example, S. J. Gunn, 'The French wars of Henry VIII' in J. Black (ed.), *The Origins of War in Early Modern Europe* (Edinburgh,1987), pp.28–51. For the nature of policy making, see for example, Susan Doran, *Elizabeth I and Foreign Policy* (2000).
6. R. B. Wernham, *After the Armada: Elizabethan England and the Struggle for Western Europe 1588–9* (Oxford, 1984) and *The Return of the Armadas: The Last Years of the Elizabethan War against Spain, 1595–1603* (Oxford, 1994).
7. Nonetheless, Wernham does identify England's 'developing sea power' and 'the maintenance of a reasonable balance between Spain and France' as two of the features of sixteenth-century policy. Wernham, *After the Armada*, p. vii.

8. See also, G. Mattingly, *The Defeat of the Spanish Armada* (1959).

9. G. Mattingly, *Renaissance Diplomacy* (New York, 1955), esp. pp. 55–63, 121–32, 162–6.

10. C. Giry Deloison, 'La naissance de la diplomatique moderne en France et en Angleterre au debut du XVIe siecle (1475–1520)', *Nouvelle Revue du Seizième siècle* (1987); Luke MacMahon, 'The Ambassadors of Henry VIII'. Unpublished University of Kent PhD dissertation, 2000; G. M. Bell, 'Elizabethan diplomacy: the subtle revolution' in Malcolm R. Thorp and A. J. Slavin (eds), *Politics, Religion and Diplomacy in Early Modern Europe* (Kirksville, MO, 1994).

11. Wallace T. MacCaffrey, *The Shaping of the Elizabethan Regime* (1969), *Queen Elizabeth and the Making of Policy, 1572–88* (Princeton, NJ, 1981), and *Elizabeth I: War and Politics, 1588–1603* (Princeton, NJ, 1992).

12. For Elizabeth's reign, see especially E.I. Kouri, *England and the Attempts to Form a Protestant Alliance in the Late 1560s: A Case-study in European Diplomacy* (Helsinki, 1981) and Simon Adams' seminal dissertation 'The Protestant cause: religious alliance with the Europeaan Calvinist communities as a political issue in England 1585–1630'. Unpublished University of Oxford DPhil. dissertation, 1973. A book by Dr Adams on England's decision to send troops to the Netherlands is forthcoming; a taster can be found in his essay in Patrick Collinson (ed.), *The Short Oxford History of the British Isles: The Sixteenth Century* (Oxford, 2001).

13. Stephen Alford, *The Early Elizabethan Polity: William Cecil and the British Succession Crisis, 1558–1569* (Cambridge, 1998).

14. N. MacDougal, *James IV* (Edinburgh, 1989); D. Dunlop, 'The politics of peace-keeping: Anglo-Scottish relations from 1503 to 1511', *Renaissance Studies*, 8 (1994), pp. 138–61; D. M. Head, 'Henry VII's Scottish policy', *The Scottish Historical Review*, 61 (1982), pp. 1–24; R. G. Eaves, *Henry VIII and James V's Regency 1524–1528* (1987); Marcus Merriman, *The Rough Wooing* (2000); Elizabeth Bonner: *The Politique of Henri II: De Facto French Rule in Scotland, 1550–1554* (1999).

2

ENGLAND'S INTERNATIONAL RELATIONS 1485–1509: CONTINUITIES AMIDST CHANGE

John M. Currin

When Henry VII seized the throne in 1485, his new realm was little more than a second-rate power in Europe. The English monarchy had lost nearly all of the Plantagenet territories in France during the last phase of the Hundred Years' War, and could no longer summon up the financial and military resources to permit effective intervention in a long European war, although its retention of Calais meant that England was still well positioned to threaten France and thus continued to be important in the diplomatic calculus of the Continental powers. By contrast, during the second half of the fifteenth century the monarchy of France had emerged politically unified and militarily strong, successfully capturing Artois and the French duchy of Burgundy in 1477 and completing the internal territorial consolidation of its realm with the conquest of Brittany in the 1490s. By 1494, the French king, Charles VIII, felt strong enough to pursue dynastic ambitions in Naples.

The two other major players in Europe were the rulers of Spain and the Empire. The new composite kingdom of Spain, formed from the marriage of King Ferdinand of Aragon and Queen Isabella of Castile in 1469, came to challenge French expansionism along the Franco-Spanish border and in Italy. Maximilian of Austria, heir to the Emperor Frederick III, meanwhile, extended Habsburg influence into the Low Countries, by marrying Mary, the duchess of Burgundy in 1477. Both as Mary's husband until her death in 1482 and as regent of the Low Countries for their son Philip the Handsome, Maximilian consistently resisted French attempts to expand into Flanders (part of the Burgundian Netherlands)

14

and tried to recover the French-held Burgundian lands, which had been conquered by Louis XI in 1477.

What did this new complexion of Europe mean in the diplomatic thinking of England's first Tudor monarch? The long-established view is that Henry VII, recognising the profound changes of the later fifteenth century *vis-à-vis* England and France, replaced the Plantagenet militant tradition of Continental conquest with a new Tudor policy of peace and accommodation with France.[1] This view emphasises Henry's adoption of an 'Anglocentric' foreign policy, making dynastic security and England's national and commercial interests the main concerns of his diplomacy. Such a nationalist emphasis, however, pays too little attention to the interactions of Henry's evolving foreign policy within the broader inter-dynastic context of early-modern European international relations. It also stresses too much the new aspects of the Tudor policy, ignoring the elements of continuity, especially the continuing influence of the Plantagenet legacy in early-Tudor foreign policy.[2] This chapter seeks to remedy these short-comings.

HENRY VII AND FRANCE

The contrast set by historians between Henry VII's policy of peaceful accommodation with France and the medieval militant Plantagenet policy of conquest in France is overdrawn. In the first place, the Plantagenet kings had vacillated between a militant and pacific policy towards France. Edward I, Edward III and Henry V had certainly embraced the policy of armed conflict in the assertion and defence of their feudal rights and sovereign claims to Guyenne and Normandy, because the political and military conditions of the time favoured military success. However, Henry III, Richard II, Henry IV and Henry VI had gravitated towards a policy of peaceful accommodation in an attempt to stabilise Anglo-French relations and preserve their hold on French lands at times when France was stronger and more unified.[3] The Plantagenets also used their claim to the French crown as leverage to force territorial concessions from the Valois kings.[4] Henry VII's French policy exhibited the same vacillation. He revived the militant policy between 1489 and 1492; then, recognising the power and vitality of France, he shifted to a policy of peaceful accommodation. However, he left open the option of a return to the militant policy if conditions were right, and did not shelve this policy until after 1504, when his declining health made it impossible for him to contemplate seriously another war with France.

During their long conflict with France, the Plantagenets often sought
to isolate their enemy through a network of alliances; in the fifteenth century, the dukes of Burgundy and Brittany had been England's principal,
albeit fickle, allies against the French king. This Anglo-Burgundian–
Breton axis was revived briefly early in Henry VII's reign, but the Tudor
king, responding to the new political circumstances in Europe, strengthened his position by forging a dynastic and political alliance with Spain
as a counter to French power and as security for his own dynasty. When
Henry came to renew the old Anglo-Burgundian political and dynastic
alliance again in the 1500s, this was not simply a continuation of later
Plantagenet foreign policy but a shrewd alignment of England with the
rising dynastic power in Europe. The French invasion of Italy in 1494,
which created a new dynamic in European politics, added a new element
to English foreign policy: the prevention of French domination of Italy by
means of countervailing political alliances. With alliances taking on wider
European dimensions, the regular conduct of diplomacy took on increased
importance. Again Henry adapted to the new conditions. He tried to
assure his ability to send and receive envoys for the conduct of timely and
complex negotiations by making ambassadors for the first time one of the
recurrent categories of state expenditure.[5]

The first phase of Henry's French policy stemmed from his time of
exile in France, when he was preparing to invade England and capture
the throne from the Yorkist usurper, Richard III. Henry's intended invasion of 1485 was caught up in the wider war waged by Anne of Beaujeu,
regent in France for Charles VIII, against a coalition of French nobles led
by Louis, duke of Orléans and Francis II, duke of Brittany, and Maximilian
of Austria, regent of the Low Countries. Anne of Beaujeu, continuing
Louis XI's policy, was plotting to supplant the Montfort dynasty in
Brittany by asserting the rival Penthièvre claim to the duchy that the
French crown had acquired. At the same time, she was supporting the
rebellion of the Three Members of Flanders (Ghent, Bruges and Ypres)
against Maximilian, hoping to expand French influence and control over
this province. In early 1485, the anti-French Anglo-Burgundian–Breton
axis appeared to be forming again. In reaction to Richard III's decision
to send 1000 archers to Brittany, the Beaujeu regime backed Henry
Tudor's invasion of England.

Henry swore an oath promising that in exchange for French help in
the winning his 'right', he would not, as king of England, favour or assist
Duke Francis II against the king of France.[6] In July, however, a pro-French
coup d'état in Brittany ended the threat of English intervention in the

duchy and the Beaujeus promptly dropped direct support for Henry. Nonetheless, they still allowed him to borrow money, hire some demobilised French troops and French ships, and launch his invasion from a French port.[7] Although Henry won his crown without direct help from Charles VIII and the Beaujeu regime, he still acknowledged his indebtedness to the French king, and during the first years of his reign kept his solemn promise not to support the duke of Brittany. Henry formalised a truce with France, beginning 12 October 1485, and extending it to January 1489.[8] Amidst increasing tension between France and Brittany and Burgundy, Henry declared his intention to remain at peace with all.[9]

Henry's neutrality tilted the political balance in France's favour. With the Anglo-French truce in place, Anne of Beaujeu signalled her intention to assert Charles VIII's claim to Brittany when the ailing Duke Francis died. In reaction, the duke revived alliances with a group of French nobles, with Maximilian of Austria (newly elected king of the Romans) and with Ferdinand and Isabella of Spain. Maximilian sent German troops to assist Francis II in 1487, and the following year Ferdinand and Isabella despatched Spanish troops to Brittany. Francis, wanting a defensive alliance with England, reminded Henry of his protection when the Tudor was a young exile in Brittany, but in July 1486 Henry agreed only to renewal of the Anglo-Breton treaty of commerce and friendship.[10] The French invaded Brittany in 1487 and again in 1488, while Henry remained neutral.

Meanwhile in Flanders, Maximilian had unwisely reopened the Franco-Burgundian wars in June 1486. The following year, he found himself on the verge of losing most of West Flanders to the French army. Desperate to revive the Anglo-Burgundian alliance, Maximilian encouraged the Lambert Simnel conspiracy of 1487, which failed to supplant Henry. The Tudor king retaliated by embargoing English trade with the Netherlands. The following year he entered into negotiations with the Three Members of Flanders, who were at that time the most implacable of Maximilian's Flemish foes.[11]

In 1488, Francis II of Brittany and Ferdinand and Isabella put pressure on Henry to join an alliance against France. He resisted and instead sent ambassadors to France and to Brittany on a mission to broker a Franco-Breton peace.[12] In March, the Spanish sovereigns proposed a marriage between the Infanta Catherine and Arthur, Prince of Wales, if Henry agreed to wage war against France. Henry wanted the dynastic alliance, but did not want to commit himself openly to war against France.[13] Frustrated, the Breton envoys persuaded Edward Woodville, Lord Scales, governor of the Isle of Wight, to come into Brittany with 300 of his men to fight the French.[14] In part to cleanse his honour in the eyes of France, Henry sent a letter of apology to Charles VIII informing the French king of the small size of Scales's force.[15] Henry pressed on with his offer of mediation, but Anne of Beaujeu and Charles VIII, sensing victory, were not interested in peace. In July, French forces routed the Breton army at the battle of St Aubin-du-Cormier. The following month, Francis II made peace with King Charles, acknowledging himself the vassal of France, promising not to appeal for foreign help, and agreeing never to marry his daughters without the consent of the king of France. Duke Francis died three weeks later, and his twelve-year old daughter Anne became duchess under the tutelage of John of Rieux, marshal of Brittany. Henry VII's neutrality in 1485–88 stemmed partly from his preoccupation with establishing his regime and rule in England and Ireland. But his solemn promise not to assist Duke Francis against the king of France seems to have been an important factor as well, for shortly after the death of Francis II, Henry radically reversed his policy and ended his neutrality. In the autumn of 1488, he agreed to send an army into Brittany at the Bretons' expense, and to build a defensive alliance with Duchess Anne, Ferdinand and Isabella, and Maximilian.[16] The traditional view is that Henry intervened in Brittany reluctantly, tried to limit his military commitment, and wanted only to prevent the Breton ports facing the windward coast of England from falling under French control. New research, however, suggests there was more to his policy at the time. The autonomy of Brittany and continued Habsburg rule of Flanders were Henry's foremost concerns, but he had in mind as well a future campaign for recovery of Normandy and Guyenne, and even for assertion of the Plantagenet claim to the French crown.

In March 1489, Henry concluded alliances with Brittany, Burgundy and Spain. These alliances were not merely defensive and indicate that Henry was also preparing the ground for asserting the old claims against France.[17] The Anglo-Breton treaty of Redon (10 February 1489) formalised the previously agreed terms for English assistance to Brittany.[18] However, this treaty also contained an article requiring Duchess Anne and her heirs to assist the king of England and his heirs should they decide in the future to invade France and recover their rights. Furthermore, an article obliging Anne to obtain Henry's consent to her marriage challenged Charles VIII's seigneurial rights over the duchy and recalled past theoretical claims of English suzerainty over Brittany. The treaty of Dordrecht (14 February 1489) between Henry and Maximilian made no mention of military action against France but, as at least one contempo-rary realised, it signalled the revival of an Anglo-Burgundian alliance, and was a threat to the French in West Flanders, Picardy and Artois.[19] The Anglo-Spanish treaty of Medina del Campo (29 March 1489) contained the contract for marriage between Prince Arthur and the Infanta Catherine, a new commercial accord, and terms for an Anglo-Spanish offensive alliance explicitly aimed at forcing Charles VIII to surrender Normandy and Guyenne to Henry and the disputed territories of Roussillon and Cerdagne, along the Spanish border, to Ferdinand and Isabella.[20] Henry may well have been preparing for a campaign to recover Guyenne once the immediate crisis in Brittany had past. Ingredients for a successful campaign in Guyenne would be a secure and autonomous Brittany in alliance with England and Spain. The support and co-operation of a powerful Gascon noble like Alain of Albret was also important. This strategic thinking may also have been behind Henry's support for Marshal Rieux's plan to marry Anne of Brittany to Albret, despite the young duchess's vociferous opposition.

In December 1488, while Henry was busy building his coalition and assembling his army and navy, the French once more invaded Brittany, hoping to conquer the duchy before the English could intervene. Between 1489 and 1491, Henry sent three land and naval expeditions to Brittany. Instead of the reluctant belligerent portrayed by historians, Henry seemed very interested in the expeditions to Brittany. He person-ally supervised the formation of his army, and even boasted of its initial success against the French.[21]

During the spring and summer of 1489, the Anglo-Breton armies held the military advantage and had the opportunity to drive the French from the duchy. Henry's field commanders wanted to co-ordinate their attacks with a large Breton army under Marshal Rieux; however, political infight-ing within the Breton government and Duchess Anne's growing mistrust of Henry undermined the military effort and gave an opening to France's counter-diplomacy against Henry's coalition. The duchess grew more mistrustful when she learned that the English commanders had negotiated a truce with their French counterparts without her knowledge and consent, a violation of the treaty of Redon.[22]

Meanwhile, Maximilian, becoming more concerned with Habsburg dynastic interests in central Europe, wanted a truce and settlement with France. The Beaujeu regime saw its opportunity to destroy Henry's coali-tion and neutralise him. In the treaties of Frankfurt (22 July 1489) and Montilz-les-Tours (30 October 1489), the French reached an agreement

with Maximilian. At the same time, Anne of Brittany wanted to partici-
pate in multi-lateral peace negotiations in France. Ferdinand and
Isabella, preoccupied with the final assault on Granada, initiated their
own secret negotiations with Anne of Beaujeu. With Henry seeming to be
isolated, the French made peace overtures to him in late 1489 and early
1490. Henry demanded as the price for his peace, the restoration of the
Plantagenet lands in France or an annual payment of 50,000 *écus d'or* as
tribute in recognition of his claim. Charging Henry with ingratitude, the
French refused his demand.[23]

In early 1490, Pope Innocent VIII tried to broker a peace between
England and France. One view is that Henry participated in the papal
mediation hoping for a settlement, but worked on rebuilding his coalition against France in case one could not be reached.[24] Yet Henry's shifting diplomacy during this initiative suggests that he was not much
interested in a settlement, but was waiting for the opportune moment to
resurrect his anti-French alliance.[25] Fearing in the meantime a French
attack on Nantes, Anne renewed her defensive alliance with Henry, who
sent to Brittany a second naval and land force of about 4780 men.[26] Then,
it seems, the English undermined the papal envoy Chieregato's mediation at a critical moment with a raid on La Hague in Normandy.[27]
Henry's policy worked, as the French agreement with Maximilian quickly
unravelled. Accusing Charles VIII of negotiating in bad faith, Maximilian
reversed his diplomacy and, in the treaties of Woking of September 1490,
formed a defensive and offensive alliance with Henry against France.

The offensive alliance of Woking indicates Henry VII's commitment
to the militant policy of conquest in France. By it he revived the
Anglo-Burgundian–Breton axis as a defensive alliance against France,
and attempted to build a still-broader Anglo-Austro-Burgundian-Spanish
bloc. These treaties set out Henry's vision for a three-pronged invasion of
France in three years' time. Henry and Maximilian agreed to a joint invasion of France by September 1493 with the specific aim of recovering territories in France claimed by Henry, Maximilian and Philip.[28] At the same
time, Henry ratified the treaty of Medina del Campo with Spain, and
then supplemented it with a new Anglo-Spanish treaty of alliance bringing Spain into the same offensive war against France.[29]

The Woking alliances and Maximilian's proxy marriage to Duchess
Anne in December 1490 spurred the French to militant action of their
own. In April 1491, Charles VIII, now in charge of his own government,
ordered a new invasion of Brittany and his army conquered most of the
duchy by the summer. Henry sent a third military expedition, numbering

about 2800 men, but it was too weak to stem the French advance.[30] In November, Duchess Anne, despairing of any assistance from Maximilian, Henry, and Ferdinand and Isabella, made peace with Charles VIII. The following month Charles married Anne, disregarding not only his own contracted marriage to Margaret of Austria, but also Maximilian's proxy marriage to Anne.

In response to the Breton debacle, Henry advanced his timetable for war, and planned an invasion of France by June 1492. He asserted his claim to France, and revived the Plantagenet symbols of the 'dual monarchy' of England and France. Tudor historians have dismissed this display as mere window-dressing, claiming that Henry only wanted to redeem his lost honour and extort respect and money from Charles VIII. However, his extensive military and diplomatic preparations seem very excessive for mere window-dressing. On 22 November 1491, Henry concluded with Spanish envoys a new treaty for a joint Anglo-Spanish attack on France by 15 June 1492.[31] Henry tried to bring the pope and the duke of Milan into his anti-French alliance, warning them of the French desire to dominate Italy and the whole Christian Commonwealth.[32] He urged the princes and electors of the Empire to support Maximilian against the treacherous French, saying that they had to vindicate the honour of the German nation by helping Maximilian take revenge for Charles's bride snatching.[33] In December 1491, Henry – who had once proclaimed himself protector of the orphaned duchess of Brittany – now encouraged, through bribes and promises, a conspiracy among disgruntled Breton nobles to depose Anne and the new French regime.[34] This Breton Plot also entailed the surrender of Brest and Morlaix to the English so that Henry could land an army in Brittany. However, the conspiracy collapsed and in June, the French repelled an attempted English landing near Barfleur.[35] The Tudor king then diverted his land and naval forces to assist the Habsburgs in a successful siege of Sluis, a base which threatened English and Dutch shipping in the Channel.

The fickleness of Henry's allies, however, undermined his war against France.[36] Ferdinand and Isabella, accusing their ambassador of exceeding his instructions, refused to attack France. Maximilian, it seemed to Henry, failed him as well. The official Tudor story, told by Polydore Vergil, is that Henry, his army fully assembled and ready for war, suddenly learned from his ambassador returning from the Habsburg court that Maximilian was unprepared for war. Unable to withdraw without loss of honour, Henry went forward with the invasion of France but he opened secret peace negotiations with Charles VIII.[37] This story lacks credibility. During 1491 and 1492,

Henry and Maximilian exchanged resident ambassadors and frequent
messages, and thus Henry would have known the state of Maximilian's military preparations long before he had committed himself to the invasion of
France. Indeed, Henry's councillors doubted Maximilian's readiness. They
urged the king to postpone the invasion until his allies were better prepared, but the king rejected this advice. Both Maximilian and Henry carried
on negotiations with Charles VIII in the summer of 1492.[38] In the Anglo-
French peace concluded in early November, Henry accepted from Charles
750,000 *écus d'or*, or two-thirds of his initial demand. When the English army
landed at Calais, Charles concluded that Henry had used negotiations
deceptively to put him off his guard.[39]

Historians have argued that because Henry launched his invasion of
France so late in the season he did not have in mind any strategic objective in France, and was trying to secure his honour and a profit. However,
the deliberations of Henry's council of war show that the invasion began
with the goal of capturing Boulogne-sur-Mer, the strategic anchor of
France's defences along its north-eastern frontier and the portal to
Normandy and to the Île de France. If taken, Boulogne would have
expanded the English pale in France and provided a base from which to
launch the next season's English attacks into Normandy, or even against
Paris. Henry and his commanders began the invasion in the belief that
Boulogne could be taken before the onset of winter, but discovered during the siege that late improvements to the town's defences made this
objective impossible to attain. It was then that Henry's commanders formally advised him that it was honourable and prudent to make peace.

The treaty of Étaples (3 November 1492) is significant because it was
not another truce, but a full Anglo-French peace lasting until one year
after the death of either monarch. This treaty marks a shift in Henry's
French policy from the militant phase he had embraced in the treaties of
Woking to a phase of peaceful accommodation. In a side agreement,
Charles VIII undertook to pay Henry 750,000 *écus d'or* in annual instalments of 50,000 *écus d'or*, not as tribute, but as the money owed him by
Anne of Brittany.[40] The treaty of Étaples became the point of reference
in early Tudor diplomacy for subsequent treaties of Anglo-French peace.
Maximilian again turned hostile towards Henry, believing that he had
violated the treaties of Woking and betrayed Habsburg interests. Ferdinand
and Isabella repudiated their unconsummated alliance with Henry in
their own treaty of peace with France. By 1493, Henry was once more isolated in Europe, facing a Yorkist pretender backed by his foreign foes,
and again dependent on French good will.

Henry did not abandon completely the militant policy towards France after 1492; his policy was ambivalent. In December 1497, the Milanese ambassador in England observed that Henry did not want always to remain at peace with France, but that he would not act unless he saw France submerged in turmoil.[41] This observation was confirmed by Henry's reaction to news of Charles VIII's death in the spring of 1498. Anticipating possible turmoil in France and Brittany's reassertion of its autonomy, Henry pondered a return to the militant policy. He told Rodrigo de Puebla, the Spanish ambassador, that he intended to take advantage of divisions within France, invade, and conquer what belonged to him by right, and that he had made overtures through an agent to the *vicomte* de Rohan, the man he had planned to make duke of Brittany in 1492.[42] Henry wanted to know what Ferdinand and Isabella might do, because he would not act against France without them. The Spanish monarchs, however, were uninterested in Henry's overture, since they were already negotiating a treaty with the new French king, Louis XII, who quickly proved his firm hold on a stable France. His marriage to Anne of Brittany restored the Franco-Breton composite union. Consequently, on 28 June 1498, Henry renewed the Anglo-French peace with Louis, ratifying it the following April.[43]

Following the renewal of the Anglo-French peace, Henry seemed indifferent to the old Plantagenet claims. Some royal councillors advised him to reject the Anglo-Spanish defensive alliance of 10 July 1499 as prejudicial to English claims in France because it applied only to the lands actually held by each monarch on this date.[44] Ignoring this advice, Henry ratified the treaty in May 1500.[45] During the Franco-Spanish War of 1502–04, Isabella tried to draw Henry into the war on the Spanish side by promising to help him recover Normandy and Guyenne,[46] but Henry declined the Spanish offer because at the time he wanted to keep and strengthen his peace with France. He sent Matthew Baker to France in June 1502 to discuss with Louis XII and his leading ministers preservation of Anglo-French amity and a marriage between Prince Henry and Claude of France, the daughter of Louis XII and Anne of Brittany.[47] Henry's proposal may have been an attempt to circumvent a Valois–Habsburg marriage.

In the treaty of Blois (September 1504), Louis XII and Philip the Handsome of Burgundy formally agreed to the marriage between Claude of France and Philip's son, Charles of Ghent. Henry tried to counter this treaty by proposing to Ferdinand and Isabella in October that his daughter Mary marry Charles of Ghent, who was their grandson (Philip had married their daughter Joanna in 1496).[48] In fact, Louis repudiated the treaty of Blois in May 1505 because of opposition to it in France, and married Claude to Francis of Angoulême, his heir apparent. The following month, Charles Somerset, Lord Herbert, arrived in France to negotiate a new Anglo-French treaty of friendship and alliance.[49] Two years later, in April 1507, Henry expressing affection for the French king responded favourably to Louis's invitation to join a confederation between France, the papacy, Venice and Aragon.[50]

Despite his amity with Louis XII, Henry remained wary of the French king's territorial ambitions, especially towards the Habsburg Netherlands, and he disliked in particular the alliance between Louis and Ferdinand of Aragon, which was formed in October 1505, when Philip of Burgundy, claiming the rule of Castile by right of his wife, Joanna, challenged Ferdinand's right to govern Castile in her name. Partly to counter Ferdinand's alliance with Louis XII, Henry cultivated alliances with the Habsburgs and backed Philip's right to rule Castile, though he urged Philip to establish good terms with Ferdinand lest their quarrel further Louis's ambitions.[51] In the summer of 1506, Henry signalled his opposition to Louis's support of a rebellion in Guelders; blaming the French king for inciting war in the Low Countries, Henry promised Philip's lieutenant general there the assistance of 7000 English troops.[52] Henry's desire to drive a wedge between Ferdinand and Louis was probably the purpose behind the offer he made to Queen Anne and to Cardinal d'Amboise in December 1507 that he would 'with all our heart' work for peace and reconciliation between Louis XII and the Habsburgs.[53]

Although Henry was suspicious of Louis, he did not want strained relations with the French monarch, especially as his health deteriorated. When Margaret of Austria invoked the defensive alliance with England in June 1508 and requested English troops to help defend the Low Countries against Guelders and the French, Henry refused her request. He advised her instead to make a truce with Louis and concentrate on neutralising him by securing Habsburg control of Castile.[54] At the time of his death in April 1509, Henry seemed apprehensive about the expansion of French power in northern Italy. Still, he had no intention of opposing France, and was said to have expressed from his deathbed the wish that his son and heir preserve the Anglo-French peace.[55]

HENRY VII AND THE ITALIAN WARS

Tudor historians have underrated Henry VII's political interest in Italy as well as his concerns about Charles VIII's invasion and conquest of Naples in 1494–95. A few historians have even argued that Henry welcomed, if not encouraged, Charles's Italian adventure.[56] Political, cultural and economic contacts between England and Italy had increased during the fifteenth century. Following this tradition, Henry cultivated close relations with the papacy before his accession, and as king he obtained from Pope Innocent VIII important papal bulls anathematising opponents of the Tudor dynasty.[57] He employed at the Curia a cardinal protector for England, making sure, after careful scrutiny of papal politics, that an influential curial cardinal always held this office. Moreover, Henry built upon the diplomatic legacy of his predecessors in developing relations with other major Italian powers. Early in his reign, Christopher Urswick, Henry's almoner, undertook goodwill visits to Naples and the papacy.[58] Henry also appointed a procurator for matters in Italy.[59] The 1489 treaty establishing an English wool staple at Pisa was intended to help develop English commerce in the Mediterranean.[60]

The evidence indicates that Henry did not favour Charles's conquest of Naples, but between 1493 and 1495, he was isolated in Europe, facing Habsburg hostility, a rebellion in Ireland, and a war with Scotland. He consequently needed French friendship and good will and was not in a position to oppose or openly criticise the French king's Neapolitan enterprise. Nevertheless, Henry signalled a close affinity with the Aragonese dynasty of Naples that Charles intended to depose. He tried to have King Ferrante I and his heir, Alfonso, duke of Calabria, included in the treaty of Étaples as allies of England. In 1493, he conferred on Duke Alfonso the Order of the Garter, an important symbol of fellowship and alliance with the English monarch.[61]

Aware of Henry's difficulties, Charles VIII offered him friendship in August 1494, and promised help against Maximilian who was supporting the Yorkist impostor, Perkin Warbeck. The implicit *quid pro quo* of the French offer was that Henry would give financial and military assistance to Charles VIII against Alfonso, who became king of Naples in 1494. Henry acknowledged his past debt of gratitude to Charles and wished him well, but he refused material and political support for Charles's Neapolitan campaign because of the Garter 'brotherhood' he had with King Alfonso.[62] Charles kept pressuring Henry, and the following year Henry agreed to remit a year's instalment of the French pension. In December 1494, he sent Richmond Herald to join Charles VIII's camp in Italy and report daily on the state of Italian affairs.[63] Yet, after Charles's triumph, Henry exhibited his continuing affinity for the exiled

Aragonese king of Naples by maintaining the Neapolitan ambassador at his court at his own expense.[64]

Spain took the diplomatic lead in forming a new European coalition against France. On 31 March 1495, the Holy League of Venice was formed as a political and military alliance between Spain, the Empire, Venice, Milan and the papacy to force Charles from Naples under the guise of defending Italy and Christendom. Although forced to withdraw to France in 1495, Charles VIII planned another campaign in Italy to relieve the small French army he had left behind. His enemies consequently wanted Henry VII to join the Holy League because England was well placed to harass France and divert Charles's ambitions from Italy. Before he would consider doing so, Henry needed the security of an alliance with Spain and an end to Maximilian's enmity and support for Warbeck.[65] Spanish diplomacy worked on reconciling Henry and Maximilian and on dissuading James IV of Scotland from attacking England. Maximilian initially refused to abandon Warbeck, and would only accept Henry into the League if he first agreed to wage war on France. Under pressure from the allies, however, Maximilian finally dropped his opposition to Henry's membership.

Henry decided to join the Holy League because he thought Charles's Italian ambitions were a grave threat to the papacy and the whole Christian Commonwealth.[66] In the spring of 1496, he sent the French king a formal protest denouncing his actions in Italy.[67] Yet, Henry wanted to thwart Charles's Italian ambitions while preserving the Anglo-French peace. He thus cast his participation in the League as a pious action taken in concert with other Christian princes to defend the Church and Christendom and to bring Charles back into obedience to the pope. He joined the Holy League on 18 July 1496, but strictly as a political, non-military, ally.[68] Henry believed that the existence of the Holy League was sufficient to deter another French invasion of Italy and in December 1497, he told the Milanese and Venetian ambassadors that Italian unity would defeat France.[69]

But the Italian states could never remain united for long. Henry expressed to the Milanese envoy his deep disappointment at the break-up of the Holy League the following year and with the mutability of Italian politics. For a while, Henry became wary of any alliances with Italian states. In late March and early April 1499, however, he changed his mind, and suddenly warmed to Duke Ludovico Sforza of Milan, who was under threat from the French king. His various diplomatic overtures at that time to Milan, Rome, the Low Countries and to Maximilian suggest Henry was thinking of organising a coalition to deter Louis XII from attacking Milan, but Maximilian showed only disdain for Henry's overtures, dashing Sforza's hopes for a possible Tudor–Habsburg alliance.[70] Henry remained neutral during the Franco-Spanish War of 1502–04 over Naples. The Anglo-Spanish defensive alliance of July 1499 did not apply to the Neapolitan lands conquered and partitioned by Ferdinand and Louis XII under the terms of the secret Franco-Spanish treaty of Granada of November 1500. In July 1502, Queen Isabella proposed renewal of the Anglo-Spanish defensive alliance, changing nothing in the treaty except the date.[71] Henry was not fooled. He rejected the offer, and refused to be drawn into helping Spain defend its ill-gotten Neapolitan gains. The war ended in Spanish victory.

No sooner had this Italian war ended than another was brewing. Pope Julius II, wanting Venice to relinquish papal lands it occupied in the Romagna, was trying to draw the greater European powers into a grand anti-Venetian coalition. Maximilian, Louis and Ferdinand harboured their own animosities and ambitions against Venice, and formed with the pope an anti-Venetian coalition at the Congress of Cambrai in December 1508, a meeting convened ostensibly for reconciling the differences between Maximilian and Louis XII over Guelders. Henry's ambassador who attended the congress was told of its secret aim: the defeat and dismemberment of Venice. However, Henry wanted to turn the congress to his own purpose of isolating Ferdinand, overthrowing his rule in Castile, and using the French wish to negotiate marriage between Prince Henry and Margaret of Angoulême as a wedge to separate Louis from Ferdinand.[72] Henry's scheme failed, and he therefore not only abstained from the League of Cambrai formed at the congress, but also tried to undermine it by warning Venice of its true purpose and by offering to help reconcile Venice with Maximilian. Apart from the papacy, France had the most to gain from Venice's defeat, for Venice was the one remaining Italian power blocking French domination of northern Italy. For this reason, perhaps, Henry tried to assist Venice diplomatically. However, he died before the Venetian ambassador could arrive in England to take up his offer of mediation.[73]

HENRY VII AND THE CRUSADE

Ongoing calls for a new crusade were a reaction to the advancing power of the Muslim Ottoman Empire, the spectre that haunted Christendom in the fifteenth and sixteenth centuries. The papacy and the monarchies of Western Europe, more concerned with advancing and defending their political and dynastic interests, did little more than issue plans and proposals for uniting in a new crusade against the Turks. Nonetheless, actions in defence of the Christian Commonwealth, even if verbal, expressed a noble and pious ideal, and might earn a pious monarch honour and renown within the wider area of Europe. Henry VII, like his fellow princes, clothed his diplomacy in rhetoric evoking the greater good of Christendom; and on two occasions he celebrated publicly reception of the sword and cap, papal acknowledgement of his pious support and defence of the Church.

The Venetian–Turkish War from 1499 to 1503 once again focused European attention on the Ottoman menace. Pope Alexander VI issued another papal call to crusade, and in 1502 Henry responded. He published in England papal bulls for collection of a crusade tax, and even allowed papal collectors to take up the tax, despite warning from his allies that Alexander would misappropriate the money for his own use. Henry himself contributed £4000 for the crusade, but he declined Alexander's request for an English army because of the expense involved in assembling, equipping and despatching a fleet from England to distant Italy. In a published letter to Pope Alexander, Henry claimed that the kings of France and Spain were better positioned to assist the pope, but then added that if these monarch failed to act, he would come to Italy in his own person, provided that the pope allowed him sufficient time to prepare, commanded in person the Christian forces against the Turks, secured first the contribution of men and money from other Christian princes, and made available adequate Italian ports for the landing of English forces.[74] This letter to Alexander should not be quickly dismissed as 'eloquent lipservice'.[75] Henry's reasons for not wanting to send military forces were sound, and the conditions he asked Alexander to meet before he would send an English army took measure of the seriousness of the pope's intention to carry out an actual crusade. The printing of the letter shows that Henry wanted his support for the crusade, as well as his conditions for support, made public. His personal interest in a crusade is reflected in his attempt to negotiate an alliance with Hungary against the Turks the same year.[76] Three years later in 1505, he supported King Manuel of Portugal's plan for a crusade, sending Lord Herbert to France to discuss it with Louis XII.[77] Henry was not discouraged by Louis's tepid reception of the idea, and the following year he entered into negotiations for a crusade undertaken by England, Castile and Portugal.[78] Henry wrote to Pope Julius II in 1507 urging peace and unity among Christian princes so that they could launch the crusade.[79] The pope praised Henry but, fixated on his own quarrel with Venice, he refused to endorse it until the arrogant republic had been humbled. Henry's diplomatic endeavours in support of a crusade suggest that he did not see himself as an insular ruler concerned only with England's national interests, but as a pious Christian monarch who was also concerned with the defence of Christendom.

HENRY VII AND THE PRETENDERS

In the later fifteenth century, European powers, especially France and Burgundy, interfered in England's dynastic wars and supported either Lancastrian or Yorkist pretenders in an effort to influence the direction of English foreign policy, or at least limit England's ability to intervene on the Continent.[80] Henry VII had similarly to contend with hostile princes who encouraged and supported rival Yorkist pretenders in order to weaken him and force a change in his foreign policy. Henry held one important advantage: the person of Edward, earl of Warwick, the surviving legitimate male heir to the house of York. The lack of alternative Yorkist males forced Yorkist leaders, especially Margaret of York, the dowager duchess of Burgundy and Edward IV's sister, to use impostors as stand-ins for legitimate Yorkist princes. The first Yorkist impostor was a young boy named Lambert Simnel, possibly of Walloon origin, who was sent against Henry in 1487 as Warwick.[81] The Simnel Conspiracy had support from anti-Tudor Anglo-Irish lords, and Maximilian allowed the Yorkists use of a band of battle-hardened *landsknechte* commanded by Martin Schwartz, one of the most brutal of Maximilian's mercenary captains.

One historian has argued that Henry brought the Simnel Conspiracy on himself because of his refusal to placate Margaret of York and his failure to renew with Maximilian the Anglo-Burgundian treaties of commerce and friendship, thereby endangering the stability of Burgundy.[82] Yet, Henry did agree to short-term renewals of the existing Anglo-Burgundian treaties of commerce, and only held back from a longer-term commitment because he wanted to continue negotiations for the removal of Burgundian restrictions on the importation of English cloth into the Netherlands. Furthermore, in June 1486, Henry granted the subjects of Maximilian and Philip permission to take refuge in English ports, where they could buy provisions.[83] This agreement, however, did not satisfy the Habsburgs, as Henry then extended the privilege to the subjects of all other princes allied to England, including the king of France.[84]

Although Henry did not ignore completely Habsburg interests, between 1485 and 1488 he would do nothing to compromise his declared neutrality in the Franco-Burgundian–Breton wars. Henry's neutrality was a problem for Maximilian. On the defensive in 1487, in danger of losing control of Flanders, Maximilian needed to revive the Anglo-Burgundian alliance against France, and the main obstacle to this plan was the neutral Tudor king whose regime, it seemed to many at the time, had only been established by France. Maximilian hoped a Yorkist restoration through the Simnel Conspiracy would result quickly in a new Anglo-Burgundian alliance. However, Simnel's army was defeated at the battle of Stoke in June and instead of an Anglo-Burgundian alliance, Maximilian earned only Tudor enmity.

When Henry shifted from neutrality to opposing France in Brittany and Flanders, thereby reviving the Anglo-Burgundian–Breton axis against France, it was Charles VIII who supported Yorkist conspiracies to neutralise Henry and punish him for his ingratitude. In 1490–91, the French encouraged two failed plots to murder Henry VII, and then they became involved with a new Yorkist impostor, Perkin Warbeck, who appeared in Ireland in late 1491 masquerading as Richard, duke of York, Edward IV's youngest son. Charles VIII's support for the impostor was a factor in Henry's 1492 war against France, and included in the treaty of Étaples was Charles's promise not to support Henry's rebels. After the peace was signed, Charles expelled Warbeck from France.[85] During the mid-1490s, Warbeck was used by Maximilian and then by James IV of Scotland to create trouble for Henry.[86] Warbeck accompanied James during his invasion of England in September 1496. There was no Yorkist uprising, and after a bit of looting and pillaging, James withdrew his army.[87] The pretender's value in Scottish diplomacy depreciated rapidly, and in 1497 James expelled him from Scotland. After trying to raise rebellion in western England, Warbeck was defeated, forced to confess his impersonation, and imprisoned in the Tower of London. In 1499, Henry executed both Warbeck and Warwick, eliminating them as potential threats to his dynasty.[88]

In 1501, Edmund de la Pole, earl of Suffolk and Edward IV's nephew, fled to Germany with his brother, Richard, in the belief that Maximilian would support him against Henry. Maximilian did not support Suffolk as he had Simnel and Warbeck, and instead used the fugitive earl to extort 50,000 crowns from Henry for his intended campaign against the Turks.[89] Giving in to the blackmail, Henry agreed in the treaty of Antwerp of June 1502 for friendship and commerce to pay Maximilian

£10,000 and marry Henry, duke of York, to Eleanor, Maximilian's grand-daughter, provided that Maximilian revoked his safe conducts to Suffolk and his followers and denied them all aid and comfort.[90] Maximilian failed to comply promptly with the terms of this treaty. In 1503, Henry sent his controller of Calais to demand that Maximilian publish an Imperial ban against Suffolk and prevent the exiles from receiving assistance.[91] Suffolk fled to Guelders the following year to escape his creditors. The duke of Guelders used Suffolk to extort money from Henry.[92] Archduke Philip warned Henry that he would regard payments to Guelders for Suffolk as a violation of the Anglo-Burgundian treaty of friendship.[93] Philip captured Suffolk in 1505, thinking he could use the earl to 'bridle' Henry.[94] Henry replied with another trade embargo against the Habsburg Netherlands. However in 1506, locked in a struggle with Ferdinand over Castile and needing an alliance with Henry, Philip had Suffolk delivered to Henry over the objections of his councillors.

HENRY VII's DYNASTIC DIPLOMACY

Marital ties between ruling dynasties strengthened political alliances and encouraged amity and peace between kingdoms. For Henry VII, inter-marriage with the established houses of Europe had the additional function of gaining European acceptance for his new dynasty. The alliance with the Trastámaras of Spain was the first and most complicated of Henry's dynastic negotiations. The alliance treaty of Medina del Campo of March 1489 included the contract for the marriage of Catherine of Aragon and Prince Arthur but the agreement failed. Henry delayed its ratification until September 1490, while Ferdinand and Isabella wanted to re-negotiate the financial terms for Catherine's dowry and the Anglo-Spanish commercial agreement. In 1493, they repudiated Medina del Campo in the treaty of Barcelona with Charles VIII, promising not to conclude a marriage alliance with England without the consent of France.

The Tudor–Trastámara dynastic alliance might well have died had it not been for Charles VIII's invasion of Italy. It was revived by the treaty of London of 1 October 1496, and ratified by Henry the following July.[95] Arthur and Catherine were married by proxy in May 1499, and again in November 1500 when Arthur turned fourteen.[96] Ferdinand and Isabella again tried to modify the financial terms of the marriage, and fretted that Henry might break the contract. Nonetheless, Catherine landed in England in October 1501, and after a lavish welcome in London, she solemnly wed Arthur on 14 November.

After Prince Arthur's untimely death in April 1502, Ferdinand and Isabella wanted the Tudor–Trastámara dynastic bond restored as soon as possible with a marriage between Catherine and Arthur's brother, Prince Henry.[97] Anglo-Spanish dynastic negotiations became entangled in Habsburg–Valois dynastic politics. In 1501, Philip of Burgundy and Louis XII started negotiations for marriage between Claude of France and Charles of Ghent. These negotiations culminated in the formal marriage contract of the treaty of Blois of September 1504, which stipulated that Claude's dowry would consist of Burgundy, Brittany, Milan, Genoa, Asti and Naples. In 1502, Louis, trying to frustrate renewal of the Tudor– Trastámara dynastic alliance, offered as part of an Anglo-French defensive alliance marriage between Prince Henry and Margaret of Angoulême. Henry proposed instead the marriage of Prince Henry and Claude, which, if accepted by Louis, could have made Prince Henry the duke of Brittany. However the French told Henry's ambassador that Claude was intended for Charles of Ghent.[98]

In due course, the treaty of Richmond for the marriage of Prince Henry and Catherine was concluded on 23 June 1503.[99] Two days later Prince Henry, still a minor, wed Catherine by proxy. Henry and Ferdinand and Isabella agreed to obtain papal dispensation from the pope on the assumption that Catherine had consummated her marriage to Arthur, even though Catherine insisted that she had not. Uncertainty over this important issue delayed the papal bull of dispensation for more than a year. In the fall of 1504, Pope Julius II agreed to issue the bull to comfort the dying Queen Isabella. He avoided the difficult matter of Catherine's first marriage by saying that *perhaps* she had consummated her marriage to Arthur. This hedge fixed the immediate diplomatic problem; the matter emerged as an issue years later when Henry VIII sought an annulment of his marriage to Catherine.

When Henry VII himself started looking for a new queen following the death of Elizabeth of York in February 1503, Ferdinand and Isabella proposed Ferdinand's niece, the young Queen Joanna of Naples, widow of King Ferrantino. The Catholic Kings favoured this match because it would not only provide for a widowed relative, but also strengthen the Tudor–Trastámara alliance.[100] In 1506, amidst the brewing conflict between Ferdinand and Philip over Castile, Henry sent envoys to Spain to survey the physical and financial attributes of the young queen, and assess the depth of political support for Philip and Ferdinand in Castile but these overtures proved fruitless.[101]

The new Tudor–Trastámara dynastic alliance nearly collapsed in the last years of Henry's reign as a result of the changing dynastic politics in Europe following the death of Isabella of Castile in November 1504. Philip of Burgundy, claiming to be king of Castile by right of his wife, supported by Castilian nobles, contested Ferdinand for the rule of Castile. Civil war in Spain seemed possible, as did a war between Ferdinand and the Habsburgs. Ferdinand therefore sought, and obtained, an alliance with France. In April 1505, Louis XII repudiated the Habsburg–Valois dynastic alliance, and in October he concluded at Blois an alliance, which was cemented by Ferdinand's marriage to Louis's niece, Germaine of Foix.

Ferdinand wanted Henry VII to be the guardian of the new Franco-Aragonese peace, hoping to form an alliance between England, France and Aragon against Philip and Maximilian.[102] Henry, however, was shifting towards a political and dynastic alliance with the Habsburgs, partly to counter the Franco-Aragonese alliance, but more importantly to preserve England's alliance with Castile, which, it was clear by 1505, would be inherited by the Habsburg heir, Charles of Ghent. Henry supported the Habsburgs with an estimated £226 000 in unsecured loans paid to Maximilian and Philip between 1505 and 1509.[103] Some of this money was meant to help finance the Habsburg take-over of Castile. On 27 June 1505, Prince Henry made a formal declaration before Bishop Richard Fox, in the presence of Catherine and the Spanish ambassador, renouncing his marriage contract to Catherine on the grounds that it was made when he was a minor.[104] According to Bishop Fox, one of king's closest councillors, Henry wanted this declaration made, but always intended that his son would marry Catherine.[105] He may have wanted this declaration in hand in case he needed justification for breaking the treaty of Richmond.

In January 1506, the ship carrying Philip and his wife Joanna to Castile was blown into Melcome Regis. Henry, taking advantage of the unexpected visit, concluded with Philip treaties of alliance, marriage and commerce. The treaty of Windsor of 9 February established an Anglo-Burgundian defensive alliance and committed Henry to help defend Philip's right to Castile and his lands in the Netherlands.[106] The treaty of London of 20 March, providing the dynastic component of the new alliance, was a contract for marriage between Henry VII and Margaret of Austria, Maximilian's daughter and the recently widowed duchess of Savoy.[107] The marriage with Margaret of Austria was one of Henry's most important diplomatic priorities in the last years of his reign, but Margaret, resisting great pressure from her father, steadfastly refused to marry the English king.[108] The Anglo-Burgundian commercial treaty of London of 30 April, the so-called *Intercursus Malus*, would have removed restrictions on the sale of English cloth in the Netherlands, except in Flanders, had it been ratified and implemented.[109] Following Philip's landing in Castile, Ferdinand surrendered the government to him and withdrew into Aragon. Philip, however, died unexpectedly in September 1506, and Ferdinand returned to govern Castile in the name of his grieving and apparently deranged daughter.

Despite the changed circumstances, Margaret continued to reject Henry, but she did agree to the marriage of her nephew Charles of Ghent with Mary Tudor, a match which Maximilian had proposed in September 1506 in reaction to Louis's repudiation of the treaty of Blois.[110] On 21 December 1507, English and Burgundian commissioners finalised in the treaty of Calais the contract of marriage and a renewal of the Anglo-Burgundian defensive alliance. The following year, Maximilian and Margaret ratified the marriage contract, and Charles and Mary were married by proxy.[111] Completion of this marriage, which would link the Tudors with the future ruler of Burgundy-Austria, Castile-Aragon and Naples, became the most important issue in Henry's diplomacy. He tried to allay French fears, saying that the marriage of Charles and Mary would promote amity with France and his other allies and was for the good of all Christendom.[112] Henry wanted Ferdinand to approve it as well. In fact, Ferdinand was outraged that he had not been consulted on a matter of great importance to his realms and withheld his consent. Since Ferdinand, allied to France and refusing to approve the marriage of Charles and Mary Tudor, could not be trusted, Henry – who had once mocked and mistrusted Maximilian – now felt that his rule of Castile was the best means for insuring the succession rights of Charles and Mary.

At the time of Henry's death, his relations with Ferdinand were very strained. The king of Aragon nevertheless hoped that the marriage of Prince Henry and Catherine would happen.[113] According to the Spanish ambassador, as Henry lay on his deathbed, some royal councillors argued for the marriage of Prince Henry to Margaret of Angoulême and an alliance with France, while others favoured his marriage with Eleanor of Burgundy or with the daughter of the duke of Bavaria and a strengthening of the alliance with the Habsburgs.[114] Bishop Fox testified years later that Henry always intended that his son should marry Catherine and never heard that he wanted the prince to marry Eleanor.[115] The dying king may have left the decision to his son. In any event, Henry VIII married Catherine in June 1509, fulfilling, he said, the promise he made to his dying father.[116]

DYNASTIC DIPLOMACY: ANGLO-SCOTTISH RELATIONS AND THE TUDOR–STUART ALLIANCE

Marriage diplomacy also played an important part in Henry's long quest for stable and peaceful Anglo-Scottish relations. In the fifteenth century, the old English claims of suzerainty over Scotland were not actively pursued and the 'Auld Alliance' between Scotland and France had atrophied. Law and order, and security in the borderlands became the main concerns in Anglo-Scottish relations, but memories of the old claims were not entirely forgotten. They focused on the strategically important city of Berwick. Conquered by England in 1482, James III and James IV regarded recovery of Berwick a matter of honour, and likewise Henry VII saw keeping it under English control as a matter of security and honour. Yet, at the onset of Henry's reign, both English and Scottish monarchs wanted, and needed, a calm and stable relationship.[117]

In July 1486, Henry and James concluded a three-year truce. Henry wanted time to consolidate his regime in England while James III needed to overcome baronial opposition to his rule.[118] The following November, the truce was extended until September 1490 and a triple Anglo-Scottish marriage alliance was agreed.[119] James III would marry the dowager Queen Elizabeth Woodville; James, earl of Ormond (James III's younger son) would marry Catherine of York; and James, duke of Rothesay (the heir to Scotland) would marry an unnamed daughter of Edward IV. The status of Berwick was left to future negotiations. Any hope that the treaty of Edinburgh might become the basis for a perpetual Anglo-Scottish peace was dissolved following the *coup d'état* against James III and his death at the battle of Sauchieburn in June 1488. The Scottish lords who dominated the minority government of James IV were viscerally hostile to England and the idea of permanent Anglo-Scottish peace. Thus, the best Henry could get in the treaty of Coldstream of 5 October 1488 was a three-year extension of the truce.[120]

The growing hostility between England and France from 1489 until 1492 created an environment for reviving the old Franco-Scottish alliance.[121] Moreover, the hostile Scottish court developed links with the anti-Tudor Anglo-Irish lords and Gaelic chieftains in Ireland. To keep Scotland weak and distracted while he waged war against France, Henry was willing to stir internal Scottish conflicts[122] and even contemplated quite extreme measures, plotting with his Scottish allies to kidnap James IV and his younger brother.[123] Henry did obtain, in the treaty of Edinburgh of 25 June 1493, an extension of the existing truce to 30 April 1501, after agreeing to pay the Scots 1000 marks as compensation for past wrongs.[124]

Anglo-Scottish relations quickly soured after the mature James IV took over control of his government. Intent on winning honour and renown as a warrior king by recapturing Berwick, James rejected Henry's peace overtures and the offer of marriage to his eldest daughter, Margaret. He plotted war against England and backed the impostor Warbeck.[125] Henry, meanwhile, tried to get Charles VIII's co-operation in a scheme to destabilise Scotland by backing the rival Scottish claim of the son of James III's exiled brother, the duke of Albany.[126]

When it finally came in September 1496, the Scottish attack on England was little more than an inept border raid. However the Western Rebellion of 1497 disrupted Henry's 'substantial war' of revenge against Scotland.[127] This situation paved the way for the seven-year truce of Ayton of 30 September 1497, which, in the treaty of Stirling of July 1499, was extended to one year after the death of either king. Negotiations for a permanent Anglo-Scottish peace began in September 1499, and culminated on 24 January 1502 in three separate treaties, collectively known as the treaty of Perpetual Peace.[128] The first treaty restored procedures for resolving border disputes; the second established a 'perpetual' peace between England and Scotland; and the third was a contract for marriage between James IV and Margaret Tudor, which took place in Scotland in August 1503. The allies of England and Scotland were included in the treaty of Perpetual Peace. James, however, refused to renounce the 'Auld Alliance', as Henry wanted, and agreed only to consult Henry should he renew it.

Although war did not break out again during Henry VII's reign, Anglo-Scottish relations remained tense. Henry feared that James might renew his alliance with France or once again attempt the conquest of Berwick and other disputed borderlands. For his part, James IV used the threat of the 'Auld Alliance' and his new proximity to the English throne as leverage against Henry.[129] The murder of Sir Robert Ker of Ferniehurst, the Scottish Warden of the Middle March, and arrest of Scots travelling through England without safe conducts, especially the earl of Arran while on his way to France, angered James and imperilled the Anglo-Scottish peace. In the spring of 1508, Henry made concessions to ease Anglo-Scottish tensions. He and James managed to preserve the Perpetual Peace despite tense moments, and its collapse in 1513 resulted from the changed dynamic of Anglo-Scottish relations under Henry VIII.[130]

CONCLUSION

In December 1507, Henry pondered the successes of his diplomacy in the course of a letter to the mayor and aldermen of London announcing the marriage contract between Mary and Charles of Ghent. Henry expressed pleasure and pride that he had aligned his dynasty with the prince who would one day rule the Low Countries and Castile, among other lands. Because of this marriage, Henry noted, English merchants would be able to trade freely in the vast territories inherited by his son-in-law.[131] Henry not only linked England's commercial prosperity with his dynastic diplomacy, but also England's own security and peace. He said that the Tudor marriages to Charles and to James IV had enclosed England on all sides with firm friends and allies, thereby enhancing the peace and security of the kingdom.

Continued peace with France and Scotland and protection of Tudor–Habsburgs dynastic alliance were the main concerns of Henry's foreign policy between 1507 and 1509, a marked change from 1488–92 when Henry was reviving the Plantagenet militant policy against France. The shelving of this militant policy in 1492 and 1498 in return for a treaty of peace with France was a significant change in English foreign policy; but the tenuous and vacillating nature of this change is illustrated in the king's attempts, as late as October 1504, to revive the militant policy as an option in English foreign policy, an option exercised by his son in 1512 and 1513. Henry recognised the growing influence of Spain, based on the wealth and power of Castile, and his dynastic alliances first with the Trastámaras and then the Habsburgs were meant to preserve this important new alliance. The Anglo-Spanish alliance initiated by Henry, despite stresses and strains, lasted until Elizabeth's reign. The Tudor–Habsburg alliance illustrated the enduring importance of the old Anglo-Burgundian alliance, which was based on an even older Anglo-Flemish alliance. There were continuities amidst the changes in Henry's foreign policy, and some vacillations. Despite the contracts and proxy marriages, the peace and prestige Henry envisioned for England coming from his dynastic diplomacy were far from consummated, and as the king lay dying there seemed to be ambivalence and confusion over the direction of England international relations during the transition to the new reign.

NOTES

1. The traditional 'anglocentric' interpretation of Henry VII's foreign policy is found in J. D. Mackie, *The Earlier Tudors, 1485–1558* (Oxford, 1953), pp. 81–121, 134–9,

143–88; R. B. Wernham, *Before the Armada: The Emergence of the English Nation, 1485–1588* (New York, 1966), pp. 27–76; S. B. Chrimes, *Henry VII* (London, 1972), pp. 272–97; P. S. Crowson, *Tudor Foreign Policy* (London, 1974), pp. 47–66. Three recent brief surveys of Henry VII's foreign policy incorporate some new research and perspectives: S. Doran, *England and Europe, 1485–1603*, 2nd edition (London, 1996), pp. 18–27; R. Lockyer and A. Thrush, *Henry VII*, 3rd edition (London, 1997), pp. 74–90; and D. Potter, 'Anglo-French relations 1500: the aftermath of the Hundred Years War', *Franco-British Studies*, 28 (1999), pp. 41–66.

2. On the changing configuration of European politics in the late fifteenth and early sixteenth centuries, see E. Fueter, *Geschichte des Europäischen Staatensystem von 1492–1559* (Munich, 1919); D. J. Hill, *A History of Diplomacy in the International Development of Europe* (3 vols. New York, 1911–14), ii, pp. 83–276; G. Zeller, *Les Temps Modernes I: De Christophe Colomb à Cromwell* (Paris, 1953), pp. 90–111; G. Mattingly, *Renaissance Diplomacy* (Boston, 1955), pp. 121–61; J. R. Hale, 'International relations in the West: war and diplomacy', in *New Cambridge Modern History: The Renaissance* (Cambridge, 1957), pp. 259–91; R. Bonney, *The European Dynastic States, 1494–1660* (Oxford, 1991), pp. 79–99; M. S. Anderson, *The Origins of the Modern European State System, 1494–1618* (1998), pp. 52–85.

3. For surveys of England's medieval foreign policy and the Plantagenet policies of war and peace with France, see G. P. Cuttino, *English Medieval Diplomacy* (Bloomington, IN, 1985); Nigel Saul (ed.), *England in Europe 1066–1453* (New York, 1994); M. Jones and M. Vale (eds), *England and Her Neighbours, 1066–1453* (1989).

4. C. S. L. Davies, ' "Roy de France et Roy d'Angleterre": the English claims to France, 1453–1558', *Publication du centre européen d'etudes bourguignonnes (XVIe – XVIe s.)*, 35 (1995), pp. 123–4.

5. J. M. Currin, ' "Pro Expensis Ambassatorum": diplomacy and financial administration in the reign of Henry VII', *EHR*, 108 (1993), pp. 589–609.

6. Guillaume de Jaligny, 'Histoire de plusieurs chose memorables advenues du règne de Charles VIII, roy de France, és années 1486, 1487, 1489' in T. Godefroy (ed.), *Histoire de Charles VIII, Roy de France* (Paris, 1684), p. 51.

7. For these events, see A. V. Antonovics, 'Henry VII, King of England, "By the Grace of Charles VIII of France" ' in R. A. Griffiths and J. W. Sherbourne (eds), *Kings and Nobles in the Later Middle Ages* (Gloucester, 1986), pp. 169–84; C. S. L. Davies, 'Richard III, Brittany, and Henry Tudor', *Nottingham Medieval Studies*, 37 (1993), pp. 110–26; M. K. Jones, 'The myth of 1485. Did France really put Henry Tudor on the throne?' in D. Grummitt (ed.), *The English Experience in France, c.1450–1558: War, Diplomacy and Cultural Exchange* (Aldershot, 2002).

8. Proclamation of Anglo-French truce, 20 September 1485, P. L. Hughes and J. F. Larkin (eds), *Tudor Royal Proclamations* (3 vols, New Haven, CT, 1964–69), i. no. 3; Rymer, xii, pp. 281–2.

9. Giovanni de Giglis, Papal Collector in England, to Pope Innocent VIII, 6 December 1485, *CSPV* i, no. 506.

10. Rymer, xii, pp. 303–12.

11. Henry VII to the Three Members of Flanders, 13 August 1488; Declaration of Thomas Billesden, English Envoy, to the Three Members, in I. L. A. Diegerick (ed.), *Correspondance des Magistrates d' Ypres Deputes à Gand et à Bruges pendant les Troubles de Flandre sous Maximilien* (Bruges, 1835), pp. 302–5.

12. C. Giry-Deloison, 'Henri VII et la Bretagne: aspects politiques et diplomatiques' in J. Kehervé (ed.), *Bretagne: Terre d'Europe* (Brest, 1992), pp. 232–5.

13. Rodrigo Gonzales de Puebla, Spanish ambassador to Henry VII, to Ferdinand and Isabella, King and Queen of Spain, 15 July 1488, in *CSP Sp.* i, no. 21.

14. For Scales's expedition to Brittany, see Adelstan, Marquis de Beauchesne, 'Expédition d' Edouard Wydeville', *Revue de Bretagne, de Vendée, et d'Anjou*, 46 (1911), pp. 185–214.

15. Henry VII to Charles VIII, 23 May 1488, in Louis de la Trémoille (ed.), *Correspondence de Charles VIII et Ses Conseillers avec Louis II de La Trémoille pendant le Guerre de Bretagne* (Paris, 1875), no. 213; Beauchesne, 'Expédition d' Edouard Wydeville', pp. 197–9.

16. Instructions to Olivier de Coëtlogon and Jean le Prêter, Breton ambassadors to England, 16 November 1488, Real Academia de la Historia (Madrid), MS Salazar y Castro, N-22, fos 18r–19v.

17. The following is based on J. M. Currin. 'Henry VII and the Treaty of Redon (1489): Plantagenet ambitions and early Tudor foreign policy', *History*, 81 (1996), pp. 343–58.

18. Rymer, xii, pp. 362–72.

19. Ibid., xii, pp. 359–62; Currin, 'Henry VII and the Treaty of Redon', p. 354.

20. Ibid., xii, pp. 417–29; *CSP Sp.* i, no. 34.

21. On the English expeditions to Brittany, see J. M. Currin. ' "The King's Army into the Partes of Bretaigne": Henry VII and the Breton Wars, 1489–90', *War in History* 7 (2000), pp. 379–412. The following discussion is based on this article.

22. Ibid., pp. 393–400.

23. J. M. Currin, 'Persuasions to peace: The Luxembourg-Margny-Gaguin embassy and the state of Anglo-French relations, 1489–90', *EHR*, 113 (1998), pp. 882–904.

24. Giry-Deloison, 'Henri VII et la Bretagne', pp. 239–40.

25. The following is based on J. M. Currin, 'To play at peace: Henry VII, war against France, and the Chieregato-Flores mediation of 1490', *Albion*, 31 (1999), pp. 207–37.

26. Rymer, xii, pp. 397–89; Currin, ' "The King's Army" ', p. 403.

27. Ibid., p. 405.

28. The treaties between Henry and Maximilian for the defensive and offensive alliances are in Rymer, xii, pp. 397–410.

29. Henry's ratifications of the treaty of Medina del Campo and of the offensive alliance with Spain are in Rymer, xii, pp. 411–29.

30. Currin, ' "The King's Army" ', p. 409.

31. Rymer, xii, pp. 462–63.

32. Henry VII to Pope Innocent VIII, 8 December 1491, *CSPV*, i, no. 613; Henry VII to Ludovico Sforza, duke of Milan, 10 January 1492, in CSP Milan., i, no. 452.

33. Henry VII to Pope Innocent VIII and the Princes and Electors of the Empire, 8 February 1492, in J. P. Datt (ed.), *Volumen rerum Germanicarum novem sive de pace imperii publica etc.* (Ulm, 1698), pp. 502–4.

34. A. de la Borderie (ed.), *Le Complot Breton de M. CCCC. XCII* (Nantes, 1884); J. M. Currin, 'Pierre le Pennec, Henry VII of England, and the Breton Plot of 1492: a case study in diplomatic pathology', *Albion* 33 (1991), pp. 1–22.

35. On this raid, see Guion d' Estouteville and Guion de la Haye, officers of the Bailliage of Cotentin, to Charles VIII, 18 June 1492, BN, MS français 15540,

fo. 132r; Guillaume Carreau to Jean de Chalon, Prince of Orange, BN, MS français 15541, fo. 97r, printed in *Le Complot Breton*, nos. 39, 41.

36. The following discussion is based on J. M. Currin, ' "To traffic with war?" Henry VII and the French Campaign of 1492' in Grummitt, *The English Experience in France*.

37. Denys Hay (ed.), *The Anglica Historia of Polydore Vergil* A.D. *1485–1537*, Camden Series, 74 (1950), pp. 49–57.

38. Charles VIII to Marshal d`Esquerdes, 28 August 1492; Instructions to Gilles Rivault, 18 August 1492 in P. Pélicier (ed.), *Lettres de Charles VIII, Roi de France* (5 vols, Paris, 1895–1905), iii, no. 691, and Pièces Justificatives, no. 25.

39. Charles VIII to the inhabitants of Reims, 9 May 1492, *Lettres de Charles VIII*, iii, no. 671.

40. Rymer, xii, pp. 497–504, 506–11. On the payment of the pension and the diplomatic personnel exchanged between Henry VII and France see C. Giry-Deloison, 'Le personnel diplomatique au début du XVIe siècle. L'exemple des relations franco-anglaises de l'avènement de Henry VII au camp du drap d'or (1485–1520)', *Journal des Savants* (July–December 1987), pp. 207–53.

41. Raimondo de Raimondi de Soncino, Milanese ambassador in England, to Ludovico Sforzo, duke of Milan, 18 December 1497, *CSP Milan* i, no. 553. This is the sense of the original Italian lost in A. B. Hinds's translation.

42. De Puebla to Ferdinand and Isabella, 17 July 1498, *CSP Sp.* i, no. 203.

43. Rymer, xii, pp. 681–82, 710–12.

44. For this new alliance treaty, see *CSP Sp.* i, no. 244. On the advice given to Henry, see de Puebla to Ferdinand and Isabella, 16 June 1500, *CSP Sp.* i, no. 268.

45. Rymer, xiii, pp. 6–10.

46. Isabella to Duque de Estrada, 12 July 1502, *CSP Sp.* i, no. 327.

47. Louis XII's Response to Sir Matthew Baker, *c.* June 1502, in J. Gairdner (ed.), *Letters and Papers Illustrative of the Reigns of Richard III and Henry VII* (2 vols, 1861–63), ii, pp. 340–62.

48. De Puebla to Ferdinand and Isabella, 23 October 1504, *CSP Sp.* i, no. 401.

49. Instructions of Louis XII to Charles Somerset, Lord Herbert, summer 1505, *Letters and Papers, Richard III and Henry VII*, ii, pp. 125–46.

50. Henry VII's response to Normandy Herald, 30 April 1507, BN, MS français 2930, fo. 11r–v.

51. Vincenzo Quirini, Venetian ambassador to Philip, king of Castile, to the Signoria of Venice, 25 June 1506, *CSPV* i. no, p. 883.

52. Memoire touchant les affaires de France, de Castile, d' Aragon, and autres matieres, July 1506; Instructions of Henry VII to François Marezen, Henry VII's ambassador to France, 12 August 1506; François Marezen to M. de Chievres, Lieutenant General of the King of Castile, 17 September 1506, in J. Godefroy (ed.), *Lettres du Roy Louis XII et du Cardinal d'Amboise avec Plusieurs Lettres, etc.*, (4 vols, Brussels, 1712), i, pp. 60–61, 78–91; Louis XII to Henry VII, 31 August 1506; Henry VII to Philip, King of Castile, 16 September 1506, *Letters and Papers, Richard III and Henry VII*, i, pp. 289–300.

53. Letters of Henry VII to Queen Anne of France and Cardinal d'Amboise 29 December 1507, BN, MS français 2960, fos 11r–12v.

54. Van Theimseke to Margaret of Austria, 20 June 1508, *Letters and Papers, Richard III and Henry VII*, i, p. 361.

55. Alessandro Nasi and Francesco Pandolfini, Florentine ambassadors to Louis XII, to the Board of the Ten, 8 May 1509, A. Desjardins, *et al.*, *Négociationes Diplomatiques de la France avec la Toscane* (6 vols, Paris, 1859–86), ii, p. 319.

56. Mackie, *Earlier Tudors*, pp. 115–16; Wernham, *Before the Armada*, pp. 13, 45; Crowson, *Tudor Foreign Policy*, p. 61.

57. C. S. L. Davies, 'Bishop John Morton, the Holy See, and the accession of Henry VII', *EHR*, 102 (1987), pp. 2–30; W. E. Wilkie, *The Cardinal Protectors of England: Rome and the Tudors Before the Reformation* (Cambridge, 1974), pp. 10–15.

58. Rymer, xii, pp. 283–4; W. Campbell, *Materials for a History of the Reign of Henry VII* (2 vols, 1873–77), i. pp. 275–77.

59. PRO, SP 46/123, fos 29v–30r.

60. M. E. Mallett, 'Anglo-Florentine commercial relations, 1465–91', *Economic History Review*, 2nd series, 15 (1962), pp. 250–65.

61. Rymer, xii, pp. 502, 517, 528. King Ferrante was already a knight of the Garter.

62. Instructions to Richmond King of Arms, 10 August 1494, *Letters and Papers, Richard III and Henry VII*, ii, pp. 292–6.

63. Instructions of Richmond, King of Arms, 31 December 1494, BL, Cotton MS Caligula D. vi, fo. 21r.

64. PRO, E 36/131, pp. 97, 143, 198, 224, 249, 292, 411, 453.

65. Ferdinand and Isabella to de Puebla, 30 January 1496, *CSP Sp.* no. 121.

66. Letter of an ambassador in England to Ferdinand and Isabella, *c.* 1495, L. Suárez Fernández (ed.), *Política Internacional de Isabel la Católica* (5 vols, Valladolid, 1965–72) iv, no. 111.

67. De Puebla to Ferdinand and Isabella, 13 June 1496, *CSP Sp.* i, no. 136; PRO, E 30/1651.

68. BL, Cotton MS Cleopatra E III, fos 140r–143v.

69. F. Stefani, *et al.* (eds), *I Diarii di Marino Sanuto* (58 vols, Venice, 1879–1902), i, col. 567 (summarised in *CSPV*, i. no. 736); Raimondo de Soncino, Milanese ambassador to Henry VII, to Ludovico Sforza, duke of Milan, 6 December 1497, *CSP Milan* i, no. 550.

70. See the letters of Soncino to Ludovico Sforza, 20 March and 9 April 1499, *CSP Milan* i, nos 607, 611.

71. Isabella to Hernan Duque de Estrada, Spanish ambassador to Henry VII, 12 July 1502, *CSP Sp.* i, no. 327. G. A. Bergenroth, the editor of the *Calendar of State Papers, Spain* incorrectly identified this ambassador as the duke of Estrada.

72. Edmund Wingfield (Winkenfield), English ambassador at the Congress of Cambrai, to Margaret of Austria, November–December 1508, *Lettres du Roy Louis XII et du Cardinal d'Amboise*, i. pp. 124–30 (summarised in *CSP Sp.* i, no. 600).

73. For Henry's offer to mediate between Venice and Maximilian, see the dispatches of the Council of Ten and the Junta of Venice to Nicolo Ponte, merchant, and Lorenzo Guistinian, 29 December 1508; 19 January, 30 January, 12 February 1509; Appointment of Andrea Badoer, ambassador to England, 30 January 1509; Instructions to the ambassador to England, 19 March 1509; Instruction from the Council of Ten and Junta to Luca de Renaldi, Imperial ambassador, 16 February 1509; the Doge and Senate of Venice to Andrea Badoer, 19 March and 24 and 28 April 1509; *CSPV* i, nos 915–16, 918–23, 926–30, 936, 941.

74. 'The Contents of the King's Letters sent by His Grace to the Pope's Holynes, concernyng provision to be made to resiste the malicious disposicion of the the grete

Turke, enemy of the Cristen faith. An. 17 Hen. VIIth' in Henry Ellis (ed.), *Original Letters Illustrative of English History*, First Series (3 vols, 1825), i. pp. 48–59.
75. Chrimes, *Henry VII*, p. 304.
76. Rymer, xiii, pp. 4–5.
77. Instructions of Louis XII to Lord Herbert *c.* 1505, *Letters and Papers, Richard III and Henry VII*, ii, pp. 127–32.
78. Juana, Queen of Castile to Manuel, King of Portugal, 5 April 1506, *Letters and Papers, Richard III and Henry VII*, ii, pp. 150–2.
79. Pope Julius II to Henry VII, 9 July 1507; Henry VII to Pope Julius II, *c.* 1507, *Letters and Papers, Richard III and Henry VII*, ii, pp. 170–9.
80. C. S. L. Davies, 'The Wars of the Roses in European context' in A. J. Pollard (ed.), *The Wars of the Roses* (1995), pp. 162–85.
81. M. Bennett, *Lambert Simnel and the Battle of Stoke* (New York, 1987).
82. C. Weightman, *Margaret of York, Duchess of Burgundy, 1446–1503* (Gloucester, 1989), p. 151.
83. Henry VII, King of England, to Maximilian, King of the Romans, 7 June 1486, BN, Mélanges Colbert 81, no. 541.
84. 16 July 1486, *Tudor Royal Proclamations*, i, no. 7.
85. I. Arthurson, *The Perkin Warbeck Conspiracy, 1491–1499* (Stroud, 1994), pp. 16–24.
86. N. MacDougal, *James IV* (Edinburgh, 1989), pp. 118–25; D. Dunlop, 'The "Masked Comedian": Perkin Warbeck's adventures in Scotland and England from 1495 to 1497', *Scottish Historical Review*, 70 (1991), pp. 99–108; Arthurson, *Warbeck Conspiracy*, pp. 121–5, 133–5, 140–5.
87. Conway, *Henry VII's Relations with Scotland and Ireland*, pp. 108–10; MacDougal, *James IV*, pp. 130–3.
88. De Puebla to Ferdinand and Isabella, 11 January 1500, *Letters and Papers, Richard III and Henry VII*, i, pp. 113–4.
89. Instructions to Sir Charles Somerset and William Warham, Ambassadors of Henry VII to Maximilian, King of the Romans 1501, *Letters and Papers, Richard III and Henry VII*, i, pp. 152–77.
90. Rymer, xiii, pp. 6–10.
91. Memorandum to Wiltshire, *c.* 1503, *Letters and Papers, Richard III and Henry VII*, i, pp. 230–55.
92. De Puebla to Ferdinand and Isabella, 23 October 1504, *CSP Sp.* i, no. 401.
93. Archduke Philip to Henry VII, 29 October 1504, *CSP Sp.* i, no. 402.
94. Quirini to the Signoria of Venice, 26 July 1505, *CSP V* i, no. 850.
95. *CSP Sp.* i, no. 163; Rymer, xii, pp. 658–66.
96. De Puebla to Ferdinand and Isabella, 27 December 1500, *CSP Sp.* i, no. 292.
97. Powers to Hernan Duque de Estrada, *CSP Sp.* i, nos 317–18.
98. Louis XII's response to Sir Matthew Baker, *c.* June 1502, *Letters and Papers, Richard III and Henry VII*, ii, pp. 340–62.
99. *CSP Sp.* i, no. 364; Rymer, xiii, pp. 76–87.
100. Ferdinand and Isabella to Duque de Estrada, 24 January 1504, *CSP Sp.* i, no. 390.
101. The report of Henry's ambassadors is printed in J. Gairdner (ed.), *Memorials of King Henry the Seventh* (1858), pp. 223–39.
102. Letters of Ferdinand to de Puebla *c.* 1505–06, *CSP Sp.* i, nos 450, 471.
103. B. P. Wolffe, *The Royal Demesne in English History: The Crown Estate in the Governance of the Realm of England from the Conquest to 1509* (1971), p. 224.

104. Protestation of Henry, Prince of Wales, 27 June 1505, *CSP Sp.* i, no. 435.
105. Deposition of Richard Fox, Bishop of Winchester, 5–6 April 1527, *LP* iv, no. 5791.
106. Rymer, xiii, pp. 123–7.
107. Ibid., xiii, pp. 127–32.
108. R. Wellens, 'Un épisode des relations entre l'Angleterre et les Pays-Bas au début du XVIᵉ siècle: le projet de marriage entre Marguerite d'Autriche et Henri VII', *Revue d'histoire moderne et contemporaine*, 29 (1992), pp. 267–90.
109. Rymer, xiii, pp. 132–41.
110. Maximilian, King of the Romans, to Henry VII, 14 September 1506, *Letters and Papers, Richard III and Henry VII*, i, p. 303.
111. Rymer, xiii, pp. 171–200, 219–22, 236–9.
112. Henry VII to Anne of Brittany and Cardinal d'Amboise, 29 December 1507, BN, MS français 2960, fos 11r–12v.
113. King Ferdinand's instructions to an unnamed ambassador going to England, *c.* late April or early May 1509, *CSP Sp.* ii, no. 1.
114. Mattingly, *Catherine of Aragon*, pp. 116–9.
115. Deposition of Richard Fox, 5–6 April 1527, *LP* iv, no. 5791.
116. Henry VIII to Margaret of Austria, 27 June 1509, *LP* i, no. 84.
117. For Anglo-Scottish relations at this time, see A. Conway, *Henry VII's Relations with Scotland and Ireland, 1485–1498* (Cambridge, 1932), pp. 9–23; N. MacDougall, *James III: a Political Study* (Edinburgh, 1982), pp. 214–35.
118. Rymer, xii, pp. 285–94.
119. Ibid., pp. 328–31.
120. D. Macpherson *et al.* (eds), *Rotuli Scoti in Turri Londinensi et in Domo Capitulari Westmonasteriensi asservati* (2 vols, 1819), ii, pp. 488–90.
121. The following is based on Conway, *Henry VII's Relations with Scotland and Ireland*, pp. 24–41; MacDougall, *James IV*, pp. 87–99.
122. Memorandum of Henry VII's agreement with the Earl of Angus, 16 November 1491, *Letters and Papers, Richard III and Henry VII*, i, pp. 385–7.
123. Rymer, xii, pp. 440–1.
124. Ibid., pp. 434–40, 548.
125. Conway, *Henry VII's Relations with Scotland and Ireland*, pp. 108–10; MacDougal, *James IV*, pp. 130–3.
126. Instructions to Richmond King of Arms (1495/96?), BL, Cotton MS Caligula D. vi, fos 26r–27r.
127. I. Arthurson, 'The king's voyage into Scotland: the war that never was' in D. Williams (ed.), *England in the Fifteenth Century: Proceedings of the 1986 Harlaxton Symposium* (Woodbridge, 1987), pp. 1–22.
128. Rymer, xii, pp. 786–804.
129. MacDougall, *James IV*, pp. 248–64; D. Dunlop, 'The politics of peace-keeping: Anglo-Scottish relations from 1503 to 1511', *Renaissance Studies*, 8 (1994), pp. 138–61, 50.
130. Dunlop, 'The politics of peace-keeping', pp. 152–161.
131. Henry VII to the Lord Mayor and Alderman of London, 1507 in R. Steele (ed.), *Kings' Letters* (2 vols, 1907), ii, pp. 72–4.

3

ETERNAL PEACE, OCCASIONAL WAR: ANGLO-FRENCH RELATIONS UNDER HENRY VIII

Glenn Richardson

The first place in the decorated garden is owed to the roses
The white lilies hold the next to the first.
The former are dyed with the crimson of the people of Sidonia
The latter are whiter than the Thracian snow.
Our prince loves the former as his crest,
The Frenchman reverences the latter with the highest honour.
Let the gods join the white lilies with the crimson roses
So that quiet, the nursling of peace, may bloom on earth.

John Leland, *The Union of the Rose and the Lily*[1]

This short poem, published in the fourth decade of the sixteenth century, expresses a remarkable idealism about Anglo-French relations. At the time the poem was written, when its author was a young student in Paris, Henry VIII was taking his first, tentative, steps down the path towards becoming the best known king in English history. In 1527 he began the process of making Catherine of Aragon merely the first of his six wives. In so doing, he broke from Rome and established himself as the Supreme Head of the Church in England. He also broke from England's long-established alliance with the Habsburgs and created significant enmity with the Holy Roman Emperor, Charles V. Henry was only able to do any of this because in 1527 he also agreed to an 'Eternal Peace' and alliance with his erstwhile enemy and greatest rival, Francis I of France.

Traditional diplomatic history of Anglo-French relations in this period has quite rightly focused on the evidence of wars, of treaties between the kingdoms and on questions of trade and strategic advantage. Histories of the period have highlighted the complex double-dealing between European princes in the early sixteenth century, in which the kings of England and France took an active part. However, such discussions have usually owed more to nineteenth-century conceptions of statecraft than sixteenth, and often strike a variety of bemused, critical, uncomprehending and even cynical notes at the conduct of relations between the two kingdoms. Until relatively recently the personal interactions between Henry VIII and Francis I tended to be dismissed as empty rhetorical gesturing or deceptive theatrics designed to mask the two princes 'real' aims which were to safeguard their own strategic advantages and undermine those of the other. That Henry and Francis were intent upon outdoing each other strategically is beyond question, but there is a wealth of evidence, much of it material rather than documentary in nature, which shows how remarkably competitive and politically significant their personal dealings were. These interactions were centred firmly on the values of personal honour enshrined in the chivalric code of the nobility which was a vital element of Renaissance kingship.

The conduct of relations with France was of fundamental importance to Henry VIII throughout his reign and came before all else in the field of foreign policy. Henry made his international debut as a warrior against France in 1513. During the 1520s competing with Francis I in war and in peace was Henry's principal means of remaining at the heart of European affairs. In the early 1530s peace with Francis encouraged, and to some extent enabled, Henry to take direct action to end his first marriage and to re-define his authority over the English Church. Thereafter, it gave England such influence in Europe as it had following the break with Rome and it largely determined Henry's stature among European princes for the remainder of his reign.[2]

OLD ENEMIES: ENGLAND AND FRANCE 1509–25

As a young man Henry VIII considered that his first duty was to be a magnificent and successful warrior and thereby to establish his international reputation. Initially he hoped to do this by asserting his dynastic claim to the crown of France and conquering the kingdom in emulation of his great hero Henry V. Warfare was a complex and expensive undertaking in the early sixteenth century and Henry could only hope to achieve his ambition if allied with other European princes. Such alliances proved difficult to secure in the first three years of his reign and even harder to sustain beyond one fighting season. In 1513 and 1523 English armies did invade France in alliance with the forces of the Holy Roman Emperor and the king of Spain. The first campaign, led by the king himself, did not result in conquest of France but in the capture of the town of Thérouanne and the city of Tournai. The campaign in 1523 made no territorial gains for Henry. In both instances Henry's allies then abandoned him before he was able to press home his attack, leaving him once more isolated in Europe.[3]

Despite the very limited success he enjoyed as a warrior-king, Henry was still able to capitalise politically on his military adventures. It was not so much his willingness to wage war on the Continent, although that was important, as his response to diplomatic isolation that forced Henry's European contemporaries to take him seriously. Guided by Cardinal Wolsey, the king of England accepted that he could not always make war in France magnificently, but that making sudden and ostentatious peace with France might enable him to play a role on the international stage out of all proportion to the size of his realm and its military resources.

Finding himself abandoned by Ferdinand of Aragon and the Emperor Maximilian at the end of 1513 fighting season, Henry made a dramatic *volte-face* by allying himself with his enemy, Louis XII of France. The key to the alliance, which was secured by the marriage of his younger sister Mary to Louis, was that the French king agreed to pay Henry one million crowns, in annual instalments of 100,000 crowns. This Henry regarded as 'tribute' for 'his' crown of France and its payment publicly satisfied, at least temporarily, his claim on the kingdom of France.[4]

The example of 1514 was repeated on an even grander scale in 1518. In October that year Wolsey organised an international agreement, known as the treaty of London or the treaty of Universal Peace. Although its ostensible aim was a European peace and a crusade against the Ottoman Turks, its real intent in the minds of Henry and Wolsey was to curb the ambition of Francis I of France who had succeeded Louis XII in January 1515 and then burst on to the international stage in September by conquering the duchy of Milan. He secured his conquest by agreements with the pope, the king of Spain and the emperor, leaving Henry VIII enraged but isolated in Europe once more. Now, under the treaty of Universal Peace, warfare in Europe was outlawed. Disputes between nations were to be submitted to Henry VIII's arbitration. All of this was to be underpinned by a new Anglo-French alliance. In return for his participation in Wolsey's grand scheme, Francis I was allowed to purchase the city of Tournai back from Henry for 600,000 crowns. He also agreed to pay Henry an increased annual pension, and his son Francis was betrothed to Henry's VIII's daughter Mary.[5]

On the basis of this alliance, Henry VIII and Francis I established an extraordinarily ambivalent and competitive personal relationship. This competition was expressed, paradoxically, through extravagant claims of friendship and mutual respect. Precluded by agreement from fighting Francis, Henry instead treated him, in the persons of his ambassadors, with warmth and generosity. Francis I reciprocated and between 1518 and 1522 they often sent close friends and servants as representatives, exchanged expensive gifts and in all their dealings strove to show the highest regard for each other.[6] They enacted in a very self-conscious way the knightly friendship which the early-modern chivalric code of honour demanded between allies. By showing magnanimity to his 'good brother and friend', as they now began to call each other, each king demonstrated his own princely strength and prestige. This way of relating was seen at its most intense and theatrical at the Field of Cloth of Gold in June 1520. Virtually the whole English nobility and a sizeable proportion of the French aristocracy parked themselves for a month at the edge of English territory near Calais to witness the two kings meet and personally affirm their alliance of 1518. Tournaments and banquets succeeded each other in a daily round of entertainments. As the kings reminded each other at their first meeting, they were not there to celebrate peace for its own sake, but as the fruitful consequence of an agreement between them which each expected the other to keep absolutely.[7]

Like Henry, Francis was never committed to peace *per se* but only for as long as it remained an effective means of asserting his own international status. Within three years he became engaged in a military struggle with the newly elected Holy Roman Emperor, Charles V, over a multitude of disputes centring on the duchy of Burgundy which Charles claimed by dynastic right and which Francis held from his predecessors. Their hostile agenda was far too big for Wolsey or Henry to control but both were happy enough to condemn Francis for breaching the universal peace of 1518 and join with the emperor against him.[8] The Franco-Habsburg war ended in Francis's defeat and capture by Imperial forces at the battle of Pavia in February 1525. Henry was bitterly disappointed that a projected Anglo-Imperial invasion of France did not follow. This was partly because Charles was not interested in it and partly because Henry's people refused to pay the so-called 'Amicable Grant' demanded by Wolsey for the cost of another invasion.

Faced with these setbacks, Henry was once more persuaded by Wolsey to use peace as the way to avenge himself on his Habsburg ally. In the

summer of 1525 he brought the war with France to an end by signing
five agreements with representatives of the French regent, Francis's mother,
Louise of Savoy. These together constituted the treaty of The More under
which Francis was committed to paying Henry two million crowns in
yearly instalments of 100,000 crowns.[9] Meanwhile Francis himself was
taken prisoner to Spain and was only released after agreeing to the treaty
of Madrid signed in January 1526. He promised to cede Burgundy to
Charles and to give his two eldest sons to the Emperor as hostages. He
was finally exchanged for them and returned to France in March 1526.[10]

NEW FRIENDS: THE ANGLO-FRENCH TREATIES OF 1527

The first 15 years of Henry VIII's reign had demonstrated that despite his
bellicose ambitions in France, Anglo-French peace was not an alien concept to the king. Indeed it was one by which he had already profited and
he planned to do so again now. An English embassy led by Sir Thomas
Cheyne bore Henry's congratulations to Francis on his release from
Spain. Cheyne was a gentleman of the king's privy chamber and thus one
of a group of courtiers with very high status at the English court. The gentlemen had access to the king at all times and attended to him personally
as trusted friends. Sending such a personal servant to Francis as ambassador was at once a mark of Henry's high regard and a statement of
Henry's own princely magnanimity. Francis had often sent to Henry men
who held the equivalent French office of *gentilhomme de la chambre du roi*
in the period before the 1522–25 war.[11] According to Cheyne's instructions, Henry metaphorically visited Francis, in the person of the ambassador who embodied, or impersonated, his master in the truest sense of
the word. They stated that Henry could not forbear:

> or be satisfied [until] such time as his grace immediately and with all
> diligence up[on the] said deliverance had visited, seen and saluted the
> said French king by some one of his most secret familiars of his privy
> chamber.[12]

Francis responded by welcoming Cheyne warmly and allowing him,
like his predecessors between 1519 and 1522, to enter the private royal
apartments whenever he wished to do so, without awaiting a formal invitation. This gesture expressed trust and favour for the ambassador and
Henry, but was also a calculated expression of Francis's own princely
munificence. Servants of chamber status were used frequently, although

never exclusively, as ambassadors in the decade after 1526.[13] The two
kings resumed the exchange of expensive and high-quality gifts which
had been a regular feature of their relations since 1518. In 1526 Francis
sent Henry miniature portraits of himself and his two eldest sons,
the hostages in Spain. Henry reciprocated with portraits produced by the
Horenbout family of himself, Catherine and Princess Mary.[14]

After his release Francis I was desperate to find friends who would help
him avoid ceding Burgundy to Charles as he had agreed to do and to get
his sons returned safely to France. In May he concluded the league of
Cognac with the pope, Venice, Florence and the Sforza family of Milan
which was designed to throw the victorious Imperial armies out of Italy.
Henry VIII was named as its 'protector' but was not actually one of the sig-
natories. By the end of 1526 English ambassadors had begun discussion of
proposals for a new marriage alliance with France. In February 1527 a
French embassy arrived in England to conclude the negotiations. Wolsey
confronted its members with a demand that they confirm, once and for
all, Henry's huge annual pension and a share in the profitable salt trade
agreed under the treaty of The More.[15] This in effect meant buying out
Henry's dynastic claim on the French crown. Only by offering a permanent or 'eternal' peace, as it would quickly become known, could Henry
demand such a high price.[16] The French ambassadors were perplexed by
this turn of events. However, the league of Cognac had failed to intimidate
the emperor into releasing Francis's sons or altering in any way the terms
of the French king's release. Francis was forced to agree to Wolsey's terms.
The treaty of Westminster was signed on 30 April 1527. It provided for a
marriage between Princess Mary and Francis's second son, Henry of
Orléans. Francis confirmed Henry's annual pension of 100,000 crowns.

Henry VIII ratified the treaty of Westminster in person at Greenwich on
5 May 1527. As elaborate celebrations for the new Anglo-French 'eternal
peace' got under way at the palace, unpaid mercenary troops hired by the
emperor to defeat the armies of the league of Cognac in Italy broke
through the walls of Rome and sacked the Eternal City. The event was
deeply embarrassing for the emperor but also politically useful. Pope
Clement VII had been part of the league of Cognac and was now virtually
Charles V's prisoner. Wolsey's quick intelligence seized on the outrage
caused by this affront to the Holy See. In the summer of 1527 he travelled
with a huge entourage to meet Francis I at Amiens. He was greeted in
France with the kind of protocol normally reserved for monarchs and
hailed as 'the Cardinal-Peacemaker'. By then Wolsey was also working to
solve another problem. The king wanted his marriage to Catherine of

Aragon annulled. Wolsey was nothing if not ambitious. He planned to use an Anglo-French alliance either to ensure Clement VII's freedom to annul Henry's marriage, or to persuade Clement to appoint him as his deputy in Europe. This would allow the cardinal to annul the king's marriage himself. In August Wolsey signed the treaty of Amiens with Francis I. It amplified the Anglo-French peace agreed in the spring into a full alliance, ostensibly for the protection of the papacy and the good order of Christendom.[17]

In the autumn of 1527 large embassies crossed the Channel in both directions to receive each king's personal ratification of the treaty of Amiens. Grand ceremonies, reminiscent of those of a decade earlier were held in Paris and at Greenwich to inaugurate the peace. At Francis I's suggestion, the two kings also exchanged membership of each other's chivalric orders as an expression of their new alliance. Francis became the first French monarch to be made a knight of the Order of the Garter and Henry the first English king to become a *chevalier* of the Order of Saint Michael. Henceforward the two monarchs abandoned the ancient term of address between kings, 'most high and mighty prince' and instead habitually titled each other 'our most well beloved brother, cousin, good confederate and perpetual ally'. In the chivalric ethos to which they both subscribed such titles flattered the recipient but according honour to someone of equal status was primarily a way of asserting it oneself.[18]

Wolsey worked hard between 1527 and 1529 to establish an effective basis of cooperation between the two kings against Charles V. However it was not this ambitious scheme but the connection between peace and profit for Henry which Wolsey used to sell the Anglo-French peace to a sceptical English political establishment. In an address to Henry VIII's council and other officials after his return from France in 1527 he told his audience that Henry would by peace 'have more treasure out of France yearly than all his revenues and customs amount to' and that he would thereby become the 'richest prince of the world'. The implied promise was that parliamentary subsidies, and more importantly perhaps, extraparliamentary levies like the 'Amicable Grant' of 1525 were things of the past. It is significant that Wolsey made no mention of international peace as such, or the honour accruing to Henry from managing the affairs of Christendom in the manner of 1518. He understood that the real predecessor of the treaty of Westminster was the 1514 treaty of London in which the king of France had bound himself financially to acknowledge the English king's rights in France and the value of his alliance.[19]

Wolsey wanted to persuade his audience that he had turned a military war into a monetary one and that Henry was its undoubted victor.

However, he was unable to do this and solve Henry's matrimonial problems in a single operation. Henry and Francis declared war on Charles in January 1528. Francis lost more battles and allies in Italy and England was dragged into a futile trade war with the Netherlands, its biggest trading partner. Instead of magisterially directing Europe's affairs to Henry VIII's advantage, Wolsey became enmeshed in the conflict between his international and domestic responsibilities.[20] By 1529 he had not secured a straightforward annulment of the king's marriage but had at least obtained papal approval to establish, with Cardinal Campeggio, a legatine court at the monastery of the Blackfriars, to hear Henry's annulment case in England. However Catherine refused to recognise the jurisdiction of the court and the case was finally revoked to Rome. Meanwhile the French were not prepared to subsume the whole conduct of their relations with the emperor to Henry's matrimonial difficulties. In August 1529 they reached a comprehensive settlement with the emperor under the treaty of Cambrai in which England was only notionally included. Wolsey's enforced absence from these negotiations due to his role at the Blackfriars court was the final blow to his hopes of securing an annulment by diplomatic means. His enemies swiftly capitalised on his predicament. As Jean du Bellay, the French ambassador in England, reported, Wolsey was attacked by Anne Boleyn and her supporters and Henry's trust in the cardinal was at last undermined. In October 1529 Wolsey fell from power. He died a little over twelve months later while being escorted back to London from York to face trial for treason.[21]

Wolsey had not been able to give Henry everything he wanted but he did give him much of what he needed. Through maintaining an advantageous relationship with France, Henry gained the sort of international prominence he had not really enjoyed while in harness with the unreliable Habsburg emperors, Maximilian and Charles V. By the late 1520s there were also more genuine grounds for co-operation between the two royal regimes. The power of Charles V encouraged a belief among the English elite, fostered by Wolsey, that the best way to achieve their individual aims was for Henry and Francis to work together. It is doubtful that Francis I saw his relations with Henry in such concrete terms. He recognised that Henry's friendship was worth having but, as the treaty of Cambrai showed, he was quite determined to conduct his affairs as suited him. Nevertheless, by the late 1520s, France, or rather idealised Frenchness, was politically and culturally fashionable at the English court. Anne Boleyn's place in Henry VIII's heart owed much to her personal sophistication born of her training at the French court a decade or so earlier. This romanticised view of France had served Wolsey's plans for Anglo-French peace but he was unable to control the political reality of France. Ironically it was the French-trained Anne Boleyn who destroyed him and then used her influence with the king to promote members of her family and friends who became the core of Henry's regime after the cardinal's fall.[22]

FRANCE AND THE BREAK WITH ROME

Having removed Wolsey from power, it fell directly to Anne and her supporters to do what he could not: namely, to give Henry an annulment, a new wife and a legitimate son – in that order. Because there was no immediate consensus among Henry's advisors about how to do this unilaterally, the years between 1529 and 1532 have often been described by historians as ones without a policy.[23] In fact, Anne and her supporters actively revived Wolsey's policy of using relations with France as a platform for action on Henry's 'Great Matter'. Wolsey's successor as principal royal advisor was the duke of Norfolk. He was assisted by Anne's father Thomas Boleyn, a former ambassador in France and now earl of Wiltshire. Anne's brother George, Viscount Rochford, was appointed ambassador to France in the autumn of 1529. Later her cousin Sir Francis Bryan and Sir John Wallop replaced members of an earlier generation of privy chamber ambassadors such as Sir Thomas Cheyne. Anne also had her own friends at the French court, notably Francis I's sister Margaret, queen of Navarre. In October 1529 Jean du Bellay wrote to Anne de Montmorency, the Great Master of France and Francis I's most powerful and trusted advisor, of the growing dominance of the Boleyn family. He advised that their pretensions to conduct relations between the two kings should be flattered.[24]

Francis's advisors were aware that they, too, needed to keep Henry favourably disposed. The king of France was obligated under the treaty of Cambrai to pay Charles V two million *écus* in ransom for his two sons, still held in Spain, and as compensation for the duchy of Burgundy which he agreed formally to cede to Francis. As a result, the French regime was reasonably united in its decision to work with, but not become beholden to, the new players in England. By 1530 Henry also needed help with his divorce case. At Francis's request, he assigned to the French king 50,000 crowns of debt which Henry had been owed by Charles's grandfather, Maximilian, in return for a jewel called the *fleur-de-lis* pawned in England in 1508. This debt Francis could then set against what he owed Charles.

Henry also gave him the jewel itself and forwent an instalment of his French pension for 1529 provided that Francis spent the money on securing the release of his two sons. In return, Francis agreed that two newly elevated French cardinals, Du Bellay and Grammont, would fully support Henry's case in the Curia at Rome. He had already agreed in 1528 that English scholars could consult the Faculty of Theology of the University of Paris on the question of the validity of Henry's marriage. The team which did so in 1530 was headed by Boleyn protégés, including Edward Foxe, and Thomas Cranmer. Francis then pressured the faculty into giving a favourable verdict but not before his two sons were finally released by Charles in July 1530.[25]

During July, the king, the duke of Norfolk and the earl of Wiltshire all sent letters to Francis and to Montmorency thanking them for the university's help, congratulating them and expressing unremitting joy at the release of the young French princes. Confidence was high in the Boleyn circle that Henry's recent generosity would pay real dividends in co-operation from France on the marriage question.[26] For his part, Francis carefully cultivated these hopes while also maintaining contacts at the English court beyond the Boleyn circle. For example, Sir Nicholas Carew had been one of his personal favourites since their first meeting in 1518. He was now a supporter of Queen Catherine, yet he continued to enjoy Francis's favour in these years. He visited the French court and for some time in the late 1520s his illegitimate son Charles was a page in the French royal household. He was also educated while in France at the king's expense.[27]

Professor Scarisbrick has convincingly demonstrated that it was in the summer of 1530 that Henry VIII first began openly to question the extent of papal jurisdiction in England.[28] By then he was searching for two separate but related resolutions of the annulment issue. The first was the case being conducted in the papal Curia over the validity of the marriage itself which was supported by the French. The second potential resolution was through English law, based upon Henry's growing assertion that his was a wholly self-sufficient, imperial, kingship beholden to no external power in any matter, including his marriage. During the remainder of that year Henry nervously pushed matters forward on both fronts offering conditional loyalty to the papacy mixed with specific actions against the Church and vague threats of more to come. This was designed partly to overawe opposition and partly to sound its true depths. Francis's opinion about all of this obviously mattered to Henry. He instructed the English ambassador, Sir Francis Bryan, to explain the justice of his cause and to assure Francis that the legislation passed against the Church by the

November 1530 Parliament struck only at the invalid exercise of papal authority in England and proceeded from Henry's 'prerogative and dignity royal'.[29] In April 1531 Cardinal Grammont was despatched to Rome with further instructions to support Henry's case. Francis also allowed Edward Foxe to return to France and to obtain a statement from the universities of Paris and Orléans that Henry's case should indeed be tried in England, but by a papal delegate. This verdict actually confirmed a valid papal jurisdiction in the case and took matters no further forward than they had been at Blackfriars in 1529. Nevertheless, it was trumpeted to the Imperial ambassador Eustace Chapuys and in Rome as a ringing endorsement of Henry's claims to direct ecclesiastical control. In September 1531 Francis also requested that the case be returned to England and assured the pope that he would not countenance any censure against Henry.[30] By the end of 1531, therefore, Henry and the Boleyn group had apparently secured what Wolsey never could, namely Francis's continued public support for Henry's divorce. This apparent support is an important, but often overlooked, factor in explaining why, in 1532, Henry suddenly went on the offensive domestically.

A more direct and aggressive approach to the divorce question is certainly evident from February 1532 when a new programme of legislation was introduced to parliament. It culminated in the Submission of the Clergy and More's resignation of the Chancellorship in May. This parliamentary action has usually been interpreted as evidence of Thomas Cromwell's debut as the new 'fixer' in the Tudor regime, showing the pragmatic way forward. In this view, French support for Henry became irrelevant because Cromwell had convinced Henry that he could proceed with the divorce as a purely domestic matter while, if necessary, deceiving Francis I into believing that he still favoured a conventional solution to the matrimonial case.[31] In fact the bulk of the evidence from that year suggests that Henry saw it quite otherwise. A legislative approach to the divorce in 1532 did not render French support redundant. Instead it was continued French support which enabled parliamentary action to be contemplated seriously for the first time.

Late in 1531 the new French ambassador in England, Gilles de La Pommeraye had reported that he was being treated 'more like a prince than an ambassador'.[32] The reason for such treatment was that in November Henry had become aware that Francis was intriguing with group of German princes who objected to the domination of the Habsburgs in the German lands.[33] Henry wanted Francis to encourage this discontent in order to distract Charles from English affairs. In early

January 1532 Stephen Gardiner, the king's ambassador in France, was instructed to tell Francis that Henry considered they should 'enter some new and more special conjunction than hath been yet between us'. While this new alliance was to be 'separate and apart from all former' treaties Gardiner should ensure that it was still:

> ... as near as you can after the form and upon like occasions and suggestions, as the obligation reciproque is which beareth the date [8 August 1526].[34]

The date refers to a treaty signed between Henry and Francis as part of the attempt to draw England into the league of Cognac in 1526. Francis had agreed not to negotiate with the emperor to Henry's prejudice and, as Wolsey confidently assured the king at the time, 'or give him any assistance in any enterprise, for whatever cause soever the same shall be set forth against your Highness'.[35] Henry seized on this in 1532 because he wanted another offensive alliance, not like that negotiated by Wolsey at Amiens in 1527 for the protection of some third party, but one specifically designed to protect him as he contemplated moving against the Church in England. He would send an initial 10,000 crowns (and promised 100,000 in the longer term) for the German princes provided that the proposed agreement between himself and Francis extended 'to war offensive and defensive on both sides'. Gardiner was further to remind Francis that Charles V would be in northern Europe for the foreseeable future:

> During which time, if any exploit should be done against us by our enemies, we think it very necessary that we might be put in some assurance of their [the French] mutual aid for our money to be sent now for their defence.[36]

The personal connection between the two kings was again to be reinforced by reference to the French princes. Gardiner was to request new portraits of the dauphin Francis, of Henry duke of Orléans and of Francis himself:

> In that form and favour as it now is, specially considering that few years do always change a man's countenance ... which to behold shall be always unto us a great rejoice and comfort.[37]

Francis was cautious but expressed some interest in the plan and Henry's offer was confirmed in February at 50,000 crowns provided absolutely that Francis agreed to:

> ... conclude with us what special aid, and sums of money, ships,
> soldiers or artillery he will be contented to assist and succour for his
> part, in case the emperor by himself, his subjects friends, allies, or
> other confederates shall hereafter, not only for our said contribution,
> but for any other occasion, pretended matter or quarrel whatsoever it
> be, directly or indirectly, privily or apertly invade us.[38]

Francis baulked at such an explicit but open ended commitment.
However, negotiations in Germany and in England continued throughout the spring. On 26 May 1532 Guillaume du Bellay concluded the
treaty of Scheyern with the leaders of Saxony, Hesse and Bavaria. Francis
was thereby committed to paying these allies 100,000 *écus* for a war
against the Habsburgs.[39] Henry's offer of cash now looked much more
attractive. La Pommeraye was recalled to France and returned with
instructions to conclude the treaty with Henry. On 23 June 1532 a new
Anglo-French agreement was signed under which Francis promised to
provide 500 lances of cavalry (about 1250 men) together with a naval
fleet of 1500 men in the event of an Imperial attack on England.[40] With
such small forces, the treaty constituted a largely symbolic commitment
on Francis's part and the details of the agreement were kept secret in
England and in France. Doubtless, as Paul Friedmann noted in his study of
Anne Boleyn, Henry 'ascribed undue importance to the treaty', worried
as he clearly was about the prospects of international action against him
if he proceeded too far domestically too quickly.[41] He evidently reposed
a good deal of confidence in the new alliance, boasting in February to
Cuthbert Tunstall, the bishop of Durham and a staunch opponent of the
anti-clerical legislation, that 'no Christian princes will, we think, abandon
us for obeying Christ nor withdraw their benevolence from us'.[42]
Misplaced as that confidence may have been, even the Imperial ambassador acknowledged at the time that the alliance was still a political coup
for Henry. No French king had ever before specifically agreed to commit
troops and resources to England's defence.[43]

Evidently the bold ideas about Henry's imperial authority which were
contained in the *Collectanea satis copiosa* and which had lately been reinforced by Christopher St German's thesis on the king-in-parliament,
Doctor and Student, had borne fruit in legislation by early 1532.[44] Cromwell
was indeed instrumental in securing this shift to a legislative approach
but there is some unusual evidence which suggests that he, too, appreciated

that Henry might still need international assurance. We have no direct documentary evidence of Cromwell's attitude to French involvement in the divorce campaign at this time. It is particularly intriguing therefore, that his New Year's gift to the king in January 1532, at the time when he was working on anti-papal legislation and Gardiner's negotiations with France began, was 'a ring with a ruby and box with the images of the French king's children'.[45] In other words some kind of presentation box containing miniature portraits of the French princes. This very personal gift is quite distinctive in Henry's pile of presents for that year. It immediately recalls the portraits of the two princes given to Henry by Francis in 1526. It cannot have been presented without careful thought as to its appropriateness and likely effect on Henry.

Cromwell was certainly no Francophile like Anne Boleyn. However, the well-being of the two princes in Spain had been used since 1526 by both kings, by Wolsey, by Louise of Savoy and the duke of Norfolk as the emotional touchstone in co-operation between the two regimes. Cromwell's gift clearly fitted into this recent tradition and may have been designed to remind Henry of the help he had given in getting the two princes released in 1530 and that he was still entitled to expect Francis's help in return. The gift certainly seems unexpected when Cromwell's later, albeit temporary, support for an Imperial alliance is considered. Nevertheless, in 1532 it may have been intended to stiffen Henry's sinews and to assure him that Cromwell understood that parliamentary action and continued friendship with France were complementary, not opposed, strategies as some historians have maintained.

On Sunday 1 September 1532 Henry VIII created Anne Boleyn marchioness of Pembroke in her own right. Immediately after this gracious ceremony, the French ambassador swore to the Anglo-French defensive treaty agreed in June.[46] The coincidence was deliberate. Henry had agreed to meet Francis in the autumn of that year so that he could 'by his own mouth, declare the abundance of goodwill and desire towards him as if he were his own natural brother'.[47] He also wanted Anne by his side so that she could receive Francis's public recognition. The meeting duly took place in Boulogne and Calais between 21 and 29 October 1532. The official English description of the event emphasises the equality of the two kings and the strength of their friendship.[48] The meeting recalled the Field of Cloth of Gold twelve years earlier with lavish banquets and exchange of expensive gifts. Francis introduced his three sons to Henry outside Boulogne on 21 October as the man who had delivered the two eldest boys from the hands of the emperor. To emphasise his apparent devotion to them, and to their father, the king of England kissed each of them on the mouth when he greeted them, a gesture of great paternal intimacy.[49] On Tuesday 22 October Francis gave Henry a set of white velvet and satin robes, identical to a set made for himself. They then appeared at Mass dressed identically in these outfits, the symbolic significance of which presumably delighted Henry. The dukes of Norfolk and Suffolk were made members of the Order of Saint Michael, while Montmorency and the Admiral of France, Philippe de Chabot, became knights of the Garter.[50] Following the meeting, Henry's natural son Henry Fitzroy, the duke of Richmond, and Norfolk's son Henry Howard, the earl of Surrey stayed for a year in the French court as the guests of Francis and the dauphin.[51] All of these activities were taken by Henry's leading advisors as signs of how the English and French regimes now understood each other and were committed to working together against their common enemy, Charles V.

This impression was reinforced when, according to Henry, at their meeting Francis I promised that he would not conclude negotiations he had begun for a marriage between his son Henry and Pope Clement VII's niece Catherine de' Medici unless and until the pope granted Henry VIII an annulment. Francis later denied that he had promised anything so explicitly but in the winter of 1532 Anne Boleyn was sufficiently convinced that everything would turn out as she hoped that she finally slept with Henry. She and the king were secretly married in January 1533.[52]

News of Anne's pregnancy appalled Francis I when it was communicated to him confidentially by George Boleyn in March 1533. Henry's recent actions had complicated his ally's international relations considerably. The support he had given Henry on the narrow issues of the annulment case had spurred on the English king. Francis did not actually endorse any direct action against the Church in England, still less Henry's precipitate and bigamous marriage to Anne. This development seriously threatened his chances of resolving Henry's matrimonial problem as part of the Valois–Medici marriage plan then being negotiated with Clement VII. Jean de Dinteville, the new French ambassador in London from February 1533, was directed to assure Henry of Francis's continued support but also to urge the king to keep his marriage to Anne secret and to trust Francis.[53] The French were not particularly supportive of Anne personally although Jean de Dinteville was part of a circle who were perhaps hopeful that her evangelical religion would influence Henry and that he in turn would encourage Francis to champion moderate reform of the Church in France and beyond. His reformist concerns are alluded to fully, if cryptically, in Hans Holbein's 1533 double portrait, *The Ambassadors*, which was commissioned by Dinteville.[54]

Whatever longer term hopes the ambassador may have harboured, he saw that in the short term Henry should do nothing to antagonise the pope or the emperor. He acted according to his instructions but his pleas fell on deaf ears because Henry was now suddenly running out of time. At all costs the child, naturally assumed to be a boy, had to be born legitimate. It was now that Cromwell really took charge. The Act in Restraint of Appeals was passed in April 1533, depriving Catherine of the means to fight any further. The following month, Thomas Cranmer, the new archbishop of Canterbury, pronounced Henry's marriage to Catherine annulled and on 1 June 1533 Anne was crowned Queen of England. In July Henry was ordered by Clement VII to take Catherine back under pain of excommunication. On 7 September his daughter Elizabeth was born at Greenwich.

When Jean de Dinteville rode through the streets of London in Anne Boleyn's coronation procession, he was welcomed by the Londoners with their traditional greeting to a Frenchman of 'whoreson knave, French dog'. Unfortunately for him and Anne, by the end of 1533 Henry was saying rather similar things himself about Francis I. In October Francis met Clement VII at Marseilles and there Henry of Orléans married Catherine de' Medici with no resolution of Henry's matrimonial dilemma. The duke of Norfolk was due to have attended the meeting but was recalled when Henry panicked because Francis refused to call it off as a protest at Clement's threat of excommunication. Worse still, Henry's eventual representative at the Marseilles meeting alongside Stephen Gardiner was the decidedly undiplomatic Bishop Edmund Bonner of London. He burst in on the pope as he waited to receive Francis for one of their meetings and berated Clement, telling him that Henry would call a General Council of the Church if the pope excommunicated him. As Francis later explained, it was not himself but Bonner who had revealed the depth of Henry's antipathy towards the pope. There was nothing Francis could do for him in such circumstances.[55]

At Marseilles the ideal of a special relationship between Henry and Francis suffered a blow from which it never fully recovered. Henry felt betrayed while Francis was frustrated that Henry could not see that an alliance with the Medici pope would help rather than hinder his efforts on Henry's behalf. The death of Clement VII in 1534 eased tensions somewhat but Francis was anxious to secure the goodwill of the next pope, Paul III, against Charles V. In the aftermath of the 'Affair of the

Placards' in October, Francis was also determined to crush heresy within his kingdom. In England the Act of Supremacy was passed in November, cementing Henry's break with Rome. Francis was eager to distance himself from Henry, at least as far as religion was concerned.

Anne Boleyn sponsored several attempts at reconciliation between 1534 and 1536 trying to use her connections with Margaret of Navarre to promote a new marriage alliance. These came to nothing due mainly to French nervousness over the illegality of Henry's royal supremacy outside England and consequent doubts over the status of his two daughters. As she began to lose favour with Henry and as her opponents manoeuvred against her in early 1536, even Anne finally abandoned all support for the French alliance. In May Jean de Dinteville made strenuous but unsuccessful efforts to rescue one of Anne's co-accused, Sir Francis Weston, but he could do nothing for the queen.[56]

WAR: COLD AND HOT

In 1536 Francis I and Charles V went to war for a third time. Henry hoped to profit from this situation by allying himself with one or the other. However neither of them was much interested in friendship on his terms. Francis wanted monetary support for his war against their mutual enemy and sent frequent requests for money to help him with his immediate costs in fighting the war.[57] For Francis, Henry's refusal to help him now that he was at war, under the terms of the treaty of mutual assistance agreed in 1532, was as clear a breach of faith as anything alleged against him. He ceased paying the annual pension because he could not, his honour saved, pay Henry any money without receiving something in return. As far as Henry was concerned however, Francis's predicament was his own fault. The Valois-Medici marriage of 1533 and the suspension of annual payments to him were fundamental breaches of the treaties of 1527 and 1532. Henry maintained that his honour would not allow him to assist Francis until he resumed payments.[58]

In October 1537 the birth of Prince Edward, the legitimate male heir for whom Henry had longed, gave the king immense pride and satisfaction. His joy was tempered by the death shortly afterwards of the boy's mother, Jane Seymour. They had been married within two weeks of Anne Boleyn's execution on 19 May 1536. Having at last reached this personal milestone by such a slow and torturous route, Henry now wanted the path ahead made straight. He felt that the papal censure of him over his marriage career to date should be lifted. From 1537 he wanted Edward to take his place alongside the royal princes of France and Prince Philip of Spain as a full member of the coming generation of monarchs. He also wanted Francis I to keep paying the 'tribute' of pensions agreed ten years earlier, despite the fact that he was no longer actively co-operating with him. And he wanted all of this without having to undo any of the changes made in England under the royal supremacy.

A traditional but very effective way of re-establishing relations between monarchs was a marriage alliance and after the death of Jane Seymour in October 1537, Henry first sought a new wife in France. The most likely candidate was Mary, the daughter of the duke of Guise. Henry was keen but James V of Scotland was keener, or at least quicker. While Henry dithered about whether he might not, after all, prefer the sixteen year old Christina of Denmark, already the widowed duchess of Milan, the Scots reached a matrimonial agreement and in May 1538 James and Mary of Guise were married. The 'Auld Alliance' was thereby renewed and greatly strengthened. It gave James V support in his defiant indifference to his uncle Henry's claim to supervise Scottish affairs. The Guise marriage had profound dynastic implications for Anglo-Scottish relations for over a century to come.

Within a few months of this personal affront, Henry faced the much greater potential danger of a genuine, if temporary, reconciliation between Francis I and Charles V. Francis I's invasion of Savoy in the spring of 1536 had been followed by an Imperial invasion of Provence. After taking Aix, Charles was forced to retreat and Francis counter-attacked into Piedmont until a truce was agreed between them in October 1537. Peace talks were mediated by Pope Paul III and culminated in a meeting between the two sovereigns at Aigues-Mortes in July 1538. Late the following year, Charles V travelled through France to the Netherlands as the guest of the king of France. This new-found friendship was built upon an understanding that Charles would shortly cede the duchy of Milan to one of Francis's two younger sons.[59]

This is the immediate context for a series of disputes which arose between Henry VIII and Francis I between late 1537 and 1542 and which culminated in a return to war in 1544. Most of them seem irritatingly trivial and prolonged to the modern observer. Yet they were very important to Henry VIII because, isolated as he was, they offered him his only real chance of disrupting the new-found harmony between the emperor and the king of France. Each of them turned on the question of royal honour and the mutual obligations between Henry and Francis. At their heart lay assertions by each king that he had always met all his obligations to the other monarch and that this had not been reciprocated. Having competed as warriors, Henry and Francis now began to compete with each other as governors, or more precisely, as law-givers and judges.

The first of these disputes arose in April 1537 when Cardinal Reginald Pole arrived in France from Rome, apparently to sponsor some form of joint Franco-Imperial action against Henry. Sir Francis Bryan was sent to France to demand Pole's extradition to face charges of treason. Pole was received politely by Francis but was not encouraged to remain at court and this enabled Francis to evade the English extradition requests. In fact he maintained that the resident English ambassador, once more Stephen Gardiner, never even formally asked for Pole to be extradited.[60] A related dispute arose two years later over one Robert Brancestor who was travelling in Charles V's entourage when the emperor passed through France in the autumn of 1539. He was accused of treason for having allegedly acted as Pole's agent in secret negotiations with the marquis of Exeter. Sir Francis Bryan demanded that Brancestor be apprehended while he was in France. Henry wanted to embarrass the French king during the emperor's visit but it was he who was embarrassed when rebuffed by Francis. Brancestor was actually arrested by Francis's officials but Charles V successfully demanded his release as one of his own servants.[61]

Another group of disputes arose over the boundaries, geographical and legal, between the two kings' jurisdictions and over the application of property law. Between 1537 and 1539 Anne de Montmorency's brother François, seigneur de La Rochepot, was involved in a complicated case of piracy when a German ship operated by Hanse merchants was taken by the crew of a ship owned by La Rochepot. This ship had in turn been taken by the crew of an English vessel and both the French and English kings claimed exclusive jurisdiction in the case. Despite, or rather because of, a long and complicated case in the French courts, the dispute was never satisfactorily resolved.[62]

As La Rochepot's case dragged on, it became entangled in another legal problem over some bibles in English which Cromwell had printed in France in 1538. According to one document in the case, the so-called 'Matthew' Bible, had been licensed for printing in France by Francis I in July or early August 1538. It had been printed in Paris apparently because the paper then available in the French capital was of better quality than any in England. Once printed, the bibles were inspected on the orders of the chancellor, Antoine du Bourg, to ensure that the material in them conformed to the terms of the printing licence. Nothing of great concern was found by the chancellor's investigator and the bibles were cleared for export. Cromwell was apparently informed to this effect.[63] Chancellor du Bourg, however, died in the early autumn of 1538, and in November his successor, Chancellor Poyet, seized the bibles on suspicion that they contained doctrinally suspect translations which differed from those in the Vulgate, the official Catholic bible in Latin. The matter was referred to the conservative Faculty of Theology of the University of Paris which subsequently condemned the 'Matthew' edition as heretical. Cromwell never succeeded in getting the print-run sent to England despite repeated efforts to involve Francis personally in the case. These were blocked by Anne de Montmorency who was eager to keep direct control over the case himself probably in order to pressurise Cromwell into a satisfactory settlement of his brother's claims in the dispute over his ship.[64]

In all these legal and quasi-legal cases, ambassadors and senior politicians were quickly involved and accusations of double standards, injustice and incompetence were exchanged between the two regimes. Matters quite unrelated to the high politics of the moment were still seen by the councillors of both kings as of vital concern to their sovereign's status because they touched upon his authority as judge and governor. At the time of the dispute over the bibles, Francis was much occupied with asserting his authority within the kingdom. In a series of reforming edicts, most notably that of Villers-Cotterêts in August 1539, he worked to ensure that royal law was superior over local and customary law and attempted to make the king's writ run as far into the kingdom as possible. He was also keen to show his Catholic credentials more overtly.[65] The distinction between acceptable debate about reform of the Church and Lutheran heresy appeared to be clearer by the late 1530s. Earlier in the decade Francis had clashed several times with the Sorbonne over his support for reformist thinkers but in 1538 he was content to allow the university and the chancellor, acting under his authority, to take such action as they believed necessary in respect of the English bibles.[66]

Henry VIII was also increasingly concerned with his authority over the realm in both the secular and sacred spheres at this time. His concept of his kingship had been challenged and altered to some degree by his struggle with the papacy and Charles V. Like Francis, as he grew older, Henry began to see himself less immediately as the chivalric warrior-prince, and more as the father of his people. The propaganda produced in these years explicitly linked his apparent concern for his realm's spiritual welfare and its international safety. In 1539 the frontispiece of the *Great Bible* showed him as a prophet and judge, distributing the word of God to a grateful people. The same year Richard Morison had praised Henry as the protector of the English who would 'diligently watch that we may safely sleep', protected from the malign powers of Europe, including France.

The iconography of the *Great Bible* was designed to declare to his own people and those abroad, the independent and imperial status of Henry's sacred monarchy. Paradoxically, it was during these same years of rancorous argument with Francis I, that Henry also drew, as never before, on the French king's example of using architectural and artistic patronage to advertise these claims of imperial status. As the proceeds of the dissolution of the monasteries began reaching Henry's coffers in the late 1530s he began spending on an unprecedented scale, building new palaces and renovating older ones. He built the entirely new residence of Nonsuch and substantially increased the size and amenities of Whitehall palace. Henry's ambassadors in France kept him abreast of developments in Francis's artistic patronage at the châteaux of Chambord in the Loire Valley, Madrid near Paris and especially at Fontainebleau.[67]

A number of architects and designers who had worked for Francis I also worked for Henry in the late 1530s. The best known of them was Niccolò Bellin of Modena who did much of the decorative work at Nonsuch. These artists did not slavishly imitate all things French, but adapted ideas and expertise acquired in the service of the French king in their work for Henry. The king also employed French cartographers, horologists and jewellers. It was also from a Frenchman, one Jean Mallard, that Henry commissioned a Book of Hours at the end of 1530s. The seven illustrations Mallard provided are, after Hans Holbein's, the most famous images of the king. The two best known show the king playing a harp in the manner of King David and reading his bible in an idealised and ornately classical privy chamber at Whitehall.[68] Relations with France also prompted a very different sort of architectural patronage. It was during Francis I's brief rapprochement with Charles V between 1538 and 1540 that Henry began building the extraordinary chain of fortifications around the southern coasts of England, many of whose block houses and castles, such as Deal, Walmer and Camber can still be seen. The result of this expenditure, alongside that for building up the royal navy, is one of the more impressive legacies of Henry's reign.

Constructing fortifications and investing in the navy indicated Henry's readiness for war but the king knew better than to seek it openly in the late 1530s when his two great rivals were united, however briefly. Frustrated at his own isolation during these years and full of indignant self-righteousness, Henry instead tried to use the legal disputes referred to above as a way shaming Francis with the folly of his dependence on the goodwill of Charles. As Henry told his ambassador, Sir John Wallop, in the autumn of 1540 he had wanted certain criminal persons apprehended in France:

> To prove the inclination and zeal of the French king towards us and for the observation of his treaty than for any other report, thinking verily that he would have considered and esteemed our amity and friendship heretofore showed unto him.[69]

This was a test of honour which Francis had clearly failed, and therefore he did not deserve Henry's serious attention. Henry castigated Francis for trusting Charles V, a prince who had never respected him, while ignoring the reasonable demands of the powerful friend who had helped him escape the emperor's clutches in 1526. Charles V still held Milan and would never willingly or easily cede it to Francis. He should therefore stop equivocating and re-establish the alliance with Henry by resumption of the pensions he had agreed to pay Henry back in 1527.

Needless to say, this did not happen. Nonetheless, when it became clear in late-1540 that Charles V was not going to cede Milan to the French, Francis ordered Charles de Marillac, his ambassador in England, to try to secure another Franco-English alliance but upon favourable terms. Given that Henry had been trying to split Francis and Charles for the best part of two years and that he had been seriously worried by the prospect of an invasion in 1539, it is curious that he did not now show much interest in finally binding a disappointed Francis to him more closely. Relations warmed slightly in the winter of 1540–41 and in the spring, Marillac began negotiations with Norfolk who was again in the ascendant following his niece Catherine's marriage to Henry in August 1540. At their heart was a proposed match between Francis's youngest son, Charles Duke of Orléans and Princess Mary.[70] The negotiations were, however, clouded by further disputes about whether the French were comprehended in new legislation concerning the status of foreigners in England and over an area of land on the border between English and French territory outside Calais, known as 'the Cowpasture'.[71] There was also the question of Francis's outstanding debts to Henry under previous treaties. Although he had refused to hand over Milan immediately, Charles V still held out the promise of its being given in the future to Charles of Orléans and the French now wanted to set the prospect of Mary eventually becoming duchess of Milan off against Francis's pension debts, or see them remitted as part of her dowry. This did not interest the

English at all and the negotiations had not got far before Henry's progress to York in the late summer. Neither side wanted to appear too eager for an alliance but by the autumn Marillac was anxious that Anglo-Imperial overtures were in the wings.[72]

The French ambassador had good reason to worry because some time before the end of 1541 Henry decided, as a result of the recent disputes and with the international situation now more in his favour, that he would rather fight Francis I than ally with him. War broke out once more between Charles V and Francis in the summer of 1542. Towards the end of that year Henry turned his hand against Scotland, a sure sign that he was once more contemplating war on the Continent. After a series of vindictive raids across the border in the autumn, James V responded with an invasion of England but was defeated at the battle of Solway Moss in November. He died within a few weeks of this defeat, leaving his infant daughter Mary as queen of Scotland. Henry now planned to split the Scottish nobility and create an English party in Edinburgh. These plans culminated in the treaty of Greenwich signed in July 1543 under which Mary of Scotland was to be married to Henry's son Edward but the agreement was never put into effect.meanwhile, in February 1543, the Scots having been dealt with to Henry's satisfaction at least, he signed an offensive alliance with the emperor against France.[73]

In July 1544 Henry crossed the Channel to direct the English siege of Boulogne. The last Anglo-Imperial campaign of Henry's reign was as muddled and strategically ineffective as the first in 1513. Those old warhorses, the dukes of Norfolk and Suffolk, jointly commanded an army of 42,000 men and were supposed to rendezvous with a similarly large Imperial army in northern France before together marching on the French capital. Remembering that he had twice before been deserted by an Imperial ally and thinking that Charles V's armies would be held up for many weeks on France's north-eastern border, Henry was determined first to take Boulogne and nearby Montreuil. The siege of Boulogne lasted until mid-September but, contrary to Henry's expectations, Charles breached French defences at Saint-Dizier by mid-August and had reached Soissons by 7 September.[74] With his money running out and seeing Henry make no attempt to meet him, Charles decided instead to make peace with Francis. The treaty of Crépy was agreed on 18 September, the day Henry entered Boulogne in triumph. Once more, Henry saw himself betrayed by his Habsburg ally.[75]

Henry and Francis did not finally end their war for another two years and not before Henry had witnessed the loss of his prized warship the

Mary Rose in an engagement with a French fleet on the Solent in July 1545. Peace was finally agreed in the treaty of Ardres, of 7 June 1546, under which Henry was to keep Boulogne for eight years and then sell it back to the French for two million crowns.[76] The retention of Boulogne on these terms gratified Henry VIII but angered Francis I and neither side spoke of 'eternal' peace. After long months of wrangling the treaty's negotiators finally told each other plainly what had caused the conflict. As the French put it; 'this war ... between our masters has been for the preservation of their honours, than for any enmity between their persons'. For the English the breach of honour occurred with 'the not payment of our pension, which you are bound to pay to the king's majesty'. This, the French retorted, was because the English 'had [broken] the treaty first for that [they] gave not aid being asked, according to treaty'.[77] This clear summary of the points at issue shows how contemporaries thought primarily in personal terms in Anglo-French relations. Both kings felt disappointed and vengeful towards the other because of lost opportunities. For Francis it was adding insult to injury to expect him to pay pensions without an immediate return of his lost coastal city. For his part, Henry saw the taking of Boulogne as a clear conquest in a just war and an appropriate compensation for the payments owed to him in the first place. Within a month of the signing of the treaty new disputes arose over trading privileges and fortifications around Boulogne. It is probable that had both kings lived they would have been at war again within a short time.

CONCLUSION

The last Anglo-French peace agreement of Henry's reign was celebrated with all the fulsome rhetoric of its predecessors. In June 1546, 20 years after he had been sent to welcome Francis back to his kingdom from Spain, Sir Thomas Cheyne was once more despatched to re-establish cordial relations between the two kings. He stood as proxy for Henry as god-father to the dauphin Henry's daughter, Elizabeth.[78] In the months that followed there were the now familiar exchanges of large and impressive embassies and assurances of personal friendship on both sides. On the surface, a new start had once more been made and both sovereigns expressed hopes of close future co-operation on religious reform and against the emperor. Yet, unlike its predecessors, the peace of 1546 did not really restore the vital balance of honour between the two kings. The Imperial ambassador in France reported that Francis hated Henry more than ever before. He was probably right but the hatred he noted sprang not from deep-seated personal animosity as is so often assumed, but from frustrated expectations. There was little novel or compelling about the idea of peace between them by this time.[79]

As tattered and dog-eared as the idea of magnificent Anglo-French peace had become by 1546, it had, nevertheless, been of great benefit to Henry VIII. Maintaining advantageous peace had enabled him to play the role on the international stage which he desired in 1514, in 1518 and from 1527 onwards. As the discussion of the 1532 alliance treaty has shown, there was also a close connection between Henry's expectation of support and protection from Francis I, seen as his due, and his willingness to adopt a more aggressive approach to the resolution of his marriage dilemma through extending his personal control over the English Church. The importance for Henry of this support has not hitherto been sufficiently appreciated in accounts of the break with Rome which have Henry acting unilaterally under the influence of Thomas Cromwell. Anne Boleyn also played a crucial role in pushing Henry forward. Anne and her supporters continued to sponsor the close relations with France first fostered by Wolsey. The difficulties which Henry's second marriage posed for Anglo-French co-operation became apparent almost as soon as its potential benefits were first appreciated in late 1532.

After the Franco-Papal agreement of 1533 and his decision to break from Rome Henry was once more faced with international isolation. In 1536 he tried, as Wolsey had first done twenty years earlier, to make himself indispensable to European monarchs. Rebuffed by all sides he then tried to show Francis, through the numerous disputes between 1537 and 1545, how much he still depended upon his English ally if he were ever finally to achieve his Italian ambitions. During Francis's brief *entente* with Charles V in 1538–40, Henry suffered painful memories of his isolation in 1514. These European agreements, however transitory, threatened his long-held idea of how he best proved his greatness in the world; by making magnificent war on the Continent or orchestrating spectacular peace there. Isolated Henry may have been, but he was able to insist that he should not be ignored for very long either by Francis or Charles V. By 1541 he had decided to act on what he had first learned in 1513–14. In order to overcome his isolation, Henry once more traded his supposed independence from the Continent for the old Habsburg alliance. This achieved the same result that it had twice before, a strategically confused but politically effective invasion of France.

The intensely personal and competitive style of Anglo-French relations became much more muted after the deaths of Henry VIII and Francis I.

The later Tudor monarchs were conscious of their duty to maintain the patrimony handed on to them by Henry, but sought to do this more through the defence of England and its religion rather than through aggressive claims against France. Even Mary I's brief involvement in the on-going Franco-Habsburg conflict in 1557 was not prompted by any desire to renew her father's policies. Of course it resulted in the disastrous loss of Calais and with it any plausible Tudor claim to rule even part of the old Plantagenet dominions. Henry VIII never rebuilt England's medieval empire as he had longed to do, but in dealing with France as he did, he was at least able to keep his relatively small and marginal kingdom at the forefront of European affairs for nearly forty years. However, it was only under his daughter Elizabeth that England's interest in maritime power beyond the English Channel really developed and it was not until the latter seventeenth century that the newly-emergent Britain began creating for itself an empire, far beyond France, of a kind which Henry VIII could hardly have imagined.

NOTES

1. J. P. Carley, 'John Leland in Paris: the evidence of his poetry', *Studies in Philology*, 83 (1986), pp. 1–50, esp. pp. 49–50.

2. G. J. Richardson, *Renaissance Monarchy: The Reigns of Henry VIII, Francis I and Charles V* (2002), pp. 36–62 for a discussion of the chivalric model of war and peace-making which underpinned Anglo-French, and indeed Franco-Imperial, relations throughout Henry VIII's reign. Henry sent an army to attack Gascony in 1512, but it was diverted by his ally, Ferdinand of Aragon, to assist his own attempts to take Navarre and it saw no action in France.

3. S. J. Gunn, 'The French Wars of Henry VIII' in J. Black (ed.), *The Origins of War in Early Modern Europe* (Edinburgh, 1987), pp. 28–47.

4. Rymer, xiii, pp. 413–21 for the peace agreement with Louis. On the origins of the French pensions paid to English kings, see Chapter 2 by John Currin in this volume.

5. Ibid., pp. 625–42; Hall p. 595.

6. It was Dr David Starkey who first noted the political significance of this reciprocity, particularly in the English reception of the French embassy of 1518 and the subsequent establishment of what is sometimes called 'privy chamber' diplomacy between England and France. See D.R. Starkey, 'Representation through intimacy: a study in the symbolism of monarchy and court office in early-modern England' in I. Lewis (ed.), *Symbols and Sentiments: Cross-cultural Studies in Symbolism* (1977), pp. 187–224.

7. G. J. Richardson, 'Anglo-French political and cultural relations during the reign of Henry VIII'. Unpublished University of London PhD dissertation, 1996, pp. 58–151 for a fuller account of the context and elaboration of Anglo-French peace between 1518 and 1520; J. G. Russell, *The Field of Cloth of Gold: Men and Manners in 1520* (1969).

8. P. Gwyn, 'Wolsey's foreign policy: the conferences of Calais and Bruges reconsidered', *HJ*, 23 (1989), pp. 735–72.

9. Rymer, xiv, pp. 48–74 [*LP* iv (i), 1600–06].

10. R. J. Knecht, *Renaissance Warrior and Patron: The Reign of Francis I* (Cambridge, 1994), pp. 239–48.

11. Starkey, 'Representation', pp. 201–3.

12. BL, Cotton MS Caligula D ix. fo. 172v [*LP* iv (i), 2039].

13. G. J. Richardson, ' "Most highly to be regarded": The privy chamber of Henry VIII and Anglo-French relations, 1515–1520', *The Court Historian*, 4 (1999), pp. 119–40 for further discussion of the role played by the gentlemen of the privy chamber in Henry's relations with Francis I.

14. R. Strong, *The English Renaissance Miniature* (1983), pp. 27–9. For evidence that these gifts were indeed those of the French king and not, as is usually believed, those of his sister Margaret, see Richardson, 'Anglo-French relations', pp. 162–66.

15. The French ambassadors in London to Francis I, 21 March 1527, PRO, 31/8/137, fos 296–8 [*LP* iv (ii), 2974]; John Clerk to Wolsey, 24 March 1527, BL, Cotton MS Caligula D x, fos 34–5 [*LP* iv (ii), 2980]; Clerk to Wolsey, undated, *c.* April 1527, BL, Cotton MS Caligula D viii, fos 222–3 [*LP* iv (ii), 3042].

16. BL, Additional MS 12192, fos 43–79, esp. fos 44–5. This is a copy of Claude Dodieu's account of the embassy. The original is BN, MS NA 7004.

17. PRO, E30/1112/3/4 Treaties for the marriage of Princess Mary and the duke of Orléans; Mercantile Treaty; Treaty to withhold consent to a General Council of the Church while the Pope remains a prisoner. All signed at Amiens 18 August 1527. On the documents themselves see M. Orth, 'A French illuminated treaty of 1527', *Burlington Magazine*, 122 (1980), pp. 125–6.

18. Francis to Henry, 2 February 1529, BN, MS français 3005, fo.1; Henry to Francis, 5 October 1530, MS français 3015, fo.1.[*LP* iv (iii), 6665]; K. Neuschel, *Word of Honor: Interpreting Noble Culture in Sixteenth-Century France* (Cornell, 1989), esp. pp. 72–4, 128–9.

19. Hall, p. 732.

20. S. J. Gunn, 'Wolsey's foreign policy and the domestic crisis of 1527–28' in S. J. Gunn and P. G. Lindley (eds), *Cardinal Wolsey: Church, State and Art* (Cambridge, 1991), pp. 149–77.

21. R. Scheurer (ed.), *Correspondance du Cardinal Jean du Bellay* (2 vols, Paris, 1969), i, p. 22; E. Ives, 'The fall of Wolsey' in Gunn and Lindley, *Cardinal Wolsey*, pp. 286–315.

22. E. Ives, *Anne Boleyn* (Oxford, 1986), pp. 33–7.

23. J. Guy, *Tudor England* (Oxford, 1990), p. 124; G. R. Elton, *Reform and Reformation: England 1509–1558* (London, 1977), pp. 116–33.

24. Du Bellay to Montmorency, London, 4 and 12 October 1529, *Correspondance*, i, pp. 94–8 [*LP* iv (iii), 5983] and pp. 104–6.

25. Copy of Francis I's letter to Pierre Lizet, the President of the University, ordering him to silence opposition to Henry VIII's cause in the Faculty of Theology led by Noël Beda, dated 17 June 1530, PRO, SP1/57, fos 166–7 [*LP* iv (iii), 6459]. See also *LP* iv (iii), 6449, 6458 for a report of the proceedings at the Faculty of Theology and a letter from Guillaume du Bellay to Anne de Montmorency, also dated 17 June at Bordeaux, explaining how Francis had dismissed the Imperial ambassador's objections to the king's intervention in the debate on the divorce case in the Faculty.

26. BN, MS français 3037, fo. 47 [*LP* iv (iii), 6509]; MS français 2997, fo. 11 [*LP* iv (iii), 6508].

27. Payments in September 1529 from the king to the principal of the College of Tournai for one 'Charles Caro, Englishman, page of the chamber of the said lord', AN, KK 100, fo. 88. On Carew senior's visit to France at this time, see R. J. Knecht (ed.), *The Voyage of Sir Nicholas Carew to the Emperor in the year 1529* (Cambridge, 1959), pp. 48–9.

28. J. J. Scarisbrick, *Henry VIII* (1968), pp. 260–75.

29. Bryan to Henry VIII, 21 November 1530, *St. P.* vii, pp. 211–15 esp. p. 214.

30. Rymer, xiv, p. 146; Henry VIII to Benet, 10 July 1531, *St.P.* vii, pp. 305–16, esp. pp. 306–7; Chapuys to Charles V, 17 July 1531, [*LP* v, 340].

31. Elton, *Reform and Reformation*, pp. 174–5; Guy, *Tudor England*, pp. 131–4.

32. N. Camusat, *Meslanges Historiques ou Recueil de plusiers actes, letters, missives et autres mémoires qui peuvent servir en la deduction de l'histoire depuis l'an 1390 jusques à l'an 1580* (Troyes, 1619), p. 78.

33. Knecht, *Renaissance Warrior*, pp. 294–5 on Francis's agreement with the German Protestant princes.

34. N. Pocock, *Records of the Reformation, The Divorce 1527–1533* (2 vols, Oxford, 1870), ii, pp. 157–65. Henry VIII's instruction to Gardiner, 12 January 1532. The date given is '8 ° Aug. anno millesimo quinquagesimo vicesimo sexto'.

35. Wolsey to Henry VIII, 11 August 1526, *St. P.* i, pp. 169–71; for the treaty see Rymer, xiv, p. 185ff. Francis confirmed the treaty on 20 August 1526 [*LP* iv (ii), 2382, 2411].

36. Pocock, *Records of the Reformation*, p. 165.

37. Henry VIII to Gardiner, 9 February 1532, ibid., pp. 169–84 [*LP* v, 791].

38. Henry VIII to Gardiner, 16 February 1532, ibid., pp. 190–206, esp. p. 199 [*LP* v, 807].

39. Knecht, *Renaissance Warrior*, p. 295.

40. Rymer, xiv, p. 435 [*LP* v, 1117]. See also 1109, 1110 [*CSP Sp.* iv (ii), 962].

41. P. Friedmann, *Anne Boleyn: A Chapter in English History, 1527–1536* (2 vols, 1843–49), i, p. 154.

42. *LP* v, p. 820.

43. Chapuys to Charles V, 5 September 1532, *CSP. Sp.* iv (ii), 993.

44. Scarisbrick, *Henry VIII*, pp. 276–80 for a detailed discussion of the influences upon Henry's justification and definition of his authority. See also D. MacCulloch, 'Henry VIII and the reform of the Church' in his *The Reign of Henry VIII: Politics, Policy and Piety* (1995), pp. 159–180, esp. p. 162.

45. PRO, E101/420/15 fo. 2v [*LP* v, 686, p. 329 Cromwell listed under 'gentlemen'].

46. *CSP* iv, 802, 804; A few days later Francis I swore to the treaty which the Venetian ambassador in France was told was made 'for the king's security when crossing the Channel'.

47. BN, MS français 3039, fo. 60. Henry VIII to Francis I, 23 July 1532.

48. *The Maner of the Triumphe at Caleys and Bulleyn* (published by Wynken de Worde in 1533) Printed in E. Arber, *An English Garner, Tudor Tracts 1532–1588* (New York, 1964), pp. 3–8.

49. Hall, p. 789; Zuam Antonio Venier to the Venetian Signory 31 October 1532 *CSPV* iv, 822. On the significance of the kiss in this context see J. Russell-Major, 'Bastard feudalism and the kiss: changing social mores in late medieval and early modern France', *Journal of Interdisciplinary History*, 17 (1987), pp. 509–35.

50. Hall, pp. 791–2; BN MS français 10388, fos 154–5 for the robes made for Henry recorded in the French expenditure accounts for the meeting.

51. Richard Tate to Cromwell, 11 December 1532, BL, Cotton MS Caligula E II, fo. 192 [*LP* iv, 1627]. See also W. Sessions, *Henry Howard Earl of Surrey* (Boston, 1986), pp. 5–6.

52. Jean de Dinteville to Montmorency, 7 November 1533 PRO, 31/3/6, fos 374–7 [*LP* vi, 1404].

53. Montmorency's instructions to Dinteville, 26 March 1533 BN, MS Dupuy 547, fo. 214.

54. On this circle and on Dinteville's friend, Georges de Selve, who visited him in London in the spring of 1533 and who appears with him in the painting 'The Ambassadors', see S. Foister, A. Roy and M. Wyld, *Holbein's The Ambassadors: Making and Meaning* (1997).

55. Dinteville to Montmorency, 7 November, *LP* vi, 1404, 1479 and Dinteville's memorandum of conversations with Henry; Scarisbrick, *Henry VIII*, pp. 317–20.

56. *DNB* sub Weston. Francis Weston's uncle, William, was Prior of the Knights of St John in England. He knew, and had fought alongside, the Grand Master of the Order, Philippe de Villiers l'Isle-Adam who was Jean Dinteville's cousin. *LP* v, 81, 579. Jean himself had been in England on the Order's business as recently as 1531. His interventions on young Weston's behalf seem likely to have been prompted in some way by these connections.

57. Henry VIII to Gardiner, 19 September 1536 and Henry VIII to Gardiner and Wallop, 11 October 1536, BL, Additional MS 25114, fos 209–12, 216–26 [*LP* xi, 469,656].

58. Henry VIII to Gardiner, 29 January 1537 and 17 February 1537, ibid., fos 241, 244–45 [*LP* xii (i), 274, 445].

59. Knecht, *Renaissance Warrior*, pp. 329–41; 385–97.

60. For letters of instructions and reports on the attempts to have Pole detained, BL, Additional MS 25114, fos 253–8, 262–3 [*LP* xii (i), 817, 625, 865, 939, 1032].

61. J. J. Scarisbrick, 'The first man around the Cape of Good Hope?' *Bulletin of the Institute of Historical Research*, 34 (1961), pp. 165–77 for an account of Brancestor's extraordinary career and the attempt to arrest him during the emperor's tour through France in late 1539. See also Richardson, 'Anglo-French relations', pp. 286–7.

62. D. L. Potter, 'Diplomacy in the mid-sixteenth century: England and France, 1536–1550'. Unpublished Cambridge University PhD Thesis, (1973), pp. 3–34 for the fullest account of this case.

63. AN, J 966, no.13/5 fos 1–3. Louis de Caillaud's report to the Chancellor. On the 'Matthew Bible' and its contribution to the Great Bible of 1539 see F. F. Bruce, *The English Bible: A History of Translations from the Earliest Version to the New English Bible* (1961), pp. 64–6.

64. Castillon to Anne de Montmorency, 31 December 1538, *LP* xiii (ii), 1163; Chapuys to Charles V, 9 January 1539, *LP* xiv (i), 37; Montmorency to Marillac, 6 May 1539, *LP* xiv (i), 934.

65. Knecht, *Renaissance Warrior*, pp. 352–3.

66. R. J. Knecht, 'Francis I, "Defender of the Faith"?' in E. W. Ives, R. J. Knecht and J. J. Scarisbrick (eds), *Wealth and Power in Tudor England: Essays presented to S. T. Bindoff* (1978), pp. 106–27 on Francis's attitudes to religious debate and heresy over the course of his reign.

67. Wallop to Henry VIII, 11 November 1540, *St. P.* viii, p. 482.

68. BL, Royal MS 2 A xvi, fo.63v; P. Tudor-Craig, 'Henry VIII and King David' in
    D. Williams (ed.), *Early Tudor England, Proceedings of the 1987 Harlaxton Symposium*
    (Woodbrige, 1989), pp. 183–201.

69. The Council at Court to the Council at London, 16 October.1540, *St. P.* i,
    pp. 652–3.

70. Francis I to Marillac, 2 June 1541, J. Kaulek (ed.), *Correspondence politique de MM. de
    Castillon et de Marillac, ambassadeurs de France en Angleterre 1537–1542* (Paris, 1885),
    no. 347 [*LP* xvi, 885].

71. On the long-running dispute see Potter, 'Diplomacy' p. 48 and following.

72. Marillac's letters to Francis I, August/September 1541, *LP* xvi, 1089, 1090,1208.

73. *LP* xvii (i), 754, 759; Scarisbrick, *Henry VIII*, pp. 424–39.

74. The Council with the King to the Council with the Queen, 19 September 1544,
    St. P. x, pp. 75–7; Knecht, *Renaissance Warrior*, pp. 490–3.

75. W. Blockmans, *Emperor Charles V 1500–1558* (2002), pp. 72–4.

76. Rymer, xv, p. 93 [*LP* xxi (i), 1014].

77. *St. P.* xi, pp. 128–9.

78. Minutes of meeting of the Privy Council, 18 June 1546, *LP* xxi (i), 1086.

79. *CSP. Sp.* viii, 360.

4

TOWARDS AN IDEOLOGICAL FOREIGN POLICY: HENRY VIII AND LUTHERAN GERMANY, 1531–47

Rory McEntegart

In September 1539 an English stranger arrived unannounced at the free imperial city of Strassburg. He explained to those who received him that he had come to the city on account of the Act of Six Articles, the reactionary religious legislation that had been passed by the English parliament earlier in the summer. He asked that he be allowed to speak about the situation in England to the Strassburg council and the city's leading theologian, Martin Bucer. At first sight he must have appeared, like so many of his confessional leanings, as merely another godly Englishman escaping the feared consequences of religious persecution. Yet this man was different from the other religious refugees fleeing England in the late summer of 1539: this man had been sent by an elite group within the inner circle of the English regime with a message for the Protestants of Germany.[1]

The Englishman delivered his message to the council and Bucer in the second week of September. He told the Strassburgers of the reasons for the turn which religion had taken in England. He acknowledged that much that had happened was due to the activities of religious conservatives at the court of King Henry VIII. But there were other reasons. In particular, there was the question of diplomatic contact between England and the alliance which the German Protestants had formed to defend their faith in 1531, the League of Schmalkalden. He said that leading English evangelicals believed that the League had failed in its diplomatic practice with England to support the cause of the gospel, and that this had given the upper hand to those of a conservative religious inclination. Since the middle of the decade the king had sought a great embassy from the League of Schmalkalden, but had only received minor legations. The king had been especially desirous of discussing theology with Martin Luther's conciliatory deputy, Philip Melanchthon, yet he had been refused permission to go to England on a number of occasions. As Bucer explained in a letter of 16 September to Landgrave Philip of Hesse, the nobleman who shared the leadership of the League with the duke of Saxony, the king had perceived 'that we negotiated with him so slowly and, as he took it, regarded him but little'.[2] As a result of this, the conservatives now stood

> in special fame and trust, whereas the evangelicals at this time are somewhat askew and in very little repute. This has mainly been caused by the fact that those pious men had much assured the king of our princes and allies and yet have still not been able to gain anything from us that would be well regarded by the king. Moreover, the fact that Master Philip has been denied him so often, that embassies too have not been sent, and that all negotiations with him have been set to our advantage and have offered him nothing which he might appreciate; these things he has taken to be a great contempt of his person.[3]

But the messenger had not been sent simply to offer a litany of complaints. He explained that the evangelicals wanted the League to make good the damage they had helped cause:

> now the pious, dear people, who have preached Christ with the greatest risk and diligence, know no counsel better (through which they will be able to remain in the liberty of Christ's Church), than that we gravely undertake right now to despatch Master Philip along with other zealous people to the king. For there are two things which have brought them into this pass. One is that the king thinks that we have held him in contempt and demonstrated with our own affairs that we are uncertain and risky – that is to say, that no one could rely on our help. The second is that he was persuaded to accept the aforementioned articles [the Act of Six Articles] by pretty periphrasis and crafty sophistry. Thus the pious people have hope that if our princes and allies were to despatch a considerable embassy to England and with true devotion look after the religion and the pious Christians there, it would yet be of great benefit to them.[4]

The picture this episode suggests of a foreign policy intimately engaged with domestic affairs, riven by faction and driven by ideology, is at odds with the traditional historiography of the Henrician Reformation. Conventionally, Henry's Reformation diplomacy has been cast in terms of great power politics: his chief concern was to prevent a papal alliance from attacking England, in the main by encouraging hostilities between the two likely underwriters of such an alliance, Charles V and Francis I. During those periods when the balance of power was threatened by a peaceful intermission in Franco-Imperial relations, Henry would turn for help to the emperor's subjects in Protestant Germany, enticing them with the prospect of a political and religious agreement; as soon as Charles and Francis resumed hostilities Henry would distance himself from the Germans, not renouncing them entirely but stringing them along with vague talk of future co-operation in case they be needed again at some later time. According to this view, Henry's foreign policy was based on secular calculation; his only care was to keep Francis and Charles apart, his movements towards the Germans no more than finely judged adjustments in a diplomatic balancing mechanism, reflecting nothing in terms of an ideological engagement with Protestantism or a clash of ideas among the king's men.[5] This chapter offers a different view. It suggests that while the possibility of a Franco-Imperial enterprise always occupied royal thinking, the Reformation introduced an ideological element to English foreign policy which has been underestimated in the historiography. A review of Anglo-Schmalkaldic relations in the second half of the reign suggests that religious ideas played an important part in the making of foreign policy: the king had a genuine interest in the Schmalkaldic League and its religious ideas; his reform-minded counsellors came to be staunch advocates of a Lutheran alliance for the opportunities it might provide for the advance of the gospel; and his conservative advisors equally firm opponents. The result was an ideological and faction-ridden foreign policy, at once influenced by and influencing domestic political changes; a messy complex of diplomatic interaction far removed from the modernist historiographical model of measured, secular international relations.

OPENING GAMBITS

The story begins in late 1533. By the end of that year the king's affairs were at crisis point: with the marriage to Anne Boleyn and the renunciation of Catherine of Aragon complete and the bulk of the Reformation legislation on the statute book Henry now faced the wrath of Catholic Europe largely alone. The need for friends was acute; towards the end of the year Henry directed that approaches be made to Germany. The policy of diplomatic engagement with Germany was not entirely new. Since his difficulties with the Habsburgs first emerged Henry had pursued diplomacy in the Holy Roman Empire, searching for possible ways of exerting pressure on Charles V. In 1533, however, this policy underwent a fundamental change. Previously, Henry had engaged in diplomatic practice with both the Catholic and Protestant princes of Germany: now, in a series of meetings during December, he turned exclusively to the Lutheran side of the German confessional divide.[6] Instructions prepared for the ambassadors at the end of the year provide an early sign of this.[7] The ambassadors were directed to stress that Henry had decided to 'reduce the said pope's powers'.[8] To this end, the Germans were to be requested 'to give unto his highness their assistance and best advise how he shall proceed to the accomplishment of his desired purposes'.[9] They should advise Henry of anything touching the common weal or abuses 'which in their opinion shall be thought meet to be reformed and redressed', in which case they would find Henry ready to support just causes.[10] And all this was only to be taken up with those Germans who themselves stood in opposition to Rome:

> for as much as it is doubtful of what mind, intention and purpose the said princes be, or at least some of them, that is to wit whether they be so dedicated to the pope's devotion that there is no likelihood of any good success touching the king's purposes. ... [the ambassadors should seek to] in[sea]rch, inquire and know the disposition and inclination of the said princes, and of every of them severally. And so thereafter according to their wisdoms and discretions to deliver or retain the king's said letters with declaration or without declaration of their said charge.[11]

Henry's movement towards Protestant, rather than bi-confessional, Germany must in large part be explained by his growing isolation in Europe at this time; in late 1533 his options for diplomatic partners were effectively limited to those who were themselves at odds with papal Europe. However, the growing interest in the Schmalkaldic League was also a result of changes in the English body politic, reflecting the emergence of new ideological influences and imperatives. Certainly, the ambassadors who went to Germany in 1534 would suggest to their hosts

that such was the case. In May of that year a Schmalkaldic League diet at
Nuremberg reported that the English ambassadors had told them that
there was a group of leading people about the king '*who favour the gospel*
[my italics]' with a special interest in diplomacy with Protestant Germany.[12]
The embassy to Germany had, '*though unknown to the king* [my italics],
been promoted and effected by some of the realm's distinguished councillors and people, who are of the opinion and hope that the League will
prepare and despatch there an embassy with articles etc'.[13] With the
despatch of a Protestant embassy to England:

> the English councillors and distinguished people who favour the
> gospel and have requested such an embassy will have greater cause to
> prompt the king, so that through this means, which the Almighty in his
> grace has now miraculously set forth, the gospel might be brought
> into England, and from a persecutor will be made a lover of the word
> of God.[14]

The Nuremberg diet made no mention of the members of this mysterious group of prominent evangelicals at the king's court, but some names
immediately suggest themselves as likely candidates. First among them is
the man who in the course of 1533 had emerged as the most probable
replacement for Cardinal Wolsey as king's minister, Thomas Cromwell. In
the council meetings which first discussed the despatch of the embassy to
Germany Cromwell had been at the forefront, preparing the order of
business, marking drafts for correction and informing the king of
progress.[15] As the embassy's concentration on Protestant Germany was
refined in the preparing of the instructions and the adminstrative materials for the ambassadors, Cromwell's hand or those of men in his service
produced all the relevant documentation. What is more, the men chosen
as ambassadors were all Cromwellian appointments: Christopher Mont, a
native of Speyer who would become Cromwell's chief German agent in
the years ahead; William Paget, who had been drifting away from his former patron the disgraced Stephen Gardiner and was about to come
under Cromwell's formal control as clerk of the signet; Thomas Legh,
who would be employed as one of Cromwell's most notorious commissioners for the dissolution of the monasteries; and Nicholas Heath, who
in spite of his later defence of orthodoxy in the reigns of Edward, Mary
and Elizabeth, was of Cromwell's circle and seems to have been partial to
evangelical ideas in the 1530s. Apart from these men directly involved in
the preparing and staffing of the embassy, there were probably others

too. Cromwell had risen to prominence on the back of a series of political alliances, notably with the group attached to Anne Boleyn; this group was known for its evangelical sympathies, and included among its number two men who would be associated with Cromwell and his German diplomacy during the remainder of the decade: the king's almoner Edward Foxe and Thomas Cranmer, who upon his return from a posting as Imperial ambassador had been appointed archbishop of Canterbury in early 1533.

It would seem that this core group of 'councillors and distinguished people who favour the gospel' had quietly been agitating for the despatch of an embassy to Protestant Germany.[16] Though Henry had been actively involved in the plans to send an embassy to Germany, the words 'though unknown to the king' suggest that to some extent the group had promoted the embassy without the king being aware of their motives. As to those motives, it is here that the question of religious ideology comes into the foreground. The initial evidence suggests that Cromwell and his circle wanted closer relations with the Schmalkaldic League because of the opportunities they would bring for the gospel; these were, after all, men 'who favour the gospel', or evangelicals. For such men, Anglo-Schmalkaldic relations represented a great opportunity. In the immediate aftermath of the break with Rome, the theological direction of the English Church was as yet unclear, still in the earliest stages of being determined; those who hoped that the new Church would take on a reformist colour could make good use of help from foreign Protestants. A visiting Schmalkaldic embassy would be able to discuss and advocate Lutheran theology around the king with much greater latitude and freedom from the risk of persecution than any Englishman or group; an embassy might lay the groundwork for a religious and political agreement between England and the League; and such an agreement might in turn pave the way for a fully reformed Church of England.

An English Embassy to Protestant Germany, 1535–36

As fortune would have it, these plans made little progress in 1534. For the greater part of the year the Schmalkaldeners were preoccupied with a succession dispute in the duchy of Württemberg and delicate peace negotiations with the Habsburgs; they had little time for the diplomatic complications which the English envoys proposed. The applications from England made no headway and for a time Anglo-Schmalkaldic relations lay dormant.

The following year, however, England turned to the League again. As before, the European situation favoured the advocacy of diplomacy with the Germans. Pope Paul III had revived the idea of a general council of the Church as a means to solve Christendom's problems. Both Henry and the German Protestants feared a general council for the threat it presented of a resolution imposed by the papacy on their respective dominions. In England plans quickly developed: initially it was intended to request the despatch to England of Luther's deputy Philip Melanchthon, whom Henry had come to respect for his reputation as a moderate reformer and feared might be tricked by the papacy into giving ground on a general council. By the summer of 1535 this had become something more significant: a plan to send a major embassy to Germany to discuss a range of religious and political matters and the possibility of Henry's admission to the Schmalkaldic League. An exploratory mission led by Robert Barnes was sent to Germany in late July to announce the despatch of ambassadors from the king; in October 1535 this embassy, led by Edward Foxe, recently promoted to the bishopric of Hereford, left for Germany. The evidence for Cromwell's leading role in all this is persuasive. As in 1533–34, he took the main part in arranging for the despatch of both the exploratory and main embassies. His office memoranda for the summer of 1535 are replete with references to 'the sending into Almayne and also Doctor Barnes', 'to send forth doctor Barnys', 'to despatch doctor Barnys with his letters and other writings', 'how I have spoken with doctor Barnes, and that he is ready to go', 'for the despatch of my lord of hereford', '298 l. 13 s. 4 d. to my lord of Hereford', 'letters to be assigned to all the princes', and the like – from March to October 1535 well over a dozen separate references to the German embassies appear in the papers of Cromwell or men in his service.[17] Also noteworthy are the Cromwellian associations and reformist inclinations of the embassy personnel. Edward Foxe was one of the most prominent of the new men who had risen in the Boleyn-Cromwell circle, a figure sufficiently associated with the reform movement for the Imperial ambassador Eustace Chapuys to lump him with Cromwell and Cranmer as 'among the most perfect Lutherans in the world'. Christopher Mont and Nicholas Heath, already noted as Cromwellian appointments to the embassy of the previous year, were reassigned to the German venture of 1535. And there was Robert Barnes, an associate of Cromwell and widely known as England's foremost Lutheran. Hints as to Cromwell's particular ideological interests may also be detected in his correspondence. Robert Barnes wrote to him in unmistakeably confraternal terms. He noted in one letter to the minister that although he had concerns about some of Edward

Foxe's theological views, 'I trust at length so to use him that there shall be no great variance, for he is gentle and may abide all manner of honest communication, wherefore I doubt not but to draw him at length to me through god's grace';[18] the words, confidential and knowing, resonate with the tones of a shared view of the world. On another occasion he bid Cromwell farewell in language whose evangelical nuances are again transparent: 'Your mastership knoweth my faith. Thus Jesus keep you in honour and virtue. Amen.'[19] Significant too is a letter dated 9 April 1536 to Cromwell from Martin Luther himself, in which the father of the Reformation excused himself for not having replied sooner to a letter which he had received from Cromwell, and returned the compliment which the minister had paid him in that letter (tantalisingly, Cromwell's letter and its complimentary sentiments do not survive). He then went on to note that:

> Dr Barnes rejoiced me wonderfully, as he told me of the earnestness and propensity of your lordship's goodwill in the cause of Christ, and in particular because of your authority in the entire kingdom and about the king, with which you can do much.[20]

This, it hardly needs to be said, is the sort of letter which Luther would only have written to someone whose religious position he considered to be close to his own. It is also a letter which for the first time in Germany identified Cromwell as a leading English evangelical. At Nuremberg in May 1534 the talk had been of a nameless group promoting reform about the king; increasingly, from 1535–36 the Germans would identify Cromwell as the man whose words and deeds represented the best hope for the gospel in England.

Yet if all this support for Anglo-Schmalkaldic relations was forthcoming from Cromwell and his friends, none of it could come to anything without the king. In some part Henry gave his backing to the development of contact between England and the League for reasons that have already been mentioned: he faced considerable external pressures in the years following the divorce and the Germans represented one of the few alliance possibilities open to him against Catholic Europe. But the European situation was not the sole motive for Henry's interest in diplomacy with the League, for he would continue to pursue active contact with the Germans through much of 1536, long after the death of Catherine of Aragon in January 1536 and the recrudescence of Franco-Imperial hostilities in Italy in April 1536 had reduced the level of the external threats facing the king. There were other reasons, and these went further than the practicalities of foreign policy. Henry had an interest in the Germans that arose out of his own religious concerns. These were different from those which guided his evangelical advisors like Cromwell, but they were important nevertheless. Henry's religious interest in the Schmalkaldic League was a result of the condition of his newly created Church: the Church of England, free now from the dictates of Rome, had no theological standard of its own to which it could bind the faithful. Henry needed to define the theology of his Church, and although he had no more desire to take directives from Wittenberg than he did from Rome, he was very interested in the possibility of engaging in consultations with the Germans with a view to helping him arrive at a codification of the faith for the Church of England. Henry had given signs in the early 1530s that he did not want the break with Rome to lead to a diversity of religious practices in England. As early as 1534 he complained to Cranmer that in spite of the repeated councils summoned to promote unity in religion 'there swarmeth abroad a number of indiscreet persons which being neither furnished with wisdom, learning nor judgement be nevertheless authorised to preach and permitted to blow abroad their folly'.[21] Henry instructed Cranmer and his prelates to take greater care with the choice of preachers, 'to th'intent our people may be educate[d], fed and enriched with wholesome food'.[22] Though there is no talk here of the need for a definitive statement of the faith to guide the clergy and people, it may be seen that Henry was not far from considering such a measure. By August 1534 he was a bit closer still with a document headed 'how the false heresies which the bishop of rome hath taught the people should be brought out of their consciences and heresies'.[23] This directed the archbishop of Canterbury to summon a council of bishops and doctors, and have them sign their decision on each of the articles contained in the 'book of the charge'.[24] Nothing more is known of what became this conference or the mysterious 'book of the charge', but it is clear that Henry was beginning to push his theologians towards establishing a codification of the English faith.

In establishing such a codification, Henry could use the advice of those European Christians who had themselves formulated a theological code to replace that of the Roman Church. It was Philip Melanchthon's European-wide reputation as the moderate face of Protestantism, as the conciliatory author of the Confession of Augsburg, that led to his being asked twice in 1534 to come to England,[25] and to his being approached by Robert Barnes early in 1535.[26] It was also one of the reasons why he was sought later in the year, and explains the abiding interest Henry showed in consulting with him during the remainder of the decade.[27] There is also the example of a group of ambassadors who came from Hamburg and Lübeck to England in 1534 to discuss the succession to the Danish throne; they soon found that Henry regarded contacts with Germany as affording the opportunity to discuss German theology. Chapuys reported in December 1534 that the ambassadors had been put into conference with the king's bishops, to discuss 'the sacrifice of the mass, and whether faith alone without works is sufficient for our salvation'.[28]

Thus, when Edward Foxe was sent to Germany it was not purely with the royal intention of negotiating a political alliance. His instructions explained that Henry wished to arrive at a settlement of religion and would like the advice and assistance of the Germans in the task. Henry wanted the embassy 'to confer, consult and devise with them in certain other things wherein his majesty minding to proceed according to the very truth of the gospel hath thought good to know their advice and counsel'.[29] The Germans were to be told that Henry intended to put his kingdom's Church in order, bringing a true understanding of religion 'to the knowledge of his people and subjects intending also so further and further to proceed therein as his grace by good consultation shall perceive may tend and pertain to the augmentation of the glory of god and the true knowledge of his word'.[30] The League should know that Henry would not 'without good advisement and mature deliberation, consultation also and conference with his friends go in any part beyond the said truth'.[31] He wished 'to be ascertained in what points and articles the learned men there be so constantly and assuredly resolved as by no persuasion of may they can be turned from the same'.[32] Thus he wanted the Germans to 'entertain in conferences and conversations the said bishop so friendly and familiarly concerning the matters aforesaid'.[33] Accordingly, when the time came for Foxe to speak to the League at Schmalkalden in December, he declared that Henry wished to be 'informed as to the state of religion, and receive advice as to what to reform in England in matters relating to faith and religion'.[34] It is not difficult to see why Cromwell and his evangelical circle must have regarded the king's interest in theological consultations as a golden opportunity. It seems likely that as early as 1533 they were aware that Henry had developed an interest in how the Lutherans had gone about separating from Rome and establishing their own Church. No doubt it was this awareness that informed the exhortations to the League recorded at the diet of Nuremberg in May 1534 to send an embassy to England where it might discuss theology with Henry and, if things went well, perhaps persuade him to go further in the direction of reform. However, there was one crucial qualification to the king's interest in theological consultations with the League, and in the years ahead this would emerge as a serious point of weakness in the evangelicals' Schmalkaldic policy. Henry wanted to discuss theology with the Germans, but he did not want simply to accept a Lutheran formulary of the faith. Foxe's instructions provide clear evidence of this: if the League should require that Henry 'receive the whole confession of Germany word for word as it is imprinted', Foxe should say that Henry would accept it only when he had received an embassy from the League and 'shall have seen and perused the articles of the said league and shall perceive that there is in it contained none other articles but such as may be agreable with the gospel whereof the said league is named'.[35] This was reiterated after Foxe met with the League at Schmalkalden in December 1535 for preliminary discussions and received from the Germans the demand that if Henry wanted to enter into an alliance with them he would first have to adopt the Confession of Augsburg. The king wrote back to Foxe, instructing him to reply in the following terms:

> forasmoch as his majesty desireth much that his bishops and learned men might agree with theirs But seen that it cannot be unless certain things in their confession and Apology should by their familiar conferences mitigate, his grace therefore would the orators and some excellent learned man with them should be sent hither to confer, talk, treat and commone upon the same.[36]

Just as the king's interest in consulting with the Germans represented an opportunity for the evangelicals, so his unwillingness blindly to accept the dictates of Wittenberg offered an opening for his counsellors of a conservative religious temper. Stephen Gardiner was perhaps the first of the conservatives to pick up on this, when in early 1536 he wrote for the king an opinion on Anglo-Schmalkaldic relations suggesting that 'if this article [this is a reference to the first of a set of articles given to the English ambassadors at the preliminary discussions at Schmalkalden in December 1535; it indicated that an alliance would be conditional upon English acceptance of the Confession of Augsburg] be granted unto, then shall the King's Highness be bound to the Church of Germany, and, without their consent, may not do that the Word of God shall permit, unless their common consent doth concur thereunto'.[37]

Gardiner was careful not to disagree with the king on the virtue of theological consultations with the League, noting that 'to hear their ambassadors, to commen also with them, to entertain them, and with them to discuss the very truth, were very good'.[38] But he emphasised that a thoroughgoing religious and political alliance would rob Henry and his Church of that independence for which the king had so recently fought:

> I would rather advise the King's Highness to give them money where-with to defend truth, than to enter any league with such men, which, as I fear, cannot be fast bound again, and also dwell so far of ... but upon the Word of God, to make a new knot, whereof the one end shall be in Germany, shall declare rather a change of a bond of dependence than a riddance thereof.[39]

Gardiner and his conservative allies would have much to work with in this regard over the following years, for although from the beginning the king was clear with the Germans that he expected a compromising approach to theological discourse, they were equally firm from the out-set that the king must accept their confession as they had established it. From the Lutheran point of view this attitude was understandable, but it offered the hope for the conservatives that Anglo-Schmalkaldic relations, far from being the Trojan horse for further reform that the evangelicals envisaged, might ultimately antagonise the king; and rather than open the door to Lutheran reform only bring into sharper definition any resid-ual royal misgivings about Lutheranism.

And indeed, the outlines of those concerns were soon to appear. After the preliminary alliance discussions concluded at Schmalkalden in late 1535, Foxe and his retinue left for Wittenberg, where they entered into a three-month-long series of intense theological discussions with the lead-ing Lutheran divines, among them Luther himself, Philip Melanchthon, Justas Jonas and John Bugenhagen. Initially there took place some incon-clusive disputations on the divorce. From February, however, the focus shifted to Lutheran theology itself. These discussions are fascinating, for they provide the first indication since the break with Rome of the specific nature of Henry's misgivings about Lutheranism. The discussions were based largely on an examination of the doctrine in the Confession of Augsburg, which had been presented by Philip Melanchthon to the Imperial party at the diet of Augsburg in 1530. The Confession of Augsburg was, of course, a doctrinal statement of Lutheranism in two parts, the Confession and the Apology. The first part, the Confession, was the longer but was composed largely of non-contentious matter such as the creed, the nature of the Church and the like; even when it turned to issues of a more controversial nature such as justification the doctrine was presented in relatively moderate terms. The second part, the Apology, was shorter but much more contentious, focusing on what the Lutherans believed were unacceptable abuses in the Catholic Church, among them private masses, the dispensing of communion in one kind only and the belief in the sanctity of clerical vows, such as celibacy. It soon emerged that the English ambassadors were able to indicate in principle the king's general acceptance of the doctrine contained in the Confession. By March, however, it was clear that no such assurances could be given with regard to the doctrine from the Apology. Specifically, the disputants were able to narrow down the seven abuses in the Apology to four which, in spite of their own personal views, they were not sure the king could accept as the Lutherans wished to formulate them: private masses, communion in one kind only, priestly marriage and the observance of monastic vows. As Martin Luther wrote in March, 'since they are not sure how their king will take the articles, especially the last four, they have decided to take time in which to show the same to his majesty'.[40]

With the specific areas of theological contention thus narrowed down, the Germans were invited to send a theological delegation to England to reach a conclusion of the matter with the king; once an acceptable theological position was thereby established in London, a political alliance between England and the League could be settled. In April the League began to discuss the sending of such an embassy. After some initial difficulties, these discussions began to develop promisingly. However, in early June they suddenly ground to a halt. The reason was the arrival in Germany of news on the fall of Anne Boleyn. The Schmalkaldeners knew that Anne had been sympathetic to the new religion. The League wondered whether her fall was merely the prelude to a wider reaction against Protestantism in England and decided to wait for further news before proceeding with the embassy plans. But there was to be no news from England for some time. In the second half of 1536 the Pilgrimage of Grace commenced and, occupied with it well into the following year, the English government had little time for foreign affairs. Anglo-Schmalkaldic relations fell quiet, not to revive again until the summer of 1537.

THE REVIVAL OF CONTACT, 1537–38

It was the League which took the first step towards re-establishing contact. In response to renewed papal efforts to summon a general council in late 1536, the Germans decided the following year to send an ambassador to the king of England to sound him out on the matter. This, however, was not the much discussed major legation which the king had been given to expect following Foxe's return. Rather, the League sent a common Hamburg sailor to the king's court with a letter on the proposed general council; so diplomatically inept was the man that upon delivering the letter he departed unannounced, not waiting for leave to go, still less for a reply from the king. This not only greatly offended Henry, it also infuriated Cromwell and his friends, who in the wake of the defeat of the Pilgrimage of Grace saw an opportunity to advance the cause of reform. After some deliberation they decided independently to contact the League. As chance would have it, they had at that very time just the man for the task. Recently an itinerant English Protestant named Thomas Theabold had arrived in England. Theabold had spent the last couple of years studying with reformers in Tübingen and Strassburg and had returned to England for the purpose of bringing some reformist literature to the king. Thomas Cromwell, Thomas Cranmer and Edward Foxe combined to brief Theabold on their concerns about the League's diplomacy and the need for a greater effort; they asked that he convey these concerns to the League. Accordingly, upon his return to Germany Theabold went to Strassburg and passed on the messages from the English evangelicals to the city's leading theologian, Martin Bucer. On 23 October 1537, Bucer wrote to Thomas Cranmer in response to the information he had received 'by these letters, and by the conversation of Thomas'.[41] He noted his optimism at what he heard as to the existence of a group of evangelicals at the upper level of government, for 'the Lord has united with you (not as Theseuses, but as Barnabases) the Latimers, the Foxes, and other endued with so much courage, so much activity, and, in fine, with so much zeal'.[42] Nevertheless, he accepted the evangelicals' criticisms conveyed by Theabold, lamenting 'that senselessness and all but treason of ours, who in a place and time so convenient and desirable have not aided you by the slightest exertions'.[43] Subsequently, the town council communicated the matters raised by Theabold in a report for the Schmalkaldic League's two leaders, John Frederick of Saxony and Philip of Hesse. The report explained that 'today a man from England was here, who brought to our preacher [Bucer] a letter, in which was written that as a result of the recent uproar in England [the Pilgrimage of Grace], the evangelical bishops very much have the king's ear'.[44] The evangelicals believed that a golden opportunity had been let slip by the League: 'in relation to this, however, the Englishman has also told me how all the kind-hearted have complained bitterly that the embassy from my gracious lord the duke of

Saxony, your grace and the other League members has not gone ahead and been sent to England, where it might promote the gospel'.[45] Edward Foxe, at this stage the senior English political figure with the greatest repute in Protestant Germany, went so far as to allow his name explicitly to be attached to the recommendation that the League send immediately an embassy to England to make good the damage that had been caused.[46] For all that, Foxe was clearly aware of the unofficial nature of these moves by the evangelicals and the risks that attended giving his name to such an initiative: in an interesting post-script to the report the writer warned that Foxe's involvement must be kept secret, 'so that he does not come into any danger with his lord the king'.[47]

The messages conveyed by Theabold resulted in a flurry of activity. The League sent a Saxon ambassador to the king in November for the purpose of reviving contact; around the turn of the year instructions began to be drafted for Christopher Mont to go to Germany to declare the king's views on a general council, reiterate his desire to enter into an alliance with the League and request that a theological delegation be despatched to England to clear up the outstanding matters from 1536.[48] On this last point Henry specified that he wanted the Germans to 'appoint Philipp Melancton to be coming in that legation specially for that his highness hath conceived a very good opinion of his virtue, learning, temperance and gravity, and would gladly confer with him at his coming in sundry of the points of Religion'.[49] Mont arrived in Germany in February and passed on the king's letters. However, besides the official dispatches he also conveyed a private oral message from Thomas Cromwell. A month earlier, Cromwell had written to Philip of Hesse to declare his support for the furtherance of Anglo-Schmalkaldic diplomacy; in the letter he also mentioned that he wanted Philip to grant credence to an oral message to be delivered by Mont.[50] Normally, this message would have left no trace. However, Mont was unable to arrange a private meeting with Philip; thus on 27 April he wrote to him instead.[51] Though Mont did not mention Cromwell by name – the letter was in place of an oral and therefore untraceable message, after all – it would be reasonable to assume that the sentiments in his letter reflected those which Cromwell had directed him to declare by word of mouth. The substance of the letter bears this assumption out. The chief theme was the same as expressed at the diet of Nuremberg in 1534 and by Theabold in 1537: Philip was exhorted to send an embassy to Henry, for such a 'despatch should be the way and preparation for a great and powerful act for God and the world; I trust that through your ambassadors the king and the whole kingdom of

England will be won and conquered for God, the Almighty'.[52] Mont enumerated the progress that had been made with reform in England, pointing to the expulsion of the papacy and the availability of the gospel in English.[53] However, touching on the key evangelical motivation for all this, he emphasised that more needed to be done, and that this was where the Germans could help: the League should not 'let this opportunity slip to bring a whole kingdom to the holy gospel and to conduct them further into a recognition of God's word, in which they have already made good progress'.[54] Mont assured Philip that he had seen signs that things would progress well in England if only the League would lend a hand and begged that 'your grace will ensure that your ambassadors are despatched most expeditiously to the king's majesty; for I trust that the result of all this will be in accordance with God's honour and glory'.[55] The consistency of these ideas with those of 1534 and 1537 is striking and must be significant. Manifestly, there is a common policy, a common group of advocates, a common thread. Now, as the Germans finally assented in April 1538 to despatch the embassy to England the evangelicals had long sought, it remained to be seen whether it would live up to expectations.

The Schmalkaldic embassy departed for England in May 1538. It was led by the Saxon vice-chancellor, Franz Burchard, and a Hessian nobleman named Georg von Boineburg. There was no Melanchthon. Explaining that he must remain in Germany in case a general council be summoned, the League sent instead a worthy but much less prestigious theologian, Friedrich Mykonius of Gotha. At the introductory royal audience on 2 June, the matters of Melanchthon's absence, the king's particular interest in him and indeed Henry's attitude to the entire consultative process were raised. Henry said to the ambassadors that Philip Melanchthon surely should have been sent to discuss theology with him, 'for his majesty doubts not that in such Christian affairs his presence should be most useful and beneficial'.[56] To this the ambassadors replied that if, as they doubted not, Henry was willing to accept the League's religious principles and defend them at a council, Melanchthon would be sent with the next embassy. Henry answered that he would happily accept the German confession:

but his majesty noted that some articles of the confession require explanation and discussion, and that some are widely contended, concerning which he would gladly talk with Master Philip. And each side must concede to the other, so that one may well achieve complete unity for the promotion of the holy truth and all Christendom.[57]

However, the League had little inclination to offer Henry any compromise beyond that in the Confession of Augsburg. The ambassadors informed the Supreme Head that their confession was grounded in scripture, and that the League would not consider any alteration to it. Though this revealing exchange offered a clear hint as to the gulf between Henry's and the League's attitude to theological negotiations, an immediate impasse was avoided. The ambassadors hastily added that, knowing Henry's reputation as they did, they were sure any problems he had with the Confession of Augsburg would be easily resolved in discussion. To this end, it was agreed that a committee should meet with the Germans for a theological disputation forthwith.[58]

The underlying difficulties thus smoothed over, attention shifted to the theological discussions. As in Wittenberg in 1536, these initially focused on the doctrine in the Confession. However, the examination of this doctrine did not proceed quite as easily as it had two years earlier. Henry had directed that the committee to discuss the Confession with the Germans should represent the full spectrum of theological opinion. This probably represented his own view of how theological discussion should take place. As Cranmer had written to a continental reformer who had sent Henry some religious literature in 1537:

> The king, who is a most acute and vigilant observer, is wont to hand over books of this kind that have been presented to him, and especially which he has not the patience to read himself, to one of his lords in waiting for perusal, from whom he may afterwards learn their contents. He then takes them back, and presently gives them to be examined by some one else of an entirely opposite way of thinking to the former party. When he has thus made himself master of their opinions, and sufficiently ascertained both what they commend and what they find fault with, he at length openly declares his own judgement respecting the same points.[59]

Thus, when the discussions opened at Lambeth on 14 June the Germans found before them a seven-man committee composed not only of such sympathetic souls as Thomas Cranmer and Robert Barnes, but also rabid anti-Lutherans such as Bishop Stokesley of London and Bishop Sampson of Chichester. Ultimately, the relatively innocuous nature of much of the Confession meant that most of the articles eventually passed through, even if sometimes accompanied by a fair amount of ill-feeling (especially so when justification by faith came up for discussion). One article, however, proved to be unresolveable in any manner or form: auricular confession. In spite of long hours and the best efforts of the Germans and their English supporters, at the close of the discussions Stokesley and Sampson remained unyielding in their refusal to renounce the sacramental status of confession, as Lutheran theology demanded.[60] The one crucial point of theological difference to emerge from the examination of the Confession was soon to be joined by four others, as attention shifted to those areas of dispute from the Apology that the discussions of 1536 had disclosed. The Germans probably expected difficulties with these. Prior to the despatch of the embassy to England in May 1538, John Frederick instructed his ambassadors to 'stop on your way at Wittenberg to consult with Dr Martin, Philip and the other divines, and also take copies of the agreement which was made with the king's ambassadors two years previously'.[61] With an eye to the theological differences on the abuses which had been revealed in the second part of the 1536 disputations at Wittenberg, John Frederick directed his ambassadors to consult on:

> the four points which remain unresolved, and which must almost be considered the pillars and very foundations of the pope and his adherents: the permitting of communion in both kinds, the abrogating of the private mass ... [the article] concerning monastic vows, and the fourth article concerning the marriage of the priesthood, or celibacy.[62]

Ominously, the duke pointed out that 'if the king persists in these articles, which are almost the most important points in the struggle with the pope and papacy, then there will remain a great shortfall in the agreement between his majesty and us'.[63] As it happened, the discussions on the Confession went on longer than planned, so that by the time they were over Henry had departed from London for the summer progress. The Germans decided that rather than extend their stay indefinitely and wait for Henry to return for a face-to-face disputation, they would send him a paper setting out the Lutheran position on the contentious points from 1536. They sent their letter to the king on 5 August.[64] What happened next is most instructive. For, having received the letter, Henry did not simply pass it on with some general directions for one of his clerics to prepare a response. Instead, he decided that he would involve himself directly in the examination of Lutheran doctrine. Calling to his side the sophisticated conservative theologian, Bishop Cuthbert Tunstall of Durham, Henry worked at fashioning a response to the Germans for over a month. Quite apart from the substance of the reply, the sheer depth of the king's labours on the matter is illuminating. This king, who famously took any opportunity to avoid the act of writing, now copiously annotated position papers prepared by Tunstall, carefully wrote up arguments and opinions of his own and closely supervised the succession of notes and drafting papers that led to the final document.[65] The quality and quantity of the king's personal involvement in the examination of the doctrine in the Apology during August and September 1538 is the equal of any other theological project on which he worked over his entire reign.[66] It is hard to see Henry's engagement in the process as the behaviour of a man who regarded the Schmalkaldeners as little more than diplomatic pawns in a much larger scheme of great power politics and who had no interest in their religion, as the historiography has customarily claimed. The very extent of the king's labours on the reply to the Lutherans' paper in the summer of 1538 is among the best evidence for the argument that Henry had a serious and deep interest in the League's religion for its own sake.

Yet the substance of Henry's reply is highly significant also, for it shows that after a painstaking examination of the Lutheran doctrine Henry held firm to a conservative position. The final copy of the reply to the Germans was a comprehensive rejection of the Lutheran view on private masses, communion in one kind only, priestly marriage and clerical vows. Moreover, in Henry's mind the work he had done with Tunstall had advanced the process of consultation and moved him towards considering action on the contentious issues the summer deliberations had thrown up. In closing the reply to the Germans, Henry wrote that 'concerning these articles which we have discussed, we will as soon as possible consider them with our theologians, and only then establish that which we judge to advance the glory of Christ and the propriety of his covenanted Church'.[67]

The embassy had not gone quite as planned by the evangelicals. Cromwell and Cranmer tried to get the Germans to stay still longer, holding out the hope of a satisfactory resolution if they stayed to discuss the matter personally with the king and his men. Reluctantly, the Germans agreed to tarry a while longer, writing back to Germany that because 'the archbishop and lord Cromwell showed us the importance attached to such a postponement, we agreed to wait the designated time for the promotion of God's word and to please the king'.[68] But nothing came of the wait other than some inconclusive preliminary exchanges with the episcopal bench on the abuses. In spite of the entreaties from Cromwell

and Cranmer to discuss matters fully with Henry when he returned from
the progress, by the time the king finally arrived back in London at the
end of September the Germans were determined to go. Upon Henry's
return to London, the ambassadors asked for leave to depart immediately; they set off for home in early October. They left behind them a
changed religious situation. Far from the springboard for reform the
evangelicals had foreseen, the Schmalkaldic embassy had instead crys-
tallised five key areas of contention, destined to form the crucial battle-
ground between the forces of reform and conservatism in the months
ahead: from the initial discussions in committee, auricular confession;
and from the examination by the king with Tunstall of the abuses, private
masses, communion in one kind only, priestly marriage and clerical vows.

THE ACT OF SIX ARTICLES

In the closing months of the year, signals appeared of the change in religious direction of the realm. The most well known of these was the move
against denial of the real presence, also known as sacramentarianism.
This began with the trial of the sacramentary John Lambert and the issuing of a royal proclamation dealing with the matter in November 1538.
In fact, this had little to do with the Schmalkaldeners or their evangelical
advocates, for they shared the view that sacramentarianism was a heretical doctrine. The League had actually sent the king intelligence on the
activities of sacramentarian cells in England and the subsequent investigations were pursued by leading evangelicals, among them Cromwell,
Cranmer and Robert Barnes. Still, as an indication of official concern
about the extent of reform the sacramentarianism issue was significant;
and in the months ahead the opportunity to taint the evangelical cause
with the same brush as denial of the real presence would not be lost by
the opponents of reform. Of greater moment to Anglo-Schmalkaldic
relations, however, were the five issues which had identified themselves as
crucial areas of theological difference during the summer of 1538. In the
closing months of the year and into the next, these continued to be contested. The royal proclamation of November 1538 included a require-
ment, directly influenced in the drafting stage by corrections in the
king's hand, that vows of chastity made to God must be kept. Discussions
on the other matters from the summer also remained under scrutiny; a
joint letter by John Frederick and Philip to Henry in early 1539 spoke of
an ongoing debate in England in which 'our articles of the mass, of the

use of the whole sacrament of the Lord's supper, and of celibacy, be still called into question'.[69]

If the situation were to be retrieved, diplomatic action would be necessary. The king had expressed firm doubts about certain key Lutheran beliefs, but he still desired consultation with a full Lutheran delegation led by Philip Melanchthon. Intervention from Germany might yet prove fruitful. Furthermore, the advocates of diplomacy with the League could play not only on the king's interest in theological discussions; they could also point to the threatening foreign policy situation, with the papal bull of excommunication against Henry issued in December 1538 and the possibility that Francis and Charles, since the summer at peace again, might combine to enforce the decree. But even religious discussion and political necessity as means of persuasion were no longer enough to satisfy Cromwell, for he had opened up yet a third point of Anglo-German contact: marriage. During the summer of 1538 Cromwell had entered into discussions with Franz Burchard on the question of marrying Henry and perhaps also Princess Mary into Germany.[70] The discussions had continued into the new year and had made some progress with the ducal house of Cleves – not a member of the Schmalkaldic League, though directly related to John Frederick of Saxony.

Henry appears to have responded favourably to each of the proposed points of contact. In January Christopher Mont went to Germany armed with instructions from the king to 'solicite the sending of the notable legation hither to his Majestie that was spoken of at the said duke's orators last being here' and to investigate whether the duke of Cleves 'be of the old popish fashon and the same to be observed yet in their contrys'.[71] The point of these investigations was not specified in the king's instructions, but Mont carried supplementary instructions signed by Cromwell, directing him to go to Franz Burchard, refer to the 'conference between his lordship and the said Burgartus [at] such time as he was here orator concerning an alliance of marriage' and declare that 'the lord Cromwell much tendering the king's alliance in Germany, if he could find any occasion would be glad to employ himself earnestly to induce and persuade the king's highness his sovereign lord rather to join with them, then otherwise, specially for the duke of Saxony's sake, who is allied there, and to make across marriage between the young duke of Cleves and my lady Mary as is aforesaid. And of the king's highness with the said older daughter of Cleves'.[72] Mont was able to initiate positive movements on the marriage front, though the complexity of the proposals meant that the matter would need some time yet for further development. In the meantime, he pressed hard for the sending to England of an embassy led by Philip Melanchthon in order to bring to a satisfactory close the discussions from the previous summer and to conclude an alliance. To begin with, Mont seems to have made good progress, the League indicating that it would be interested in sending a delegation to Henry. Suddenly, however, this all changed. The League had been engaged for some time in discussions with the emperor on the question of a cessation of hostilities while an answer was sought to the problems of religious division in the Holy Roman Empire; in March these discussions unexpectedly came to fruition in the form of a truce known as the Frankfurt Interim. This truce changed the League's attitude; whereas a few weeks earlier it had suggested to Mont that an embassy would be despatched to England shortly, now it backed away from any such commitment. In the light of the news coming back from Germany, Cromwell was forced to tone down his prognostications, writing to the king that 'Christopher doth diligently instant and sue for the sending of an honourable ambassiate, but he hath yet no answer'.[73] Mont, though, was nothing if not persistent. He kept on at the Schmalkaldeners into the following month and, finally, was able to persuade them to relent a little. In April the League consented to send to England a minor legation to inform Henry of the current situation – though without a theologian of any description, let alone Philip Melanchthon.

The situation was rapidly turning against the evangelicals. The king had already decided by this time to settle by statute the question of sacramentarianism (ironically, in view of the five articles which would soon be appended to the proscription of denial of the real presence, on the suggestion of a leading evangelical, Thomas Audley).[74] As for the matters that had emerged as key disputes with Lutheranism in the Anglo-Schmalkaldic discussions of 1536 and 1538, they had been examined continuously since the departure of the previous Schmalkaldic embassy from England, awaiting final resolution in a disputation between the king and a follow-up German delegation under Philip Melanchthon.[75] But now, in April, it was merely a minor legation which arrived from the League. And not only did it have little to say on the question of a political understanding, on the matters of theological difference it could only offer Henry the unilateral declaration that there would be no further theological discussion, for 'we judge the opinion of our men is sufficiently known to the serene king, and the learned in England, as well by our confession as by those disputations which the ambassadors of the most serene king [had] three years ago, and lately the English bishops had with our men, sent thither'.[76] It is hard to imagine that if a full theological delegation from the League led by Philip Melanchthon had arrived in London in April 1539 to discuss the five contentious issues from the previous summer that those very same questions would have appeared inside a couple of weeks as the latter five articles of the Act of Six Articles. But with the arrival of the puny Schmalkaldic retinue at the court Henry's patience had run out: If the Germans had no further interest in discussing theology with him, he would settle the five questions without them. Not even Cromwell could help now, for just as the small legation arrived he fell chronically ill and was confined to bed for the best part of a fortnight. With their high-handed refusal to discuss theology further and their most powerful English advocate confined to bed at the crucial moment, the Schmalkaldeners would have no further part to play in working out an official English position on the five issues their diplomacy with England had identified as requiring settlement. On 10 June 1539, after a series of discussions and drafts in which Henry displayed a close and continuous interest, an act to settle diversity in religious opinion became law; the Act of Six Articles, with its one and originally single article proscribing denial of the real presence, and those additional five which emerged directly from the Anglo-Schmalkaldic discussions of 1536 and 1538 and the failure to continue those discussions in 1539: communion in one kind only, private masses, clerical marriage, vows of widowhood and auricular confession.[77]

THE FINAL MONTHS

This brings us to the episode which began this chapter. In the wake of the Act of Six Articles, the evangelicals decided to approach the League again. As had been the case in 1534, 1537 and 1538, the initial contact was at the unofficial level: a Protestant fleeing England on account of the act was directed to go to Strassburg, where he should explain how the king's disenchantment with the League had led him to pass the Act of Six Articles and beg for the despatch of the much desired embassy led by Philip Melanchthon. The question of who actually directed the stranger to go to the Strassburg council and Martin Bucer in July 1539 is an interesting one. It seems that Cromwell and Cranmer were behind the initiative. For one thing, the letter by Martin Bucer to Philip of Hesse on the stranger refers throughout to the provenance of the Englishman's urgings from 'pious people', the 'kindhearted' and so on around the king; this evidence on its own, given the associations with Schmalkaldic advocacy of Cromwell and Cranmer would be enough to suggest that they were the men who briefed and sent the man to Strassburg in July 1539. But more specifically still, Bucer's letter mentions that these 'pious men' were the very same who had done everything they could to persuade the 1538 embassy to stay longer in England; it will be recalled that there were just two such men who had done all they could to forestall the return to Germany of the Schmalkaldic embassy: the king's minister and the arch-bishop of Canterbury.[78] Yet if it is worth noting this direct involvement of Cromwell and Cranmer in the despatch to Strassburg as still another example of their independent Schmalkaldic advocacy, the intervention itself came to nothing; Bucer's letter to Philip of Hesse was passed on to John Frederick of Saxony, who dismissed the entreaties, saying that the Act of Six Articles demonstrated that Henry had 'never been serious about the gospel', pouring scorn on the view that 'the guilt should be ours for the king of England's enacting his unchristian articles against our doctrine' and rejecting the suggestion that Melanchthon should go to England, adding caustically that since Bucer was so keen on the idea he could go himself.[79]

Given the German antipathy for Henry following the Act of Six Articles, it could all have ended there. But Cromwell had kept open through the year that third point of contact with Germany he had first investigated the previous summer, the marriage of the king to the duchess of Cleves (the plans to marry Princess Mary into the duchy as well had made little progress and had been quietly dropped). By July, even as John Frederick roundly condemned the thought of further con-tact with England, these plans had reached an advanced stage; by September they had gone further still, with an embassy prepared for despatch from the duchy to England in order to finalise a contract of marriage. These developments forced John Frederick to change his mind. After hasty talks with his Schmalkaldic partners he decided that, in spite of his suspicions of Henry, his close relationship with the Cleves family meant he must keep an eye on the marital negotiations and any conse-quent alliances; when the Cleves embassy went to England in September it was accompanied by two Saxon ambassadors, Franz Burchard and Hans von Dolzig. The ambassadors found an improved situation in England. They wrote back to Saxony that Cromwell had told them that 'the opponents of the gospel are very frightened at our arrival and would prefer that the king only enter into negotiations with Cleves. But the king wants very much to have the friendship of our gracious lord the duke; and so it [i.e. the marriage] will with God's grace achieve all that is beneficial.'[80]

Cromwell assured them that in the new situation created by the Cleves marriage, the Act of Six Articles would soon be revoked.[81] The king told Burchard that religious matters could be discussed further and expressed yet again his hope 'that Master Philip should come to his majesty, for his majesty wants very much that a concord will be made in religion'.[82] The treaty of marriage was concluded on 6 October; on the return of Burchard and Dolzig to Germany the League reconsidered its English diplomacy at a meeting at the diet of Arnstadt. The diet decided that in view of the impending marriage the League should send an embassy to England to investigate the possibility of concluding an Anglo-Schmalkaldic alliance. On 22 November Burchard and Dolzig left for England once again, this time joining the bride-to-be and her wedding party not merely as observers for the local familial interests of the duke of Saxony, but as the representatives of the Schmalkaldic League. Against all the odds, Cromwell had used the Cleves match to open the way to an alliance with Protestant Germany.[83]

It was a brilliant performance – and it might well have worked out brilliantly. But then, on New Year's Day, Henry met Anne; and from the first exchange of glances at Rochester he did not like the look of her.[84] Unhappily, he could not back out; the matter had gone too far, and with France and the empire making threatening noises at England Henry needed all the friends he could get: the wedding went ahead on 6 January 1540. Yet marriage, far from improving the situation, only made things worse; now Henry did not like the feel of Anne either. Suddenly, the whole ingenious edifice began to crumble. It seems hard to credit, but in the blink of an eye all Cromwell's high statesmanship and clever backroom machinating was undone by his 'storybook misjudgement of the king's fantasy'.[85]

Within a few months, as the implications of Cromwell's blunder became clear, the minister's enemies grouped around him. He fought back with characteristic energy and ruthlessness, locking away opponents, drawing new offices upon himself and urging yet again the despatch to England of an embassy led by Melanchthon.[86] But his opponents had a young and beautiful alternative consort for the king in Catherine Howard; and unlike 1536 with Anne Boleyn, Cromwell was too closely associated with the king's bride this time to be able to switch sides and work with those ranged against him. Cromwell was accused of religious radicalism, counterworking the king's settlement of religion and uttering treasonous words concerning the king. The long Schmalkaldic advocacy of the minister helped buttress these charges. The French ambassador Marillac wrote on the day of Cromwell's arrest that 'Cromwell, as attached to the German Lutherans', had favoured the new religion against the old, and was determined to see it triumph before all opposition, including the king's.[87] The following day Marillac reported that Cromwell's house had been searched and that in it 'were found several letters he wrote to or received from the Lutheran lords of Germany. Cannot learn what they contained except that this king was thereby so exasperated against him that he would no longer hear him spoken of, but rather desired to abolish all memory of him as the greatest wretch ever born in England.'[88] In July 1540 Cromwell was executed. Henry decided that the international situation was suitable for him to divorce Anne and marry Catherine Howard; as a final renunciation of the Lutheran alliance Robert Barnes was burnt at Smithfield.

Anglo-Schmalkaldic relations were effectively at an end. Though there were some movements towards a revival of Anglo-German diplomacy from 1544 on, they were entirely political in motivation and came to nothing. Only with the swing towards Protestantism near the end of the king's life and the increasing threats faced by the League from Charles were relations pursued with any great alacrity, but before the efforts could get far the king's death in January 1547 and the demise of the League at the hands of Charles V a couple of months later brought the affair to a close.

CONCLUSION

The first Protestant foreign policy venture in English history was that which King Henry VIII pursued with the League of Schmalkalden. In this chapter I have not sought to dismiss the influence of great power politics on Anglo-Schmalkaldic relations. Rather, I have tried to show how practical, secular foreign policy calculations could be influenced by ideological considerations. Throughout the history of Anglo-Schmalkaldic relations Henry and his men constantly had to take account of the attitudes and actions of the French king, the Holy Roman Emperor and the pope. It was not that the historiography was wrong in pointing to the importance of the larger European powers when assessing Anglo-Schmalkaldic diplomacy; rather, it was that it distorted the true picture by failing to give due weight to the influence of ideology: the king's interest in consulting with the League on theological grounds, Cromwell and his evangelical faction's belief that closer relations with the League would advance the cause of reform, their conservative enemies' perception that such relations would endanger their position; the Germans' suspicions of Henry's religious good faith and their fears that associating with the king might draw the ire of Charles V and thus cast a shadow over the survival of their own Reformation. Ideas mattered: they informed the actions of the principals, they defined the lines of political division and they shaped the perceptions and reactions of the participants. With Anglo-Schmalkaldic relations we see in English foreign policy something new; a concern that would remain of central importance to the realm's diplomacy for the rest of the Tudor century and long beyond: the Protestant cause.

NOTES

1. The material in this and the following paragraph is largely based on a letter from Martin Bucer to Philip of Hesse: M. Lenz (ed.), *Briefwechsel Landgraf Philipps des Grossmüthigen von Hessen mit Bucer* (Leipzig, 1880–87), hereafter *BwP*, i, pp. 99–105 (transcribed from the original at Marburg) [C. G. Bretschneider (ed.), *Corpus Reformatorum* (Halle, 1834–60), hereafter *CR*, iii, pp. 775–82; *LP*, xiv (ii). 186. *CR* is a transcript of the Hessian copy sent to Saxony and is not always reliable; *LP* is an abstract of *CR*]. Bucer's letter is about three thousand words long. For convenience, in what follows only the reference from *BwP* will be given. Fuller detail on much of what follows in this chapter can be found in Rory McEntegart, *Henry VIII, the League of Schmalkalden and the English Reformation* (2002); the book also includes in the footnotes the original German and Latin versions of all translations in the main text.

2. *BwP*, i, p. 100.

3. Ibid.

4. Ibid., pp. 102–3.

5. For the historiography, see McEntegart, *The League of Schmalkalden*, pp. 1–6.

6. G. W. Bernard, 'The making of religious policy, 1533–1546: Henry VIII and the search for the middle way', *HJ* 41 (1998), p. 343, fails to see the difference between the bi-confessional Anglo-German contacts of the late 1520s and early 1530s (on the divorce) and the exclusively Protestant Anglo-Schmalkaldic relations that developed from 1533–34. For a detailed narrative of the diplomatic moves from 1531 to 1533 see Rory McEntegart, 'England and the League of Schmalkalden, 1531–1547: faction, foreign policy and the English Reformation'. Unpublished University of London PhD dissertation, 1992, pp. 33–54.

7. Draft of instructions for Heath and Mont, PRO, SP 1/82, fos 20–31 [*LP* vii, 21 i] and 32–9 [*LP* vii 21 ii] (inferior draft of instructions for Heath and Mont); draft of instructions for Paget, BL, Cotton MS., Vit. B.xiv, fos 61–9 [*LP* vii, 148].

8. Draft of instructions for Heath and Mont, PRO, SP 1/82, fos 29v [*LP* vii, 21 i] and 37v [*LP* vii. 21 ii] (inferior draft of instructions for Heath and Mont). This passage does not appear in Paget's instructions due to injury of the manuscript by fire. The quoted matter in this and the following two footnotes is taken from the first folio reference.

9. Draft of instructions for Heath and Mont, PRO, SP 1/82, fos 30 [*LP* vii, 21 i] and 38 [*LP* vii 21 ii] (inferior draft of instructions for Heath and Mont); draft of instructions for Paget, BL, Cotton MS Vit. B.xiv, fo. 69 [*LP* vii, 148].

10. Draft of instructions for Heath and Mont PRO, SP 1/82, fos 30v [*LP* vii, 21 i]) and 38v [*LP* vii, 21 ii] (inferior draft of instructions for Heath and Mont); BL, Cotton MS Vit. B.xiv, fo. 69 [*LP* vii, 148] (draft of instructions for Paget).

11. Draft of instructions for Paget, BL, Cotton MS Vit. B.xiv, fo. 69v [*LP* vii, 148].

12. Hessisches Staatsarchiv Marburg, hereafter HStMar, PA 409, fo. 23v; Thüringisches Staatsarchiv Weimar, hereafter TStWei, Reg. H. 91, fo. 77 [E. Fabian (ed.), *Die Schmalkaldischen Bundesabschiede, 1530–1536* (Tübingen, 1958), hereafter *SchmBa*, ii. 50].

13. HStMar, PA 409, fos 23-v; TStWei, Reg. H. 91, fo. 77 [*SchmBa* ii. 49–50].

14. HStMar, PA 409, fo. 23v; TStWei, Reg. H. 91, fo. 77 [*SchmBa* ii. 50].

15. For detail on the remainder of this paragraph see McEntegart, *The League of Schmalkalden*, pp. 114–23.

16. HStMar, PA 409, fo. 23v; TStWei, Reg. H. 91, fo. 77 [*SchmBa* ii. 50].

17. For detail on the preparations and staffing of the embassy, see McEntegart, *League of Schmalkalden*, pp. 26–35.

18. BL, Cotton MS Vit. B.xxi., fo. 123v [*LP* ix, 1030].

19. BL, Cotton MS Vit. B.xxi., fo. 121 [*LP* ix, 543].

20. BL, Harleian MS 6989, fo. 56 (final copy written and signed in Luther's hand) [*Weimarer Ausgabe der Werke D.M. Luthers, Abteilung Briefe* (Weimar, 1930–48), hereafter *WABr*, vii. 396; *LP* x, 644]. There was also a letter dated 13 April from the Wittenberg divine Justas Jonas to Cromwell, urging that a religious agreement be closed between England and the League, from which he believed would naturally flow a political alliance (BL, Harleian MS 6989, fo. 57 [*LP* x, 665]).

21. PRO, SP 6/2, fo. 126v [*LP* vii, 750].

22. PRO, SP 6/2, fo. 127v [*LP* vii, 750].

23. PRO, SP 1/85, fo. 99v [*LP* vii, 1043].

24. PRO, SP 1/85, fos 99v–100 [*LP* vii, 1043].

25. *LP* vii, 1147.

26. There is very little evidence for this mission; Melanchthon simply wrote to Henry, telling the king that he had commented on the articles Barnes had brought him, as requested (*LP* viii, 384–5).

27. Henry's later interest in Melanchthon will be discussed below.

28. *LP* viii, 1432.

29. PRO, SP 1/96, fo. 13v [*LP* ix, 213 i].

30. Ibid., fo. 14v [*LP* ix, 213 i].

31. Ibid.

32. PRO, SP 1/96, fo. 15 [*LP* ix, 213 i].

33. Ibid., fo. 15v [*LP* ix, 213 i].

34. *LP* ix, 979.

35. PRO, SP 1/96, fo. 23 [*LP* ix, 213 i].

36. BL, Cotton MS Cleo. E.vi., vol. 2, fo. 307v [Gilbert Burnet, *History of the Reformation of the Church of England*, in N. Pocock (ed.) (Oxford, 1865), vi, p. 160. *LP* x, 457].

37. J. A. Muller (ed.), *The Letters of Stephen Gardiner* (Cambridge, 1933), p. 72. Muller prints the original draft in Gardiner's hand, as opposed to the seventeenth-century copy used in *LP* x, 256.

38. Ibid.

39. Ibid.

40. *WABr*, vii 383.

41. H. Robinson (ed.),*Original Letters relative to the English Reformation* (Cambridge, 1846), p. 520 [*LP* xii (ii), 869].

42. Robinson, *Original Letters*, pp. 520–1 [*LP* xii (ii), 869].

43. Ibid., p. 521 [*LP* xii (ii), 869].

44. TStWei, Reg. H. 137, no. 64, fo. 156 (copy sent as enclosure to undated letter from Philip to John Frederick: fo. 155). The author of the council's report was probably Jakob Sturm; he would soon after be written to on the subject of Anglo-Schmalkaldic relations by Philip of Hesse: H. Virck and O. Winckelmann (eds), *Politische Correspondenz der Stadt Strassburg im Zeitalter der Reformation*, (Strassburg, 1892–98), hereafter *PC*, ii. 464.

45. TStWei, Reg. H. 137, no. 64, fos 156r–v (copy sent as enclosure to undated letter from Philip to John Frederick: fo. 155).

46. Ibid.

47. TStWei, Reg. H. 137, no. 64, fo. 157 (copy sent as enclosure to undated letter from Philip to John Frederick: fo. 155).

48. The instructions were drafted by Cromwell's clerk Wriothesley: PRO, SP 1/129, fos 140–55 [*LP* xiii (i), 367]. A close German paraphrasal of these instructions is in TStWei, Reg. H. 165, no. 78 i, fos 1–10. Mont carried brief and colourless letters of credence for the landgrave and the duke of Saxony. Letter for Philip: HStMar, PA 1800, fo. 11 (final copy); BL, Cotton MS Vit. B.xxi, fos 170–2 (draft) [*LP* xiii (i), 353]. Letter for John Frederick, BL, Cotton MS Vit. B.xxi, fo. 173 (good draft) [*LP* xiii (i), 352].

49. PRO, SP 1/129, fo. 150 [*LP* xiii (i), 367].

50. HStMar, PA 1800, fo. 7 (Latin final copy, signed in Cromwell's handwriting at the foot 'Obsequendi studiossis, Thomas Crumwell). A contemporary German translation is at fo. 9. The key sentence is: 'I have directed that something be explained to your excellency in my name, to which I heartily request you give certain credence, and not burden yourself but to judge me most studiously.'

51. This private letter from Christopher Mont to Philip of Hesse was written as the English agent was making his way back to England and happened upon a messenger near Grave in the province of Brabant. HStMar, PA 1800, fos 19–20 [Friedrich Prüser, *England und die Schmalkaldener, 1535–1540* (Leipzig, 1540), pp. 304–6].

52. HStMar, PA 1800, fos 19r–v [Prüser, *England und die Schmalkaldener*, p. 305].

53. HStMar, PA 1800, fo. 19v [Prüser, *England und die Schmalkaldener*, p. 305].

54. Ibid.

55. HStMar, PA 1800, fo. 20 [Prüser, *England und die Schmalkaldener*, p. 306].

56. Ibid., fo. 181.

57. Ibid., fo. 181v.

58. Ibid., fos 181–3.

59. Robinson, *Original Letters*, p. 15 [*LP* xii (ii), 315].

60. For detail on this opening phase of the discussions, see McEntegart, *The League of Schmalkalden*, pp. 108–14.

61. G. Mentz, *Johann Friedrich der Grossmütige, 1503–1554* (Jena, 1903–08), iii, p. 381.

62. Ibid., ii, pp. 381–2.

63. Ibid., iii, p. 382.

64. TStWei, Reg. H. 165, no. 78 i, fos 122–3 (early draft of opening section), pp. 124–60 (draft); BL, Cotton. MS, Cleo.E.v. fos 186–221 (final version) [Burnet, *History of the Reformation*, iv, pp. 352–72; *LP* xiii (ii), 37].

65. Scriptural and patristic sources which have marginal notes in Henry's hand: PRO, SP 1/135, fos 157–77 [*LP* xiii (ii), 166 i–iii]; BL, Cotton MS Cleo.E.v., fos 167–70 [*LP* xiii (i), 1307 xx], fos 174–7 [*LP* xiii (i), 1307 xxii]; PRO, SP 1/134, fos 41–5 [*LP* xiii (i), 1307 xvi; printed in J.E. Cox (ed.), *Miscellaneous Writings and Letters of Thomas Cranmer* (Cambridge, 1846), pp. 480–2]. Notes in Henry's hand in preparation for drafting: BL, Cott. MS., Cleo.E.v., fo. 133 [No *LP* reference. Printed in J. Strype, *Ecclesiastical Memorials, Relating Chiefly to Religion, and the Reformation of it, and the Emergencies of the Church of England, under King Henry VIII, King Edward VI, and Queen Mary I* (Oxford, 1822), i (ii), p. 392]. Drafts with corrections in the hands of Henry and Tunstall: PRO, SP 1/135, fos 151–6 [*LP* xiii (ii), 165 iii], fos 178–91 [*LP* xiii (ii), 166 iv]; BL, Cotton MS Cleo.E.v., fos 151–60 [No *LP* reference], fos 144–50 [*LP* xiii (ii), 165 ii]; Corpus Christi College Cambridge, hereafter CCCC, MS 109, fos 7–57 [No *LP* reference]. Tunstall's summary of the German letter: BL, Cotton MS Cleo.E.v., fos 222–4 [*LP* xiii (ii), 37 ii]; this was 'reabridged' in an anonymous hand at ibid., fo. 266 [*LP* xiii (ii), 37 iii]. Final copy of reply to the German letter of 5 August: BL, Cotton. MS Cleo.E.v., fos 228–38 [Burnet, *History of the Reformation*, iv, pp. 373–91]. For a detailed analysis of the process of producing the reply to the Germans, see McEntegart, *The League of Schmalkalden*, pp. 115–27.

66. This view, of course, can only apply to those projects for which evidence survives. It may be that Henry gave greatly of his theological energies in the writing of *Assertio septem sacramentorum*, but there is little extant documentary evidence for the making of that work. For Henry's involvement in the Ten Articles, Bishops' Book and King's Book, see J.J. Scarisbrick, *Henry VIII* (1968), pp. 403–20.

67. Burnet, *History of the Reformation*, iv, p. 391.

68. Letter from Burchard to John Frederick, HStMar, PA 2575, fo. 250 (copy sent as enclosure to letter from John Frederick to Philip, 21 September, fo. 245).

69. Strype, *Ecclesiastical memorials*, i (ii), p. 400 [*LP* xiv (i), 698]. Latin draft: TStWei, Reg. H. 260, no. 111, vol. 1, fos 6–12. Latin final copy: BL, Cotton MS Cleo. E.vi, vol. 2, fos 297–302.

70. The first definite evidence of this plan appeared on 23 August 1538, in a letter from Franz Burchard to John Frederick. In this letter Burchard reported that 'lord Cromwell, who is most favourably inclined to the German nation, wants most dearly that the king should wed himself with the German princes': HStMar, PA 2575, fo. 251v (copy of a letter from Burchard to John Frederick; sent as enclosure to letter dated 21 September 1538 from John Frederick to Philip: ibid., fo. 245). Cromwell subsequently engaged in a private correspondence with John Frederick on this question: see Cromell's instructions on the marriage plans for Mont in early 1539, referring to John Frederick, 'as he hath written by his letters to his lordshipp' (BL, Cotton MS Vit.B.xxi, fo. 174 [*LP* xiv (i), 103 ii]).

71. PRO, SP 1/142, fo. 106v (final version, signed at the head by the king) [*LP* xiv (i), 103 i].

72. BL, Cotton MS Vit. B.xxi, fos 174-v (final version, signed at the foot by Cromwell) [*LP* xiv (i), 103 ii].

73. BL, Cotton MS Vit. B.xxi., fo. 96v [*St.P.* I, 605; R.B. Merriman, *Life and Letters of Thomas Cromwell* (Oxford, 1902), ii, p. 201; *LP* xiv (i), 552].

74. Stephen Gardiner provides the evidence for this. He wrote in the next reign: 'And I shall never forget that the Lord Audelay, late Chauncelor, told me … that when our late soveraigne lord devised with hym how to resist the detestable heresie

against the Sacrament of thAltar, he advised the King's Majestie to make an acte of parliament of yt.'. Gardiner to the privy council, 30 August 1547, Muller, *Gardiner's Letters*, p. 369. Gardiner said that Audley had told him this during Easter 1543. The example was cited as part of a thesis arguing that acts made by parliament could only be undone by the same.

75. See the letter by John Frederick and Philip to Henry in early 1539, cited above, speaking of an ongoing debate in England in which 'our articles of the mass, of the use of the whole sacrament of the Lord's supper, and of celibacy, be still called into question': Strype, *Ecclesiastical Memorials*, i (ii), p. 400 [*LP* xiv (i), 698]. Latin draft: TStWei, Reg. H. 260, no. 111, vol. 1, fos 6–12. Latin final copy: BL, Cotton MS Cleo. E.vi, vol. 2, fos 297–302. See also a letter of 8 March 1539 to a continental reformer which mentioned that 'nothing has as yet been settled respecting the marriage of the clergy, although some persons have very freely preached before the king on the subject'; alluding to another point of dispute from 1538, it was also noted that 'the mass is not asserted to be a sacrifice for the living and the dead, but only a representation of Christ's passion', a comment which if rather optimistic does reflect the fact that the private mass too was a subject under discussion at this time. Robinson, *Original Letters*, p. 624 [*LP* xiv (i), 466].

76. Letter to Henry from John Frederick and Philip. Strype, *Ecclesiastical Memorials*, i (ii), pp. 399–400 [*LP* xiv (i), 698]. Latin draft: TStWei, Reg. H. 260, no. 111, vol. 1, fos 6–12. Latin final copy: BL, Cotton MS Cleo. E.vi, vol. 2, fos 297–302.

77. The argument presented here for the emergence of the act differs from the usual. It is more fully set out (with an historiographical discussion) in McEntegart, *The League of Schmalkalden*, pp. 163–6.

78. The key passage is in the postscript to Bucer's letter: 'our previous embassy, the vice-chancellor [Burchard] and Mykonius, are pious and learned men, but the belief that they were the measure of those practised sophists which England has is, I fear, mistaken. Moreover, they proceeded most illadvisedly, [*CR* iii. 781, has mistakenly transcribed this clause and all of the previous sentence, which is the reason for the nonsensical translation at *LP* xiv (ii), 186] when, *in spite of the fervent requests and applications of the pious men in England* [my italics], they hurried back home before the disputations had been concluded': *BwP* i. 104.

79. TStWei, Reg. H. 260, no. 111, vol. 1, fos 210–12v [Mentz, *Johann Friedrich*, iii. pp. 440–2].

80. Burchard's and Dolzig's ambassadorial account, TStWei, Reg. H. 260, no. 111, vol. 2, fo. 33.

81. Letter from Burchard and Dolzig to John Frederick, TStWei, Reg. H. 260, no. 111, vol. 1, fo. 171v (final version); HStMar, PA 2582, fos 239v–40 (copy sent as enclosure to letter from John Frederick to Philip, 22 October: fos 230–4).

82. Burchard's and Dolzig's ambassadorial account. TStWei, Reg. H. 260, no. 111, vol. 2, fo. 36v.

83. For detail on the marriage treaty, the diet of Arnstadt and the decision by the League to join the wedding party to England, see McEntegart, *The League of Schmalkalden*, pp. 184–8. On the Cleves match as a whole, see Retha Warnicke, *The Marrying of Anne of Cleves: Royal Protocol in Early Modern England* (Cambridge, 2000). Warnicke suggests that the Cleves match was an entirely diplomatic arrangement. She fails to explain Cromwell's private words to the Schmalkaldic ambassadors in

September 1539 mentioned earlier in the paragraph and, even more critically, why, if the marriage had no Protestant implications at all, the Schmalkaldic League (a Protestant alliance) should have been invited or chose itself to send representatives to accompany the Cleves wedding party to England.

84. This is the straightforward view, which I prefer. For a stress on contemporary attitudes to witchcraft and homosexual relations, see Warnicke, *Anne of Cleves*, pp. 225–8.

85. Diarmaid MacCulloch, *Thomas Cranmer: A Life* (New Haven, 1996), p. 262.

86. For detail on this paragraph, see McEntegart, *The League of Schmalkalden*, pp. 190–202

87. *LP* xv, 766.

88. Ibid., 804.

5

MID-TUDOR FOREIGN POLICY AND DIPLOMACY: 1547–63

David Potter

The weakness of England vis-à-vis its neighbours in the mid-Tudor decades has long been a commonplace of historical writing. It has been assumed that the minority of Edward VI, the inexperience of Mary I and the initial precariousness of Elizabeth I seriously undermined the strong power-base established by Henry VIII, while the faction-ridden politics of those years fatally weakened the bargaining ability of any English government. A.F. Pollard saw the treaty conceding the loss of Boulogne in 1550 as 'the most ignominious treaty signed by England during the century'; W. K. Jordan thought it a result of a policy of 'peace at any possible price'.[1] For R. B. Wernham, the year 1558 saw England 'at its lowest ebb of weakness and demoralisation'.[2] This gloomy diagnostic lent itself all too easily to a propensity to view Elizabeth I's accession as a blessed relief and in addition the idea of a 'mid-Tudor crisis' was readily adapted to this view of English weakness abroad.[3]

English policy in the mid-Tudor years was certainly overshadowed by the legacy of Henry VIII's wars in France and Scotland and complicated by rapid internal religious upheaval. French intervention in Scotland from 1548, coupled with the debilitating drain of resources for the defence of Boulogne, led to a serious re-appraisal of policy after the peace with France in March 1550. In part this was the result of an inability on the part of England, in the throes of religious change, to use the Emperor Charles V as a counter-weight to France in those years. The brief alliance with France during the Northumberland years (1551–53), though not unprecedented (see Chapter 2) was uneasy in view of continued French dominance in Scotland and took place in the context of the opening of the last great phase of Habsburg-Valois war in 1551. The return to the Habsburg alliance by Mary I in 1553 was in part a natural reaction in view of the convergence of England's religious and diplomatic position. That alliance, however, became increasingly controversial, caught up as it was in religious controversy, and was blamed for the English loss of Calais in 1558. Elizabeth's predicament between 1558 and 1563 stemmed from the continuing threat posed by France, especially in Scotland, as well as from the deep unease in her relations with Philip II.

The main objective of this chapter is not so much to narrate these diplomatic and military events as to point up the evolution of attitudes and outlooks on the part of the people who shaped English policies and to ask how English politicians, diplomats and active propagandists sought to cope with and then understand an increasingly dangerous and complex world. The first point to understand here is that the absence, between 1547 and 1558, of a firm monarchical grip on foreign policy and of the traditional driving forces of policy, most notably a king's ambition and pursuit of glory, posed problems that were quite specific to the period and in some ways proved fruitful. Such conditions prompted a more complex and dispassionate analysis of international affairs than was possible for English diplomats overshadowed by the need to serve the interests of a dominant and vainglorious king. They could thus tentatively step out of the shadow traced by a powerful monarch into the bleak light of geo-politics. Mary's accession in 1553 and the alliance with Philip of Spain added a further ingredient; the religious upheavals attendant on the restoration of the Catholic Church prompted the intervention of Protestant propagandists in print (at first based abroad) in questions of foreign policy, hitherto the exclusive preserve of the court.

One further structural characteristic of the period should be borne in mind and is too often overlooked. England remained a second-rate power in comparison with the great dynastic states of the Valois and the Habsburgs in terms of its population, resources and economy. English intervention was always a rather peripheral matter in the relations between France and the emperor, complicated from 1512 onwards by the problem of Scotland. A balance-sheet of military expenditure since 1544 drawn up in the early 1550s provides a devastating insight into the ruinous costs of war.[4] At a time when ordinary peacetime revenues could not have been much more than £160 000, the total cost was £3 501 453 and of that £1 342 552 was represented by the siege and maintenance of Boulogne since the start of 1544. The arguments against war put forward in the Privy Council in 1557 stressed most notably the parlous economic state of the realm (caused by two disastrous harvests):

> The wars the Queen's Majesty is utterly unable to maintain ... the
> common people of this realm being presently many ways grieved and
> some pinched with famine and want of payment of money due to
> them, some miscontented for matters of Religion and generally all
> yet tasting of the smart of the last wars it might be very dangerous to
> entangle them now with new wars.

The blame, it was argued, would be put on Philip, and failure in war 'is
both dishonorable, and may be many ways dangerous for this realm.'[5]
Three years later, Nicholas Bacon summed up the odds neatly in 1559:

> who is so ignorant, that knows not that the kingdom and dominions that
> be under the governance of the crown of France to be four times as
> much as the realm of England, and the men in them four times as much
> or more, and therewith that the French [king] hath and useth as large
> an authority and commandment to levy money and treasure upon his
> people for the maintenance of his enterprises, as the prince here hath
> and more.

What was more, the French King's credit was commensurately greater, his
army and commanders experienced and he had access to German mercenaries 'where we cannot without great dangers do the like to defend
us', while he had an extensive network of allies.[6] The disparity to some
extent had been concealed by Henry VIII's formidable personality and
ambition and the injection of resources allowed as a result of the confiscations of Church lands but this had led ultimately to defeat and the
apparently insuperable problems of French and Spanish intervention.[7]

A pessimistic view of the predicament of England in these years, then,
is not just an historians' construct and can be demonstrated in many
ways. William Paget's stark analysis of 1546 and doom-laden writings in
the crisis of 1549–50 (of which more below) make it quite clear that this
leading Henrician diplomat and minister had lost confidence in the ability of England to defend its extended interests in Scotland and France.
France had waged war for 25 years 'whereof four were but as playing with
us to speak of.' England on the other hand had been exhausted by eight
years of war.[8] Armagil Waad's much quoted summary of 1558: 'wars with
France and Scotland: the French King bestriding the Realm, having one
foot in Calais and the other in Scotland: steadfast enmity but no steadfast

freindship abroad'[9] could be amplified by another view of England in 1559 as a 'bone thrown between two dogs'.[10] In a starkly realistic analysis of the problem during peace negotiations at Cercamp in November 1558, John Mason told Cecil that 'our state can no longer bear these wars'; if the best conditions were not available, then we should have to settle for 'such as we can get.'[11] The general gloom of 1558–59 is reflected in Paget's assumption at the end of Mary's reign that the recovery of Calais would be 'that ... which we never looked for.'[12] In 1559, Paget's deeply pessimistic note to William Cecil of 'things that you have known in our days' argued that the French were natural enemies and that their power was increasing; the only hope was to be had from the Habsburgs but:

> If we take part with neither of them, they will fasten their feet both of them here, and make a Piedmont of us: If we take part with one, we our selves shall be afterwards made a prey of by the victor.[13]

Common to all of these views is a deep and traditional antipathy to France coupled with a certain disquiet about Habsburg power. Paget was out of favour in 1559 but his view is closely paralleled in the contemporary judgment of Nicholas Wotton, still very much a trusted diplomat, that if Philip II were to make a separate peace

> we were not able long to resist the French and the Scots, and others whom the French would set in our tops; wherof might ensue, that the French should be Lords of England and Scotland too: and what would ensue thereof, a blind man can see.[14]

England, then, depended on Philip but Wotton was by no means blindly convinced of his benevolence. Foreign observers, with their own dyspeptic view of the English, shared these views. Philip II's representative, the count of Feria, in March 1558 thought the country unwilling to contribute to the recovery of Calais, in a worse mess than 'any country has ever fallen into'.[15]

Given all these gloomy perceptions and structural problems, who were the people who both expressed them and shaped a re-assessment of England's position in the world? Diplomacy was beginning tentatively to emerge as a career for specialists but was still confined to a relatively small group.[16] In terms of personnel and working methods, as in other areas of government, there was a substantial degree of continuity in those who served abroad from the 1540s to the 1560s.[17] Of the 17 men who held resident embassies in the years 1547–63, ten had been employed by Henry VIII (Thomas Thirlby, Philip Hoby, Richard Morison, Nicholas Wotton, John Mason, Christopher Mont, Edmund Harvel, Peter Vannes, Edward Carne and Thomas Chamberlain). Some (Wotton, Mont, Carne and Harvel) had been born in the 1490s,[18] the rest in the first decade or so of the century; indeed, Wotton by 1556 could claim to be 'broken through age' during his last period as resident envoy in France.[19] John Mason, one of the most important residents abroad in the period, could serve equally well under Edward VI and Mary. Of the 13 men employed in more than one isolated special embassy, half had served Henry VIII in diplomacy (the oldest was Sir Thomas Cheyne, born in 1482 and still going strong with missions to the emperor and the Low Countries between 1549 and 1553). Morison and Hoby, though they had served Henry VIII, represented a younger generation of a more humanistic training while other younger resident envoys (Nicholas Throckmorton, Henry Killigrew and Thomas Smith) were to go on to extensive foreign employment under Elizabeth. Specialists sent abroad for legal negotiations who proved themselves 'meet to serve' later emerged as ambassadors under Elizabeth, though William Petre seems to have thought there was a dearth of men suitable to be sent abroad.[20] While several of the men who served as secretaries to embassies in the period were old hands, Roger Ascham as secretary to Morison 1550–53 was one of the most important humanists to be employed abroad, though never as an ambassador.[21] There were younger men who emerged as trusted ambassadors under Elizabeth (John Shers, Thomas Dannet, John Somers, Henry Killigrew and Henry Middlemore). The precipitate decline of clerical ambassadors apparent under Henry VIII continued. With the exception of Thirlby, none of the resident ambassadors was a bishop.[22] Peers were still thought fitting for special and ceremonial embassies (nine served in some role during these years) though in some cases it is clear they were also experienced diplomats.[23] Continuity was assured through the work of high diplomatic administrators such as the secretary William Petre.[24] Finally, the work-horses of English diplomacy in the period, the couriers and heralds who not only carried despatches but also acted as spies, continued through the period without much change.

There were, of course, circumstances peculiar to the mid-century years. As a result of the youth of Edward and the personality of Mary, there was no revival of Henry VIII's 'chamber diplomacy' of the 1520s and 1530s; the need for personal representation of an active monarch with his co-equals was not so pressing. Then, the sharp changes in religious establishment as well as the development of more radical Reformed Protestant ideas among the social and cultural elite inevitably influenced the choice of ambassadors by one regime or another. Certain ambassadors who served under Edward VI were shunned under Mary (Thomas Smith, Philip Hoby, William Pickering, Richard Morison, Christopher Mont, the long-standing envoy in Germany) while others out of favour under Edward came into their own under Mary. Thomas Thirlby, who ceased to be ambassador to the emperor in July 1548, returned to that post just before the death of Edward VI and was much employed under Mary. The first Viscount Montagu, a noted Catholic, only began service as a special envoy under Mary. Lord William Howard, an unsuccessful ambassador to France in 1541 and thereafter an officer at Calais, was not reemployed abroad until 1558–59. Thomas Chamberlain, who first served as agent in Flanders in 1544, was active under Edward, shunned under Mary for his religion, but appointed the first resident in Spain for decades in 1560 despite his Protestantism. Elizabeth's accession saw the advent of a small but important group of Protestant activists in the ranks of foreign envoys, the most important of whom was Nicholas Throckmorton, gentleman of the privy chamber in Edward's reign, spectacularly acquitted of treason after Wyatt's rebellion and then in quasi-exile in France. Protestant sympathies or anti-Marian attitudes did not necessarily imply any automatic attitude to the great dynastic powers and, though anti-Marian exiles often gravitated to France, they did not necessarily love the French. Throckmorton, who knew France well, got on badly with the regime there and recommended others such as Mason, Mewtas, Challoner and Sidney 'of whom I know they have a good opinion'.[25]

On balance, it could be argued that the English diplomatic network of the mid-century years was rather more limited than had been the case under Henry VIII (there were no missions to the Levant, Poland, Sweden, Switzerland and only the unofficial visit of Willoughby and Chancellor to Russia in 1553–54). In Italy, only Venice had a resident English agent and the restoration of relations with the papacy in the mid-1550s was brief. After Mary's marriage to Philip, there seems to have been a decline in the functioning of normal diplomatic channels; the Venetian ambassador reported in December 1555 that Mary intended to recall all her ambassadors, except Wotton in France, and rely on Philip's agents.[26] Mason was recalled from the Low Countries (where he was accredited to Philip) after Charles V's departure in September 1556 and Vannes recalled from Venice and not replaced.[27] With the end of the embassy to France in June 1557, Carne was left the only resident abroad (in an anomalous position at Rome representing Philip and Mary during a period when the pope was at war with Philip) and there were no foreign resident ambassadors in England in the last 18 months of Mary's reign.[28] These changes may have been planned but they happened only slowly and do not imply any intention to subsume English diplomacy in the Habsburg network. But Mary's role as Philip's wife, however circumscribed by the marriage treaty, was bound, in view of the conventions of the time, to influence the role of English diplomats. Elizabeth's accession necessarily refocused English diplomatic activities. After the return of Carne from Rome in 1559, Elizabeth sent no more embassies to Italy but she restored resident embassies at the Imperial court (intermittently) from 1558, the French court from 1559 and to Philip II from 1558 in Brussels and from 1560 in Spain. She also continued the contacts with Russia established in 1553 and sent envoys to Poland, Turkey and Sweden from the 1580s. Her envoys were in the main attuned to the new religious and political dispensation but their appointments reflected political and personal rivalries at court.

How did these diplomats and advisers relate to the regimes they served? The first point to bear in mind is that the unusual circumstances of the Somerset Protectorate and then the dominance of Northumberland encouraged discussion of foreign affairs and diplomacy in a way which had been virtually impossible under Henry VIII. The position of Somerset, standing in the king's place, could not fail to be a weaker one in the formation of foreign policy than that of an adult reigning monarch. For instance his colleagues could speak and write to him more frankly than they could have to Henry VIII.[29] Northumberland's position as faction leader without the formal role of Lord Protector was weaker still. Liberty of expression, though, depended partly on the diplomat's personality and partly on his relationship with the Principal Secretary and ruling group. John Mason, for instance, felt free to pronounce on topics as diverse as Ireland and economic policy while on mission in France.[30]

We need at this point to consider a number of examples of the thinking of highly-placed ambassadors and 'civil servants' which will serve to show how foreign affairs could be handled from a position of weakness. William Paget is an unusual example of a leading royal councillor and administrator who was also an active ambassador.[31] Paget was a skilled and subtle diplomat; he was noted by the French ambassador in 1547 as 'the one I have found most favourable to the king's cause here'; he certainly posed as 'only begetter' of the Anglo-French peace of 1546 and of

Somerset's offers to return Boulogne, swore to de Selve that 'never was Englishman so good a French as was he', though all this was probably no more than a device to convince de Selve of his credentials, since he was equally persuasive with the Imperial envoy van der Delft.[32] Paget was essentially a pragmatic traditionalist in his approach to foreign relations; in other words he saw the principal dangers to England as stemming from French enmity over Boulogne and papal incitement to the emperor to attack, the main fear being too close an alignment between France and the emperor, though the latter as ruler of the Low Countries was more of a natural ally. He had written a remarkable *tour d'horizon* for Henry VIII in the summer of 1546 which insisted on the dangers posed both by France and the emperor but which inclined to suggest closer relations with the latter buttressed by efforts to reconcile him with the German princes.[33] This view only evolved under the stress of the Scottish war after 1547 in a series of remarkable letters and memoranda for Somerset in 1548–49 which anticipated the Privy Council memorandum of 1557 mentioned above. Somerset wished to maintain Henry VIII's late acquisitions in France and his ambitions in Scotland but, while for Henry the yearly schemes against Scotland from 1541 onwards were a major element of his policy towards France, for Somerset they became the centre-piece.[34] Probably under Paget's prompting, he even considered selling Boulogne early to the French in 1547–48 in return for a free hand in Scotland but the French would not accept this. They in their turn demanded Calais, an impossible condition.[35] Somerset related his thinking on the matter in a despatch a year later to Wotton which showed both his preparedness to give up Boulogne and also his unrealistic expectations of the French.[36] Nothing came of this and the regime found itself saddled with demands in Scotland and France. By February 1548 Paget was cautious, to say the least, about new adventures in Scotland,[37] but in the first surviving of his memoranda to Somerset in February 1549, he was, given the normal conventions, brutally frank.[38] If war with the Scots continued alongside the underhand war with the French he prophesied 'certain and undoubted ruin and destruction to the whole realm'. There was no money to pay an army and, if relations with the emperor deteriorated, it would be impossible to raise revenues, while there were those at home who would take his part. In a masterly survey of the affairs of Germany since the emperor's triumph at Mühlberg, he was quite clear that neither the Germans nor the Poles could do anything. A league for religion would fail if England provided no cash and, even then, the emperor would find the means to divert the German Protestants.

All which things laid together I conclude to my simple understanding ... you are not able with your own force only, nor with your
own force nor any other that you can have abroad, withstand the
imminent and present dangers.

What was the answer? Certainly first of all to cut one's coat according to
one's cloth ('It is evil having a lord's heart and a beggar's purse
together'); then to 'fain friendship with the emperor' by holding out the
hope that the religious changes made hitherto could be reversed. This
would possibly 'win a respite to breathe'.[39]

Rapprochement with the emperor was really all Paget could suggest in
practice, even though he admitted in a memo of April 1549 that the
emperor was no friend in view of the religious changes in England. Paget
had been asked what could be done about the Franco-Scottish alliance.
He was adamant that the Scots would not accept English rule and that the
'broken friendship' and barely concealed war with the French could not
be accepted. Should England challenge them? His answer was a decided
no: they had 'waxen rich', were prepared for war and were stronger,
besides being aware of English 'misery.' Again his only answer was 'to see
what were best to be done' with the emperor.[40] The failure of his mission
to Brussels and of any hope of using it to get better terms from the
French was clear by the time of the French declaration of war on 8 August
1549 and rendered Paget even more pessimistic. The war with Scotland
and capture of Boulogne, he argued, had been honourable in their time
'but now having felt the charges of both to have been so great and the
inconvenience of them such as we are not (for any thing that I know)
able to avoid' it was time to cut losses. The king of France was never prepared to accept the loss of Boulogne or the occupation of Scotland (even
when encumbered by a war with the emperor) 'wherefore without peace
with Scotland I believe that the French king will never be at peace with
England.' Thus the policy in Scotland automatically entailed war with
France and Paget was determined to ask the awkward question: 'whether
we be able to maintain war with France' long enough to force it to accept
English power in Scotland. His conclusion was, no. His advice was therefore in effect to liquidate the Scottish adventure (after all, if Henry VIII
could live without war with the Scots for so many years so could the present government), revictual Boulogne and see to internal disorder.[41]

Opinion within the diplomatic world remained divided on the question of France with both the older generation and younger generations
remaining hostile. Nicholas Wotton, ambassador to France from 1546–49

and 1553–57, is an obvious example here; notoriously blunt in manner,[42] he remained hostile to the French despite his great experience of the country, knowledge of its history, and culture and skill as an observer.[43] In January 1551 he thought that news of renewed conflict in Germany might encourage 'our trusty and welbeloved friends of France, perceiving the emperor to have both his hands full in Germany' to attack Calais, which he was convinced they were determined to have.[44] Wotton had even more reason to be suspicious of French attitudes during his arduous embassy in France of 1553–57, when he was preoccupied with the activities of English exiles and their plots and warned constantly of French intentions against Calais.[45] He was also unconvinced from the start that England could remain neutral between France and the Habsburgs.[46] By 1559, his deeply hostile view was well rooted. In a remarkably frank letter to Cecil during the negotiations that led to the treaty of Cateau-Cambrésis, he sought to discount informal French peace offers made through Lord Grey by a long *tour de force* of an historical discourse on Cato's dictum *fistula dulce canit, volucrem dum decipit auceps* ('the pipes play sweetly while the fowler snares the bird'), the summation of which was 'I cannot easily be persuaded, that we can have a true peace with France.' Since the treaty of Arras in 1435, he argued, the French had always sought to divide their enemies, usually with disastrous consequences to the latter. This record was now compounded by the fact that the greatness of the house of Guise rested on the interest of their niece Mary Queen of Scots and her 'fained title to the crown of England'. His prescription, like that of Paget throughout his career, was to anchor policy in the confirmation of alliances with the house of Burgundy (the Habsburgs) in order to get the best possible terms from the French.[47]

Wotton was a highly capable and influential ambassador of the older school.[48] The promotion of younger men such as Richard Morison (an active government propagandist since the 1530s), Philip Hoby and Roger Ascham to service abroad, especially in the unusual circumstances of the early 1550s, stimulated serious reflections from them on English interests. Morison and Hoby, for instance, sought to find an escape from the problem of the dire choice between France and the emperor by suggesting an alignment which would bring together England, Charles, the German princes and Scandinavian rulers in a grand alliance against France. A variant of this, in view of the emperor's ill-health and political collapse, would be to open contacts with the Vienna Habsburgs rather than rely on Philip.[49] There seems good reason to think this approach was already being discussed in inner circles. When Charles V, with a certain

degree of cheek, called on English aid for the war which had started late
in 1551 against the French, Cecil wrote a paper for Edward VI that
treated the idea seriously and suggested that a reversal for the emperor
would be perilous for England 'and herein the greatness of the French
King is dreadful'.[50] Cecil's preferred option (not dissimilar from Paget's
in 1546) was to limit English intervention to a general anti-French
alliance involving the German princes but meanwhile Morison was
secretly instructed to fish out the emperor's intentions in a way not to
provoke the French 'who giveth ... us lately many causes to doubt them'
and may 'perchance be the more jealous of our sending thither'.[51] It was
this project for a German alliance that came to the fore in the last months
of Edward.[52] Meanwhile Ascham, Morison's secretary, was writing, initially for the attention of the Privy Council, a 'Report of Germany', one
of the earliest pieces of serious historical and political analysis in the
English language (to be discussed below).

Nicholas Throckmorton, who had spent much of Mary's reign in effective exile in France and elsewhere, shared many of Wotton's views of the
French, though his Protestant activism led him to more positive conclusions. Throckmorton had great experience of France, was fluent in the
language, and was an expert sifter of intelligence.[53] His appointment as
Elizabeth's first resident envoy at the French court was a crucial move for
the regime. He started from the position that the French were simply
never to be trusted.[54] When he first took up his post in May 1559, he
thought that, under the Constable's guidance, they would be likely for a
while to stick to their obligations under the treaty, though this would only
happen 'in making yourselves so strong at home'.[55] Even before the
death of Henry II, he had concluded that 'we have great cause to suspect
the French meaning towards us'[56] and Throckmorton confirmed
Wotton's view that the Guise regime was bound to be hostile. He knew
himself to be 'odious' to the Guises and, by February 1560, anxious not
to be arrested on the outbreak of war, was frequently asking to be
recalled.[57] The constant drift of his reports was to take advantage of
Henry II's death. Shortly after it, he was pressing that this was 'a propi-
tious time for recovering of Calais'[58] and to enter into relations with
French Protestant leaders.[59] Like Wotton, he thought 'it is in no wise safe
for you to depend over long in doubtful and unknown terms with the
King of Spain' but, unlike Wotton, he thought Philip 'but a hollow friend
unto you'[60] and had an alternative to offer: 'you should arm to the sea
forthwith ... it is in no wise to be suffered, that either the Frenchmen
shall vanquish the Scots that now favour your religion, or that you suffer

any such number of the French there to land'.[61] It is difficult to avoid the assumption that Throckmorton's job was to provide evidence to spur Elizabeth on to action in Scotland once the rebellion had begun there; terms such as 'without delay ... for assuredly it is high time' (July 1559), 'the remedy ... is to take time as it serveth, and beat the iron while it is hot' (February 1560), 'I trust your Majesty will not let slip this occasion' (March 1560) convey the urgency of his general tone.[62] To Cecil he wrote that it depended on him 'so to foresee that the commonwealth be provided for; and that the worst being prevented, the best may save itself' and 'you never had a better time to have to do with these men, than you have at this present'.[63] The 'honied words' he received at length from the cardinal of Lorraine to stay English intervention in Scotland were to be warded off; 'if this be not followed, and now in time handled while it is hot; we shall, I fear, I fear, within few years say to our cost, that all this of the French came but from the teeth forward'.[64] As for the Conspiracy of Amboise, 'if ever time were to work for your surety, and to do that you have need to do; it is now'.[65] Nevertheless, Throckmorton was not a fanatic; the end of the Guise regime in December 1560 and the onset of factional struggles offered new opportunities and he took the view that it was in English interests that none should triumph, in this very much in alignment with Cecil's initially sceptical attitude to intervention in France. He had to change his view towards more active intervention, however, once the fighting opened in the spring of 1562 and the prospect of Spanish aid to the Catholics loomed.[66]

It is clear from Throckmorton's didactic despatches that he was extremely close in his objectives and assumptions to William Cecil. The role of Cecil and the nature of his thinking on foreign affairs have to be considered, of course, since it throws direct light on policy formulated at the very centre and Cecil's papers provide such a rich source. He had been peripherally involved in policy formation during the later 1540s when, in Somerset's service, his circle included many who were then pushing for a union between England and Scotland.[67] It should be remembered that, though only once an ambassador, his experience of policy formation went back to the early 1550s and his first period as Principal Secretary and he had an intimate knowledge of affairs through his close relations with figures such as Wotton and Paget. His thoughts on overall strategy in 1551–53 have already been discussed. The outlook was, of course, undoubtedly more sombre by the time Cecil took up his post again in November 1558 at the moment Paget seems to have been definitively excluded from affairs by the new regime.[68] It has been suggested that Cecil had prepared a coherent programme based on his connections in Cambridge and the Protestant exile community.[69] In foreign affairs, however, policy had to be shaped according to opportunity. Like that of his mistress, Cecil's view of the world was shaped by the dangers of the 1550s and there is little doubt that they both saw France and its ambitions in Scotland as the main threat, since a French invasion from Scotland was more feasible than one from Calais.

It has been argued that Cecil had a more coherent 'British' perspective to his policy and that, although Elizabeth saw the dangers, she preferred short-term expedients.[70] Throckmorton's policy formulations were therefore apposite at a time when the cautious Elizabeth, who knew her own mind from the start, was anxious not to commit herself to war and when other councillors, for example Nicholas Bacon, were pessimistic about the possibilities of military action. The queen, Bacon argued, was short of money and had no allies, the economy was shaky, support for rebels unjust and the French too powerful; in short, he was able to rehearse brilliantly and convincingly most of the arguments against war which had been put forth for the previous generation.[71] The Council, under Cecil's prompting, concluded the opposite, arguing that 'the French mean, after their powers are brought into Scotland, first to conquer it ... and next, that they and the Scots will invade this realm principally upon the north parts'. In December 1559, though, they could not persuade the queen.[72]

In Cecil's 'Brief Consideration of the Weighty Matter of Scotland', drawn up initially in August 1559 and revised in the spring of 1560 he dwelt on the long-standing threat from France, 'how brickle, how false, how double their pacts of peace have been ... the insolency of the French nation ... the old rooted hatred of the house of Guise'. On 23 March the Privy Council again drew up a paper reflecting Cecil's opinions and stressing the opportunity provided by internal French weakness (much of it supplied by Throckmorton[73]) and the revolt of the Lords of the Congregation in Scotland.[74] However, 'the Queen's Majesty never liketh this matter of Scotland' he wrote to Throckmorton on news of the reverse at Leith, 'you know what hangeth thereuppon; weak hearted men, and flatterers will follow that way ... I have had such a torment herein with the Queen's Majesty, as an ague hath not in five fits so much abated.'[75] Cecil's 'Memorial of certain points meet for restoring the Realm of Scotland to the ancient weal' (written probably on early 1560) developed the arguments for the eventual union of the two countries which had been sketched out by Ascham in the *Toxophilus* of 1545[76] and is apparent within Somerset's propaganda of 1547–48[77], in which

Cecil had had a part:

> the best worldly felicity that Scotland can have is either to continue in
> a perpetual peace with the kingdom of England or to be made one
> monarchy with England as they both make but one isle divided from
> the rest of the world.

As long as the French, England's ancient enemies, retained power in
Scotland, they would always seek 'to make Scotland an instrument to
exercise thereby their malice upon England to make a footstool thereof
to look over England as they may'. It is clear that Cecil saw the only
answer to this as the removal of Mary Queen of Scots' power or her
dethronement in favour of Hamilton.[78] Cecil was similarly ruthless in his
attitude to intervention in France; in 1560 he was sceptical about offers
made by French conspirators: 'surely France is disturbed', he noted, and
the offer of towns in Normandy and Brittany 'liketh me well ... but I can
not give your Majesty counsel to embrace things so far off'. Nor could he
accept the viability of an intervention on behalf of a 'devotion popular
upon religion'.[79] By the spring of 1562, though, he could ask Mont in
Germany (again using his allies among foreign ambassadors to back his
case) to write to the queen 'that if she do not now attempt the furtherance of the Gospel in France and the keeping asunder of France and
Spain, her peril will be the most of any prince in Christendom.'[80]
However, the advent of the French civil war initiated a new phase in the
making of English policy, one in which Cecil and his allies would no
longer dominate the queen's confidence but would have to share it with
Leicester and one in which the alliance between Cecil and
Throckmorton would be fractured. Cecil's attitude to military intervention was guarded and lukewarm.[81]

So far, we have considered analyses of policy which emerged essentially
out of the turmoil of practical day-to-day politics. We should now turn to
some more reflective longer works which were produced by humanists
close to government circles in the 1550s. Of these Ascham's 'Report on
Germany' (a fragment, published later but circulated in manuscript) is
pre-eminent as a work both of historical and political analysis, composed
at a time (1552–53) when Anglo-German relations were crucial to the
calculations of the English government.[82] To some extent all diplomats
were expected to report on the affairs of the courts to which they were
accredited (Chamberlain's 1553 analysis of the Low Countries is a case in
point), but Ascham's discussion draws on his classical learning, reading

of Commynes and Machiavelli and personal observation in order to understand the reasons for the unexpected collapse of Charles V's power. [83] As a humanist, Ascham assumed a certain constancy in human nature and a framework of ethical principles, but his reading of Machiavelli led him towards a much more interesting analysis of motive which would still have been difficult in English politics. In particular, he sought to show how the emperor's unwise ill-treatment (his 'unkindness') of his subjects and allies had alienated them and led them to ally with France and the Turks. Thus, though he had some regard for the emperor and little time for the king of France, he contributed significantly to the suspicion of Habsburg policy being generated in English Protestant circles, while skilfully delineating how Maurice of Saxony's devious ambition (the besetting problem of mid-Tudor politics) led him to turn first against his own family and then against the emperor, achieving great benefits for religion and the Empire at the expense of ethical conduct.[84]

For all its pioneering techniques of political analysis, Ascham's work was confined to foreign politics and therefore had limited circulation at the time. One of the most interesting *tours d'horizon* of English foreign policy to emerge from the Northumberland years is William Thomas's discourse 'Touching his Majesty's outward affairs' probably written in the summer of 1551, one of a series addressed to Edward VI for his enlightenment on state affairs.[85] Thomas was, like Ascham, strongly Protestant, had travelled widely, particularly in Italy, and part of his strategy for winning government favour after the disgraceful episode of his flight in 1545 was to publish *Il Pellegrino inglese*, a sustained eulogy of Henry VIII and his foreign policy, written first in exile in English then published in Italian in 1552. In April 1550, with the backing of William Cecil and Walter Mildmay, he emerged as clerk of the Privy Council. He was also attached as secretary to Northampton's important embassy to France in May 1551 that was to lead to the treaty of Angers.[86] The astonishing point is that, given his strong religious views, his analysis of foreign policy could be so close to that of the conservative Paget in 1549; moreover, the most cogent modern studies of Thomas have argued convincingly for the influence of Machiavelli on him.[87] This is amply demonstrated by the discourse on 'What prince's amity is best' also written in 1551; in this he asked the stark questions 'to what end the amity of foreign princes doth serve, and what need one prince hath of the other's amity'. His answer is also stark and akin to the later dictum that countries do not so much have permanent allies as permanent interests: princes, he says, need alliances 'to maintain their own', all the more necessary as 'few princes are of themselves able to maintain their own'. 'Lack of foresight' in alliances leads some states to a point where 'they neither could maintain peace, nor sustain war'.[88] When he deals directly with 'outward affairs',[89] he begins, like Paget, with a profoundly pessimistic analysis of the general English position 'both hated and contempned [*sic*] of them all.' His initial advice is either to seek friends to help or gain time to recover. The first would prove diffi- cult because of religion: 'it is impossible we should have any perfect amity with any foreign prince that dissenteth from us in Religion' a point made also in the 'Discourse on Amity'. In the absence of a strong English power or any neighbour of like religion 'our extremest shift is to work by policy.' He deliberately put the worst case:

> The French king is a doubtful friend, and the emperor a dissembling too. The one hath done us already displeasure: and the other we are sure will do it if he can. For what quarrel hath he to the Germans but Religion? Wherein he hath sworn rather to spend his life than not to reduce it to his own manner. And when he shall have overcome those few that rest (which are of small account in respect of his power) where shall he end his fury but against us ? ... On the other side the French king is already in possession of Scotland and practiseth in Ireland amongst a people that loveth liberty: and that for every small hope of gain will be ready to revolt. Wherein if he should prevail we might reckon ourselves besieged.

The main objective must, he thought, be to gain time. Like Paget, he advised an embassy to the emperor to show him how the French domi- nated Scotland and Ireland and that England wished for a closer alliance with him. What would he require? It would be likely that the emperor's chief objective in an alliance would be 'alteration of Religion.' Again, like Paget, he advised 'the matter to be dissembled with such practices of delays as may best serve to the winning of time'. This would give the French King pause for thought and gain time 'to establish Religion within your Realm: but also to put your subjects in a readiness', while on the emperor's death any obligations would be dissolved and England free of both him and France. Finally, in Scotland the earl of Arran was to be pressed to taking the crown for himself and the Irish to be 'entertained' until the end of the summer. Nothing was to be hoped for from the Danes; negotiations could be started but they were never true friends and their services (available only for money) could not be afforded. It was true that Papists in England might be encouraged by all this and

Protestants in Germany discouraged. The emperor might learn the truth
and become even more hostile. These arguments are dismissed. The
main objective – of gaining a breathing space – must be used to build up
English strength.

The obvious conclusion from these remarkably similar analyses of foreign policy is that English success abroad was directly related to internal
cohesion and preparedness. Thomas thought diplomacy and good government both necessary for stability. Both Paget and Thomas thought
that internal religious policy, though a determinant, could be finessed if
necessary; both Thomas and Cecil attached importance to Scotland and
the thinking of Cecil and Paget was in many ways similar.

For all the interest and sophistication of analysis in the views of professional diplomats, discussion of foreign affairs was no longer confined to
the highest reaches of government and at this point it becomes important to consider the influence of those outside the inner circle of affairs.
Foreign observers, for whom the English language remained an impene-
trable barrier,[90] thought the English people proverbially hostile to foreigners, even though they suspected the upper classes were rather less so,
and the advent of Philip's entourage in 1554 sharply accentuated this
problem.[91] Although they did not fully understand why, they agreed that
'the people', especially in this period of relatively insecure governments,
constituted an element in the making of English policy. That the peace
commissioners at Cercamp in 1558 even suggested putting the unpalatable terms on offer to parliament could only confirm such a view.[92]
Indeed the devious dealings of both French and Imperial ambassadors
with a whole range of the political elite make it quite clear that they
assumed the existence of such a political culture.[93] The famous English
tendency to changeability ('mutacion') observed by foreigners led them
to note that rebels and pretenders who had been 'expelled from this
country have often been brought back by this people with very little help
from abroad'.[94] The Habsburg envoy d'Assonleville in 1558 thought that,
though the rulers might grasp the importance of the Habsburg alliance,
'le vulgaire' preferred another alliance, 'so unstable are they, not knowing what is good for them'.[95]

From the 1530s there is distinct evidence for the role of non-official
'projectors' who would offer advice to ministers. An interesting example
from the early 1550s is the advice proffered to William Cecil by an old
French hand, Thomas Barnaby, whose career is another example of continuity in foreign relations. As far as we can tell, Barnaby was a merchant
who had married in France about 1514 but as a result of some losses to

French pirates in 1526 (which he had never been able to resolve in the French courts) had been forced to leave his trade 'and follow the king's affairs' on 28 missions, many of them for Thomas Cromwell, to France between then and 1552, when he wrote a long letter of advice to William Cecil.[96] He claimed to know all the French ports between Boulogne and Bordeaux and to have met all the leading French ministers of his time. One further aspect of his life worth noting is that he was a radical Protestant and claimed to have incurred the displeasure of Gardiner and Wallop in the late 1530s and early 1540s for the reputation of being Cromwell's spy. Reporting initially on talks with French admiralty officials, he noted their claims that the English could no longer hope to invade France since it was no longer divided as it had been in the previous century:

> and now it is knit all to one realm and that we may see what great hurt we have done them with our wars ... and what town we can show that we do hold but only have spent out all our riches and destroyed a great number of subjects, and left all our money in Flanders, Hainault and Artois to the utter destruction of our realm.[97]

Barnaby is an interesting example of an Englishman deeply experienced in France who seems to have detested the French, particularly their leaders. His main object was to cast down the 'gloriousness' of the French:

> God knoweth my poor heart how much I do tender the wealth and prosperity of mine own nation and that I am sorry from the bottom of my heart to think that they of France accept us to be gross-natured people and covetous, and they have said unto me ere now that if we had never so rank or malicious war with them, they know how to buy us for money.[98]

The essence of Barnaby's advice was novel in that it involved the use of economic power, namely an embargo on Newcastle coal, on which he claimed that the French were heavily dependent for the manufacture of iron, steel, artillery, jewellery and which occupied a good part of their merchant fleet at certain times of the year. His plan was for the king to establish an English monopoly of shipping and establish a staple in Kent.[99] The other dimension of his plan was to have important long-term consequences, for since 1532 he had been exploring the new port of Le Havre and indeed had submitted plans of it to Cromwell. England 'needed none other rod to scourge Normandy and France'. French royal revenues depended on salt passing through it and the manufactures of Paris and Rouen passed out through it. It was crucial to the revictualling of the French fleet.[100] Le Havre was, of course, to come into its own in English calculations just ten years later.

So far, this discussion has concentrated on advice devised for the inner circles of the government machine. Foreign policy could not, though, be formulated in a vacuum and throughout the sixteenth century public opinion had a role to play in the mobilisation of forces for war, opposition occasionally voiced but seldom overtly published.[101] The shaping of public opinion became a more urgent matter in the 1540s with the propaganda formulated to defend the policy towards Scotland.[102] Claims to Scotland were a feature of John Coke's 1550 *Debate Betwene the Heraldes of Englande and Fraunce*, though the essence of his argument is a highly traditional piece of anti-French polemic by an official of the staple.[103] The advent of Mary's marriage negotiations and the prospect of Spanish rule immeasurably increased wider participation in debates on foreign policy and effected a rather clear transformation of the dominant public view from anti-French to anti-Spanish in a relatively short time. As in religious matters the regime lost the 'battle of the books', so in comment on foreign affairs it lost control of the monopoly of propaganda.[104] As early as August 1553 such pamphlets were being reported by the Imperial ambassador.[105] The views on foreign policy expressed by an anonymous 'personage of the court', to the effect that the emperor had done little to help Mary in her crisis and that Northumberland had allied with the French because the French had always helped their friends, is closely related to the contemporary 'Discours d'un seigneur Anglois', copied by Noailles. This developed a full-scale anti-Habsburg argument.[106] The Wyatt rebellion, for all its religious undertones, was a direct challenge to the queen's prerogative in foreign affairs.[107] Once the marriage was an accomplished fact, there was no shortage of vehement attacks on its consequences[108] but *A Warnyng for England*, probably printed abroad, appeared in the summer of 1555 and dealt more directly with foreign policy by hanging on an attack against the tyranny of the Spanish in Naples the suggestion both that Philip was eager to abandon his barren wife and suggesting that the real objective of the government was the restoration of monastic lands.[109] By late 1555, and the controversy over Philip's coronation, such pamphlets, probably including *The Lamentation of Napelles* and *The Mourning of Mylayne*, were becoming alarming to the government and circulated during the parliamentary session.[110] In the spring of 1556, the 'Letter' of John Bradford, who claimed to have read these tracts, concluded: 'I think there is no law confirmed and passed, whereby the Queen may lawfully disinherit the realm of the crown.'[111] Bradford developed anti-Spanish arguments of extreme vituperation supposedly from the perspective of a Catholic who claimed to have realised how horrible the Spaniards were when, as chamberlain to one of Philip's councillors, he set to learning Spanish secretly in order to read his correspondence; not surprisingly this turned out to harbour dastardly plots against England and its queen. His tract was 'addressed' to lords suspected of being the Spaniards' friends and singled out others as enemies of Spain and Paget as one of those they saw as 'apt vessels to work treason by'.[112] The widely held suspicion that the Spaniards were intent on draining money out of England is reflected in a pamphlet seen by Gilles de Noailles in August 1556 called *Maria Ruyna Angliae.*[113]

Propaganda printed abroad quite evidently served the interests both of the French embassy and those opposed to war. The 1556 *Lamentacion of England* warned against a new war with France, attacking Philip's supposed schemes first to take possession of Calais by spreading rumours of its betrayal or to encourage conflict on the borders with the French in order to provoke war with the French:

> and so not only consume the greatest part of the substance and treasure of the realm ... but also will be a occasion of destruction of a great number of the noble men gentlemen & commons of this realm. It is not long since we had wars with France, which was for the emperor's pleasure, but what followed thereof, it is not unknown. Did it not almost beggar the whole realm ... Therefore I would desire the states of the realm, that they will be circumspect and well advised, how they attempt to break with France, for the pleasure of any other princes, lest they be the occasion of the destruction and beggary of the whole realm.

This reappeared in 1558 after the fall of Calais, with a conclusion drawing attention to the prediction of dire consequences of a war with France.[114] The example of the loss of Calais was taken up by Protestant propagandists. Traheron's *Warning to England*, published abroad, mounted a savage attack against the 'despiteful, cruel bloody, wilful, furious' Mary who, eager to 'betray her native country', 'began a war with a mighty king where peace was sought and desired, only to satisfy her wilful head, to increase the force of the Spaniard, & to maim ... thy best captains, & soldiers'.[115]

The anti-Spanish publication campaigns of the 1550s ushered in a new period for the interaction between foreign policy and public opinion, which did not cease with the accession of Elizabeth but rather intensified as what was portrayed as the struggle between the true religion and the papal anti-Christ gathered pace. The opening of the Wars of Religion in France saw the start of a new era of public news letters and translations of reports and relations from the French, starting with a series of documents issued by Condé in 1562. The very rapidity of their appearance in English makes unavoidable the conclusion that a concerted campaign was involved.[116]

They were paralleled by more direct government publications. Printed proclamations had long been the most obvious way to place foreign policy before a wider public, though they had only limited effect. Announcements of peace treaties were confined to the fact of conclusion and orders for the restoration of normal commerce,[117] though the 1554-proclamation on the marriage treaty with Philip was unusually detailed[118] and the March 1560 proclamation maintaining peace with France and Scotland rehearsed all the queen's grievances against the French, particularly Guise ambition, denounced French unwillingness to negotiate, and yet insisted that the peace would be maintained with France and Scotland.[119] Declarations of war were another matter since they often anticipated demands for aid. Henry VIII emphasised French dealings with the Turks and failure to pay his pension in 1543, Edward VI in 1549 the French king's 'deadly malice' and failure to fulfil the previous peace treaty, finally his attack on Boulogne, while Mary in 1557 detailed the conspiracies that Henry II had stirred up against her.[120] Supplementary texts proclaimed letters of marque, arrest of enemy persons and property, and suspension of commerce as well as sanctions for the supply of the army. Longer manifestos became more important as the need to influence opinion was more clearly perceived. A *Declaration* was published in 1542 asserting the king's rights to Scotland and a longer text on the same theme emerged in 1548.[121] Nor, despite the fury of attacks against it, was the Marian regime devoid of propaganda resources.[122] The Elizabethan regime clearly thought that the intervention in France of 1562 required serious public defence. The September 1562 proclamation justifying intervention did so on the basis that English troops were acting to defend the authority of the French king. The objective of regaining Calais was only hinted at.[123] This time, though, a longer *Declaration* was also issued justifying intervention in terms of Guise ambition and desire to subvert true religion.[124]

The mid-century years, ones of great danger and pessimism, stimulated public and private discourse on matters connected with England's foreign relations which saw some important if tentative steps towards a view of foreign policy as to some extent distinct from dynastic interest. When Thomas or Barnaby wrote about affairs they used the terms 'we' and 'us' when referring to England as opposed to foreign princes. The Protestant propagandists played the patriotic card as hard as they could: the *Supplication* called on members of parliament 'to have respect unto this their natural and free country of England'. Bradford declared himself compelled to write as 'an English man, for the natural love I bear towards my country' and summoned 'all English men' to defend their native land.[125] As yet, these views were marginalised and Elizabeth was increasingly to assert her exclusive control of policy; yet the genie was out of the bottle and it was never afterwards quite possible to put it back. Protestantism ate away at long-established English views of France as the great enemy but involved also a desire for France to join the Reformed camp. For older diplomats, Henricians, moderates or reformists as well as Protestants, it was still relatively easy to be even-handed between the powers. For the younger men, religion could not be ignored in dividing the world into good and evil; French and Spanish Catholics stood on the other side of the gulf. Even Paget in 1546 had seen the pope as a major enemy;[126] for many of the active diplomats of the 1560s onwards, it was religion rather than a dynasty that posed the problem.[127]

NOTES

1. A. F. Pollard, in *Cambridge Modern History*, ii, p. 499; W. K. Jordan, *Edward VI: The Threshold of Power* (1970), p. 116.
2. R. B. Wernham, *Before the Armada: The Growth of English Foreign Policy 1485–1588* (1968), p. 239.
3. For R. D. Jones, *The Mid-Tudor Crisis, 1539–1563* (1973), pp. 149–89, the problem lay in the combination between internal weakness and an over-ambitious foreign policy with a 'British dimension'. The crisis in foreign policy 'derived from the adoption of rash, short-sighted and ill-judged policies by the Crown and its ministers, exacerbated by polarisation of religious extremes and by the erosion of the financial, economic and social bases of national stability at home, and by the intervention of powerful forces abroad ready and able to exploit these and dynastic weaknesses'. (p. 189).
4. R. Hoyle, 'War and public finance' in D. MacCulloch (ed.), *The Reign of Henry VIII* (1995), pp. 90–1. Hoyle estimates Henry's income in his early years as £80–90,000, probably doubled by the confiscations of church lands in the 1530s. The lay subsidy should then be added to this (pp. 77, 83).

5. BL, Cotton MS Titus C vii, fos 198–9. These arguments were laid out in this memorandum of all or part of the Council, (see also Calig. E v, fos 33–9 and PRO, SP14/190, fo. 140) (discussed in D. Loades, *The Reign of Mary Tudor* (1979), pp. 241–2).

6. Speech in the Privy Council, *c.*15 December 1559, copy, BL Harl.253 (Historical coll. of Ralph Starkey) fos 83v–92v, at 87v (summary in *CSPF Eliz.* ii, pp. 197–8). The importance of the French king's access to credit was stressed by John Mason, 18 April 1551, see P.F. Tytler, *England in the Reigns of Edward VI and Mary* (2 vols. 1839), i, p. 358.

7. It is not intended here to discuss at length the old views, exemplified by Wernham and Jordan, of the Northumberland regime and Mary's reign as characterised by subservience to foreign powers. Most modern scholarship would dispute this. E.g. D. Loades, *John Dudley, Duke of Northumberland 1504–53* (Oxford, 1996), p. 205; C.S.L. Davies, 'England and the French War, 1557–59' in J. Loach and R. Tittler (eds), *The Mid-Tudor Polity* (1980), pp. 159–85.

8. B. L. Beer and S. M. Jack (eds), 'The Letters of William, Lord Paget of Beaudesert, 1547–63', *Camden Miscellany*, 4th series, 13 (1974), pp. 1–141 [hereafter 'Paget Letters'], p. 77.

9. The treatise on the 'The distresses of the Comonwelth' PRO, SP12/1, fo.77 (quoted Conyers Read, *Mr. Secretary Cecil and Queen Elizabeth* (1955), p. 124; Wernham, *Before the Armada*, p. 240). Printed in R. B. Wernham and J. C. Walker, *England under Elizabeth* (1932), p. 204. On Waad's authorship see J. E. Neale, in *EHR*, 65 (1950) pp. 91–8, 350.

10. Anon. letter from Antwerp to Cecil, October 1559 [possibly Thomas Challoner] *CSPF Eliz.*, ii, p. 3: 'To make a hard comparison, he may then liken England to a bone thrown between two dogs'. Challoner had reported in August 1559 that the count of Feria had said 'that Englande wold be another Millanne to sett the princes together by the eares.' (T. Wright, *Queen Elizabeth and Her Times* (2 vols, 1838) i, p. 7).

11. Mason to Cecil, 20 November 1558, *CSPF Eliz.* i, p. 6; see also PRO, SP12/1, fo. 5

12. Paget to the Council, 26 September 1558, 'Paget Letters', p. 123. Paget's argument was that the French pension arrears should be demanded in talks in order to forego them in return for Calais.

13. Paget and Parry to Cecil, 20 February 1558/9, Samuel Haynes, *A Collection of State Papers ... now remaining at Hatfield House* (1740), pp. 208–9 and also HMC 9 *Salisbury*, i, p. 151: 'The Necessite of Friendship with the House of Burgundy ... the naturall enmity betwene us and Fraunce'. The fear that England would become a new Piedmont was relayed by Nicholas Throckmorton in September 1559 as an opinion of Chantonnay the Imperial envoy in France: 'that we had nede to loke about us, for it wold so cum to pass, as either we shuld be made a Piemont and be devided, or els a Milain, and so constrained to stand upon our gard untill we were weried.' (P. Forbes, *A Full View of the Public Transactions in the Reign of Q. Elizabeth* (2 vols 1740–41) [hereafter Forbes, *Transactions*], i, pp. 237, 241).

14. Wotton to Cecil 8 January 1558/9, Forbes, *Transactions*, i, p. 17; Mason, in the analysis mentioned above, thought that Philip was stalling in the peace negotiations by using Calais as an excuse.

15. 'tiendo el peor en que nunca gentes estubieron jamas', Feria to Philip, 10 March 1558, Joseph Marie Bruno, baron Kervyn de Lettenhove, *Relations Politiques des*

Pays-Bas et de l'Angleterre sous Le Règne de Philippe II (11 vols, Brussels, 1888–1900) i, p. 152, trans in *CSP. Sp.* xiii, p. 366. For the Council's reasons for not contributing to a Calais expedition, see BL, Cotton MS Titus B ii, fos 59–60 (1 February 1558).

16. Luke MacMahon, 'The Ambassadors of Henry VIII.' Unpublished University of Kent PhD dissertation, 2000.

17. The detailed biographical references for the next two paragraphs have been deleted for lack of space. For brief details see G. Bell, *Handlist of British Diplomatic Representatives, 1509–1688* (1990); W. K. Jordan, *Edward VI: The Young King* (1968), pp. 232–3 for a useful overall survey of the diplomats of these years, though Jordan's argument that most of them were career diplomats is to be taken with care.

18. Wotton, bemoaning his decrepitude to Cecil in January 1559, said that he would be entering his 'climacteric' year (i.e.60th) in May 1559 (Forbes, *Transactions*, i, p. 23).

19. Wotton to Petre, 8 October 1556, *CSPF Mary*, p. 264.

20. So Wotton recalled in 1557 (to Petre, January 1557, *CSPF Mary*, p. 282). On being 'mete to serve': e.g. Dr Valentine Dale (*CSPF Mary*, pp. 68–9). He then became, first, special envoy to the Low Countries in 1564 (Bell, *Handlist*) and resident ambassador in France 1573–76 (ibid., F123). Throckmorton feared being 'made unapt to be received another tyme abrode' by being arrested on a break with France (to Cecil, 20 February 1559, Forbes, *Transactions*, i, p. 329).

21. See L. V. Ryan, *Roger Ascham* (Stanford, 1963), pp. 119–55. Ascham had also been promised the Latin secretaryship under Edward but was not actually appointed until some time after his return from Germany, in May 1554 (ibid., p. 198).

22. The problem is pointed up by the need to recall Thirlby temporarily in 1553 from the Imperial court for the meeting of parliament (*CSP. Sp.* xi, p. 236). As late as 1560, though, Throckmorton could recommend the sending of bishops on a grand embassy to the Empire: 'Mr Pylkyngton were mete to be byshopyd and to be sent also ... besyds the substance off lernynge, wheareyn he ys notyd comparable to any off owers, he ys yn cyrcumstancis ecclesiaticall policie a wyse man' (to Cecil, 4 Febuary 1560, Forbes, *Transactions*, i, p. 321). None of these appointments were made.

23. Paget is the obvious case but Clinton, a military man, 'parloyt tresbien [francoys]' (Marillac to Henry II, 27 May 1549, BN, MS français 3099 p. 17) and was sent on several missions to France and the emperor between 1551 and 1556.

24. F. G. Emmison, *Tudor Secretary* (1961).

25. Throckmorton to Cecil, 20 February 1559/60, Forbes, *Transactions*, i, p. 329; same to same, 19 May 1560, ibid., i, 452: 'In my oppynion, Mr Sydney were not the unmetyste man for thys place, for sondry respects; and yf not he, then Mr Chaloner: but that your syster wyll be angry, I cowld reamember your brother, Mr Thomas Hobie, amongst others.'

26. Michieli to Doge and Senate, 3 December 1555, *CSPV* vi, p. 270

27. On Mason's status, see Bell, *Handlist*, E60; Vannes's last surviving letter in *CSPF Mary*, p. 267 is 24 October 1556.

28. After Renard's departure in September 1555, there was no Habsburg ambassador, the count of Feria acting in 1558 as military liaison between Philip and the Council, not formally as ambassador, and was replaced by Alonso de Cordoba in July, joined by d'Assonleville in September (see M. J. Rodriguez-Salgado and S. Adams (eds), 'The Count of Feria's Dispatch to Philip II of 14 November 1558', *Camden Miscellany*, 4th series. 29 (1984), pp. 306–9. Even the Venetian envoy

Suriano, who arrived in March 1557, was officially accredited to Philip (*CSPV* vi, pp. 991, 1195).

29. Paget later claimed that in 1546 'tous ceux de son conseil n'eussent osé ouvrir la bouche pour luy en parler' (i.e. of the return of Boulogne) and that he had had 'avec ledict feu roy d'Angleterre plus de privaulté et de liberté que l'on ne sçauroyt croyre ne que le munde ne voyoit ne pensoyt', that he had more 'liberté' of speech than Wolsey or Cromwell, to the point of angering Henry in arguing for the restoration of Boulogne. This, though, must be set in the context of his trying to convince the French ambassador of his good will (G. Lefèvre-Pontalis, *Correspondance politique de Odet de Selve* (Paris, 1888) [hereafter *Selve*], 29 August 1547, p. 194–5).

30. Tytler, *Edward VI and Mary* i, pp. 303, 341.

31. Paget went on five missions between 1549 and 1556. Stephen Gardiner is another under Henry VIII but there is good reason to think that the post of Principal Secretary was increasingly incompatible with active diplomacy (William Cecil, for instance, only went on one embassy – to Scotland in 1560). Wotton was briefly Principal Secretary October 1549–September 1550. He was perhaps more useful as an ambassador and left little mark in central affairs (B. Ficaro, 'Nicholas Wotton, Dean and Diplomat'. Unpublished University of Kent PhD dissertation, 1981, pp. 153–4).

32. Letters of 23 May, 29 August, 9 September, 4 October 1547, *Selve*, pp. 147, 194–5, 200, 216. The despatch of 29 August is interestingly paralleled with Paget's letter to Somerset of 30 August ('Paget Letters', pp. 12–13). On relations with van der Delft, see *LP* xxi (i), 469, 547; *CSP. Sp.* ix, pp. 20, 30, 51, 57, 109–10, 151, 184–8, 244, 257, 184; S. R. Gammon, *Statesman and Schemer* (Newton Abbot, 1973), p. 85.

33. August 1546, BL, Cotton MS Titus B ii, fos 79–81, Paget's own copy in Northampton RO, Fitzwilliam MSS, C 21, fos 20r–21r: 'we have cause to be at the point of despaire to find any frendship in either of them ... the worst is upon the two occasions to have them both at ones joyned togethers to be our enemies or the one overcomyng furst the other to be our enemie ... The best waie is bothe to kepe them from agreing and from being either of them any greater.'

34. M. L. Bush, *The Government Policy of Protector Somerset* (Montreal, 1975), ch. 2; Wernham, *Before the Armada*, p. 153 had argued the centrality of Scotland to Henry's policy; J. J. Scarisbrick, *Henry VIII* (1968) pp. 424–6 that the Scottish war was an offshoot of the war with France. Neither is entirely correct.

35. Somerset opened the question of Boulogne as early as August 1547 and in September 1547 sent Paget to say he wished to restore Boulogne to the French early, (see *Selve*, nos. 208, 221). The project was raised again on Somerset's return from Scotland and continued until the end of the year (*Selve*, nos. 238, 248, 254 p. 237, 262 pp. 247–8). On the French counter-claim to Calais, see *Selve*, no. 264. This is the implication of a message conveyed by Somerset through Huntly in October 1548 (*Selve*, p. 464). See Somerset to Wotton, 15 October [1548], BL, Harleian MS 249, fos 18–25 at 24v.

36. Somerset to Wotton, 15 October [1548], BL, Harleian MS 249, fo. 23r, draft: 'we did consider that Boloyne standith the K. Majestie yerly in an importable charge CM li and this last yere in CCM markes, which is more then the realme is able well to beare. At thende of certaigne yeres he must restier it or elles he must fall in to a war, and in that space with kepyng of it to spend the K. Majesties treasure, consume the realme, wast men and vitailes. Iff that money could be saufed, and the

pencon paied, and Scotland com quyetly in to the K Majesties handes, in this peax his highnes shuld be so enriched that when the sword shall come in to his handes he shalbe able to get asmuche as x Boloynes be worth with that or som other quarter of Fraunce were propice.' This important despatch is difficult to interpret as it is heavily revised. The thoughts on Boulogne 'upon this consyderacion with our self' are sketched out before he described offers to de Selve as a response to Henry II's reported request for some means to peace. They involve a recapitulation of the proposals made the previous winter. The conversation referred to appears to be that on 16 November 1547, *Selve*, p. 237.

37. 'Paget Letters', p. 14
38. Charles de Marillac described him at this time as 'l'ame du protecteur et ung des principaulx aucteurs de tout le remuement de beau mesnaige qui se faict par dela' (BN, MS français,3099, pp. 39, 50).
39. 'Paget Letters', p. 24. The line that the emperor could be deceived into thinking nothing very radical was going on in England was to become well established in diplomatic moves. Wotton was to use it with the emperor in 1551 (*CSP. Sp.* x, pp. 310–17). William Thomas thought the same (see below).
40. 'Paget Letters', p. 32.
41. 'Paget Letters', pp. 76–8.
42. See Paget's remark of him as a man who 'writeth his mind plainly' and consequently incurred Gardiner's hostility (to Petre, 1 November 1544, PRO, SP1/194 fo. 200 (*LP*, xix (ii), 532)) or the remark of Scepperus that he was 'naturally and by habit a harsh (*aygre*) man (*CSP. Sp.* viii, no.93) and Renard that he was 'naturally testy and intriguing' (ibid., ix, p. 294). Richard Morison thought in 1551 'there are few men less loved of the French (*CSPF Edward VI*, p. 338).
43. See B. Ficaro, 'Nicholas Wotton', pp. 273–9.
44. Wotton to Cecil, 2 January 1551, Haynes, *State Papers*, p. 112 (HMC 9 *Salisbury* i, p. 82): 'knowing the great Desyre that they have to lyve in Peace with us, that is to say to have Caleis agayne. ... Fraunce now flourishes, and the Kinge is yonge and lustye, and of myndde to do great Acts. Wherby I rekon that it wer very harde for the Frenche Menne to be long ydle; and yet, where they might be occupyed, medling not with Themperor, excepte onlye with us, I can not perceyve.' For similar cautions against French intentions, see the report from John Abell, agent at Strassburg, 27 June 1551, *Salisbury MSS*, i, pp. 87–8 and the report, September 1552, of the agent Thomas Stukeley that Henry II had actually told him that he intended to attack Calais (*CSPF Edward VI*, p. 221; J. G. Nicholls, *Literary Remains of King Edward the Sixth* (2 vols Roxburgh Club, 1857–58), p. 455.
45. This was known in diplomatic circles. Throckmorton in 1559 feared his warnings would be ignored and pleaded that they be not judged 'as Mr Wotton's were judged of for Calais' (to Cecil, 23 September 1559, Forbes, *Transactions*, i, p. 238)
46. Wotton to Petre, 26 January 1554, PRO, SP69/3 fos 46–7 (*CSPF Mary*, p. 53): 'because of this marriage I think it will be very hard to avoid the war betwixt us and France.' The tears he is reported to have shed on taking leave of Henry II on 7 June 1557 are thus a curiosity (Montmorency to François de Noailles, 7 June 1557, AE, CP Angleterre 18, fo 457).
47. Wotton to Cecil, 8 January 1558/9, Forbes, *Transactions*, i, pp. 14–24, at 18–22. The opinions are very much the same as those of Wotton and the other peace commissioners at Arras on 18 November 1558, *CSPF Eliz.* i, pp. 3–4, in which Wotton in

particular argued that the French willingness to give up their positions in Italy in order to retain Calais was a clear indicator of their ultimate objective to subjugate England.

48. An excellent example is his smoothing out of the emperor's anger over Morison's hectoring oration at an audience in 1551 (*CSP. Sp.* x, pp. 310–17).

49. Morison to Council, 27 April 1553, *CSPF Edward VI*, pp. 269–70; Hoby to Northumberland, 5 May 1553, ibid., p. 275.

50. 23 September 1552, BL, Cotton MS Nero C x, fo. 69 is Edward VI's version (M. A. S. Hume, *The Great Lord Burghley* (1898), pp. 33–4); BL, Cotton MS Galba B xii, fos 230–31 is the draft in Cecil's hand, slightly different. It is linked to another memo by Cecil on the same subject (BL, Cotton MS Galba B xii, fo. 229). The matter had been discussed in the council in July 1552; it was first put off and then decided that England could offer mediation but that the treaty with the emperor was no longer effective, especially since the emperor had refused help in 1549 (W. K. Jordan (ed.), *The Chronicle and Political Papers of King Edward VI* (1966), p. 135; Instructions to Morison on the emperor's request for aid, BL, Cotton MS Galba B xii, fo. 224).

51. Instructions to Morison 24 September [1552], draft, BL, Cotton MS Galba B xii, fos. 232–5 with letter from Cecil, ibid., fo. 236; another dated 19 September (*CSPF Edward VI*, p. 221).

52. BL, Cotton MS Galba B xii, fos 236–7. Council to the ambassadors with the emperor, 5 May 1553: 'ye shold devise with Mr Mounte at his coming ... with what princes of Germany in what degrees and aftre what soarte it weare beste to enter and breake first'. This German project was precisely the one dismissed by Paget as useless in 1549 ('Paget Letters', pp. 23–4), though of course things had changed since then.

53. Much of Throckmorton's correspondence is published in Forbes, *Transactions*, many of them drafts from his own papers now in BL, Additional MS 35830 (the Hardwick papers). His paper of advice in 1558 is unfortunately truncated in surviving form. See J. E. Neale, 'Sir Nicholas Throckmorton's advice to Queen Elizabeth on her accession to the throne', *EHR*, 65 (1950), 91–8.

54. A good example would be his description of the chevalier de Seurre, sent as resident to England in January 1560: 'these mens disguisings and fawnings ... if eare will be given to honied wordes, if sweete languaige will persuade, if speaches well applyed and couched will be belevid ... the enchanter is cum a lande.' (4 February 1560, Forbes, *Transactions*, i, p. 316) Throckmorton was anxious that the new ambassador would persuade the queen to a compromise that would leave some French troops in Scotland.

55. 18 June 1559, Forbes, *Transactions*, i, p. 121.

56. 4 July 1559, Forbes, *Transactions*, i, p. 152.

57. To Cecil, 23 July 1559, Forbes, *Transactions*, i, p. 160: 'the disgrace I am like to be in here'; to Cecil, 20 February 1560, ibid., i, pp. 328–9: 'how odious I am to these men; and how they have ben put out of doubt (as yow know, and by whome) that I have ben the only sturrer and worker of all that is done'. Throckmorton is one of the formulators of the 'black legend' of the Guise in England: 'so long as any of the House of Guise ruleth in France, these pikes will never be fogottin; but revenge will be sought, if ever time serve' (15 March 1560, ibid., i, pp. 366–7). The same point had been made, though, by Nicholas Bacon in his Council speech of December 1559: war in Scotland would be 'because the house of Guise (who is the

foundere of this quarrelle) hath gottene the chiefe credite and governance under the Kinge'. (BL, Harleian MS 253, fos 87v–88r).

58. 13 July 1559, Forbes, *Transactions*, i, p. 157. He returned to the case in the more favourable conditions of 1562: 'It may chance that in these garboils there will be some good occasion or opportunity offered that you may again be brought to the possession of Calais or some other place of consequence' (PRO, SP70/36, fo 65).

59. N. Sutherland, 'The origins of Queen Elizabeth's relations with the Huguenots, 1559–62' in her *Princes, Politics and Religion 1547–1589* (1984), pp. 73–96.

60. 18 July 1559, Forbes I, *Transactions*, p. 165; 27 July 1559, ibid., i, p. 182. The hostility to Philip is also reflected in a letter from his informant in London, Peyto, 9 May 1560 (ibid., i, p. 441). For the general hostility to Philip's 'betrayal' over Calais in these years, see Bp. of Aquila to Arras, 30 December 1560, AGS E 814 fo. 10; Feria to Philip, 20 February 1559, Lettenhove, *Relations Politiques*, i, p. 440, *CSP. Sp. 1558–67*, p. 30); Cecil's memo on the state of the realm, *c*.1570, Haynes, *State Papers*, p. 583.

61. Throckmorton's emphasis on the use of sea-power recurs: 'bend your force, credytt, and devise to maintayne and encrease your navy ... yt is the flower of Englandis garlande.' (to Cecil, 28 April 1560, Forbes, *Transactions*, i, p. 416.

62. 18 July 1559, Forbes, *Transactions*, I, p. 165; 4 February 1560, ibid., i, p. 318; to queen, 15 March 1560, ibid., i, p. 366; to Council same date, p. 372; to Cecil same date, p. 375. Cecil responded to these promptings directly, writing to Croft in Scotland in July 1559: 'kindle the fire, for if it be quenched the opportunity will not come again in our lifetime' (*CSP. Scot.* i, p. 223).

63. To Cecil, 23 September 1559, Forbes, *Transactions*, i, p. 238; 8 February 1560, ibid., i, p. 324. Throckmorton was anxious to encourage the queen to stick to the forward policy in Scotland and prevent Elbeuf's landing there (ibid., i, p. 331)

64. Throckmorton's long interview with Lorraine on 25 February (to queen, 27 February 1560, Forbes, *Transactions*, i, pp. 334–44) interpretation (to Cecil, 27 February 1560, ibid., i, p. 345). He went on to advise strongly 'that the Queen's Majestie's ships slack not to do what service they can; and that by no meanes there be an suspence and surcease of armes in the meane tyme' (ibid., i, p. 346).

65. To Cecil, 7 March 1560, Forbes, *Transactions*, i, p. 353. This does not mean that Throckmorton was directly involved as claimed in J. Dureng, 'La complicité de l'Angleterre dans le complot d'Amboise', *Revue d'histoire moderne et contemporaine*, 6 (1904–5), pp. 249–56, refuted in N. Sutherland, 'Queen Elizabeth and the Conspiracy of Amboise' in her *Princes, Politics and Religion*, pp. 97–112.

66. Throckmorton to Cecil, 24 January 1562, *CSPF Eliz.* iv, pp. 503–4: 'our safety is for neither part to overthrow the other'; but then to the queen, 6 March 1562, ibid., iv, p. 548: 'it is time for the Queen to countenance the Protestants'; to Cecil, 14 March 1562, ibid., iv, pp. 553–4: 'it is time the Protestants were countenanced, lest all quail'.

67. J. Dawson, 'William Cecil and the British dimension of early Elizabethan foreign policy', *History*, 74 (1989), pp. 198–9.

68. For a consideration of the reasons for Paget's exclusion, see Rodriguez-Salgado and Adams, 'Feria's Dispatch', p. 315.

69. W. MacCaffrey, *The Shaping of the Elizabethan Regime* (1969), part I; N. Jones, 'Elizabeth's first year: the conception and birth of the Elizabethan political world' in C. Haigh (ed.), *The Reign of Elizabeth* (1984), pp. 27–53.

70. Dawson, 'Cecil and the British dimension', p. 205
71. BL., Harleian MS 253, fo. 83, summary in *CSPF Eliz.* ii, pp. 197–8.
72. The Council had mapped out its arguments on 24 December 1559, *CSPF Eliz.* ii, pp. 220–24, esp. 221, end. by Cecil 28 December as 'not allowed by the Queen'.
73. E.g. Throckmorton to queen, 22 May 1560, Forbes, *Transactions*, i, p. 465.
74. Cecil's paper, Forbes, *Transactions*, i, pp. 387–90 (another version of *CSPF Eliz.* i, pp. 519–24 end. August 1559); Council's opinion, 23 March 1560, ibid., ii, pp. 390–96.
75. Cecil to Throckmorton, 13 May 1560, Forbes, *Transactions*, i, pp. 454–5.
76. The first edition of *Toxophilus* was printed in 1545 (*STC* 837) but probably written in 1544 (L. V. Ryan, *Roger Ascham*, p. 49). The passage on Scotland, *English Works*, ed. W. A. Wright (Cambridge, 1904), p. 53: 'yet one thynge would I wysshe for the Scottes, and that is this, that seinge one God, one faythe, one compasse of the see, one lande and countrie, one tungue in speakynge, one maner and trade in lyuynge, lyke courage and stomake in war, lyke quicknesse of witte to learning, hath made Englande and Scotlande bothe one, they wolde suffre them no longer to be two: but cleane gyue over the Pope ... ' noting the advantages to Wales of union with England 'this felicitie ... shal chaunce [fo. 28a of 1589 Abell Jeffes ed.: 'should haue chaunced'] also to Scotlande by the godly wysedome of the moost noble Prince King Henrye the viii.' The same thinking is present in William Thomas's 'Pilgrim', written in 1547 (see below): Henry VIII might have united England and Scotland in 'one self devyded nacion and realm, one self perpetuall united people, not for the welth ... but for the uniform quiet of their approved auncient contention' (see Abraham D'Aubant (ed.), *The Works of William Thomas* (1774), p. 107).
77. Most notably the 'Proclamation' [September 1547] and 'Epistle' [February 1548]. On the publication of the latter see *Selve*, 8 February 1548, p. 282. These ideas are also similar to those of the anglophile James Henrisoun in his 'Exhortation', see M. Merriman, 'James Henrisoun and "Great Britain": British Union and the Scottish Commonwealth' in R. Mason (ed.), *Scotland and England* (Edinburgh, 1987), pp. 85–112.
78. BL, Lansdowne MS 4, no.9, fos 26–7 (holograph); Throckmorton broached the matter of dynastic union in a letter to Robert Dudley, February 1560, Wright, *Queen Elizabeth*, i, pp. 58–9.
79. Cecil to queen, 21 June 1560, Wright, *Queen Elizabeth*, i, p. 31; same to same, 9 July 1560, *CSPF Eliz.* iii, p. 184; Cecil and Wotton to the queen, same date, ibid., pp. 185–6
80. Cecil to Mont, 22 March 1562, PRO, SP70/35, fo.139 (*CSPF Eliz.* iv, p. 561) papers of July 1562, PRO, SP70/39, fo.106; 'A Memorial of the perils of France', Forbes, *Transactions*, ii, p. 2 (*CSPF Eliz.* v, no. 337).
81. MacCaffrey, 'The Newhaven expedition', pp. 7–8; see especially Cecil's letter of 11 October 1562, Wright, *Queen Elizabeth*, i, pp. 95–6.
82. *A Report and Discourse written by Roger Ascham, of the affaires and state of Germany and the Emperour Charles his court* (undated), probably 1570, in *English Works*, pp. 129–69. For a thorough discussion of the work, see Ryan, *Roger Ascham*, pp. 156–92. Ascham set aside the work as too dangerous in 1553 and Gardiner knew nothing of it, though it seems likely it was known in his own circle.
83. BL, Cotton MS Galba B xii, fos 238r–39v for Chamberlain's report.

84. On the emperor, see *English Works*, p. 128; On Henry II: 'for what cared he for religion abroad, who at home not onely followeth none him selfe priuately in his life, but also persecuteth the trouth in others openly with the sword.' (ibid., p. 164).

85. P. J. Laven, 'The Life and Writings of William Thomas'. Unpublished University of London M.A. dissertation, p. 52.

86. Ibid., pp. 75–90, on the dating of *Il Pelegrino*, pp. 75–90, Laven argues that the English version is not just a translation as does E.R. Adair, 'William Thomas' in R. W. Seton-Watson (ed.), *Tudor Studies* (1924), pp. 133–60 at p. 138.

87. Above all Laven, 'William Thomas', pp. 309–11 and S. Anglo, 'Our extremest shift is to work by policy: William Thomas and early Tudor Machiavellism', *Transactions of the Cymmrodorion Society* (1984), p. 31; Jordan, *Chronicle and Papers of Edward VI*, pp. xx–xxi thought that Thomas's writings on public affairs were 'glib'; Nicholls, *Literary Remains*, i, p. clxiv is also dismissive, though Froude, *History of England* i, pp. 308–10 was very positive.

88. Text in d'Aubant, *Works of William Thomas* and also J. Strype, *Ecclesiastical Memorials* (7 vols.1816) vi, pp. 362–6.

89. For the text, see d'Aubant, *Works of William Thomas* pp. 179–92; Adair, 'William Thomas', pp. 141–4. For the MS of these treatises, BL, Cotton MS Vesp. D xviii, fos 2–45.

90. E.G. Selve at dinner with William Howard and Paulet in 1548 could only make out the names in their conversation, unable to understand the rest of their English 'gergon' (4 April 1548, *Selve*, p. 323). No major foreign ambassadors seem to have had any significant knowledge of English and negotiated in Latin and French.

91. It should be pointed out that such foreign observations on the nature of the people increase in the 1550s in comparison with ambassadorial reports down to the 1540s. E.g. Scheyve's report that the English feared Spanish rule (*CSP. Sp.* xi, p. 228); Renard to Philip *CSP. Sp.* xi, p. 263; Renard, 15 October 1553: 'the English are said to hate foreigners because they are a thoughtless people and loathe foreign artisans' (ibid., xi, p. 301); letter of Spanish gentleman, 2 October 1554 *CSP. Sp.* xiii, pp. 60–61. Charles V's view that 'loathed as all foreigners are by all Englishmen' (23 June 1553, *CSP. Sp.* xi, p. 64) and that they 'more than any other nation abhor' foreigners (20 September 1553, *CSP. Sp.* xi, p. 246); 'de nature jalouse et abhorrissans estrangiers, et qu'ilz ont tousjours détesté gouvernement de prince ou de supérieur estrangier' (Renard, 8 March 1554, PRO Tyler transcripts i, *CSP. Sp.* xii, p. 139).

92. Arundel, Thirlby and Wotton to the Council, 29 October 1558, PRO SP69/13, fo 230v (*CSPF Mary*, p. 404); Philip's commissioners 28/ 30 October 1558, *CSP. Sp.* xiii, pp. 430, 432, 433; English commissioners, 29 October, Lettenhove, *Relations Politiques*, i, p. 260. The Council unsurprisingly vetoed this novel suggestion: a great Council would be better 'since it were not convenient to have the same broken to the whole house, but only to the nobility and some others of the best and gravest sort.' (8 November 1558, PRO, SP 69/13, fos 239v–40r). Somerset had suggested putting a proposed restoration of Boulogne to parliament in 1547 (26 October 1547, *Selve*, p. 229).

93. Point made by E. H. Harbison, *Rival Ambassadors at the Court of Queen Mary* (Princeton, 1940), p. 64; for an example, ibid., pp. 276–7. Simon Renard thought the English constitution 'populaire' in which the people were fickle and the nobility dependent on the king (to Philip, March/April 1555, *CSP. Sp*, xiii, p. 150). The

English often stressed this in order to avoid unpleasant decisions: Mary remarked herself that it was necessary to satisfy 'the people' in the question of the marriage (ibid., xi, p. 289) and Noailles thought that Paget was motivated by fears of 'quelque eslevation du peuple' (René Aubert de Vertot, *Ambassades de Messieurs de Noailles en Angleterre*, 5 vols (Leyden, 1763) ii, p. 279) and reported that Mary's subjects 'ne permettront jamais que nul estrangier arrive en ce royaulme' (ibid., ii, p. 241) and later that Petre thought of the marriage that 'la noblesse, ny le peuple ne la sçau-roient jamais aimer' (ibid., v, p. 168). Renard feared the French were stirring up 'le peuple' against the marriage (*CSP. Sp.* xii, pp. 30–1) and Noailles in 1555 thought that a Franco-Imperial reconciliation 'mortiffie le cueur à ce peuple' whatever the queen's policy might have been (27 July 1555, Vertot, *Ambassade*, v, p. 44).

94. Noailles to Constable, 10 August 1554, AE CP Ang. I–II (XII), p. 467, quoted L. Wiesener, *La jeunesse d'Elisabeth* (Paris, 1878), p. 296. See also ibid., pp. 167–8 for a selection of comments on the English character.

95. D'Assonleville to Philip, 6/7 November 1558, Lettenhove, *Relations Politiques*, i, p. 275 (*CSP. Sp.* xiii, pp. 437–8).

96. Barnaby to Cecil, 1 October [1552], BL, Lansdowne MS 2, fos 187–92 (printed with errors, Strype, *Ecclesiastical Memorials*, vi, pp. 482–9). There is no doubt that Barnaby was reporting to Cromwell from France (*LP* xiii (ii), 187, 188, 541, 581, 668). Barnaby says that he 'was marryed there for xxxviijti yeres agone' (fo. 187r), though in 1538 he was noted by the French ambassador as brother-in-law to Sir John Wallop, (J. Kaulek (ed.), *Correspondance Politique de MM. de Castillon et de Marillac* (Paris, 1885), no.49) whom by 1552 he regarded as an enemy. After Cromwell's death he had had 'many a hevye looke' from him (fo. 190r) but see *LP* xvii, 393, 409 for Wallop's deal-ings with him. His suit in France had been settled in 1541 (*LP* xvii, 283 etc). He claimed in his letter of 1552 to have been reporting to Somerset and indeed a 'Mr Barnabie' was sent to Ireland in September 1548 (PRO, E315/257 fo.79).

97. BL, Lansdowne MS 2, fo. 187r

98. Ibid., fo. 187v. He goes on to instance Wolsey's pension (which he puts at 400,000 crowns) as an example.

99. Ibid., fo. 188r. He claimed he had bought coal in Newcastle for 2/2d a cauldron and sold it in France for 14 nobles.

100. Ibid., fo. 189v–190r. He summed up his immediate plan as prohibition on French fishing, Newcastle coal and the occupation of Alderney.

101. See G. Bernard, *War Taxation and Rebellion in Early Tudor England* (Brighton, 1986).

102. See, Dawson, 'Cecil and the British dimension', pp. 198–9.

103. *The Debate Betwene the Heraldes of Englande and Fraunce compyled by Jhon Coke ... and fynyshed the yere of our Lorde MDL.* For commentary see L. Pannier (ed.), *Le Débat des Hérauts d'Armes de France et d'Angleterre* (Paris, 1877). Coke stresses French aid to the Scots, piracy, alliances with the Turks, 'that most judasly and trayterously you have envaded his maiesties domynyons ... his highnes beyng not xij yeres of age, and the realme of Englande at great sedicion amongest them selves partely by your falce and crafty meanes', ingratitude for Henry VIII's help in 1525 and 'your ryches, which elevateth you so in pride that your knowe neyther God, your soveraygne lorde the kynge of Englande, nor your selves'.

104. J. Loach, 'The Marian establishment and the printing press', *EHR* 101 (1986), pp. 135–48 on the decline of official printing; C. Haigh, *English Reformations: Religion, Politics and Society under the Tudors* (1993), p. 223 on the loss of control.

105. See that addressed to 'Noblemen and gentlemen favouring the word of God' enclosed in Renard's despatch of 16 August (*CSP. Sp.* xi, pp. 173–4), considered by Charles V to be 'scandalous and unavowable' (ibid., p. 179). See also ibid., p. 241.

106. *CSP. Sp.* xi, pp. 191–2; Vertot, *Ambassades*, ii, p. 182–90. Harbison considers the role of Noailles in the articulation of this propaganda in *Rival Ambassadors*, p. 80 and 'French intrigue at the court of Queen Mary', *American Historical Review* 45 (1940), pp. 533–51., at. 549–50.

107. For discussion of the rival political and religious dimensions of the rebellion see D. Loades, *Two Tudor Conspiracies* (Cambridge, 1965); M. Thorpe, 'Religion and the Wyatt Rebellion of 1554', *Church History*, 47 (1978), pp. 363–80.

108. E.g. *A supplicacyon to the quenes Maiestie (complaynyth ... that wher as this noble realm off England hath of long tyme out of mynd bene the most fre contre in all Christendom, now is lyke to be brought in to bondage ...* (1555) printed with the bogus colophon London, Iohn Cawoode 'Prynter to the Queenes Majestie, with her most gracious Lycence' (*STC* 17562), fo. 22v: the marriage 'will bring this noble realme int to beggery and vyle slavery'.

109. *A warnyng for Englande conteynyng the horrible practises of the Kyng of Spayne in the Kyngedom of Naples ...* (Emden: Gilles van der Erve, 1555) (*STC* 10024): 'may she thynke that the Emperour wyll put all his kyngdoms and dominions into the handes of one, of whome his sonne can haue no issue?' This has often been attributed to John Ponet.

110. Advis de Flandres, 28 November 1555; Noailles, 16 December 1555, Vertot, *Ambassades*, v, pp. 241, 254. On these works, referred to by John Bradford, see Strype, *Memorials*, vii, pp. 183–99.

111. *The Copye of a letter sent by John Bradforthe to the right honorable the lordes the Erles of Arundel, Derbie, Shrewsburye and Penbroke, declaring the nature of the Spaniards ...* (? London, 1556) (*STC* 3480), sig. Fiii v. On his reference to contemporary tracts on Milan and Naples, sig.Fi. Not to be confused with the martyr John Bradford (burned, June 1555), this author is recorded as 'serving man to Sir William Skipwith' a conformist administrator and J. P. in Lincolnshire.

112. Ibid., sig. [Dv r]. On the lords' attitudes, [Dvii v]. It would be easy to dismiss Bradford as a pathological xenophobe were it not for the fact that many of the deeply hostile plans he claimed to have discovered in Spanish circles are echoed in Renard's despatches: e.g. 'ceulx de par deçà, tant subjectz à l'avarice, que si l'on les veut practiquer et racheter de présents et de promesses, l'on les convertira où l'on vouldra.' (Weiss iv, p. 100) and *CSP. Sp.* xii, p. 14, while his virulent contempt for the English is amply documented (see Wiesener, *La jeunesse d'Elisabeth*, pp. 167–8).

113. Gilles de Noailles, 30 August 1556, AE CP Angleterre XIII, fo. 46 (Harbison, p. 304).

114. *The Lamentacion of England* (no place or date), dated internally 30 December 1556, reissued 1558 (*STC* 10015). This was sometimes attributed to Cranmer.

115. 'Benthalmai Outis' [Bartholomew Traheron, *A Warning to England to repente, and to turn to god from idolatrie and poperie by the terrible exemple of Calece given the 7 of March Ann D. 1558* (?Wesel, 1558) [*STC* 24174], pp. 5–7 (MS pagin.).

116. *A declaration made by my lord the prince of Condé* (6 April 1562) [*STC* 16849]; *A treaty of thassociacion made by the prince of Condee to maintain the honour of God, the quiet of*

the realm and the liberty of the king (16 April 1562) [*STC* 16852]; *The very truth of the conference between the queen mother and Condé* (1562) [*STC* 4813.4]; *An answer made by Condé to the request presented by the triumvirate to the French king* (London, 1562) [*STC* 5042]. There was also a demand for news: *The perfytt newes out of Ffraunce* (1562) [mentioned E. Arber (ed.), *Transcript of the Registers of the Company of Stationers of London, 1554–1640* (5 vols 1875–94, reprint 1967) i, 84r] and numerous works on the massacre at Vassy.

117. P. L. Hughes and J. F. Larkin (eds), *Tudor Royal Proclamations* (2 vols, New Haven, 1964–69): peace with France 1546 (i, p. 369); peace with France, 1550 (i, pp. 486–7); 7 April 1559, peace with France (ii, pp. 111–12).

118. Ibid., ii, pp. 21–6 (14 January 1554).

119. Ibid., ii, pp. 142–4.

120. Ibid., i, pp. 320–21 (war with France, 2 August 1543); ii, pp. 77–8 (war with France, 7 June 1557). The 1549 Declaration against France is not included in Hughes and Larkin but can be found in PRO, SP 68/4 fo.1117–27. Thomas in his English version of *Il Pellegrino*, on Henry VIII's war of 1543: 'what knowe I of the practises betwene the Turk and the French Kinge', the emperor had used 'important perswasions' to war and as for Boulogne: not the whole of Picardy was 'suffitiente to satisfie the debtes the French Kinge did owe unto the Kinges Majestie' (copy in BL, Harleian MS 353, fos 31–2).

121. *A Declaration, conteyning the iust causes of this present warre with the Scottis* (Berthelet: 1542); for the *Proclamation* of 1548 see above.

122. Under Mary official propaganda sought to celebrate the Habsburg alliance e.g. *The Copie of a letter sent into Scotlande*, ostensibly by John Elder, dated 1 January 1555 (*STC* 7552) and the regime could count on the literary support of John Heywood.

123. *Tudor Proclamations*, ii, pp. 206–7, 24 September 1562 on despatching forces to Normandy: 'saving to the crown of England ... that which of late times being evicted from ought to be restored' drafted by Cecil, see *CSPF* v, no.693.

124. E.g. *Declaration* (R. Iugge and I. Cawood: 1562) in *Harleian Miscellany* (4 vols, 1808–13) i, pp. 374–9. See also the sequence of drafts on 'Why the Queen puts her subjects to arms', 30 September 1562, *CSPF Eliz. v*, nos, 667–74; Forbes, *Transactions*, ii, pp. 69, 74, 77 and the version in French, 27 September, in H. de La Ferrière, *Le XVIe Siècle et les Valois* (Paris, 1879), pp. 76–7.

125. *Supplication*, conclusion; Bradford, Preface, sig. Aii v.

126. See Paget's 'Consultacion' of Aug. 1546 (above, n.43), fos 20r–20v: 'that we se aparently . . . the bysshop of Rome with al his membres ardently inflamed to recover agayne his usurped power and tyranny over this realme.' Paget was no doubt acutely attuned to his master's view of the Pope.

127. S. Adams, 'The Protestant cause: religious alliance and the West European Calvinist communities as a political issue in England, 1585–1630' (Oxford, D.Phil., 1973).

6

SEEKING A PROTESTANT ALLIANCE AND LIBERTY OF CONSCIENCE ON THE CONTINENT, 1558–85

David J. B. Trim

This chapter examines England's foreign policy during the early and middle part of Elizabeth I's reign and concludes that it was confessionally driven, with what can best be characterised as a Protestant programme of action prioritised by the Elizabethan government.[1] In it I attempt to shrug off the burden of past historiography, which weighs down most assessments of Elizabethan England's relations with foreign powers. In consequence, the interpretation that follows is very different from those advanced in most of the works cited; however, the differences are not indicated clearly in the notes. This is not because of any disrespect for the authors – that I do not have frequent citations 'correcting' scholars, some of whom are dead, many of whose works I greatly respect, and all of whom contributed something to our knowledge and understanding of the past, is simply because this is necessary in advancing a radically new interpretation. If points of dissent with historiographical orthodoxy were all to be fully referenced, this essay would be impossibly long. Rather than engage with other scholars, therefore, I instead concentrate on the original events and original sources, in order to reveal the reality (or as much as can be recovered) of Elizabethan foreign policy. Readers who wish to engage with the alternative viewpoints will find them in the secondary sources cited in the notes and in Chapter 7.

I

It is a commonplace of historians that Elizabeth I did not want to help European Protestants and that she did so only reluctantly and half-heartedly. Remarkably, both scholars who have praised, and those who have disparaged, Elizabeth and her foreign policy have taken for granted that the queen and the majority of her ministers were, on the whole, only unwilling supporters of their co-religionists across the narrow seas – and particularly of the Continental Calvinists who, of all Protestants, most needed, and requested, England's direct assistance in this period. When scholars are so much in agreement, surely it is likely that there is also agreement between their interpretation and the actuality of the past?

In fact, this impressive consensus is largely the result of historiographical inheritance. There has been a presumption that Elizabeth was not pro-Protestant and indeed was to a great extent confessionally neutral in her approach to foreign affairs – a presumption related to the similar assumption that she was indifferent to zealous Protestantism. Both views of Elizabeth originated with the very first historian of the last Tudor, William Camden, writing in the reign of James I. For reasons relating to politico-religious disputes at the time he was writing, Camden portrayed the queen and council as having an aversion to Calvinists abroad, as well as at home, in an attempt to disassociate the golden memory of the great queen from Jacobean puritans. Ever since, Camden's view has been transmitted and been built on by successive generations of historians and biographers.[2]

Elizabeth's reign has been continually rewritten and reinterpreted in light of the great issues facing society at the time of rewriting and for various reasons, but the traditional view of her foreign policy has always fitted very well into the worldviews of academic historians – and so it was retained as part of their more general interpretations of the queen. As for her innumerable popular biographers, they have sought new psychological insights and all seem to assume that the worthy but dull, 'dry-as-dust' area of diplomatic history has little to offer on this score. At any rate they have generally been content simply to synthesise and perpetuate the views of professional historians on Elizabethan foreign policy.[3]

This traditional viewpoint was, of course, made credible by the persistent myth of a *politique* Elizabeth, who was uncaring of religion and merely used its rhetoric while actually pursuing 'English commonsense solutions while an outside world tore itself to pieces on rival ideologies'.[4] That this *is* a myth is increasingly obvious. The queen's own devoted, personal attachment to Protestantism was demonstrated by the work of W. P. Haugaard and again in Susan Doran's recent study of her letters. It is now generally accepted that Elizabeth's personal beliefs influenced (and can be seen at work in) her government's policy at home – so why not abroad?[5]

After all, the majority of her counsellors shared her religious views, broadly speaking. Thanks largely to the work of Simon Adams the myth that the Elizabethan body politic was fractured by faction has also been shown in recent years to be false, at least until the last decade of her reign.[6] The traditional picture, painted by historians since the late nineteenth century, of the Puritan-but-Machiavellian Walsingham and Puritan-yet-feckless Leicester attempting to push the queen and her prudent (and also *politique*) chief minister, Burghley, into intervention on the Continent against their better judgements, is simply no longer tenable in the light of recent research.[7] Yet it is still widely accepted, in its basic premises, if not in its details. Thus, one of Elizabeth's most recent biographers portrays a queen 'captured by hard-line Protestantism' against her will after the pope declared her to be deposed and her subjects free of their oaths of allegiance in 1570: thereafter 'she found herself' (apparently in spite of herself) 'pursuing a more aggressively Protestant policy'.[8]

It is time to look afresh at Elizabeth's foreign policy, bearing in mind that she was a genuinely committed Protestant (though not, to be sure, a Calvinist), surrounded by zealous Protestant ministers, who, though by no means in total harmony over royal policy, had similar goals in mind. We need not be detained by the debate as to whether she had a 'foreign policy' in any meaningful sense, or merely reacted to events, since this is in itself a policy of sorts. Further, even if much help for foreign Protestants originated (or appeared to originate) with private individuals or groups, the government was usually at least aware that it was being given and to ignore such interventions in foreign realms was, again, a clear-cut choice.[9] It is also possible to dodge the vexed question of how much Elizabeth was actually responsible for her ministers' action – recent attempts to write the queen out of the policy-making process (most notably by Stephen Alford) have certainly gone too far, but this volume focuses on foreign policy, which is a function of government. An assessment of the contribution of different individuals and factions within the government to its actions can, to a certain extent, be left to one side in a study such as this – the focus is instead on showing what those actions actually were and to what purpose.

The focus here is on the period from Elizabeth's accession in 1558, to 1585, when England entered the war against Spain outright and openly. Thereafter, though there was some scope for debate about the circumstances in which peace might be made, essentially the political nation was fixed on the war effort, the exigencies of which largely dictated policy. This was not, however, the case during Elizabeth's first twenty-seven years on the throne; there were more potential policy options and the decisions reached in these crucial years set the tone for the rest of the reign.

What, then, were England's foreign policy aims in the palindromic sixteenth-century years of '58–'85? I argue that confessional factors were ultimately of primary importance in determining Elizabethan foreign policy. Other factors did influence policy, of course, but while the queen and her ministers sought to enhance the nation's prosperity and to preserve its security, 'national security' time and again was interpreted from a confessional stance. There was little concern for the balance of power on the Continent *per se*; the concern was rather to keep specifically Roman Catholic sovereigns in check. To this was added, moreover, a concern to secure, where possible, liberty of conscience (inclusive of liberty to worship) for Protestants ruled by those princes. Although England would act unilaterally in pursuit of these policy objectives, queen and council preferred to act in consort with other Reformed states; indeed they felt that the best way to achieve all their ends was by creating a pan-European alliance of Protestant principalities, kingdoms and republics. Such a coalition could most effectively combat Catholic aggression and intervene to compel toleration of the Reformed.

The goal of creating an alliance among the various Evangelical sovereigns (what has been termed a 'Protestant alliance policy') may seem quite moderate.[10] Indeed, Elizabethan policy was not Protestant in the way that, say, the Holy Roman Emperor Ferdinand II's policy was Catholic: there was no attempt to impose Protestantism by force of arms on Catholic countries. We come back, however, to the reason for seeking a Protestant alliance: namely to restrain Romanist sovereigns and obtain liberty of conscience for their reformed subjects. The quest for freedom of worship for Protestants was in fact far from moderate, because it was so antithetical to what the Most Catholic King of Spain and most of the Catholic subjects of the Very Christian King of France would accept.[11] One might just as well say that the aims of Philip II in sending the Armada were moderate, because the first goal he set the dukes of Medina Sidonia and Parma was to obtain freedom of worship for English Catholics! The Elizabethan regime was never likely to grant full rights to

English Catholics; the Guises and Catholic League would not grant liberty of conscience to French Calvinists and continually resumed hostilities even when the French crown brokered a compromise peace; and Philip II, as many foundered negotiations revealed, would not rule over heretics. The aims of English foreign policy were far from moderate and reveal a real commitment to fellow Protestants.

Now, the government sought to promote its Protestant-ish foreign policy without endangering national prosperity or security; indeed, often no choice had to be made between commercial, security and religious interests, for they generally neatly coincided. In this sense, the 'provocative question' posed in one oft-cited essay, as to whether English policy under Elizabeth 'was guided by "True Faith" ... [or] "National Interest" ', may imply a false dichotomy.[12] But when they did come into conflict, the confessional, rather than national, interest consistently took precedence for Elizabeth and her ministers.

II

On succeeding to the throne in 1558 Elizabeth could have been forgiven had she felt her birthright was akin to a poisoned chalice. She inherited a traditional foreign policy of war against France, in alliance with the house of Burgundy. More, she inherited an actual war with France, in alliance with the Spanish Monarchy, whose head, Philip II (widower of Elizabeth's predecessor), was sovereign of the remnants of Burgundy, including the provinces of the Low Countries – a war that Philip was winning, but in which England was doing very badly, having just lost to France its last Continental enclave of Calais. Peace negotiations were already underway, but England's weakened state made it increasingly unlikely that they would result in the return of Calais.

To make matters worse, Elizabeth also inherited a problematic economy and a nation that was confessionally divided. Her personal adherence to the evangelicals only made her position still more difficult, for a substantial proportion of the population was opposed to yet more reform in religious matters, especially if it was with a capital 'R' – Reformation (along Protestant lines), rather than simple regeneration or reorganisation. Even her claim to the throne was potentially tainted, since her father had proclaimed her illegitimate, and though this had been reversed, Elizabeth's alleged bastardy was likely to be seized upon by those to whom her confessional allegiance was anathema, especially since her conception was the occasion for the original Henrician schism with

Rome. This was not just a notional danger – if Elizabeth was barred from inheriting the throne then the rightful heir was arguably her cousin, Mary Stewart, whose husband was Francis, the crown prince of France. His adoption in 1559 of the arms of England, in right of his wife, was not an empty gesture, but a definite threat to Elizabeth's throne.

The best (perhaps the only) way to confront the French threat and to regain Calais was, apparently, obvious – certainly to some of Elizabeth's subjects. An elder statesman, Lord Paget, emphasised to one of the queen's secretaries of state, only three months after her accession, 'the necessity of friendship with the House of Burgundy'.[13] She needed to keep the support of Philip II – the greatest king in Christendom. But there was the rub; to Philip the title 'Catholic king' was neither nominal, nor even a job-description, but rather a vocation.[14] If the traditional Burgundian/Spanish alliance were to be maintained, Elizabeth would have to cut her policy coat according to Philip II's confessional cloth.

This might not be a problem in terms of domestic policy. Philip was unquestionably disappointed when Elizabeth, after initially giving hints that the nation's religion might be left unchanged, actually established a clearly Protestant Church of England. The compromise formulæ and gestures to placate conservative English opinion which so angered the Puritans and have so exercised many subsequent historians did not impress the Spanish – especially the former bishop of Aquila, Alvaro de La Quadra, who was the king's new ambassador in London.[15] However, in practice Philip was willing to live with the changes, partly because he, too, needed to preserve his existing alliance against France. As de La Quadra made plain to William Cecil, the new queen's principal secretary and most trusted counsellor, Anglo-Spanish co-operation remained desirable from the Habsburg perspective if the changes she made in England's religion were limited. Accepting Elizabeth's right to choose her country's confession could, after all, be justified in terms of the *cuius regio eius religio* principle, negotiated by Philip's uncle, Ferdinand and accepted by his father, Charles, at the peace of Augsburg only four years earlier. Furthermore, as long as Elizabeth also effectively accepted this principle then there was the chance that the issue of England's religion could become moot, for she might be succeeded by a good Catholic (as had happened only six years before on Edward VI's death), or the Tridentine reforms, which Philip enthusiastically supported, might ultimately lead to English re-conversion.[16]

Thus, it was really in the area of foreign, rather than domestic, policy that the English need to maintain the Spanish alliance (or at least avoid outright Spanish enmity) caused a potential policy problem for the new queen and her government. As long as Elizabethan Protestantism remained restricted to England and Wales the traditional alliance was still possible, at least in theory. But if the new regime's reformist sympathies were to be actively expressed *abroad* then the Most Catholic King might not ignore the changes his *quondam* sister-in-law had effected in her own kingdom; and it would of course be particularly provocative and dangerous were her government to dabble in the domestic affairs of any of the domains of the Spanish Monarchy. In short, for the Elizabethan regime to avoid openly affronting Spain and driving Philip II into an enmity he hoped to avoid, it had to have a care, above all, for its foreign policy. It was this which had to be tailored to meet Spanish taste.

This exigency indeed greatly influenced the *implementation* of policy for the first quarter-century of Elizabeth's reign. However, in practice it had less effect on the *formulation* of policy. In the first five years of the reign the regime was, as Andrew Pettegree argues, 'restlessly interventionist, supporting Protestant rebels and refugees in several countries with an almost reckless abandon'. Following reverses in 1563, there was an apparent U-turn in policy – even Pettegree concurs with the general historiographical trend in his description of 'a hesitant and tremulous Queen of mature middle age [who did] little justice to the much bolder spirit that characterised the first years of her rule.'[17] In fact, in the remaining twenty-two years before changes in the international political scene helped to lead to the outbreak of open war with Spain in 1585, English foreign policy remained essentially the same – but it was executed cautiously and covertly, with queen and council at pains to give 'the prudent king' hope that outright war with the Tudor state could be avoided. The initial programme of aggressive intervention foundered on England's military inadequacies, but only when that had occurred did the government adopt a more circumspect course of action. In sum, Elizabethan foreign policy aims rarely if ever reflected Habsburg objectives, but rather were meant to avoid being obviously at odds with them.

III

Pettegree's analysis of early Elizabethan policy, quoted above, has not been as widely noticed, much less accepted, as it deserves. The new government was quick to support Protestants in Scotland, France, and even the Low Countries – it did so openly in the first two states, which were declared enemies of the Habsburgs, but not in the Low Countries. We will look at early-Elizabethan foreign policy in some detail because this reveals that the regime's commitment to seeking liberty of conscience for foreign Protestants (especially Calvinists), and willingness to take action in support thereof, existed from the first years of the reign.

The new regime's international intentions were signalled very early. The new tranche of privy councillors appointed in December 1558, a month into Elizabeth's reign, were 'men of assured understanding ... and well affected to the Protestant Religion'. As well as the former Marian exiles Francis Russell, earl of Bedford, and Sir Francis Knollys, they included Sir Nicholas Bacon, Sir Ambrose Cave and Sir Edward Rogers, all of whom, like Bedford and Knollys, were reliable anti-Catholics, and soon showed themselves to be actively sympathetic to Continental Protestants.[18] Only a few weeks later, on 1 February 1559, the English ambassador to the Vatican was recalled (on the grounds that there was 'no further cause why he should make further abode there') while envoys were despatched to the Lutheran princes of Germany (to assure them that Elizabeth subscribed to the Augsburg Confession and to canvass the possibility of alliances).[19]

The first test of the new regime, however, came in Scotland in 1559, after the conclusion of the peace of Cateau–Cambrésis in April, at which Spain obliged England to accept the forfeiture of Calais in order to obtain peace terms – a peace both Philip II and Henry II of France regarded as necessary, partly due to mutual exhaustion, but partly because of their concern about the spread of heresy. Scotland's queen, Mary, was in France with her husband the dauphin, so her French mother, Mary of Guise, ruled the country as regent. French control of Scotland would always have been regarded as a potential danger by an English government but the situation was made worse by the change in England's religion. The zealously Catholic regent's repression of Protestants in Scotland triggered a rising by the country's Calvinists, but sympathy for their fellow believers' plight was not the only factor that inclined the new English regime towards intervention on their behalf. Mary was of the house of Lorraine, whose collective identity was bound up in its historic role as orthodox warriors against infidels and heretics. Because Mary Stewart's in-laws were naturally happy to embarrass their traditional English enemies, the confessional change initiated by Elizabeth actually gave the house of Lorraine a real incentive to act against her, for there was not only an opportunity to aggrandise the Guise family but to roll back the Reformation, at least in England. For this reason, Cardinal Charles of Lorraine had argued that only Francis and Mary could be accepted as England's legitimate representatives at the Cateau–Cambrésis negotiations. That peace was agreed there did not lessen the potential danger to Protestant England resulting from the Guise–Valois–Stuart connection – not least because after the accession of the dauphin in July 1559 as Francis II, the regency was in the hands of the cardinal and his brother, Francis, duke of Guise, head of the house of Lorraine. The threat posed by a potential Franco-Scottish Catholic 'crusade', possibly backed by the papacy, exercised the minds not only of Secretary Cecil and Elizabeth's Privy Council, but the wider English political nation, and was also recognised by Philip II and his ministers.[20]

The result was military intervention in Scotland. The English government, to be sure, had motives for this that had nothing to do with religion, but it is significant that throughout Elizabeth's reign there was no attempt to dominate Scottish politics and policy as there had been under Henry VIII and Edward VI. A primary concern was of course for national security, but so long as the Scottish government was Protestant dominated, English security was generally assumed to be assured. It is notable that in the negotiations of the summer of 1559 with the Protestant Scots Lords of the Congregation, even the restoration of independence from French rule 'came second, as a defining characteristic for Cecil, to the [issue of the] lords' religion', as Alford points out.[21] It would be mistaken, therefore, to interpret English action in Scotland in 1559–60 as essentially expansionist.

The exhortation to Scottish Calvinists in the spring of 1559 (when England and France were still at war) to act 'for maintenance of the Word of God' had possibly been a cynical one.[22] But when the Elizabethan regime decided to act in peacetime it was not simply to remove Scotland from French influence, or to increase the chances of a British union; rather, as Cecil's papers make clear, it was just as much to secure for Scotland the same freedom from 'all Idolatry like as England' enjoyed, and to ensure that in both countries 'the truth of Christian religion' was maintained.[23]

Moreover, the execution of the policy was entrusted to men such as Cuthbert Vaughan, a committed Calvinist. He was one of the initial liaison officers with the Scottish Protestants; when he was sent back to London after quarrelling with Lord Eure, one of the wardens of the marches, the Privy Council was not only quick to dismiss Eure's charges against Vaughan and send him back to the border, but did so with a grant of £200.[24] By the spring of 1560 it was apparent that the Lords of the Congregation alone could not bring down the Francophile and Catholic

regime in Scotland, and an English army was sent to bring about its down-
fall. The options for commanders were limited by political considerations
and the availability of experienced officers, yet within these constraints,
Protestants played a leading role. Overall command was nominally given
to the duke of Norfolk, who was confessionally conservative, as were most
of the wardens of the marches and their officials, but they had only limited influence on the actual campaign. Norfolk stayed in Berwick and
control of the expeditionary force of some 1200 horse and 6000 foot was
largely in evangelical hands. It was commanded by the Calvinist Lord
Grey de Wilton; among his officers and all-important gentleman volunteers were a hard core of zealous Protestants, many of whom later fought
for William of Orange and/or the Huguenots. Grey's men had the worst
of the engagements with the French army, largely because the French
troops were more combat effective – due in turn at least partly to continuing English use of old-fashioned military technology and tactics (for
example, their use of the long bow whereas the French used firearms) –
an important point to which we will return.[25] However, despite tactical
reversals, the campaign was a strategic success, partly thanks to the
English fleet and the death of Mary of Guise in June. Cecil negotiated
the treaty of Edinburgh (6 July 1560), by the terms of which the French
withdrew, leaving Scotland ruled (for the moment) by the Lords of the
Congregation.

It was not only in Scotland, though, that the Elizabethan regime was
active in the early years of Elizabeth's reign. As de La Quadra perceived,
its aggressive Protestant stance made it a danger 'to the faith and the
neighbouring kingdoms' – the plural is significant.[26] It was not just
Scotland where the Spanish suspected Elizabeth might intervene. As early
as the summer of 1559, de La Quadra believed 'that if she could raise a
revolt about religion in France like that in Scotland, neither fear nor conscience would prevent her from attempting it and the same thing may be
said of Flanders'. Given the security threat to Elizabeth from the
Stewart–Valois alliance, English 'meddling' in Scottish or French internal
affairs may seem like an act of *realpolitik*, even if masked under a confessional cloak, but there could be no such excuses for English interest in the
Low Countries. The Spanish bishop-turned-ambassador was not simply
paranoid, however, for he had solid grounds on which to base his fears of
Elizabeth's intentions. Protestants from the Low Countries quickly found
that England under the new queen offered a ready refuge from persecution to them; de La Quadra was 'quite astounded to see the flocks of
heretics who come hither to the city and are well received'.[27] By the winter

of 1559, with an English invasion of Scotland imminent, he warned Philip that if this were successful then Elizabeth would feel encouraged to meddle in the confessional affairs of France and the Netherlands, and that one aim of the Scottish intervention was to 'turn the French out of the island and join the kingdoms ... by a union of religion', for then 'the alliances with your Majesty might well be disposed with'![28]

In the summer of 1561, Spanish suspicions were reinforced when Elizabeth sent Walter Haddon on a mission to Bruges, in Flanders. Haddon was a member of the Protestant 'Cambridge connection' that included Cecil, and a friend of Archbishop Parker. He was, in de La Quadra's words, 'a great heretic and one of the Commissioners against the Catholics [in England]'; he had also, that January, been appointed to a commission 'to peruse the order of lessons throughout the year, to cause new calendars to be printed, to provide remedies for the decay of churches, and to prescribe some good order for collegiate churches'; and at the request of the government he wrote an answer to the epistle (in French and Latin) by the noted Spanish churchman Hieronimo Osorio, urging Elizabeth to repent. A firm Calvinist, later in the 1560s he helped to draft a proposal for thorough reform of the English Church, which Puritans tried to push through parliament. Thus de La Quadra's evident suspicion that, although Haddon was nominally to discuss contractual problems between English and Bruges textile merchants, he was in fact to encourage the Protestants of Flanders (one of the strongholds of the Dutch Reformation) to resist persecution, was credible. And as de La Quadra pointed out, Haddon was master of requests – he thus had a direct connection to the queen as well as the principal secretary and archbishop of Canterbury.[29] By 1562, de La Quadra was gloomily 'certain that this Queen has thought and studied nothing else since [Philip left the Netherlands], but how to oust him from the Netherlands, and she believes that the best way to effect this is to embroil them over there on religious questions.'[30]

The Elizabethan regime's willingness to encourage the Protestants of the Low Countries, not only later in the 1560s and 1570s (which is well known) but even in its early days, shows clearly that it was very far from allowing its foreign policy to be dictated by Spain. Rather than slavishly shaping its policy to fit a Spanish mould, the government regarded Philip II as a confessional enemy, and hence not only a clear and present danger to England's continental co-religionists, but a probable eventual threat to England as well. Pains were taken to avoid open affront to the Habsburgs, but the actual intent of English policy *vis-à-vis* the Dutch, as in Scotland and France, was to obtain liberty of conscience for local Protestants – partly out of religious fellow-feeling, and partly to secure future allies against the threat of Catholic action, spearheaded by the Spanish Monarchy. This was of course entirely at odds with the 'messianic vision' of Philip II and his attempts to preserve the existing grip of Roman Catholicism, if not actually roll back the Reformation.[31]

That English policy did not conform to Habsburg designs is also evident from Anglo-Spanish relations during the first civil war in France (1562–63), when England sent an army to aid the Huguenots. To Philip and other Catholic powers Elizabeth and her ministers carefully portrayed this open military aid to Calvinists as primarily, or solely, concerned with regaining territory lost in France in the previous decade – acceptable in terms of great power-alliance politics.[32] Yet England actually helped the Huguenots. The Spanish had already tried to delay or prevent English action against the French in Scotland, despite the long-standing Franco-Spanish enmity and the traditional Franco-Scottish and Anglo-Spanish alliances; they now expressed strong reservations about English action in France.[33] In the preceding 50 years the Habsburgs had encouraged English attacks on France, but – unlike in 1513, 1522–23, 1544 or 1557 – England was now clearly Protestant and so Spanish attitudes were different. It was to deal with this that the Elizabethan regime pretended to have the same old reasons for intervening in France, even while acting precisely as Philip II feared. Again, although Spanish priorities affected the way English foreign policy was carried out and depicted to the world, they did not determine what the policy was.

As in the Low Countries, Elizabeth had supported the Protestant cause in France from the first. Beginning in 1559, her privy councillors had been frequently in contact with prominent Calvinist nobles and their sympathisers, in several cases building on long-term relationships.[34] The appointment of the Calvinist Sir Nicholas Throckmorton, a close friend of Cecil, as ambassador to Paris was significant since he 'worked openly' with radical advocates of Huguenot resistance. In 1560 Elizabeth was implicated in the conspiracy of Amboise – an unsuccessful attempt by Louis, prince of Condé, the Huguenot leader, to seize the regency of Francis II from the grip of the Guises.[35] Francis's death and the accession of his brother Charles IX in December 1560 broke their hold on power, but only briefly. After the duke of Guise took control of the person of Charles in March 1562, Condé and Gaspard de Coligny, Admiral of France, started mustering Huguenot troops. The French Wars of Religion had begun.

Condé and Coligny sent representatives to Elizabeth to ask for military aid even before they requested it from the Huguenot churches.[36] A number of other envoys followed. Elizabeth and her ministers were open to these approaches because they believed the 'two Lorraines' had a good chance 'utterly to extinguish [and to] overthrow the Protestant religion in France'; this they had to prevent because they further believed that France's Calvinists were England's first line of defence. The victory of the Guises would, Cecil wrote, 'put us here in danger for our religion', because of their connection to Mary Queen of Scots; more generally, the leading figures in the government feared an alliance between France and Spain, aimed at destroying the Reformation, so that they saw Condé and Coligny as a bulwark also against the Spanish, who were already seen as a potential enemy, rather than an ally, on the grounds that they posed a threat to England's religion. For all these reasons, queen and Privy Council naturally supported the Huguenots.[37]

To be sure, Elizabeth and Cecil hoped to regain Calais and so hard negotiating took place before England agreed to send an army to France. However, the essential commitment of the Protestant English regime to their French counterparts is revealed by the fact that Cecil and other prominent counsellors connived at the despatch of a force of 'volunteers' to serve in Huguenot pay until the terms for the despatch of a royal army were agreed. Between four and five hundred men garrisoned the ports of Le Havre and Dieppe, while perhaps another hundred served as individual volunteers with the Protestant armies elsewhere.[38]

The 6000-strong royal army that arrived in Le Havre in October, commanded by the earl of Warwick, was an army even more Calvinist in character than Grey's in Scotland. As even contemporaries recognised, Warwick owed his appointment not to his brief military experience, but to the influence of the zealous Protestants in the government, for he was one of the leading advocates of an internationalist, interventionist, Protestant foreign policy (like his brother, Lord Robert Dudley, later earl of Leicester). Warwick's officers comprised a remarkable cross-section of militant Calvinist opinion – one wrote home that his correspondent might think him 'over holy for a soldier, indeed I received the communion this day among a great number of Christian soldiers' who believed it was now in English power 'to banish idolatry out of this Realm'.[39]

The army arrived too late to prevent the fall of Rouen, France's second city, or to reinforce Condé's army before his defeat and capture at Dreux in December. Early in 1563, though, Warwick's men marched out to join the Huguenot army in Normandy commanded by Coligny and the count of Montgommery. The offensive the English and French troops then undertook, largely at Elizabeth's expense, helped to oblige the French crown to negotiate a compromise peace – but this successful intervention jointly with the Huguenots is overlooked in both English and French narrative histories of the first civil war.[40] Things then went wrong; after the peace of Amboise was agreed in March 1563, the English aim of preserving the Protestant cause in France had, for the moment, been achieved yet Elizabeth held out for the return of Calais as well. In Huguenot eyes she thus went from a fellow-Protestant back to a traditional enemy of France and Condé joined with the royal French army sent against the English in Le Havre. Warwick's outer garrisons were taken, his men had the worse of skirmishes in the field, and he was eventually penned up in Le Havre. Plague broke out, and in August the surviving English troops surrendered and were evacuated to England. It was an ignominious end to Elizabeth's first overseas intervention.[41]

Thereafter and for the next twenty-two years the English government would prefer covert operations to open war. Nevertheless, despite the considerable embarrassment and expense caused by the hostilities of April–August 1563, we will see that English foreign policy did not change – only how it was implemented. In looking back at the first four years of Elizabeth's reign, Cecil summarised 1560 as the year that 'Scotland [was] set free from the servitude of the Pope', while the achievement of 1562 was that 'The tottering Church of Christ in France [was] succoured'.[42] This reveals very well the world-view behind Elizabethan foreign policy. As we will see, the former did not change and this is why the latter also remained substantially the same.

IV

The early years of the Elizabethan regime have been examined in some depth because they are near-universally seen as ones in which conventional English foreign policy was maintained, with Protestant internationalism only becoming a (vexed) issue in conciliar debates on foreign policy after the revolt of the Netherlands. In fact, the tone for these years was set right at the beginning, as we have seen. However, English policy was 'different' from the mid-1560s on, inasmuch as before then it was aggressive and bold. Thereafter, it tended to be more covert and cautious, albeit with moments of risk-taking. Policy *objectives* remained substantially the same – to aid foreign Protestants obtain liberty of conscience and to build an alliance that could deter Catholic powers from oppressing reformed communities in the first place. But the methods used to obtain the objectives changed in the mid-1560s. This is the other reason why it was necessary to treat the years up to then separately. Thereafter policy remained substantially the same, in means as well as ends; but at the same time, since the unambiguous approach of despatching a royal army abroad openly was no longer used, the implementation of policy became more complex. Thus, hereafter I consider English policy thematically, rather than in the straightforward narrative used for the early, formative period.

From 1567 to 1585 the Elizabethan regime consistently intervened abroad in an effort to secure friendly, godly, regimes in those foreign countries where this seemed possible, or freedom of worship for Protestants in those countries where it did not. To achieve these aims it acted in the diplomatic, financial–commercial, and military spheres. The English government encouraged foreign states to oppose Spain, France, the papacy, and their allies, and attempted to build an international Protestant defensive pact. It provided grants and loans to Protestant factions or governments and struck against the finances of Catholic regimes. It supplied (both from national resources and by mobilising and co-ordinating private enterprise) food, weapons, powder and shot, armour, and other equipment to confessional allies. Finally, it facilitated the actions of privateers, and allowed the recruiting of, or itself actively mobilised, forces of mercenaries which joined foreign Protestant armies, sometimes to great effect.

Each of these means of executing policy will be briefly considered, in turn. However, the obvious question to ask is why there was a change. If Elizabeth and her ministers were still committed to the Protestant cause then why did they restrict themselves to the provision of money, munitions and mercenaries, and not openly declare war on the Spanish or Catholic French monarchies? Because these things did not happen (at least until 1585), the Elizabethan regime is seen as uncommitted to European Protestants for most of the queen's reign. The unhappy events of 1563 are typically described as marking a shift in policy – Elizabeth had been stung once and was unwilling to grasp the nettle thereafter; the intervention in France becomes part of the young queen's maturing process and no more. The fact that from the mid-1560s England avoided open confrontation with France or Spain at first glance seems to indicate that this orthodox view is correct. Allowing companies of volunteers to serve on the Continent, letting corsairs use English ports as bases, and sending occasional sums of money or shipments of arms – such cautious undertakings may seem more suggestive of an approach governed by *realpolitik*, rather than religious fervour.

In fact, 1563 marked a changing-point, but not because Elizabeth and her ministers decided to leave the Huguenots or other Continental co-religionists to their own devices. The key issue was that England's government realised that the kingdom was unable to fight a victorious war against either of Europe's two super-powers, France and Spain, without major reforms of its military infrastructure. It was military weakness which obliged a change in the means by which English policy ends were pursued.

We have already seen that English backwardness in the art of war had caused trouble for Grey in 1560 but because of their strategic success the English were able to shrug off the clear implications of their tactical reversals. In consequence, English armies once again went to war in France in 1562 armed with the long bow that was the distinctive national weapon: thus, an English observer noted how, on the arrival of English troops to reinforce the besieged Protestant garrison of Rouen, 'they without know, by their arrows when they skirmish with them'. English captains were also reluctant to adopt the armour and weapons that had become standard for European foot in the previous half century.[43]

English shortcomings were painfully exposed in France. The long bow was simply inadequate to penetrate the heavy armour of the *reiters* (German cavalry employed by the French), in particular, but the English were also troubled by the pikemen which were commonplace in Continental, yet rare in English, armies. More profoundly, because of their dependence on outmoded technology, the English utilised an ineffective tactical system: they did not match the sophisticated deployment of combined arms (pikemen and heavy cavalry) that Continental armies now used habitually. The English learned a severe lesson in their own inadequacy.[44]

The campaigns of 1560 and 1562–63 had thus revealed that the realm lacked military strength and so 'the Queen, in peace not unmindful of war, caused such preparation to be made of armour, weapons, and all kind of furniture of the field', importing from overseas, 'beside great plenty that was forged here at home'. The acquisition of sizeable quantities of modern *matériel* was now a government priority.[45] Yet it was not enough only to buy in supplies of the latest military technology; the new tactics had also to be taught to and mastered by the kingdom's militia. It was significant that immediately after the Normandy campaign, professional 'muster masters', paid by the queen, were appointed in every shire with responsibility for improving each county's trained bands.[46]

This all naturally took time; in the words of the most authoritative study of the process, 'there was no easy road to military efficiency for Elizabethan England'.[47] Things had not improved significantly, from the Privy Council's perspective, by the end of the decade. Within six months of the 1569 Northern Rebellion, Cecil, in listing points that made the realm vulnerable, emphasised the 'Ignorance of martial knowledge in her subjects' and 'Lack of mete Captains and trained Soldiers' in England. Officials in the key Channel-coast counties were ordered to make special provision for training and equipping more arquebusiers in their trained bands: the more the better![48] Moreover, the government was forging a better-trained militia and building up supplies of munitions to 'suffice not only for necessity of defence, but for the setting forth of any enterprise that might perhaps be suddenly occasioned'. Thus, it was in two 1569 memoranda of remedies 'against the conspiration' of the pope, the kings of France and Spain, and sundry Italian potentates, that Cecil listed the need not only to pray, but to make 'Arquebusiers increased by many devices': partly in the context of the need 'To view the power of the realm, and to put it in order', but partly of 'procuring some aid secretly for the prince of Condé'. As one veteran recalled, in considering the need to support foreign Protestants, Elizabeth 'provided first for her subjects at home, training and mustering of able men in all places of the realm'.[49] Until England could be rearmed only those best fitted for doing combat with modern opponents would be sent forth to the Continent – those with experience and proficiency in 'modern' weapons, tactics and organisation would be allowed to serve in foreign armies as mercenaries.

Thus, for the two decades following the English intervention in the first civil war, the Privy Council was painfully aware that open war had to be avoided until the country was rearmed, retrained and reorganised for 'modern' war: because of this, England was simply not strong enough to confront the French crown openly. Equally, up to 1568 there were still hopes of avoiding a breach with Spain, while thereafter, with the formidable Spanish army on the other side of the narrow seas, it was even more necessary to avoid open war until England was ready. It was thus undoubtedly politic and prudent for England not to aid foreign Protestants in the 1560s and 1570s; yet during these years, the 'Protestant Cause' in Western Europe was in crisis: something had to be done. When the call came from French and Dutch Protestants, though *raison d'état* suggested otherwise, Elizabethan England responded as best it could.

V

A major element of English policy was a consistent attempt to build a coalition of Protestant states to combat the perceived threat of the 'Catholic international'. In 1562 the government had sent envoys to obtain financial support from the German Protestant princes for the Huguenots.[50] As we have seen, Elizabeth was prepared to intervene in France unilaterally, with both troops and money; thus, these overtures were not simply an effort to get others to pay for aid to the Huguenots, but were rather aimed at what today would be called collective security. An Evangelical alliance would involve mutual financial obligations, to be sure, but the purpose of a Protestant pact was to avoid the necessity for any substantial expenditure in the first place. As with all such coalitions, down to NATO, a collective security arrangement among the Reformed princes was intended as a deterrent and to prevent wide-scale war. As will be seen, this is even more evident from the provisions Elizabeth was prepared to sign up to in the 1570s.

The growing awareness that England could not act effectively alone because of military weakness made a Protestant alliance even more important – and never more so than after 1565 when Charles IX of France and his court met with the duke of Alva, special ambassador of Philip II, in a lengthy conference at Bayonne in the south of France. In fact, no firm agreements for Franco-Spanish joint action emerged, but the Swiss Protestant republics, the Huguenots, and the English government, all of which felt threatened by a potential international Catholic coalition, did not know this. The sense of threat was heightened when, in 1567, Alva led a Spanish army along the borders of Switzerland and France to the Low Countries to restore order and orthodoxy after religious toleration had been granted in the wake of an uprising. William of Nassau, prince of Orange, raised an army in Germany to oppose Alva, but was easily defeated the following year. Meanwhile, partly because of fears that Alva would aid the French crown in a pre-emptive strike against the French Reformed communities, the second civil war had broken out in France.

The Huguenots promoted the idea of Calvinist collective security. In December 1567 Condé urged that 'as those princes professing the false religion spare no pains in assembling a league to exterminate the true religion, it is necessary and most just that the kings and princes professing the true religion join themselves in one accord and union, of a will to aid each other against the violence of our enemies'.[51] In 1568 William of

Orange (who joined the Huguenots after his defeat by Alva) likewise wrote that the cause of the French and Dutch Protestants was also that of the Germans and other nations.[52] This argument was maintained right up to the time England went openly to war with Spain; in 1575 and 1585 Henry of Navarre argued to Elizabeth that the pope and the king of Spain were enemies of 'all true Christian Princes and states', which therefore had to act in concert to preserve themselves.[53]

From the beginning, many influential English figures subscribed to this position. As early as 1559 one of the crown's chief financial agents on the Continent urged the need for 'all those which love the true religion to stand together', while already in 1560 Cecil had proposed the 'soliciting of the Princes protestants in Germany' to Elizabeth. And as Alford points out, in March 1561 the Scottish lords of congregation were urged that England and Scotland should ally 'on the model of the German princes'.[54] In 1568 Throckmorton (now theoretically retired, but in practice still a government adviser) responded to the Huguenot and Dutch logic, observing grimly that 'when the general Design is to exterminate all Nations dissenting with them in Religion (as it is most apparent and probable) what shall come of us when the like Professors with us shall be utterly destroyed in Flanders and France?' The only option was to aid Condé and William of Orange, but it was also necessary that the 'princes of Germany be assistant in this cause'.[55] Cecil concurred, writing of the desirability of 'A conjunction with all princes protestants for defence' against the threat of Rome, France and Spain, and his particular hope of 'some league' with 'the princes protestants of the Empire [i.e., Germany]'.[56]

There was, therefore, a major effort throughout the 1560s to create a coalition with the Lutheran princes of Germany and Scandinavia; it is fully explored in the works of Professor Kouri, which deserve to be better known.[57] No such agreement was reached, but English efforts to persuade the German princes to act in support of the Huguenots and Dutch were not without success. They facilitated the recruiting of mercenaries by Protestants in both France and the Netherlands (though when German armies intervened in the second and third civil wars it was because they were subsidised by the Huguenots and the English government, rather than simple confessional fellow-feeling).

The peace of Saint-Germain (August 1570) brought uneasy peace to France, while the Netherlands was firmly in Alva's grip after 1568, so that there was an interval without religious war. Meanwhile, the Spanish had been implicated in a rebellion against Elizabeth in the north of England in 1569, drawn largely from Catholics and their sympathisers; and in 1570

the pope had declared Elizabeth deposed and relieved her subjects of
their duty of allegiance to her. In short, there was now greater need for a
Protestant alliance than ever before. With the brief end of the wars of religion, the Admiral de Coligny achieved a temporary ascendancy at
Charles IX's court. As N. M. Sutherland shows, in 1571–72 French and
English diplomacy (driven partly by the fervent Calvinist internationalism of Sir Francis Walsingham, ambassador in Paris, later principal secretary) helped to bring about a new, more widespread outbreak of revolt
in the Netherlands, supported by Huguenot and English incursions, and
an invasion from Germany led by William of Orange.[58] This Anglo-
Huguenot offensive was defeated but it still provoked a crisis in France
which was a major factor in the St Bartholomew's massacre (August 1572)
and the outbreak of the fourth civil war. This revolved around the siege
of La Rochelle: virtually the only Protestant stronghold in France.
Elizabeth's government aided the city in the logistical and military
spheres, as we will see, but it also undertook a new diplomatic offensive
to get the German Protestant princes to aid their beleaguered French
and Dutch counterparts. These efforts were made easier by the fact that
even Lutheran princes were appalled by the massacre of French
Calvinists and were inclined to act against Charles IX.[59] The siege of La
Rochelle petered out in stalemate; Germany remained a refuge and
recruiting ground for the Huguenots and William of Orange's followers.

In the aftermath of the fourth civil war, English envoys took the lead in
developing a coalition between moderate Catholics, the Huguenot leaders, William of Orange, and the elector Palatine. The English aim was, as
Mack Holt argues, 'complete liberty of conscience' for the Huguenots.[60]
The end result (which owed much to English subsidies and is discussed
more below) was a triumph. Armies led by the prince of Condé, Henry
of Navarre and John Casimir (a younger son of the elector Palatine)
fought the fifth civil war and ended it, 'encamped in the center of France
dictating peace terms', which Charles IX's successor, Henry III, was
forced to accept. He granted 'very generous concessions to the Huguenots'
in the edict of Beaulieu (May 1576): 'the most complete and elaborate
charter' that France's Protestants received in the wars of religion.[61]
Meanwhile, William of Orange's successes and Spanish excesses produced on 8 November the pacification of Ghent, by which most of the
provinces of the Low Countries committed themselves to expel the
Spanish army.

Such achievements gave renewed impetus to attempts to negotiate
a pan-European Protestant pact. In December 1576 English agents

conferred with representatives of Henry of Navarre, the prince of Condé, and the city of La Rochelle; the elector Palatine, the dukes of Pomerania and Württemberg, and the landgrave of Hesse; the prince of Orange; and the Swiss confederation.[62] Contemporary Catholic claims that a definitive league was agreed at this meeting were probably attempts to prevent precisely that outcome by pre-emptive publicity, but they did not succeed. The following year a concerted effort was made by the English government to achieve a concrete agreement comprehending all the German Protestant princes.

Philip Sidney, Leicester's nephew, and close friend of a number of Netherlandish, German and French Protestant intellectuals and nobles, was chosen to carry Elizabeth's condolences to the new Holy Roman Emperor on his father's death. The choice of Sidney reflected his real mission, which was, en route, to promote evangelical unity. Sidney's first stop was in the northern Netherlands, where he conferred with William of Orange. William was part of the Nassau family of German Protestant princes and nobles, and Elizabeth hoped to use their influence to develop William's hoped-for alliance of England with Holland and Zealand into a general Protestant alliance, incorporating the Lutherans. Sidney then travelled on to the emperor, via Protestant principalities.[63] Sidney's efforts were instrumental in bringing about the convention that John Casimir of the Palatinate had been promoting as a step towards bridging the sometimes bitter divides between the Lutheran and Calvinist confessions. Sidney had returned home by the time it convened at Frankfurt in September 1577, but Elizabeth was represented by a delegation that was prominent at the convention; it was not for want of their effort that it ultimately ended without reconciliation.[64]

Nevertheless, the efforts of 1577 were not without fruit, for Elizabeth did agree formal co-operation with the electors of Saxony and Brandenburg and the duke of Brunswick.[65] Moreover, what Elizabeth had been prepared to do in order to secure a pan-European Protestant league is revealed in a draft treaty between Elizabeth, the electors Palatine and of Saxony and Brandenburg, the duke of Brunswick, and the landgrave of Hesse. In order 'that the confederates may not be oppressed for their religion by the [...] Pope of Rome and his adherents [and] that the said Pope and his adherents [...] may be restrained from spreading the limits of their authority' the queen was willing 'to deposit a reasonable sum of money', which the Germans would match in proportion, in Bremen; and the actual sum she 'hath delivered into the hands of her Commissioners' to this end was a remarkable £20,000.[66]

Even though disappointed by lack of results at Frankfurt, Elizabeth continued to seek a universal Protestant coalition. However, while English relations with the Lutheran states were always cordial, a formal defensive alliance was never agreed; as R. B. Wernham argues, the problem was not a want of enthusiasm on the part of the English government, but that the German princes were reluctant to 'jeopardise the peace of the Holy Roman Empire by active hostility to the Spanish cousin of their Hapsburg Emperor or by an active anti-Catholic policy [...] particularly after the death of John Casimir [...] and the Lutheran reaction in Saxony that followed the death of Christian I'. Indeed, that the German princes were 'sous la force de l'Empereur' was a point of which Elizabeth was reminded, when she endeavoured to organise joint action to aid the Calvinist Gebhard Truchsess in the Cologne electoral succession war in 1584.[67]

Finally, in 1582–85, as the Dutch war effort began to crumble under sustained Spanish pressure, and as it became apparent that the Wars of Religion would soon resume in France, Elizabeth sent several embassies to Denmark, Sweden, and the northern German states. They stressed, firstly, the need for true believers to help afflicted brethren, as Lord Willoughby told the Danish chancellor in 1585; and, secondly, as A. J. Slavin argues, the essential importance of 'the principle of religious freedom' (i.e., freedom of worship for Protestants).[68] None of the Baltic powers actively joined the war against Spain but these diplomatic efforts did at least stop the Habsburgs making trouble for England and the Netherlands in an area that was important for the international commerce of both countries, while they were engaged in war with Spain. Moreover, Willoughby's embassy persuaded the Danish king and some Baltic princes not to allow the sale of naval stores to Spain – this benefited the Huguenot and Dutch causes alike, since Spanish sea power threatened both during the preparation of the Armada. This 'was something of value on [Elizabeth's] balance sheet', as Slavin points out.[69]

VI

The Elizabethan government provided a range of financial support to the Protestants of France and the Netherlands, from outright grants, to loans, to acting as guarantor for other loans. All were vital. Of course, money that was borrowed had, in theory, to be repaid, but in practice English loans often ended up effectively as gifts; the regime was probably aware it was unlikely to be repaid in full when agreeing to them. In any case, what early-modern governments needed most of all was cash in hand. Thus, loans that provided actual money at crucial times, as the English ones often did in these years, were of crucial importance to the recipients.

Large sums (at least £9500, and perhaps in excess of £25,000) were paid direct to commanders in Huguenot employ during the first War of Religion.[70] The English treasury disbursed sums totalling £45,309 4s 2d to Odet de Châtillon (brother of Admiral de Coligny, and the Huguenots' representative in England) between 6 November 1568 and 30 July 1569; some of this may have been part of a loan of approximately £20,000 from Elizabeth to Condé and Henry of Navarre, secured on the jewels of Navarre's queen-mother. In 1569 Elizabeth additionally advanced over £20,000 to pay for the army of German Protestant mercenaries brought into France by the duke of Zweibrücken (or Deux-Ponts as French sources name him), of which at least £15,000 was borrowed by the Huguenots, secured against salt production.[71]

In 1575–76, as we have seen, Elizabeth, covertly financed the army raised in the Rhineland by the prince of Condé and John Casimir.[72] Subsequent negotiations involving Condé, the elector and John Casimir, William of Orange, and Elizabeth's agents, resulted in a grant from the queen of 50,000 *thalers* (some £15,000), which was transported in July 1575 to the electoral capital of Heidelberg by English officers.[73] After lobbying by the earl of Sussex and other privy councillors, Elizabeth agreed to provide loans worth at least another £15,000 to the elector Palatine. He then committed himself to the enterprise, which made it possible to raise the extra mercenaries needed.[74]

Within weeks of the pacification of Ghent the Privy Council approved a loan of £100,000 to the States-General of the Netherlands of which some £20,000 was delivered in bullion immediately.[75] In 1578 a further £45,000 of this was transmitted to the States, most of it hypothecated to the expenses of the army that Elizabeth in the spring of that year commissioned John Casimir to raise for service in the Low Countries. The English government additionally guaranteed nearly £29,000 borrowed by the Dutch in Germany, using English financial agents.[76]

In 1581 Elizabeth backed the invitation to the duke of Anjou to become the United Provinces' governor-general. She then bankrolled Anjou through 1582 and into 1583. The importance of the subsidies to Anjou, which totalled £70,000 in less than twelve months, cannot be overstated – the Dutch were keenly awaiting news of whether she would finance him and her decision to do so was a great encouragement to their leaders.[77] John Casimir received another £10,000 in 1582; Anjou further received in 1584 a little over £14,000; while an additional £5000 was paid in 1581 to cover sums previously advanced to the Dutch.[78]

In addition to the forms of financial aid directly supplied by the government, a number of nobles stood security for merchants' loans to Châtillon and other French leaders during the third civil war; in 1571 the queen of Navarre's council estimated that they owed half a million *livres* (£50,000) on these.[79] In 1573, Cecil (by now Lord Treasurer and ennobled as Lord Burghley) helped to co-ordinate the raising of a loan in the city of London for the mayor and burgesses of La Rochelle, during the crisis of the fourth civil war.[80] Bishops Edwin Sandys of London and Horne of Winchester successfully appealed to sympathetic merchants in London and Southampton for both donations and loans for the count of Montgommery's 1573 relief expedition to La Rochelle.[81] The efforts of the queen's ministers and God's bore impressive fruit: reports that Montgommery raised some 300,000 *écus* in England may be exaggerated, but support was widespread and certainly by 1581 the city of La Rochelle owed about £40,000 to London merchants.[82]

In 1572 and 1573, English merchants transmitted cash raised by donations from Dutch refugees and English sympathisers to the Netherlands. Others raised on credit £20,000 to purchase and ship to Holland weapons, gunpowder and a variety of victuals. Members of the Merchant Adventurers' Company regularly advanced cash and credit to English mercenary captains in the Low Countries and all this was done with the knowledge and frequently the active encouragement of government ministers and other privy councillors.[83]

A final method of economic warfare was utilised by the Elizabethan regime – striking at an enemy's commerce and finance. In 1563 Margaret of Parma, Philip's regent in the Netherlands, suspended commerce with England. This was in response to English 'help to the cause of heresy in Scotland and France', and it was intended to threaten both royal finances and the national economy, thereby bringing the new queen to heel.[84] As intended, this threatened the cloth trade in the Antwerp market and Elizabeth's revenue from customs. So the English found an alternative market in Germany and by 1565 the dispute had been settled, though not without some pain on both sides.

This episode allows us to see the better-known mutual trade embargo of December 1568 to March 1573 in context. Elizabethan foreign policy is usually said to have been driven by the need to avoid disrupting the all-important cloth trade. The regime's willingness to act in 1572 both financially, as described above, and logistically and (deniably) militarily, as described below, is ascribed to the fact that, since in 1572 traffic between England and the Netherlands was impossible, Elizabeth had nothing to lose and might even be able to put pressure on Spain to settle on favourable terms. Now, commercial exigencies undoubtedly influenced Elizabethan policy – but when the chips were down they came second to confessional considerations.

This can be seen from the famous seizure, in 1568, of a fleet carrying treasure to Alva intended for the payment of his troops. Genoese merchants were to deliver a large store of bullion to the Netherlands, but, buffeted by the autumnal gales and harassed by Protestant privateers, the ships carrying it took refuge in ports along the English south coast, but they were taken in charge by men like Sir Edward Horsey and Sir Arthur Champernowne, who had connections to the Dutch Sea Beggars and Huguenot corsairs. The treasure, which totalled over £75,000, was used by the exchequer over the next three years as security for English borrowing (the government having agreed with the Italian merchants in question to take the cash over as a loan), but the real significance was not the financial benefit to the Elizabethan regime; it was the blow to the Spanish regime in the Low Countries.[85] Alva was obliged to take extreme measures in the Netherlands to make ends meet. Whereas in 1568 less than one million florins were raised locally, in 1569 it was over two million.[86] The imposition of the hated 'Tenth Penny' tax by Alva outraged even moderate Catholic, Dutch opinion, and led eventually to the more widespread revolt of 1572.

In retaliation for the seizure, the Spanish took all English merchants and ships in Dutch and Spanish harbours and prohibited trade between England and the Netherlands; Elizabeth responded with similar reprisals against merchants from Habsburg territories. The resulting dispute and suspension of commerce lasted until the spring of 1573; the English economy and the queen's revenues were damaged, but the effects on the Spanish Netherlands were worse.[87] Given what had happened in 1563, Elizabeth's ministers would have known that a Spanish trade embargo was the most likely response to their appropriation of the Genoese loan. This was, after all, a greater and far more immediate provocation than English military aid to Protestants in France – which, as we shall see, was still being given when the Spanish treasure ships were seized anyway. Commercial concerns were not all important to the Elizabethan regime, then, for the English government went ahead with all these actions, despite the evident danger of a new trade war, with all its potentially damaging consequences to England's economy. In the ensuing years, too, the government knew that helping the Huguenots or a renewed revolt in the Netherlands would only make resolving the dispute more difficult, yet this is precisely what it did. English actions in 1572 were thus natural developments in a consistent policy. This becomes even clearer when we consider the government's actions in supplying the Huguenots and Dutch with military stores and mercenaries.

VII

Barely had the third war of religion begun in the late summer of 1568 than Elizabeth assured a French ambassador, sent to secure her non-intervention, 'that she would never encourage or support any subject in rebellion against his prince'.[88] Nevertheless, by February 1569 France's queen-mother was complaining that Elizabeth had 'maintain[ed] overtly and covertly seditious persons and rebels with money, munitions, and artillery, all [of] which [...] Winter, the Vice-Admiral, had landed at Rochelle'. To this the English ambassador in Paris, Sir Henry Norris (two of whose sons had fought for the Huguenots in the second civil war in 1567) coolly responded if this had happened 'that it was without the Queen's knowledge or consent'.[89]

In fact, the accusations of royal complicity were accurate – from an English perspective alarmingly so. In the autumn of 1568 Elizabeth sent Walter Haddon to La Rochelle to discuss aid to Navarre, Condé and Coligny. On 8 November 1568, they agreed a treaty by which Elizabeth would 'supply ordnance and munition of war to La Rochelle'.[90] This aid took the form of a complete train of artillery of six siege guns, with 20 lasts of powder, 4000 rounds of shot, and all the necessary wagons and equipment, all transferred from the Tower of London and valued as worth £4225 12s 8d. The English government took great pains to prevent news of this leaking out but the ships were under the charge of a well-known Puritan London merchant, Nicholas Culverwell, and were escorted by the royal fleet, commanded by Vice-Admiral Sir William Winter (one of whose brothers later fought under Montgommery in the fourth civil war). Although salt was indeed shipped back to England, Culverwell and his consortium had to pay for it as part of normal commerce; the reason for the venture was to deliver the matériel. It was Throckmorton who drew up the articles for agreement between the merchants, the queen and the Huguenot princes; the instructions to the merchants were from Lord Keeper Sir Nicholas Bacon, Leicester, Cecil and the chancellor of the exchequer, Sir Walter Mildmay; while Warwick, as master of the ordnance, must have been consulted. The commitment of Elizabeth and the whole of her government is clear.[91] The government never went to such extravagant lengths again, but the episode was not unique. The crown did not always act as supplier, but royal officials helped to ensure that necessary supplies got through to beleaguered foreign Protestants, by waiving regulations, or actually orchestrating supposedly private enterprise. Powder and shot was supplied in this way to the Huguenots on an ongoing basis, occasionally through Norman ports but typically through La Rochelle. It was not just munitions that were sent, however; during the third and fourth civil wars, the English crown connived with Châtillon, Montgommery, and others to supply the Huguenot forces with all sorts of urgent requirements, from shoes to food – again, these typically went through La Rochelle, which during the fourth war was partly sustained by these covert shipments brought in by blockade runners. In the Netherlands, meanwhile, the funds raised at the behest of royal and ecclesiastical officials during the critical days of 1572–73 likewise brought in weapons, armour and food-stuffs. These supplies were especially important at this time, when the rebels were short of native resources, but they continued to be sent, with government knowledge if not always collusion, into the early 1580s.[92]

VIII

In addition to the indirect means of support explored so far, the English government also had recourse to direct naval and military action on occasion. As already noted, after 1563 this was usually undertaken covertly. The exception was in Scotland. Here the success of 1560 did not produce a permanent settlement. The active reign of Mary Queen of Scots after her return from France was less than ten years, and the country was thrown back into instability, with different aristocratic factions jockeying for power. Traditional relations with France meant that French influence could still be exerted within Scotland and there were still Scottish nobles opposed to Protestantism. The weakness of the Scottish central government after Mary's deposition meant some of the English Catholic rebels of 1569 were able to take refuge north of the border, which led to English incursions in March and April 1570 to round them up. In May and July English troops undertook punitive campaigns, campaigning along with Scottish Protestants, to take reprisals against clans and nobles that had sheltered English rebels, who supported Mary, or who otherwise opposed her son's regime backed by Elizabeth. In 1572–73 French influence led to another invasion. Edinburgh Castle was besieged in April and May 1573, and even after its fall some troops remained in Scotland until August. Later crises were settled without invasion, however, and after the (Calvinist) James VI reached adulthood and settled into governing his kingdom, Anglo-Scottish relations generally took on a different tone (see Chapter 7).

On the continent, covert operations were consistently accepted or masterminded by royal ministers – at times arguably without Elizabeth's knowledge, but at times clearly with her approval. That these apparently private enterprises by privateers and mercenaries were, like the shipments of arms, actually sanctioned by England's government was widely guessed but could rarely be proved. They allowed the government to pursue its policy objectives without involving the nation in a war for which it was not yet ready. This was also an effective use of English manpower, since very often the troops in question were some of the most skilled and experienced soldiers in the kingdom.

There are a range of detailed studies of the Huguenot '*armée de mer*' and the Dutch 'Sea Beggars' (or *watergeuzen*), all of which give an idea of the role of English privateers in their activities.[93] For this reason, I say little more about them here. It is worth stressing, however, that English corsairs joined with their Huguenot counterparts almost immediately following the beginning of the third civil war – the latter, within a month of the outbreak of war, were already envisaging co-operating with the English against Catholic shipping of all nations in the Bay of Biscay. This makes still more suspicious the eventual fate of the treasure fleet of that year.[94]

The English navy also played a role in supporting French and Dutch Protestants since their ability to operate at a distance made their involvement in any military enterprises hard to prove. Sometimes the distinction between royal ships and privateers was not clear-cut. Naval squadrons commanded by Sir William Winter helped bring the intervention in Scotland to a victorious conclusion in 1560; directly intervened in fighting in Normandy in 1562 to aid French troops led by the count de Montgommery; and escorted the artillery to La Rochelle in 1569.[95] Sir Arthur Champernowne, vice-admiral in Plymouth, had plundered Spanish shipping for at least five years, before his seizure of the Genoese ships in 1568 in the belief that the treasure they carried had been gathered by the pope for the war against Protestants. He married one of his sons to one of Montgommery's daughters in 1572; later that year, after the St Bartholomew's massacre, he helped the count to gather in Plymouth a fleet for the relief of La Rochelle that included at least one royal ship; and in 1574 he gathered ships in an (unsuccessful) attempt to rescue Montgommery during the fifth civil war.[96] Then in the sixth war of religion (1577) English privateers (including Walsingham's step-son, Christopher Carleill) made a significant contribution to the Huguenot defence of the approaches to La Rochelle – after the French had appealed to the Privy Council for aid.[97]

Carleill also served as a mercenary in the Dutch army and this brings us to the most important aspect of the government's deniable military operations: its complicity in the employment of English mercenaries ('voluntaries', in contemporary terminology) by foreign Protestants. This began in 1562, when, as we have seen, the government arranged the employment of English volunteers in order to defend the vital Norman ports until the terms by which a royal army would be sent were arranged. Throckmorton urged that 'some such as desire to adventure and see the world were let slip' to Normandy, concluding that 'the more expedition and the more secrecy that is used in this, the better it will prove for all respects. The Queen's majesty and you of her council must be ignorant of this matter.'[98] This set a pattern for what followed thereafter.

In the third war of religion, Henry Champernowne (Sir Arthur's nephew) led a force of light cavalry that made a considerable contribution to the Calvinist war-effort. The queen was said by one Huguenot soldier-historian to have chosen Champernowne and his officers, and even Camden, writing from Cecil's papers, confirms how Elizabeth personally 'permitted Henry Champernowne' to lead his men to France because, although distracted by the simultaneous threat of the Northern Rebellion, she 'would not neglect the Protestants in France'. Champernowne was no ordinary gentleman soldier, for his mother had been a lady of Elizabeth's household in 1559, while his paternal aunt, Catherine Ashley, had been the queen's governess, married one of her cousins and by the 1560s was first gentlewoman of the privy chamber. Champernowne wrote personally to Elizabeth from France in September 1569 and reported regularly to Cecil and Leicester.[99]

In 1572 English soldiers took part in three of the four fronts on which the renewed Dutch revolt was waged. English sailors and soldiers were with the Sea Beggar leader, Lumey de La Marck, when he famously captured Brille on 1 April, triggering the revolt. Thanks to Walsingham, they were in the army Louis of Nassau led into the southern Netherlands in May. In June Burghley co-ordinated the raising and shipping of a large force of about 1700 English and Welsh troops to Flushing, which controlled the waterways leading to Antwerp. 'By August the Privy Council was regulating the flow of reinforcements' to both the northern and southern Netherlands; throughout, 'Elizabeth's ministers were deeply complicit' in the actions of English troops in the Netherlands.[100] The next year, when Montgommery mounted his expedition from England to La Rochelle and then to Brittany, he raised English troops, as well as ships – again, probably with the help of Sir Arthur Champernowne. But in addition he had the blessing of at least two privy councillors, Burghley and Sussex; he certainly consulted them over his movements and they may have had a hand in his troop-mustering.[101]

The grim situation of the Dutch revolt from 1573 until 1576 meant that the English government was reluctant to invest too heavily in an (apparently) losing cause. However, although royal officials did not take a lead in supplying mercenaries to the Netherlands in these years (unlike in 1572), they never stopped Englishmen fighting for the Dutch. The Spanish repeatedly complained about recruiting by English captains commissioned by William of Orange and the States of Holland; the queen and her ministers repeatedly condemned their actions; and they kept raising men and shipping them across the narrow seas. It is no wonder that, after yet another English troop contract had been filled despite vigorous Spanish protests, Don Luís de Requesens, Alva's successor in the Netherlands, confided in two of his colleagues that the English queen and her councillors 'bore little affection and good will to the affairs of his Majesty'.[102]

On 7 January 1578 Elizabeth provisionally concluded a treaty with the States General which provided for mutual co-operation, including the dispatch of an army of 5000 foot and a 1000 horse. The utter defeat of the Dutch army at Gembloux on 31 January caused her not to ratify the treaty, but she did not rethink military aid, only whether it should be overt. Instead, she stuck with the deniable option – she paid John Casimir to bring an army into the States' service and her councillors organised the recruiting of an army of mercenaries. This in the end had an establishment of nearly 5000 – only slightly less than the royal army liable under the January treaty. Approximately 4500 English and Welshmen actually did serve in the Dutch army that summer, which would not have been much less than the actual strength of an army with an establishment of 6000. This contingent was led by the same officers who would have commanded in a royal army, save that there was no great nobleman as general, and it included many veterans skilled with pike and shot, instead of bow and bill. It was, in fact, to all intents and purposes the army contracted by treaty, save that its employer was the States General rather than the queen.[103]

From then on the Privy Council always supported and facilitated discreet recruiting for States' service. There were an average of about 3000 English troops in Dutch pay each year from 1579 through 1585 (not including the troops sent in the autumn of 1585 after England entered the war openly), averaging over ten per cent of the total Dutch establishment. They were consistently used in the field, whereas many of the native troops were kept in garrisons, so they bore a disproportionate share of the fighting. They were unable to prevent the war going against the United Provinces, but they at least helped to preserve the cause until the death of William of Orange and changing circumstances in France made open English intervention in the Netherlands essential.[104]

Neither privy councillors nor other royal officials were always directly involved in raising the English troops that fought in Huguenot and Dutch employ from 1567–85, but Elizabeth and her ministers were always aware when companies and regiments were being raised. Their acceptance of recruiting in those cases where they were not directly concerned made them as complicit in them as in those cases where they were. As a Venetian diplomat observed, Elizabeth could not keep assuring foreign sovereigns 'that she desires to be their good sister [when] she makes no attempt to put a stop to [such] practices'.[105]

IX

In sum, then, my argument is that from 1558 to 1585 there was a consensus within the Elizabethan regime that England was threatened by the Catholic powers of Europe (especially France and Spain) as part of a cosmic struggle; commercial and strategic factors informed government policy but confessional considerations took priority. There were differences between ministers, for sure, but they were over exactly what should be done in a given situation to make the policy work, not over the policy itself. The government sought to meet the Catholic threat by enlisting the support of, and giving assistance to, the other Protestant powers of Europe; and it especially hoped to establish Protestantism in the Netherlands and France, both to help co-religionists there obtain the right to worship God in a manner pleasing to Him, but also as a way of weakening the Catholic powers. These were viewed as a threat to Elizabeth personally and England as a commonwealth because of their faith, which in and of itself turned traditional friends into contemporary enemies. Yet the history of English relations with foreign states from 1558 to 1585, as outlined above, shows that the government was prepared to prioritise the defence of those who shared Reformed beliefs, *because* they shared those beliefs, over narrow national political advantage.[106] This was not a policy of exclusivist English self-interest.

There is sufficient motivation, magnitude, continuity and government-direction about the assistance given to the Huguenots and Dutch (i.e. to the Protestants actually threatened by Catholic powers in this period), and sufficient intentionality about English foreign policy initiatives between 1558 and 1585, to characterise English foreign policy in that period as, effectively, a Protestant foreign policy. That is what many of Elizabeth's ministers and prominent members of the English body politic wanted it to be; it is what most foreign Catholic observers thought it was. It is time to take their opinions seriously.

Notes

1. Earlier versions were read to the History Department Seminar, University of Reading, and the Tudor-Stuart Seminar, Institute of Historical Research, in 2001. I am grateful for suggestions and comments made on those occasions, and in particular to Ralph Houlbrooke and Susan Doran, whose critiques have been most helpful. I am also very grateful to the editors for their considerable patience when, due to sustained illness, this essay was extremely overdue.

2. On Camden's sources and bias, see Patrick Collinson, 'One of Us? William Camden and the making of history', *Transactions of the Royal Historical Society*, ser. 6, viii (1998), pp. 139–63, esp. 152, 156; and Simon Adams, 'Favourites and factions at the Elizabethan court' in John Guy (ed.), *The Tudor Monarchy* (1997), pp. 260–2. On his formative influence on subsequent generations, see Christopher Haigh's editorial 'Introduction' to *The Reign of Elizabeth I* (Basingstoke, 1984), pp. 6–11.

3. I am preparing a historiographical study of Elizabethan foreign policy, but see, Haigh, 'Introduction', pp. 11–13.

4. The summary of other historians' views by Charles Wilson, *Queen Elizabeth and the Revolt of the Netherlands* (1970), p. 5.

5. W. P. Haugaard, *Elizabeth and the English Reformation: The Struggle for a Stable Settlement of Religion* (Cambridge, 1968), and 'Elizabeth Tudor's book of devotions: a neglected clue to the queen's life and character', *Sixteenth Century Journal*, 12 (1981), pp. 79–105. Susan Doran, 'Elizabeth I's religion: the evidence of her letters', *Journal of Ecclesiastical History*, 51 (2000), pp. 699–720. Also important is Norman Jones's study of the Elizabethan settlement of religion, showing it to have been radically Protestant in its intention: *Faith by Statute: Parliament and the Settlement of Religion, 1559*, Royal Historical Society Studies in History, 32 (1982).

6. See in particular Simon Adams, 'Eliza enthroned? The court and its politics', in Haigh, *Reign of Elizabeth*, pp. 55–77 and 267–71; and also 'Faction, clientage and

party: English politics 1550–1603', *History Today*, 32 (December 1982), pp. 33–39; 'Favourites and factions', pp. 253–74; and 'The patronage of the crown in Elizabethan politics: the 1590s in perspective', in John Guy (ed.), *The Reign of Elizabeth I: Court and Culture in the Last Decade* (Cambridge, 1995), all reproduced as chs 1–4 of Adams, *Leicester and the Court: Essays on Elizabethan Politics* (Manchester, 2001). Adams's interpretation has recently been amplified by Stephen Alford, *The Early Elizabethan Polity: William Cecil and the British Succession Crisis, 1558–1569* (Cambridge, 1998). The picture of 'consensus politics' has perhaps been overdrawn, since there were still substantial disagreements amongst royal counsellors. However, as I have argued elsewhere, in the area of foreign policy, they differed over means, not ends. See D. J. B. Trim, 'Fighting "Jacob's Wars". The Employment of English and Welsh Mercenaries in the European Wars of Religion: France and the Netherlands, 1562–1610'. Unpublished University of London PhD dissertation, 2002, pp. 136, 195–96, 294, *et passim.*

7. Alford, *The Early Elizabethan Polity*, p. 216.

8. David Starkey, *Elizabeth: Apprenticeship* (2000), p. 322.

9. See Trim, 'Mercenaries', pp. 107–8, also 126–30, 194.

10. E. I. Kouri, *England and the Attempts to Form a Protestant Alliance in the Late 1560s: A Case Study in European Diplomacy*. Annales Academiæ Scientiarum Fennicæ, ser. B, no. 210 (Helsinki, 1981), p. 21.

11. *El ruy Catolico* and *le roy très chrestien* were official contemporary titles of the kings of Spain and France respectively (rather as Elizabeth was 'Defender of the Faith').

12. E. I. Kouri, 'For true faith or national interest? Queen Elizabeth I and the Protestant powers' in E. I. Kouri and Tom Scot (eds), *Politics and Society in Reformation Europe: Essays for Sir Geoffrey Elton on his Sixty-Fifth Birthday* (Basingstoke, 1987), pp. 411–36, at pp. 412, 426. The essay explicitly recognises that the two were not necessarily an either/or choice (a point some scholarly critics have missed). But though Kouri adopted this simplified, polarised model only as a starting-point for discussion, in fact he implies throughout that Elizabeth actually did prefer national to confessional interest.

13. Quoted in G. D. Ramsay, 'The foreign policy of Elizabeth I' in Haigh, *Reign of Elizabeth*, p. 147.

14. Geoffrey Parker, *The Grand Strategy of Philip II* (New Haven, CT., 1998), pp. 77–107 and 'The place of Tudor England in the messianic vision of Philip II of Spain', *TRHS*, ser. 6, 12 (2002), pp. 167–221.

15. For example, de La Quadra to Philip II, 10 May 1559, *CSP. Sp.* Eliz. i, p. 69.

16. De La Quadra to Philip, 30 May 1559, ibid., pp. 71–2; Norman L. Jones, 'Elizabeth's first year: the conception and birth of the Elizabethan political world' in Haigh, *Reign of Elizabeth*, pp. 34–36, 47; H. G. Koenigsberger *et al.*, *Europe in the Sixteenth Century* (2nd edn, 1989), pp. 219–20, 241; Alford, *The Early Elizabethan Polity*, p. 95.

17. Andrew Pettegree, 'Queen B', *History Today* (March 1995), p. 50.

18. The earl of Pembroke, another staunch Protestant internationalist (as events proved) was already a member of the council. John Hayward in John Bruce (ed.), 'Annals of the First Four Years of the Reign of Queen Elizabeth, by Sir John Hayward' *Camden Society*, o.s., 7 (1840), p. 12; John Guy, *Tudor England* (Oxford, 1988), pp. 253–4, 261; Trim, 'Mercenaries', pp. 106–7.

19. *Acts of the Privy Council*, vii, p. 50 [hereafter *APC*]; Jones, 'Elizabeth's first year', p. 34.

20. De La Quadra to Philip, 19 June 1559, and Philip to de La Quadra, 9 July 1559, *CSP. Sp. Eliz.* i, pp. 75–6, 83; Alford, *The Early Elizabethan Polity*, pp. 53–5; Jones, 'Elizabeth's first year', pp. 48–9; Julian Lock, ' "Strange Usurped Potentates": Elizabeth I, the Papacy and the Indian Summer of the Medieval Deposing Power'. Unpublished D.Phil. dissertation, University of Oxford, 1993, pp. 168–72.

21. Alford, *The Early Elizabethan Polity*, p. 56.

22. Quoted in Jones, 'Elizabeth's First Year', p. 41.

23. Alford, *The Early Elizabethan Polity*, pp. 56–61, quoting at pp. 57, 61, from PRO, SP 52/1, fo. 101 and BL, Lansdowne MS 4, fo. 26.

24. De La Quadra to Philip, 27 June 1559, *CSP. Sp. Eliz.* i, p. 78.

25. 'Hayward's Annals', pp. 51, 54, 64; Sir Philip Egerton (ed.), 'A Commentary of the Services and Charges of William Lord Grey of Wilton, K. G., by his son, Arthur Lord Grey of Wilton, K. G. With a Memoir of the Author and Illustrative Documents' *Camden Society*, o.s., 10 (1847); Trim, 'Mercenaries', p. 485; BL, Lansdowne MS 1218, fos 119r, 129v; Thomas Churchyard, *The first parte of Churchyardes Chippes, contayning twelve severall labours* (1575), fos 9r, 9v, 59v, 61v; Humfrey Barwick, *Concerning the Force and Effect of … Manuall Weapons of Fire, 1594* (English Experience in Printed Books, no. 643; Amsterdam and Norwood, NJ: 1974), sigs F2r-F3r. See Mark Charles Fissel, *English Warfare 1511–1642* (New York: 2001), pp. 114–23.

26. De La Quadra to Philip, 12 July 1559, *CSP. Sp. Eliz.* i, p. 85.

27. Same to same, 13 [August] 1559, ibid., p. 90.

28. Same to same, 3 February 1560, ibid., pp. 123–24.

29. De La Quadra to Margaret of Parma, 29 August 1561, ibid., p. 212; *DNB* (2nd edn), viii, p. 873. Thomas S. Freeman, ' "The re-formation of the Church in this parliament": Thomas Norton, John Foxe and the Parliament of 1571', *Parliamentary History*, 16 (1997), p. 132.

30. De La Quadra to Cardinal Granvelle, 2 April 1562, *CSP. Sp. Eliz.* i, p. 234.

31. Parker, 'Place of Tudor England in the messianic vision of Philip II'.

32. For example, Elizabeth I to Philip II, 22 September 1562, G. B. Harrison (ed.), *The Letters of Elizabeth I* (1968), pp. 36–9; Sir Thomas Smith to Privy Council, 22 December 1562, *CSPF Eliz.* v, p. 586.

33. De La Quadra to Philip 3 February 1560, *CSP. Sp. Eliz.* i, p. 123; Philip to Elizabeth, 11 September 1562, *CSPF Eliz.* v, p. 295.

34. See, e.g., de La Quadra to Holy Roman Emperor, 18 August 1559, *CSP. Sp. Eliz.* i, p. 93; see also, Trim, 'Mercenaries', pp. 98, 106–7, 133, and sources cited therein.

35. Guy, *Tudor England*, p. 267; N. M. Sutherland, 'Calvinism and the conspiracy of Amboise', *History*, 47 (1962), p. 134. See also David Potter, 'Mid-Tudor Foreign Policy and Diplomacy' pp. 106–38.

36. Coligny to Cecil and Condé to Elizabeth 1 and 2 April 1562, *CSPF Eliz.* iv, pp. 578–9; Condé wrote 'aux églises reformées de France' on 7 April; J. -F. Michaud and J. -J. -F. Poujoulat (eds), *Mémoires du Prince de Condé* in *Nouvelle collection des mémoires relatifs à l'histoire de France depuis le XIII siècle jusqu'à la fin du XVIII siècle*, ser. 1, vi (Paris, 1839), p. 629.

37. 'Hayward's Annals', pp. 93, 97–98; Cecil to Thomas Randolph 30 January 1561, BL, Harley MS 6990, fo. 15r; Cecil, memoranda, 1559 and 20 July 1562, PRO, SP 12/4, fo. 135r (quoted in Alford, *The Early Elizabethan Polity*, p. 218), SP 70/39, fo. 106v; Throckmorton to Cecil, 24 June 1562, *CSPF Eliz.* v, p. 127. Throckmorton is too

often portrayed simply as an extremist, for his attitudes on this issue were widely endorsed. See e.g., Elizabeth to Throckmorton, 16 July 1572 and Cecil to same 14 December 1562, PRO, SP 70/39, fo. 63r, SP 70/46, fo. 171r. For Throckmorton, see also Chapter 5 by Potter, pp. 116–17. Spanish troops *did* aid the French crown in the first civil war.

38. D. J. B. Trim, 'The "foundation-stone of the British army"? The Normandy campaign of 1562', *Journal of the Society for Army Historical Research*, 77 (1999), pp. 71–87; idem, 'Mercenaries', p. 313.

39. [John Hales?]'s notes on recent history [*c*.1563], BL, Additional MS 48023, fos 365v, 367v; 'Hayward's Annals', pp. 200–1; Patrick Collinson (ed.), 'Introduction', to *Letters of Thomas Wood, Puritan, 1566–1577* (*BIHR*, special suppt, v, 1960), pp. vi, ix; Christopher Haigh, *Elizabeth I* (1988), p. 128; Henry Killigrew to Cecil, 4 October 1562, PRO, SP 70/42, fo. 71r.

40. For some evidence, see *CSPF Eliz*, v, pp. 550, 574; vi, pp. 34, 47, 56, 61, 72, 76, 122, 170–72; PRO, SP 70/50, fos 148r–49r, 70/55, fo. 155. *Mémoires de Michel de Castelnau* in Michaud and Poujoulat (eds), *Nouvelle collection des mémoires*, ser. 1, ix (Paris, 1838), p. 482. James W. Thompson, *The Wars of Religion in France* (Chicago, 1909), p. 188. And see below, p. 161.

41. For a recent overview of the English intervention, see Paul E. J. Hammer, *Elizabeth's Wars: War, Government and Society in Tudor England 1544–1604* (Basingstoke, 2003), pp. 63–7.

42. 26 December 1562, *CSPF Eliz.* v, p. 591.

43. Smith to Throckmorton 17 October 1562, PRO, SP 70/43, fo. 53r. Both arquebuses and bow staves were shipped to Normandy, *CSPF Eliz.* v, pp. 260, 263. William Bromfield to Cecil, 20 December 1562, PRO, SP 70/47, fo. 56r.

44. Castelnau, *Mémoires*, p. 468; William Harrison, 'The Description of England' in *The First and Second Volumes of Chronicles … newlie augmented and continued … to the yeare 1586 …* (n.p., 1586), p. 198; Barwick, *Force and Effect of … Manual Weapons of Fire*, sig. F3r; D. J. B. Trim, '*Fin de siècle:* the English soldier's experience at the end of the sixteenth century', *Military and Naval History Journal*, 10 (1999), pp. 5–7, 12 n.42. And see Fissel, *English Warfare*, pp. 117, 136, 283; Hammer, *Elizabeth's Wars*, pp. 98–9

45. 'Hayward's Annals', p. 86; Harrison, 'Description of England', p. 198; R. B. Wernham, *Before the Armada: The Growth of English Foreign Policy 1485–1588* (1966), pp. 278–9.

46. Anon. [John Hales?] notes on recent events *c*.1563, BL, Additional MS 48023, fo. 356r.

47. Lindsay Boynton, *The Elizabethan Militia 1558–1638* (1967), p. 90.

48. Cecil's 'A short memoryall of the state of the realm' 1569, Samuel Haynes, *A Collection of State Papers Relating to Affairs … now remaining at Hatfield House* (1740), p. 580; privy council to deputy lieutenants of Kent, Essex and Hampshire, 30 June, 1570, *CSP. Domestic, Addenda, 1566–1579*, pp. 305–6.

49. 'Hayward's Annals', p. 86; Haynes, *State Papers*, p. 588; BL, Lansdowne MS 102, fos 145r, 146r; T[homas] C[hurchyard] and R. Ro[binson], *A true discourse historicall of the succeeding governours in the Netherlands, and the civill warres there […] with the memorable services of our honourable English generals, captaines and souldiers* (1602), pp. 67, 70.

50. Cecil to Throckmorton, 16 July 1562, BL, Additional MS 35831, fo. 49r.

51. PRO, SP 70/95, fo. 204v.

52. BN, MS français 3177, fos 45v–51v.

53. Bibliothèque Mazarine, MS 2593, fos 146v–7v, 149r–50r.

54. Christopher Mundt to Elizabeth, PRO, SP 70/45, fo. 53 quoted in Lock, ' "Strange Usurped Potentates" ', p. 192n; Cecil's memorandum to Elizabeth 25, March 1560, PRO, SP 12/11, fo. 84r quoted in Alford, *The Early Elizabethan Polity* p. 189. See also ibid., p. 88

55. Throckmorton to Cecil, 18 September 1568, Haynes, *State Papers*, p. 471; same to same 2, September 1568, PRO, SP 12/47 quoted in Alford, *The Early Elizabethan Polity*, p. 186.

56. Cecil's memorandum June 1569, PRO, SP 12/51, fo. 10v quoted in Alford, *The Early Elizabethan Polity*, pp. 189, 194.

57. See E. I. Kouri (ed.), *Elizabethan England and Europe: Forty Unprinted Letters from Elizabeth I to Protestant Powers* (*BIHR*, special suppt, xii, 1982); idem, *England and Attempts to Form a Protestant Alliance.*

58. N. M. Sutherland, *The Massacre of St Bartholomew and the European Conflict 1559–1572* (Basingstoke, 1973). It is not the case, however, that the English government abandoned the enterprise; for a corrective, see Trim, 'Mercenaries', pp. 109–19.

59. Fogaça to Alva, 25 November 1572, 16 February 1573, J.M.B.C. Baron Kervin de Lettenhove (ed.), *Relations Politiques des Pays-Bas et de L'Angleterre sous le regne de Philippe II* (11 vols. Brussels, 1882–1900), vi, pp. 589, 663. Cf. de Schomberg to Charles IX, 9 January 1573, Bibliothèque Mazarine, MS 2078, fos 120r–23r.

60. Mack P. Holt, *The Duke of Anjou and the Politique Struggle during the Wars of Religion* (Cambridge, 1986), p. 48.

61. James B. Wood, 'The Royal Army, 1559–1576' in Mack P. Holt (ed.), *Society and Institutions in Early Modern France* (Athens, GA., 1991), p. 30; Holt, *Duke of Anjou*, pp. 63–6, at 66; Thompson, *Wars of Religion*, pp. 514–16, at 516.

62. 'Concordat de Mydelbourg', 15 December 1576, BN, MS français 23040, pp. 90–3. There are at least two other copies of this in the BN MSS français plus one in the Archives des Affaires Étrangères.

63. Wilson, *Revolt of the Netherlands*, pp. 53, 55–6; Wallace T. MacCaffrey, *Queen Elizabeth and the Making of Policy 1572–1588* (Princeton, NJ, 1981), p. 223. J. A. van Dorsten, *Poets, Patrons, and Professors: Sir Philip Sidney, Daniel Rogers and the Leiden Humanists* (Leiden, 1962), pp. 48–9; idem, 'Sidney and Languet' in J. van den Berg and A. Hamilton (eds), *The Anglo-Dutch Renaissance: Seven Essays* (Publications of the Sir Thomas Browne Institute, n.s., x; Leiden, 1988), pp. 21–2, 25.

64. Van Dorsten, 'Sidney and Languet', pp. 25–7; idem, *Poets, Patrons and Professors*, pp. 53–4. John Casimir to Sidney, 12 June 1577, *CSPF Eliz.*, xi, pp. 599–600; Kouri, *Forty Letters*, pp. 40–1. See J. N. Bakhuizen van den Brink, 'Het convent te Frankfort,' *Nederlandsch Archief voor Kerkegeschiedenis*, n. s., 32 (1941), pp. 235–80.

65. 'Articuli praecipi foederis, quod Sereniss. Reginia Angliae que cum Evangelicus Germaniae Principius iuire constituit', Bod.L, Tanner MS 80, fo. 53r.

66. Bod.L, Tanner MS 79, fos 11r–13r.

67. R. B. Wernham, *After the Armada: Elizabethan England and the Struggle for Western Europe 1588–1595* (Oxford, 1984), p. 560; cf. J. B. Black, *The Reign of Elizabeth 1558–1603* (Oxford, 1936), p. 286; van Dorsten, *Poets, Patrons and Professors*, p. 175. 'Advis donne a la royne dangleterre touchant l'electeur de Cologne', BN, Cinq Cents de Colbert 401, fos 63–74 (hereafter CCC].

68. 'Relation of Willoughby' December 1585, *CSPF Eliz.* xx, pp. 255–7; Arthur J. Slavin, 'Daniel Rogers in Copenhagen, 1588: mission and memory' in Malcolm R. Thorp and Arthur J. Slavin (eds), *Politics, Religion and Diplomacy in Early Modern Europe*, Sixteenth Century Essays and Studies, 27 (Kirksville, MO., 1994), p. 256.

69. Slavin, 'Daniel Rogers', p. 265.

70. This is either much less or slightly more than I estimated in an earlier study: D. J. B. Trim, 'The secret war of Elizabeth I: England and the Huguenots during the early Wars of Religion', *Proceedings of the Huguenot Society of Great Britain and Ireland*, 27 (1998–2001), p. 191. See accounts of treasurer at Le Havre October–January 1562–63 (for £4614 13s 3d), *CSPF Eliz.* vi, p. 76; warrants and receipts January–February 1563 (for 7000 crowns, equivalent to some £1900 or 2300, depending on the exchange rate used), BL, Additional MS 5753, fos 203r–7r (and see *CSPF Eliz.* v, p. 607 and vi, p. 344) receipt to Sir Edward Rogers for £3000, n.d. (but the date can be fixed to 1562–63, see *Oxford Dictionary of National Biography* (2004), *s.n.* Rogers), BL, Additional MS 5753, fo. 208r. If the whole £20,000 referred to in Additional MS 5753, fos 200v–1r (warrants from Elizabeth to Sir Hugh Paulet, December 1562) *was* 'disbursed ... for the support of certain bands of French captains and soldiers in the Queen's pay', as Dietz suggests, then the actual total paid to the Huguenots would have been £25,300 (if, as seems likely, the £4614 was part of the £20,000): Frederick C. Dietz, *English Public Finance 1558–1641* (New York, 1932), p. 12.

71. See Ernest G. Atkinson, 'The Cardinal of Châtillon in England, 1568–71', *Proceedings of the Huguenot Society*, 3 (1888–91), pp. 226–7, 276; Jeanne de Navarre to Burghley and Walsingham to same 27 and 28 May 1572, BL, Lansdowne MS 14, fo. 170r and 15, fo. 160r; memorandum to Coligny, 1 March 1569, BN, CCC 24, fo. 369r; Mark Greengrass, 'Financing the cause: Protestant mobilization and accountability in France (1562–1589)' in Philip Benedict *et al.* (eds), *Reformation, Revolt and Civil War in France and the Netherlands 1555–1585*, Koninklijke Nederlandse Akademie van Wetenschappen, Verhandelingen: Letterkunde, n.s., 176; (Amsterdam, 1999), p. 244; Dietz, *English Public Finance* p. 14; and Kouri, *England and Attempts to Form a Protestant Alliance*, p. 42.

72. Elizabeth to elector Palatine and John Casimir, May 1575 and elector's undertaking not to mention Elizabeth's name in loan contracts, 23 July 1575, *CSPF Eliz.* xi, pp. 65, 95.

73. Obligations and quittances, ibid., pp. 95–6; Trim, 'Mercenaries', pp. 132–3.

74. Wilkes to Burghley, 29 August 1575, James Harvie to Burghley, 9 October 1575, Lettenhove, *Relations Politiques*, vii, pp. 561, 595; de Guaras to Zayas, 17 September 1575, *CSP. Sp.* ii, p. 503; Condé to Sussex, 4 and 28 October 1575 and 27 August 1576, BL, Cotton MS Titus B vii, fos 399r, 401r, 393r; Bernard Vogler, 'Le rôle des électeurs palatins dans les guerres de religion en France (1559–1592)', *Cahiers d'histoire*, 10 (1965), pp. 65–7; Dietz, *English Public Finance*, p. 38

75. Minutes of States General, 2 December 1576, Algemeen Rijksarchief, The Hague, 1.01.03: 1, fo. 44v; Dietz, *English Public Finance*, p. 39.

76. States General's bonds with Elizabeth April–July 1578, Mation Archief, 1.01.01/III: 23A-C; Dietz, *English Public Finance,* pp. 39–40.

77. Anjou's accounts, PRO, SP 78/10, nos 122 (fos 308–36) and 123 (fos 158r–9r [*sic*]); Holt, *Anjou*, pp. 196–7; Orange to burgomasters and echevins of Antwerp, 27 November 1581, Bibliothèque Sainte-Geneviève, MS 1456, fo. 420.

78. Dietz, *English Public Finance*, pp. 40, 40–41n. Cf. ibid., pp. 449–50n.; Trim, 'Mercenaries', pp. 145, 217.
79. Atkinson, 'The Cardinal of Châtillon', p. 223; Greengrass, 'Financing the cause', p. 245.
80. Conyers Read, *Lord Burghley and Queen Elizabeth* (London, 1960), pp. 92, 554 n.44; Patrick Collinson, 'England and International Calvinism' in Menna Prestwich (ed.), *International Calvinism 1541–1715* (Oxford, 1985), pp. 204–5.
81. Trim, 'Mercenaries', p. 121.
82. Léon Marlet, *Le Comte de Montgomery* (Paris, 1890), p. 130. For example, the Merchant Taylors' Company subscribed £300, 7 February 1573, Company court minutes, i, p. 634 (I owe this reference to Ann Saunders); Journal of Jean Maillet 13 November 1582, Geneva, Archives d'Etat, Pièces Historiques 2066, p. 2 (I am obliged to Simon Adams for a copy of his transcription of this document).
83. D. J. B. Trim, 'Protestant refugees in Elizabethan England and confessional conflict in France and the Netherlands, 1562–*c*.1610' in Randolph Vigne and Charles Littleton (eds), *From Strangers to Citizens: The Integration of Immigrant Communities in Britain, Ireland and America, 1550–1750* (2001), p. 71; idem, 'Mercenaries', ch. 6, esp. pp. 214–20.
84. Ramsay, 'Foreign policy of Elizabeth', p. 154.
85. Champernowne and Horsey to Cecil, 19 and 20 December 1568, Lettenhove, *Relations Politiques*, v, p. 19; Guy, *Tudor England*, p. 276. See also Wernham, *Before the Armada*, p. 296; Dietz, *English Public Finance* p. 14; also Ramsay, 'Foreign policy of Elizabeth', p. 156.
86. Geoffrey Parker, *The Army of Flanders and the Spanish Road* (Cambridge, 1972; 1990), p. 141, fig. 13.
87. Trim, 'Protestant refugees and confessional conflict', p. 69; idem, 'Mercenaries', p. 99.
88. Kouri, *England and Attempts to Form a Protestant Alliance*, pp. 42–3.
89. Norris to Elizabeth, 10 February 1569, *CSPF Eliz.* ix, p. 29.
90. *Hinc Haffield MSS*, i, p. 371. See *DNB*, viii, p. 873. Amos Barbot, *Histoire de La Rochelle depuis l'an 1199 jusques en 1575*, in Denys d'Aussy (ed.), *Archives historiques de La Saintonge et de L'Aunis*, xvii (1889), p. 326.
91. See Trim, 'Mercenaries', pp. 102–4, 481.
92. See Trim, 'Secret war of Elizabeth I', 192; idem, 'Protestant refugees and confessional conflict', pp. 71–2.
93. See P. J. Blok, 'De Watergeuzen in Engeland (1568–1572)', *Bijdragen voor Vaderlandsche Geschiedenis en Oudheidkunde*, ser. 3, ix (1896), pp. 226–63; Jean de Pablo, 'Contribution á l'étude de l'histoire des institutions militaires huguenotes, i. L'armée de mer huguenote pendant la troisième guerre de religion', *Archiv für Reformationsgeschichte*, 47 (1956), pp. 64–76; Brian Dietz, 'Privateering in north-west European waters 1568–1572'. Unpublished PhD dissertation, University of London, 1959; M. Delafosse, 'Les corsaires protestants à La Rochelle (1570–1577)', *Bibliothèque de l'école des Chartes*, 121 (1963), pp. 187–217; J. C. A. de Meij, *De Watergeuzen en de Nederlanden 1586–1572*, Koninklijke Nederlandse Akademie van Wetenschappen, Verhandelingen: Letterkunde, n.s., 77, ii (Amsterdam, 1972); M. J. French, 'Privateering and the revolt of the Netherlands: The *watergeuzen* or sea beggars in Portsmouth, Gosport and the Isle of Wight 1570–71', *Proceedings of the Hampshire Field Club and Archaeological Society*, 47 (1991), pp. 171–80.
94. M. de Blandin to the queen of Navarre, September 1568, BN, CCC 24, fo. 361r.

95. Above, pp. 148, 164; Thomas Churchyard, *A generall rehearsall of warres, called Churchyard's choise* (1579), sig. L4v.
96. Spanish merchant's petition, 1568, *CSPF Eliz.* x, p. 451; Champernowne to Cecil 1, January 1569, Lettenhove, *Relations Politiques*, v, p. 205; Trim, 'Mercenaries', p. 122; Marlet, *Le Comte de Montgomery*, pp. 136–7, 141; anon. to de Requesens, 17 May 1574, *CSP. Sp. Eliz.* ii, p. 481; Privy Council warrants, 27 January 1574, *APC*, viii, p. 182.
97. Condé to Sussex, 12 June 1577, BL, Cotton MS Titus B.vii, fo. 318r; see Trim, 'Mercenaries', pp. 138, 300.
98. Throckmorton to Cecil, 26 May 1562, BL, Additional MS 35831, fo. 34r.
99. Agrippa d'Aubigné, *L'histoire universelle* (3 vols, Maille, 1616–20), i, p. 308; William Camden, *Annales. The True and Royal History of the famous Empresse Elizabeth*, trans. Abraham Darcie (1625), i, p. 224. See Trim, 'Mercenaries', pp. 108, 415.
100. Trim, 'Mercenaries', pp. 108–19, at 109, 119.
101. Ibid., pp. 122, 282, 317. Montgomery to Burghley, 28 March and 26 May 1573, *CSPF Eliz.* x, pp. 291–2, 344–5; Montgomery to Sussex, 3 April 1573, BL, Cotton MS Titus B.vii, fo. 250r.
102. 23 April 1574, Lettenhove, *Relations Politiques*, vii, p. 110. Trim, 'Mercenaries', pp. 125–30.
103. Trim, 'Mercenaries', pp. 140–6.
104. For troop numbers, see ibid., apps 2, 10, pp. 340, 344, 512–14.
105. Giovanni Comer to the Signory, 4 May 1569, *CSPV* vii, p. 456.
106. Kouri, 'Elizabeth and the Protestant Powers', p. 412. I use here the conceptual framework of Kouri's definition of national interest as 'England's supposed political advantage' and of a faith-based policy as one involving 'the idealistic defence of Protestantism as such'. English policy, as it emerges in this essay, however, clearly leans towards the latter.

7

'THE STATE OF THE WORLD IS MARVELLOUSLY CHANGED': ENGLAND, SPAIN AND EUROPE 1558–1604

Pauline Croft

In May 1589, the 69-year-old William Cecil Lord Burghley reflected wearily on the European political situation. 'The state of the world is marvellously changed', he wrote to his old friend and fellow privy councillor the earl of Shrewsbury, 'when we true Englishmen have cause for our own quietness to wish good success to a French King and a King of Scots; and yet they both differ one from the other, in profession of religion; but seeing both are enemies to our enemies, we have cause to join with them in their actions against our enemies.'[1] Barely a year after the defeat of the Armada, Burghley still saw hostilities between England and Spain – rather than between England and France or England and Scotland – as an unwelcome reversal of traditional diplomacy. For centuries, the threat to England had come from the menacing, pincer-like 'auld alliance' of the French and Scots. In 1542, on the death of James V, his baby daughter Mary inherited the Scottish throne but in 1548 she was sent to France and educated at court, where her mother's family the Guises were prominent. In 1558 the alliance was consolidated when the dauphin Francis, son of King Henry II, married the young Queen of Scots.

By contrast England had been a friend to Castile, Aragon and Portugal since the fourteenth century. In 1489 the treaty of Medina del Campo bound Henry VII, the new Tudor king, in an alliance with Isabella of Castile and her husband Ferdinand of Aragon, whose marriage created a new power in Europe. These ties were strengthened when the accession of their grandson Charles of Ghent as ruler of Spain in 1516 also brought the 17 provinces of the Low Countries, inherited from his father the Archduke Philip, into the Anglo-Spanish alliance. The port of Antwerp provided the greatest market for broadcloth, England's key export, and during the fifteenth century the dukes of Burgundy, then rulers of the Low Countries, were close allies of England. The sixteenth-century link with the Habsburgs was a continuation of 'Burgundian' policies. From the Habsburg perspective, swift sea access to the wealthy Netherlands, in tax terms the most valuable part of their empire, emphatically required good relations with England whose navy commanded the Channel.

The peak of the Anglo-Spanish alliance came in 1554 when Charles's son Philip of Spain married Mary Tudor. The queen through her mother Catherine of Aragon had more Spanish blood than Philip, with his half-Flemish father and Portuguese mother. The marriage was a Habsburg masterstroke in outflanking France, the opposing great power; control over England, the middle-weight of the three monarchies, would add decisively to Habsburg dominance. Mary's untimely death in November 1558 was a considerable setback, coming just at the point when a half-century of struggle had exhausted both the Valois and the Habsburgs. However, both Philip II and the young Queen Elizabeth found the Franco-Scottish link still threatening, and after 1558 when France took Calais (the sole remaining English possession across the Channel) Elizabeth's advisers feared that Henry II bestrode her realm with 'one foot in Calais and the other in Scotland'. Sir William Cecil took comfort in 'the earnest and very brotherly friendship' of the Spanish king.[2] So the amity continued and for most of the 1560s Philip regarded England (on whose affairs he prided himself as being uniquely knowledgeable) as broadly within his sphere of leadership. Although he deplored Elizabeth's policy of returning her country to Protestantism, until 1570 Philip successfully protected her from a papal excommunication and continued to hope that she might eventually 'come to her senses' as he wrote to his ambassador in London.[3]

PHILIP II AND ENGLAND 1558–87

There is nothing new in emphasising the friendly relations between England and Spain in the first half of the sixteenth century. Yet there has been a strong tendency to assume that after 1558 there was an inevitable drift to war. The distinguished historian Manuel Fernandez Alvarez crisply entitled an article on Elizabeth and Philip 'Una paz imposible'. In 1959 the American Garret Mattingly in his classic *The Defeat of the Spanish Armada* described how 'Philip II and his militant advisers dreamed of a great crusade' and saw the war with England as 'forced' by history itself: 'the clash of irreconcilables could not be postponed for ever'. In 1980, R. B. Wernham's perspicacious overview did justice to the long years of peace between England and Spain, but he titled his opening chapter on the tensions of the 1560s 'The first quarrels', implying an escalating series.[4] In 1988, on the four hundredth anniversary of the Armada campaign, the best-selling account by Colin Martin and Geoffrey Parker suggested that the story began with Henry VIII's divorce from his Spanish wife Catherine of Aragon. The theme of the inevitable long term slide into war has been rehearsed most recently in a survey of English sea power, commerce and foreign policy between 1490 and 1690.[5]

Of course, the assumption that war was bound to break out is simply evidence of the constant temptation to read history backwards. The language of destiny (meaning hindsight) still creeps into modern textbooks: 'the old diplomatic friendship between England and Spain was not *destined* to last but to give way to a life-and-death struggle'.[6] The 'inevitabilist' view is reinforced by an ill-defined but pervasive belief that the conflict was essentially and primarily religious and ideological. Undoubtedly the Reformation and Counter-Reformation created grave new difficulties in international relationships: yet the Emperor Charles V allied with the excommunicated schismatic Henry VIII in 1543 and formed other alliances with Protestant princes, just as the Most Christian King Charles IX allied with the excommunicated Elizabeth in 1572 and unhesitatingly maintained France's longstanding links with Ottoman Turkey. Diplomacy bridged the ideological divide even as it recognised the problem. As Lord Burghley noted, religion gave way before the need to support 'enemies to our enemies'.

Unsurprisingly, Philip II was dismayed by Elizabeth's Protestantism, not least because he considered that during Mary's reign he had been the instrument used by God to return England to Catholicism. That had happened 'by my intervention and by my hand' as he told the duke of Alva in January 1570. This self-congratulatory comment incidentally revealed that he had not taken the measure of his late wife's resolve in religious matters. Philip was also very prone to what has been described as 'messianic imperialism', explicitly equating God's service with his own. He repeatedly assumed that any deficiencies in his planning and preparation would be made up by the direct intervention of the Almighty, since Philip was acting in His best interests. The king's unwavering confidence in miracles frequently alarmed his military and naval commanders such as Alva and Santa Cruz, and sometimes resulted in catastrophe.[7]

Yet alongside Philip's intense personal beliefs and constant use of triumphalist Catholic language, there ran a pragmatic, hard-headed appreciation of Spain's worldly interests. The two aspects of his outlook were virtually inseparable since the king held that the deepest Christian obligation laid upon him was to preserve the kingdoms bequeathed by his father. Charles V's political testament, a comprehensive review of the international situation prepared for Philip in 1548, emphasised the practicalities – constant vigilance and up-to-date information, the need to keep alliances in good order, the use of marriage diplomacy and the value of good relations with Portugal and England. Philip profoundly respected the emperor's views and once commented that things went well for him when he followed paternal advice, and badly when he did not. Both Charles and Philip thought their policies in pursuit of Habsburg interests were far more effective in serving the Catholic Church than any scheme devised by the papacy. This confidence allowed Philip for years to shrug off the argument made by successive popes that he was morally bound to depose Elizabeth in accordance with the papal bull *Regnans* of 1570. As late as July 1585 the presumption of Gregory XIII in pressing for an invasion of England greatly irritated the king.[8]

The territories that Philip inherited were so extensive and so varied – Spain, the Low Countries, the Balearics, Sardinia, Milan, Naples, Sicily, with large areas of the New World (particularly Mexico and Peru) as well as client states such as Savoy, Genoa and Malta – that for most of his reign, relations with England were far from his prime concern. In 1559, 1571 and 1574 he pondered the distant possibility of intervening directly in English affairs, but his fleeting comments should not be read as evidence for the 'inevitability' of eventual confrontation.[9] In his letters Philip was always juggling a wide variety of schemes, many of them highly impractical, as veterans like Alva were not slow to tell him. England was only one piece, albeit a significant one, on the Habsburgs' global chess-board.

After the treaty of Cateau–Cambrésis in 1559 ended the war in northern Europe, the king was mainly preoccupied with the Mediterranean. The naval power of the Turks and their expansionist policies made the coasts of Sicily, Sardinia, the Balearics and Spain very vulnerable. The successful relief of besieged Malta in 1565, and the great victory at Lepanto in 1571, were valuable but not decisive; they did, however, justify the virtual doubling of Spain's Mediterranean galley fleet that the king

had overseen after 1562.[10] At home, between 1568 and 1570 Philip confronted the bitterly fought rebellion in the Alpujarra mountains of
Granada by the Moriscos (Spanish Muslims outwardly conforming to
Christianity), who planned to ally with the Turks. In 1567 after the collapse of the Brussels government of his half-sister Margaret of Parma, in
the face of noble disaffection and widespread iconoclastic rioting, Philip
sent Alva across Europe from Italy with the main body of the Spanish
infantry. Thereafter Spain attempted to suppress the gathering revolt in
the Low Countries, and by 1572 war had broken out. From then on the
area was constantly on the king's mind. However, the crisis did not prevent Philip from further expanding his dominions. After the royal family
of Portugal died out in the male line, he claimed the throne through his
mother, a Portuguese princess. Between 1580 and 1583 Spanish military
and naval forces were sent to gain control of the Portuguese mainland
and the islands of the Azores (taken in 1582) and Terceira (1583). The
conquest of Portugal brought with it overseas dominions in Africa, South
America and the East Indies, rich but far-flung territories that added to
the king's military and financial burdens since their lengthy trade-routes
would need to be defended. The takeover of Portugal created the first
empire on which the sun literally never set, but it was to prove a poisoned
chalice.[11]

Running parallel to all these events, after 1562 the collapse of France
into intermittent civil war was a major problem for Spain. Philip was
openly delighted to hear of the massacre of Huguenots (French
Protestants) in Paris on St Bartholomew's Day 1572, because he feared
that if heresy prevailed in France it might revive the religious disorders
which had convulsed Spain in the late 1550s. The king hoped that other
French cities would follow Paris and exterminate Protestantism, but the
massacre only deepened divisions. In 1584 the death of the duke of
Anjou, heir to the throne, ensured that his childless elder brother King
Henry III would eventually be succeeded by their Huguenot cousin
Henry of Navarre. The thought was intolerable to Philip II. Henry was
not only a Protestant; he took his title from the Pyrenean state which
Spanish forces had occupied in 1512 and joined to the crown of Castile
in 1515. If Henry gained the French throne it seemed inevitable that he
would attempt to reverse the Spanish annexation of Navarre. French
affairs dominated Philip's policies throughout 1584 and in December his
envoys signed a treaty with the duke of Guise, leader of the Catholic
League. Philip agreed to provide funds and offer military assistance if –
or rather when – civil war resumed. His open-ended commitment

underlined the priority he always gave to France. Philip reacted with perfect consistency in August 1585 when he was offered French help in a
possible joint invasion of England to succour Catholics; he wrote curtly
in the proposal's margin that the French should finish off their own
heretics first, since those near at hand concerned him more than those
further away.[12]

British historians have tended to neglect the complex pan-European
dimensions of Spanish policy and over-emphasise the importance of
England. In consequence the conflict of 1588 has been depicted as a
bilateral fight between two sworn enemies. Spanish historians have sometimes concurred, writing of the '*dual* antagonism' of Philip and Elizabeth,
both 'semi-legendary' figures in their own lifetimes.[13] Yet the evidence
supports neither the 'inevitabilist' nor the bilateral view. Both monarchs
presided over courts and councils in which multiple strategies were
debated. Each contained what may roughly be described as a peace-
leaning party and an aggressive party, so policy was shaped not least by
whichever of the two factions was temporarily in the ascendant. Despite
his occasional thoughts about intervention and his frequent irritation
with Elizabeth, Philip did not seriously consider an invasion until 1585,
thirty years after his accession to the Spanish throne. His strategy in 1588
was multilateral, aiming above all to restore Spanish control over the Low
Countries. The invasion of England was a means to bring about that
greater end.

Abandoning the deceptions of hindsight, we must start from the
realisation that diplomatic and commercial relations between major
states have never been trouble-free. Frictions of one sort or another are
endemic, virtually universal – occurring even between close allies – and it
is the regular business of heads of state to finesse them. Crisis manage-
ment is the essence of high-level diplomacy and the aim is always to maintain a working consensus. Any catalogue of the problems and frictions of
Anglo-Spanish relations which assumes that war was the inevitable outcome ignores the fact that both sides had many good reasons to strive for
a viable if not wholly cordial *entente*.

The initial conflicts of the 1560s arose mostly from the trading relationships between England and the Low Countries. There was a brief
embargo in 1563 but in 1568 a more serious dispute arose. Money sent to
Alva to pay the army of Flanders frequently came by sea from Spain, and
in November 1568 French pirates and bad weather forced the ships to
shelter in west-country ports. For safety the money was brought ashore.
Just at this point news arrived at Elizabeth's court of the Spanish attack at

San Juan de Ulua in Mexico on the trading and slaving fleet commanded by John Hawkins of Plymouth. English attitudes hardened. The fiery new Spanish ambassador Guerau de Spes escalated the tensions, urging the seizure of English merchants' goods in both the Low Countries and Spain itself. This was excessive; the money in transit belonged, not to Alva but to the Genoese bankers who were loaning it to him, and in any case comprised only a small part of his budget. Alva and Philip acceded to the embargo only because de Spes wrongly informed them that Elizabeth had confiscated the money. In fact she intended to treat it as a loan to herself and left it in the Tower untouched, ignoring the pleas of the financier Sir Thomas Gresham to turn it into English coin.[14] But Alva had no wish to go further, and Philip was unsure if Elizabeth really was moving towards outright hostilities. If she was, he wanted to send funds to the Catholic leaders of the Northern Rebellion, just at this point breaking out in England, and (against Alva's advice) to offer Spanish support to Mary Queen of Scots. Philip also decided (again despite Alva's advice) to use the services of a Florentine banker, Roberto Ridolfi, in passing messages between Spain, the English rebels and Mary, who after fleeing Scotland in 1568 lived under house arrest in northern England.

It remains unclear whether Ridolfi was a double agent, working for English rather than Spanish paymasters, or just lamentably careless and naive. He used only one cipher in all his correspondence (quickly broken by English decrypters) and occasionally even wrote to Mary *en clair* (unciphered). After a brief period of sabre-rattling, Philip decided to concentrate on plotting, not least because Alva firmly told him that military action against Elizabeth was out of the question. The king also accepted the services of the dubious English mercenary and go-between George Fitzwilliam, who was almost certainly working for Burghley. The duke of Norfolk, whose role in the plot was to marry the Scottish queen once she was established on the English throne, was promptly arrested and Mary herself placed in closer confinement.[15]

The revelation that Philip had actively supported Mary as the chief contender for her throne shocked Elizabeth deeply. Together with the king's inability to protect her from the impetuous and unworldly Pius V, who launched his excommunication bull *Regnans* in 1570 without even consulting Philip, the Ridolfi plot suggested that Spain could no longer be trusted as a benevolent neutral able to offer valuable support. Thereafter the queen began to spend heavily on naval defences and she allowed, even sometimes openly supported, privateering raids on the Spanish Caribbean. Eleven substantial English expeditions sailed there between 1572 and 1577. In April 1572, following the traditional ploy of balancing Spain against France, Elizabeth concluded the treaty of Blois with Catherine de' Medici and her son Charles IX.

However, feelers were already being put out (not least by Burghley in March 1572) indicating a willingness to settle. Both Elizabeth and Philip made tentative moves towards lifting the mutual embargo, since it had proved burdensome to merchants and expensive to the rulers of England, Spain and the Netherlands. As trade faltered, all three lost valuable customs revenues. Philip soon saw additional reasons to mend the breach. The Dutch rebels exiled earlier from the Low Countries had formed themselves into bands of privateers, the Sea Beggars, who frequented English ports while keeping alive the opposition to Alva. In February 1572 the English government expelled the Sea Beggars, as a nuisance to legitimate commerce in the Channel, whereupon they mounted an attack on the port of Brill in Holland. Once they secured a base, rebellion was re-ignited particularly in Holland and Zealand where many proclaimed their loyalty to William the Silent. Even worse, large numbers of French Huguenot volunteers joined them.[16] Alva would need substantial reinforcements to put down this revived insurgency and in Madrid any lingering thoughts of intervening in England vanished.

In June 1572 Alva himself suggested negotiations. To Burghley, the new developments offered not only a reconciliation with Spain but also a way forward if French aid to William the Silent threatened to become a takeover. In a position paper drafted for the queen, he suggested that if France should attempt to control the shoreline of the Low Countries, she might secretly suggest that she would aid Spain against France if Philip would offer his subjects the restoration of the ancient liberties of the Netherlands.[17] Burghley was a committed Protestant and prone to apocalyptic memo-writing, but he was also steeped in the traditional English policy of balancing one power against another. He had few ideological objections to making offers to Spain.

The treaty of Blois quickly proved worthless, since in August the massacre of St Bartholomew re-ignited widespread religious violence. Elizabeth maintained the *entente* just reached with Catherine de' Medici, but France was no longer a powerful monarchy. Like the Soviet Union in the later twentieth century, it declined from superpower to shambles in little more than a decade. By late summer 1572 it was imperative to mend England's relations with Spain. In October terms were discussed and after a preliminary concord was reached, the ports were opened fully in spring 1573, initially for two years. The worldly wise Alva pressed Philip to agree, even though he thought it likely that Elizabeth would continue her support for 'rebels and corsairs'. Between princes there was a great difference between hostility and dissimulation, the duke remarked, and in any case (he could not resist pointing out) all this 'mud' had come from trusting Ridolfi. Burghley told the Spanish agent in London that he had pushed the accord through the Privy Council, perhaps an exaggeration but indicating his role as leader of the peace party.[18]

In 1574 Spain, England and the Low Countries resumed full diplomatic and commercial relations. The treaty of Bristol is often overlooked but it was a major success for diplomacy. It reinforces the basic point that friction is endemic in the relations of sovereign powers, but not necessarily the preliminary to war. The claims of seizures and counter-seizures arising from the embargo at the outbreak of the troubles were settled; Elizabeth returned Alva's money; and in some other areas Philip conceded more than the queen required. When she asked for the expulsion from the Low Countries of those she had exiled from England (in other words Catholic plotters) Philip ordered the expulsion of *all* English Catholics.[19]

In August 1574 the queen went on an unusually long progress to Bristol, to ratify the treaty personally. Acknowledging that the realm was entrusted to her by God, she prayed 'that in the end I may render up and present the same again unto Thee a peaceable, quiet and well-ordered state and kingdom'. In a week of civic ceremonies she watched a vigorous mock battle between War and Peace staged by arquebusiers and pikemen. The citizens made it plain that they wanted the renewal of good relations with Spain. 'Our trade doth stand on civil life, and there our glory lies: and not on strife, the ruin of states, a storm that all destroys.' A well-ordered polity must take into account the interests of mercantile cities like London and Bristol. Strife was the ruin of states, certainly of commerce. Peace won the civic battle as the queen looked on.[20] Although the English continued to offer some unofficial support to the Dutch rebels, they balanced this in October 1575 when a large Spanish fleet carrying troops for Flanders was forced by bad weather into English ports. The ships were re-provisioned and given courteous treatment.[21]

Burghley was promoted to the Lord Treasurership in 1572 and thereafter showed particular concern for England's overseas trade. The customs duties formed a significant part of royal revenues while the leading merchants and trading companies of London exercised great influence, not least because in emergencies they were a vital source of loans. The disturbances in the Low Countries were undermining the Antwerp mart, which in the 1560s took 65 per cent of London's cloth exports. Many merchants were relocating to Hamburg, which lessened English dependence on Antwerp and with it the Privy Council's sensitivity to the views of Spanish governors at Brussels. At the same time, however, English direct trade with Spain was growing, recovering from the doldrums of mid-century to the extent that in 1565, Spanish goods provided around 11 per cent of London's imports and took around 10 per cent of the capital's direct cloth exports, with another steady stream of re-exports from the Low Countries.[22]

The Spanish trade divided into two branches, one trading to the north coast and the other to Andalusia, especially Seville which absorbed quantities of English goods destined for the New World fleets. The upsurge in the Indies trade after the recession of 1550–59 inaugurated a forty-year boom, and Andalusia's buoyancy increased its attractions for English merchants. During the embargo from 1569 to 1573, a steady current of English illicit trade flowed south, testimony to the lure of the Iberian market.[23]

Once the ports re-opened in 1573, English ships increasingly vented commodities such as the lighter new draperies (coloured woollen fabrics) and fashionable knitted stockings, as well as corn, hides and calfskins, and haberdashery. In return, along with wine and fruit came commodities vital for English cloth production; oil to soften raw wool for carding, alum to prepare it for dyeing, and cochineal for expensive scarlets. The Spanish trade supported employment (particularly in the clothing counties), helped to train English mariners in sea skills, and encouraged the expansion of the mercantile marine. By 1576 the London port-books indicate that commerce had fully recovered and was expanding vigorously. The foundation of the regulated Spanish Company, chartered by the Crown in 1577 to bring together merchants in London and the outports such as Bristol, provides further evidence of its importance. Increasingly the two-way traffic was conducted almost entirely in English vessels, adding to the profits of English ship owners, and the distances travelled required vessels larger and sturdier than the small barks that crossed the North Sea. After 1573, not merely English tonnage as a whole, but the more valuable sector of it, was stimulated by the flourishing Iberian route. There is also evidence to suggest that English merchants conducted lucrative business in the indirect trades, in ships which never entered English ports (and hence were never listed in the port books) but plied directly between northern European and Spanish entrepots.[24]

In the later 1570s, commerce began to push through the Straits, with Malaga attracting English importers of wine and currants. English ships sailed on to Leghorn, the new port of the Grand Dukes of Tuscany; to

Venice; and in the 1580s to Crete and Istanbul. A safe passage beyond Gibraltar depended on good relations between England and Spain, so these new trades increased the importance to English merchants of a working diplomatic relationship between the two countries. English involvement in the Iberian and Mediterranean commercial world formed part of a much greater movement whereby the north–south trade axes of Europe were steadily rising in significance, as the cross-Channel and central European trades focused on the Low Countries began to decline. The result was an increasing traffic southwards from all northern states, including England, the Dutch and the Hanse. Hostilities between England and Spain temporarily weakened this trade-flow but war proved unable to roll back a major economic shift in European commerce. After the peace of 1604, Anglo-Spanish trade boomed.[25]

However, after 1577 new developments began to divide the London merchant community. Expeditions to the Caribbean suggested that extraordinary profits might be made there, despite Spain's claims to a monopoly. Drake's circumnavigation of the globe between 1577 and 1580 demonstrated both English navigational abilities and the hollowness of Spain's pretensions to control its far-flung empire. Elizabeth frequently backed expeditions which in Spanish eyes were flagrantly aggressive, and she even knighted Drake on the deck of his *Golden Hind*, but Burghley declined to accept Drake's gift of ten gold bars taken from sacked Spanish vessels, describing them as stolen goods.[26] Elizabeth seems never to have appreciated how hostile and duplicitous her actions appeared to Philip II, and as late as 1601, speaking to parliament, she portrayed her policies as wholly defensive. By contrast English merchants in the Iberian trades were well aware that her provocations were dangerous, and lobbied constantly after 1577 to remind the Privy Council of the value of peaceful commercial links. They joined with the Spanish ambassador Mendoza to emphasise that steady customs revenues and regular profits were being jeopardised by English adventurers, whose boasts of huge gains usually failed to materialise.[27]

British historians have taken the queen too much at her own valuation. Support for Drake and other privateers was bound to undermine the restored 1574 amity with Philip II. They also fail to appreciate how her actions appeared to impartial observers. It has become a mantra that Elizabeth disliked rebels, and in 1601 she claimed that no ruler had been more careful to conserve the loyalty of subjects to their prince. Yet her deeds hardly support her words. In 1560 the queen encouraged the Protestant rebels in Scotland and continued to assist the pro-English party in the struggles for control of James VI's government. In 1562 she aided the Huguenot rebels in France. Both these interventions were supported by Sir William Cecil. After 1573 she refused to stem the flow of English volunteers serving the rebellious William of Orange and successfully urged the Scottish Regency to permit the exodus of Scotsmen taking service with him, but to stop mercenaries recruited for Alva's forces. She supported the illegitimate pretender Dom Antonio de Crato after 1580, although his claim to the Portuguese throne was far inferior to that of Philip II. In 1585 she capped over a decade of violent English incursions into Spanish America with Drake's descent on the coast of mainland Galicia, followed by his raids on Spanish and Portuguese subjects and their property in the Azores and West Indies. Above all, in the treaty of Nonsuch in August 1585 she contracted a formal alliance with the leaders of the Dutch revolt and began to send them substantial military aid. It is not surprising that Spanish historians have pointed to the discrepancies between Elizabeth's words and her actions.[28]

The parting of the ways between England and Spain began in July 1584, when an assassin intent on winning the Spanish reward offered for the head of William of Silent shot and killed him in Delft. The rebels were already beginning to retreat before the campaigns of the prince of Parma, and lacking William's leadership they would stand much less chance of survival. France was wracked by internal struggles and might even decline into a Spanish puppet state. To the English Privy Council the situation was a nightmare: Philip II might soon control the entire European coastline from the western Mediterranean to north Holland. Burghley was particularly concerned about trade, after a survey of ships in English ports commissioned in autumn 1584 revealed the large number employed in the Iberian trade with the quantity and value of their cargoes.[29] Then in May 1585 Philip embargoed Dutch, English and Hanseatic ships in Spanish ports, an ill-advised step that silenced the voices for peace among English merchants. Many were forced to seek redress for their losses in Spain by joining those privateers already at sea preying on Spanish shipping. The treaty of Nonsuch was seen by foreign ambassadors as tantamount to a declaration of war, although no formal statement was ever made.

Philip did not immediately respond. In October 1585 he announced to the pope and the Grand Duke of Tuscany his intention of invading England, but it was one thing to decide on an invasion in principle, quite another to bring it about. Revealingly, some Spanish councillors still described English actions as merely 'insolencies'. Various strategies were reviewed in June 1586 and Philip decided on an initial landing in Ireland, followed by a joint operation in the Channel between a Spanish fleet and Parma's army of Flanders. Although this came near the final plan, in September the king's attention was diverted by the Babington plot to kill Elizabeth, which might render any invasion unnecessary. Until the execution of Mary Queen of Scots in February 1587 clarified the situation, Philip was also profoundly exercised over the question of what to do with the English throne if he captured Elizabeth. The assembling of a fleet went on steadily for most of 1586 but did not in itself irreversibly commit the king to action against England, and he still toyed with the idea of a punitive raid. It seems likely that Drake's assault on the ships in Cadiz bay in April 1587 was the final straw – 'their audacity is intolerable' raged Philip – but it was not until September 1587 that he issued the first detailed instructions to his commanders. As late as spring 1588 Elizabeth was prepared to grasp at a last chance for peace, sending her envoys to Bourbourg to negotiate with Parma, who deeply disliked Philip's invasion strategy even as he professionally implemented royal orders to prepare for action. Most of the Privy Council thought Bourbourg not only pointless but a sure way of alienating the Dutch, but they could not derail the queen's insistence on one last attempt to avert war. The talks continued until the Armada set sail.[30]

THE ARMADA OF 1588

The story of the Spanish Armada has been brilliantly told and does not need repeating here. Some points, however, require emphasis. First, the scale of the action was enormous. On the vessels themselves were 19,000 troops, almost all Spanish, and a further 27,000 veterans were readied by Parma for transporting to England. The fleet that the duke of Medina Sidonia led out of Corunna, after a refit necessitated by storms off Finisterre, consisted of around 130 ships with the combined fire-power of 360 guns. Parma commanded a further 81 vessels and 194 transport barges. The campaign cost 45,000 ducats a day and tied down all the military and naval resources of the Iberian peninsula, gravely affecting the defence of other parts of the Spanish monarchy. All that stood between England and conquest was the navy.[31] The situation was even more dangerous than the Privy Council realised, since they misread Spanish intentions and gathered troops at Tilbury in Essex. In fact, Medina Sidonia intended to land his formidable forces in Kent, establishing a base for Parma's men before storming to London.

Second, the contest was not as unequal as is often assumed. Largely constructed in the 1570s, the navy's 'race-built' vessels were fast, heavily armed and weatherly. They were more manoeuvrable than anything in the Spanish fleet, which never managed to implement its planned tactic of grappling and boarding them.[32] The English on board, unlike the Spanish, were all skilled seamen and even the aristocrats in command, men like Lord Admiral Howard of Effingham and Lord Henry Seymour who led the eastern squadron, had some sailing experience and joined in the crew's labours. The royal navy was backed up by 143 vessels, some of them fighting ships equipped for privateering. The best of the fleet was superb, but it was an alarmingly small force to hold off the massive, crescent-shaped formation coming up the Channel.

Third, English strategy was superior to the over-ambitious plan imposed by Philip II. If English land forces were in the wrong place, the navy was not, for Sir Francis Drake correctly divined Spanish intentions. The English ships had failed in their first efforts to engage the Armada in Spanish waters and returned to Plymouth. Over a hundred ships assembled in the Sound on 30 July, and as soon as the tide permitted they warped out of harbour and under cover of darkness skilfully tacked across the face of the oncoming Armada and round its southern tip. Now advantageously placed upwind of their opponents, they could continually harass the Spanish formation as it sailed eastwards. Parma could not move his men safely across to Kent until the Armada had cleared the Channel of English warships. He also faced a threat from Dutch vessels that were attempting to blockade him in and were ready to fire on his unarmed barges if they put to sea. Provided the English navy remained capable of fighting, Parma's forces would never embark.[33] In a considerable feat of leadership, Medina Sidonia brought most of his great fleet relatively unscathed into Calais roads, but the English still controlled the Channel.

Fourth, the English won the key battle. In the commemorations of 1988, some fashionably revisionist writers asserted that the weather defeated the Armada, a view at first sight supported by the Dutch medal that proclaimed 'God blew and they were scattered'.[34] However, the argument confuses the military outcome of the campaign with the damage done to Spanish vessels. On the night of 7 August, eight fire ships bore down on the galleons clustered together off Calais. The English intended to create confusion and panic, and before the burning vessels most Spanish captains cut their anchors and fled. 'At a stroke the Armada had been transformed from a cohesive and still formidable fighting force to a scattered gaggle of panic-stricken ships.' They managed to regroup, but the following day off Gravelines, the English came within range and the battle lasted nine hours. Morale on the Armada was broken and Medina Sidonia hanged a captain who ignored his orders to continue fighting: in all twenty officers were arrested. Some leading commanders openly deplored his leadership of the campaign and surrender was even considered, albeit briefly. Yet although the Armada sustained great damage, so far only six major vessels had been lost. Much worse was to come on the way home, for more than thirty ships, already weakened by English artillery, went down off the west coasts of Scotland and Ireland in severe summer storms. Nevertheless, as the experienced admiral of the Biscayan squadron observed in his campaign journal, the whole venture was lost at the moment in August when they were forced away from the banks of Flanders and prevented from linking up with Parma.[35] This was not luck, or a draw, but an outstanding English naval victory.

AFTER THE ARMADA

The years that followed, including the failure of the incoherent English counter-attack, the 'Portugal expedition' of 1589, are usually seen as a dreary aftermath leading to the treaty of London in 1604. Again, this view wrongly assumes that conflict between England and Spain was bilateral. In fact Elizabeth was faced with the opening of two new major theatres of war, in France and Ireland. She had little choice but to commit her forces to both, to fight off threats less dramatic than the Armada but almost equally menacing. In August 1589, the assassination of Henry III led Philip II to intervene directly in France, instead of merely funding the Catholic League. Spanish control of the French coastline posed an intolerable threat, quite apart from the strong feelings of solidarity felt by many English Protestants for their Huguenot brethren. For five years English troops and English money supported the Huguenot Henry of Navarre, whose accession to the French throne was determinedly contested by Spain. The burdens were heavy, since out of an annual royal revenue of around £300,000, the campaigns in Brittany, Normandy and Picardy cost around £290,000 – nearly one fifth of the queen's total income during the years of her involvement in France.[36]

In July 1593 Henry IV converted to Catholicism, removing the Catholic League's *raison d'etre*, and by 1594 the Spanish threat was receding. However, as English troops withdrew from France another war sprang up in Ireland. Troubles there were endemic and a revolt broke out in Ulster in 1593–94. The situation worsened in 1595 when Hugh O'Neill, earl of Tyrone and the greatest magnate in the north of Ireland, joined the rebels. Philip II had considered a descent on Ireland in 1586–87, as part of his strategic review, since it was a fixed conviction of Spanish military thinking that an assault force operating from an established Irish base would divert English troops away from the Low Countries.

Tyrone's defection could not have come at a worse time, since it coincided with the revival of Spanish naval strength. The disaster of 1588 left Philip with an abiding thirst for revenge, to save his honour in the eyes of Europe. The loss of so many vessels did terrible damage, not least to Spanish morale, but did not permanently destroy Spain's capacity to wage war at sea. Rapidly the fleet was rebuilt on more modern lines, with twelve new galleons named 'the Apostles' planned to form the core of a permanent Atlantic strike-force. Meanwhile, between 1589 and 1591, English privateers made very profitable assaults on Spanish merchant shipping, taking 299 recorded prizes. Ironically, both the defeat of the Armada and these later English successes convinced the king that he must focus his rebuilt forces on the Atlantic, not as previously the Mediterranean.[37]

In July 1595 a small fleet of Spanish galleys based at Blavet in Brittany appeared off the Cornish coast and burned Penzance, Mousehole and Newlyn in a brief raid.[38] The shock was palpable since the English had come to think their shores were inviolable. In response Drake and Hawkins sailed for Panama in August 1595, intending to cut the vital route by which Peruvian silver crossed the Isthmus prior to shipment for Spain. The plan was too ambitious and failed, though it further fuelled Philip's anger. However, as the expedition limped home in spring 1596, having lost both its leaders, information was coming in from the network of intelligencers maintained by English funds that another great fleet was gathering in Spain. Elizabeth opted for diplomatic action, concluding in May 1596 an offensive and defensive pact offered to her by Henry IV which was further strengthened in October when the Dutch joined, forming a triple alliance against Spain.[39]

Nevertheless diplomacy alone could not tackle resurgent Spanish sea power. It was thought that the fleet gathering in Lisbon would sail for Ireland the following year, so a pre-emptive strike was planned, following the pattern of Drake's Cadiz raid of 1587. However, the young earl of Essex, who commanded along with Lord Admiral Howard, had grander aims. He hoped not merely to attack Cadiz, but to garrison it and hold it as 'a continual diversion … a thorn sticking in his foot' that would permanently impede Philip II.[40] The expedition was reinforced with 2000 Dutch soldiers under Count Louis Gunther of Nassau. Essex's capture of Cadiz was a major victory, although he bungled the opportunity of taking the Indies ships gathering in the bay with their rich cargoes. Yet his aim to create a base was too unrealistic to succeed. Cadiz might be held for two weeks, but not much more. The speed and surprise of the attack caught Medina Sidonia unawares, but as Captain-General of Andalusia he was energetically rallying troops for an assault all the time Cadiz was in English hands. Howard refused to hold the town without an explicit commission or instruction from the queen, which they did not possess. As they sailed away, the bitter disagreement between the two commanders weakened the impact of their victory, since Essex always insisted he was forced to abandon Cadiz.[41]

On the Spanish side Cadiz was seen as a further humiliation, a disaster that 'increased the strength and morale of the enemy and weakened that of Your Majesty'.[42] The great writer Cervantes, a veteran of Lepanto, composed a bitter sonnet deploring Spain's impotence. The blow was all the more unexpected since in May 1596 the Spanish court was celebrating the death of Drake in the West Indies, assuming it meant the end of English raiding. The Adelantado of Castile, Martin de Padilla, who in 1589 had defended the mouth of the Tagus against the English fleet, addressed a scathing memorandum to the king. Current policy would never end the war: Spain must make a final, resolute attack to settle the score. Honour regained, Philip could enter negotiations to ensure that Spain achieved her ends – Elizabeth's withdrawal of support for the Dutch.[43]

Padilla was instructed to gather an Atlantic task force, an order which he set about fulfilling with impressive efficiency. Initially Philip considered that the Adelantado should land in Cork or Baltimore and make contact with the Irish rebels, but if that proved too difficult against the autumn storms, he should land at Milford Haven and summon support from Welsh Catholics. Working from Lisbon, Padilla was unable to collect his ships together speedily enough and on 21 October 1596 the king decided it was too late to sail for Ireland. Writing from the Escorial, Philip instructed Padilla to head for Brittany and take Brest, the deep-water port that Spanish forces had briefly held until they were driven out in 1594 by English troops.[44]

The king aimed to capitalise on the surprise Spanish capture of Calais in March 1596 by Archduke Albert and his Flemish forces. 'England may not endure this town to be Spanish' wrote Burghley grimly to his son Robert. In October Philip instructed Albert to prepare Calais for an attack on England the following year, spring 1597. If Spanish forces also took Brest they would command the whole southern shore of the Channel. Spain was exhausted, but so was England, where successive harvests had failed since 1594. Moreover Philip scored a tactical success in ensuring the continuation of the Irish struggle, for in May 1596 just as Tyrone was contemplating making peace, Spanish envoys arrived promising aid and much-needed munitions. He decided to fight on.[45] The king had reasonable grounds for hoping that Elizabeth would negotiate once she was faced with revived revolt in Ireland and Spanish galleons ranging her shores from the Lizard to Dover.

It was not to be. After Padilla faced down a near-mutiny by his men, the fleet of around a hundred vessels and 15,000 soldiers sailed for Corunna on 24 October 1596. An autumn storm struck four days later off Finisterre, with the loss of 32 ships and 2000 men. Four royal galleons including the largest, the 900-ton *Santiago* which was carrying the troops' wages, went to the bottom with few survivors.[46] In November 1596 the combined disasters of the English sack of Cadiz and the loss of Padilla's fleet forced Philip to renege on his creditors, postponing payments on his debts for a year. However, over the winter and spring of 1597 the Adelantado refurbished his surviving vessels and gathered more men, arousing renewed English alarm. Essex was anxious to repeat his exploits at Cadiz and Burghley supported another pre-emptive strike. 'I hope God will prosper the purpose' he wrote to Essex.[47] In June 1597 the queen gave orders for an assault on Padilla's fleet gathering at Ferrol. Essex set out in July but was blown too far out to sea, and in August decided to make for the Azores with hopes of intercepting the Spanish plate fleet. This was dangerously irresponsible since it left the Channel open to Padilla's ships, which were untouched.

In spring 1597 Philip II had considered a plan to land troops from the army of Flanders in northern England, where he was assured that most of the population was militantly Catholic. When the Council of War vetoed the idea the king turned back to his previous designs. He asked Padilla to consider either Brest or Milford Haven as targets, but again changed his strategy at the last minute: instead they were to seize Falmouth. The imposing fleet, with 136 vessels and over ten thousand men sailed from Ferrol but bad weather forced them back into Corunna. When they set out again they came almost in sight of the Lizard but were scattered by storms, almost exactly a year after the previous disaster.[48]

The campaigns of 1596 and 1597 were described by R.B. Wernham in the final volume of his three-decker study of Elizabethan foreign policy.[49]

His title, *The Return of the Armadas*, has entered historians' vocabulary but is profoundly misleading. Writing long after retirement, Wernham relied exclusively on English sources and gave undue prominence to panicky rumours about Spanish intentions. His repeated use of the word 'armada' (in Spanish, simply 'fleet') confused readers with its echoes of 1588. It ignored the fact that the *Gran Armada* (properly styled) was planned as only one part of a unique combined operation with Parma's army. After 1588 Philip II abandoned his project to conquer England, and infantry forces were never again mustered across the Channel. His aim after July 1596 was to revenge Cadiz by a similarly powerful raid on England or Ireland. It would also demonstrate that revived Spanish naval power posed a formidable threat in English home waters. He would force negotiations, either by raising insurrection among Elizabeth's Catholic subjects or by direct Spanish involvement in the Irish rebellion. Padilla's fleets of 1596 and 1597 were substantial, fully comparable to the English fleet that sacked Cadiz in June 1596, but far inferior to the total Spanish forces of 1588.

Moreover, the story of these two lesser 'armadas' when reconstructed from Spanish sources indicates that the Privy Council was woefully ill-informed about the enemy's intentions. At best they received news of ships and men gathering in various harbours – Lisbon, Corunna, Ferrol – or learned of recent events in Spain from sailors captured by English vessels. At worst the Privy Council was misled by distant sightings at sea that frequently turned out to be fleets of Hanseatic or Dutch merchant ships, or even complete flights of fancy. In 1596 Sir Robert Cecil and his father Lord Burghley compiled a list of intelligences required, but neither they nor Essex, who was also gathering European news, came anywhere near penetrating Spanish intentions. There was never an English 'mole' with accurate information about plans discussed in the Spanish Council of State or Council of War, and in any case Philip II frequently imposed fresh orders at the last moment. The English were forced to resort to guesswork. The tense debate on 3 November 1596 revealed almost as many views as there were privy councillors present. There was no consensus on where Padilla's men might land, whether they planned incursion or invasion, or what strategy would best counter the threat. The whole discussion was unnecessary, since unknown to the Privy Council Padilla's fleet had been scattered at sea more than a week earlier. [50]

The same points can be made about the so-called 'third armada' of 1599. On his accession in August 1598, the twenty-year-old Philip III was unrealistically aggressive, partly because he assumed that the 1598 treaty of Vervins, releasing Spanish troops from France, would permit new campaigns against the English and the Dutch. He personally backed a plan to revive the strategy of 1588, seizing a bridgehead in England before transporting the army of Flanders across the Channel. This was a fantasy: the young king soon learned that his resources would not even permit him to provide adequate support for his regular troops in the Low Countries. Nevertheless he continued to make belligerent noises.[51]

The death of Burghley in August 1598 forced Sir Robert Cecil to take responsibility for England's preparedness in spring 1599. News of ships gathering in Spanish harbours struck him as 'great and suspicious', and by July, as rumours grew of an impending invasion, soldiers were mobilised in the maritime counties. In August there were further rumours that Spanish troops had landed on the Isle of Wight and that a great fleet lay off Brest, waiting to attack. The panic seems to have escalated spontaneously into one of those 'great fears' which from time to time plagued all early-modern societies. The English military and naval mobilisation approached the scale of 1588 itself, with plans to muster over 40,000 horse and foot. As the navy was in home waters, unlike 1597, ships were set to patrol the mouths of the Thames and the Medway; guard the Channel at Dover; patrol between Scilly and Ushant; and stand off the Irish coast.[52]

By 20 August 1599 nothing had happened and no armada had been sighted. Elizabeth, irritated by the panic as well as by the heavy costs incurred, ordered a gradual stand-down despite some opposition from the Privy Council. All the evidence suggests that Cecil, for the first time facing an emergency on his own, over-reacted out of excessive caution. Essex was away in Ireland, leading the largest expeditionary force the queen had ever sent there, so responsibility for England's safety rested squarely on the secretary. He had not entirely believed the reports of Spanish strength but thought them too risky to ignore. 'I have given way to these Preparations ... preferring therein the ways of safety, before any matter of charge.' He asked Sir Henry Neville in France if he could find a French merchant to live in Spain and send better intelligence, in return for generous pay. Cecil was beginning to appreciate the inadequacies of the Privy Council's information, a learning process accelerated by some scalding comments from Elizabeth a few days later.[53]

What had actually happened? Philip III considered an assault on England but did nothing to prepare for it. Between January and autumn 1599, he was completely taken up with his journey to Valencia to meet his new bride Margarita of Austria. Astonishingly, the Council of War met sixty-eight times during the progress, to plan Spanish defences against a rumoured English invasion fleet and to discuss the king's views on policy towards England and Ireland, but there was no concerted strategy.[54] Spain was suffering from an acute shortage of money, soldiers and mariners, but in spring, as usual, Padilla set about gathering such naval forces as he could muster, in case he was ordered out into the Atlantic. He left Ferrol in August, after hearing news of a hostile descent on Las Palmas in the Canaries. His quarry was the Dutch admiral Pieter van der Does, whose forces were responsible for sacking the city. By the time the Adelantado's fleet was at sea the Dutch had abandoned the Canaries, so he was unable to find their ships. They achieved little more, wandering across to equatorial San Tomé (where van der Does died of fever) before turning for home. The contemporary Spanish chronicler Cabrera de Cordoba heard rumours in Madrid that the enemy fleet boasted of sending a ransom from Las Palmas back to Elizabeth, and it may be, as Cabrera de Cordoba obliquely implied, that some English privateering ships joined in the Dutch attack. No royal fleet sailed from England in 1599, so the Spanish account again illustrates the lack of accurate information plaguing both sides.[55] The 'third armada' of 1599 was a myth, born of rumours and misleading reports. It was entirely in keeping with this campaign of mirrors that the councillors riding to Valencia feared that they might be facing another English descent on Spain.

Philip III made a last effort in September 1601, sending a small fleet of 33 ships with over 4000 men to Ireland. The aim was to establish a base from which to harass England, but as the experienced Padilla pointed out, the task force was far too small for the purpose. Contrary winds forced it to land at Kinsale in the south, instead of close to Tyrone's strongholds in the north, and despite the arrival of reinforcements from Spain the English forces under Lord Mountjoy quickly compelled their enemy to surrender.[56]

CONCLUSION

Philip III made peace with England in 1604. He was encouraged by his sister Isabella and her husband the Archduke Albert, presiding together over their splendid court in Brussels. In his last months Philip II had granted the couple a joint suzerainty over the ten Southern Netherlands provinces still held by Spain. By 1604, France was regaining strength and stability under the leadership of Henry IV and his brilliant treasurer Sully. Europe was returning to the stasis of the mid-sixteenth century, with France and Spain warily keeping the peace of Vervins between them, and the conflict in the Low Countries steadily winding down.

By 1604, Elizabeth was dead and James VI of Scotland had succeeded peacefully to her throne. Crucially, the treaty of London was made possible not merely by Spanish willingness to treat, but by the final defeat and surrender of Tyrone in March 1603, which removed the long English nightmare of a Spanish base in rebel territory. The years of crisis in Anglo-Spanish relations were over. After the conclusion of negotiations in August 1604, James feasted the Spanish envoy, the constable of Castile, and showered him with gifts. A myriad of lesser problems remained unsolved, not least the question of continuing English encroachments in the New World, but until the outbreak of the Thirty Years War in 1618, the three Western monarchies of France, Spain and England were once again intent on handling the frictions of mutual co-existence by diplomacy, not force of arms.

NOTES

1. E. Lodge (ed.), *Illustrations of English History* (2nd edn, 1838) ii, p. 373.
2. 'The distresses of the Commonwealth', PRO, SP12/1/7; BL, Cotton MS, Vespasian C.vii, fo. 110, quoted in Stephen Alford, *The Early Elizabethan Polity* (Cambridge, 1998), p. 72.
3. Philip II to Guzman de Silva, 4 February 1568, *CSP. Sp. Eliz.* xii, p. 3.
4. M. Rodriguez-Salgado provides an outstanding critique of 'inevitabilism' in 'Paz ruidosa, guerra sorda. Las relaciones de Felipe II e Inglaterra', *La Monarquia de Felipe II a Debate* (Sociedad Estatal para la Conmemoracion de los Centenarios de Felipe II y Carlos V, Madrid, 2000). Manuel Fernandez Alvarez, 'Felipe II e Isabel de Inglaterra (una paz imposible)', *Revista de Historia Naval*, 23 (1988), pp. 19–35. Garrett Mattingly, *The Defeat of the Spanish Armada* (1962), pp. 41, 426; R. B. Wernham, *The Making of Elizabethan Foreign Policy 1558–1603* (1980), p. 23.
5. Colin Martin and Geoffrey Parker, *The Spanish Armada* (2nd edn, Manchester, 1999), p. 57; David Loades, *England's Maritime Empire* (Harlow, 2000), pp. 79–137.
6. My italics. Philip Edwards, *The Making of the Modern English State, 1460–1660* (2001), p. 242.
7. Geoffrey Parker, *The Grand Strategy of Philip II* (1998), pp. 75, 93, 106, and his Prothero Lecture, 'The place of Tudor England in the messianic vision of Philip II of Spain', *Transactions of the Royal Historical Society*, 6th series, 12 (2002), pp. 167–223.
8. Parker, *Grand Strategy*, pp. 77–80, 179.
9. In 1559, writing from the Low Countries, Philip considered ordering a fleet to be prepared to carry men to England, but the context of his inconsistent, stream-of-consciousness letter was his own imminent voyage to Spain. It is possible that he briefly contemplated arriving in London to overawe Elizabeth. *CSP. Sp. Eliz.* i, pp. 41–2. For 1571 see below pp. 11–12: for 1574, Magdalena Pi Corrales, *Espana y las potencias nordicas: 'La Otra Invencible' 1574* (Madrid, 1983).
10. I. A. A. Thompson, *War and Government in Habsburg Spain 1560–1620* (1976), pp. 13–14, 168.

11. Geoffrey Parker, 'David or Goliath: Philip II and his world', in Richard L. Kagan and Geoffrey Parker (eds), *Spain, Europe and the Atlantic World: Essays in Honour of John H. Elliott* (Cambridge, 1995), pp. 245–66.

12. J. Calvar Gross, J. I. Gonzalez-Aller, M. de Duenas Fontan, Maria del Campo Merida Valverde (eds), *La Batalla del Mar Oceano*, i (*Genesis de la empresa de Inglaterra de 1588, 28 Junio 1568–30 Enero 1586*) (Madrid, 1988), p. 497.

13. My italics: Rodriguez-Salgado 'Paz ruidosa', p. 79

14. G. D. Ramsay, *The Queen's Merchants and the Revolt of the Netherlands* (Manchester, 1986), pp. 86–102. Parker, *Grand Strategy*, p. 156 reinstates the significance of the attack on Hawkins.

15. The argument that Ridolfi was an agent was first put forward by Francis Edwards, *The Marvellous Chance* (1968). It is supported by Parker, 'Place of Tudor England'.

16. R. B. Wernham, *Before the Armada: The Growth of English Foreign Policy 1485–1588*, (1966), p. 319.

17. Ibid., p. 321. J. M. B. C. Baron Kervin de Lettenhove (ed.), *Relations Politiques des Pays-Bas et de L'Angleterre sous le règne de Philippe II* (11 vols, Brussels, 1882–1900) vi, p. 421.

18. L. P. Gachard (ed.), *Correspondance de Philippe II sur les Affaires des Pays Bas* (5 vols, Brussels 1848–79), ii, p. 320. Lettenhove, *Relations Politiques*, vi, pp. 719–37.

19. Parker, *Grand Strategy*, p. 164. It is however incorrect to suggest that Philip also closed the English seminary at Douai; it was not closed until 1578, and for other reasons.

20. Leah S. Marcus, Janel Mueller and Mary Beth Rose (eds), *Elizabeth I: Collected Works* (Chicago, 2000), pp. 310–11; Mary Hill Cole, *The Portable Queen: Elizabeth I and the Politics of Ceremony* (Amherst, MA. 1999), pp. 110, 158.

21. October 1575, PRO, SP12/105/123; Wernham, *Before the Armada*, p. 328 wrongly dates this incident to 1574, but the fleet expected from Spain that year was cancelled.

22. This and most of what follows is taken from Croft, 'English Commerce with Spain and the Armada War, 1558–1603', in M. J. Rodriguez-Salgado and Simon Adams (eds), *England, Spain and the Gran Armada* (Edinburgh, 1991), pp. 236–63.

23. P. Croft, 'Trading with the Enemy', *HJ*, 32 (1989), pp. 281–302.

24. Croft, 'English Commerce'.

25. Carlos Gomez-Centurion Jimenez, *Felipe II, La Empresa de Inglaterra y el Comercio Septentrional (1566–1609)* (Madrid, 1988).

26. Harry Kelsey, *Francis Drake: the Queen's Pirate* (1998), pp. 82–111; Mendoza to Philip II, 9 January 1581, Archivo General de Simancas, Estado leg. 835 fo. 164, 'haviendo sodo robado'.

27. T. E. Hartley (ed.), *Proceedings in the Parliaments of Elizabeth I, vol. 3, 1593–1603* (1995). pp. 275–6; Croft, 'English Commerce'.

28. Hartley, *Proceedings*, p. 279; Wallace MacCaffrey, *Queen Elizabeth and the Making of Policy, 1572–88* (Princeton, 1981), pp. 194–5; John Cummins, *Francis Drake* (1995), pp. 135–160; Rodriguez-Salgado, 'Paz ruidosa', p. 78.

29. Croft, 'English Commerce', p. 241; The survey (BL, Lansdowne MS 41, arts. 37–43) refutes the claim made by Loades, *England's Maritime Empire*, p. 101, that by the 1580s Anglo-Spanish trade had sunk to 'statistical insignificance'.

30. Parker, *Grand Strategy*, pp. 179–203; M. J. Rodriguez-Salgado, 'The Anglo-Spanish War: the final episode in the Wars of the Roses?' *England, Spain and the Gran Armada*, pp. 1–44, 96.

31. Martin and Parker, *Spanish Armada*, pp. 15–27, 104, 112, 261–65. NB: all dates in their account are New Style; Parker, *Grand Strategy*, pp. 198, 235–45.
32. N. A. M. Rodger, *The Safeguard of the Sea* (1997), pp. 214–20, and for an excellent brief account of the action in the Channel, pp. 254–71.
33. Kelsey, *Drake*, pp. 300–26.
34. Cf. the view put out in the *National Trust Magazine*, 53, spring 1988. For the most extreme version, Felipe Fernandez-Armesto, *The Spanish Armada* (Oxford, 1988).
35. Martin and Parker, *Spanish Armada*, pp. 175, 180,183, n.17; G. Parker, ' "No se si vinieron estas": dos cartas de Don Alonso Martinez de Leyva con motivo del desastre de la Gran Armada en agosto de 1588', *Revista de Historia Naval*, 79 (2002), pp. 7–16.
36. Susan Doran, *Elizabeth I and Foreign Policy* (2000), p. 69.
37. Thompson, *War and Government*, pp. 192–3; Thompson, 'The Spanish Armada: naval warfare between the Mediterranean and the Atlantic' in *England, Spain and the Gran Armada*, pp. 70–94; K. R. Andrews, *Elizabethan Privateering* (Cambridge, 1964), pp. 124–34. David Goodman, *Spanish Naval Power 1589–1665: Reconstruction and Defeat* (Cambridge, 1997), surveys the rebuilding process.
38. All previous accounts of Spanish strategy in these years have been superceded by the meticulous researches in Spanish archives of Edward S. Tenace, 'Spanish intervention in Brittany and the failure of Philip II's bid for European hegemony, 1589–1598', unpublished University of Illinois PhD dissertation, 1997. C. Fernandez Douro, *Armada Espanola desde la Union de los Reinos de Castilla y de Aragon*, iii (Madrid, 1897), pp. 92–3.
39. Wallace MacCaffrey, *Elizabeth I: War and Politics 1588–1603* (Princeton, 1992), pp. 202–3.
40. Essex to the Privy Council, 13 June 1596, PRO, SP12/259/12; Paul Hammer, *The Polarisation of Elizabethan Politics: The Political Career of Robert Devereux, 2nd Earl of Essex, 1585–97* (Cambridge, 1999), pp. 249–63, 361–74.
41. Peter Pierson, *Commander of the Armada: the Seventh Duke of Medina Sidonia* (1989), pp. 202–10; Hammer, *Essex*, pp. 251–2.
42. Pierson, *Commander*, p. 208.
43. 'Memorial de Don Martin de Padilla conde de Sancta Gadea', AGS Estado leg. 177 partly quoted in Henry Kamen, *Philip of Spain* (1997), pp. 307–8.
44. 21 October and 22 October 1596, Philip II to the Conde de Santa Gadea (Padilla), AGS Estado leg. 176, and AGS Estado 434 fo. 59, 22 October 1596, quoted in Tenace 'Spanish intervention', pp. 397–401. Padilla opposed the new instructions, pointing to the dangers of navigating along the Breton coast.
45. Thomas Wright, *Queen Elizabeth and her Times* (2 vols, 1838), ii, pp. 459–60; Philip II to Albert, AGS Estado 2223 fo. 114, 5 October 1596, quoted in Tenace, 'Spanish intervention', p. 398; Hiram Morgan, *Tyrone's Rebellion* (1993), pp. 206–10.
46. 'Relacion del viaje del Adelantado', October 1597, PRO, SP94/5/23; Kamen, *Philip*, p. 308; Fernandez Douro, *Armada Espanola*, iii, pp. 129–31.
47. PRO, SP 12/263/74.
48. Consulta of 9 July 1597, AGS Estado leg. 2855. Tenace, 'Spanish intervention', pp. 416–24; Fernandez Douro, *Armada Espanola*, iii, pp. 162–6.
49. R. B. Wernham, *The Return of the Armadas: The Last Years of the Elizabethan War against Spain 1595–1603* (Oxford, 1994).
50. Holograph by Cecil with last line by Burghley (?1596), PRO, SP 94/5/166; Wernham, *Return of the Armadas*, pp. 136–9.

51. Paul C. Allen, *Philip III and the Pax Hispanica* (2000), pp. 18–24.

52. Wernham, *Return of the Armadas*, pp. 264–7.

53. Edmund Sawyer (ed.), *Winwood's Memorials* (3 vols, 1725), i, pp. 91, 97.

54. Allen, *Philip III*, pp. 20–1.

55. Wernham, *Return of the Armadas*, pp. 251–62; Fernandez Douro, *Armada Espanola*, iii, pp. 210–1; Cabrera de Cordoba, *Relaciones de las Cosas Sucedidas en la Corte de Espana desde 1599 hasta 1614* (reprinted Salamanca 1997), pp. 27–8, 35–41; Allen, *Philip III*, p. 27 has been misled by Cabrera de Cordoba into assuming that the whole fleet was English.

56. Allen, *Philip III*, pp. 72–6.

8

LOVING AND AFFECTIONATE COUSINS? THE RELATIONSHIP BETWEEN ELIZABETH I AND JAMES VI OF SCOTLAND 1586–1603

Susan Doran

The starting point for this essay is the treaty of Berwick concluded between Queen Elizabeth of England and James VI of Scotland on 5 July 1586, a treaty that is usually seen as marking a watershed in Anglo-Scottish relations. With its signature, it appears, the backdoor to England was securely locked, the 'Auld Alliance' of Scotland and France finally shattered, the centuries of hostility and warfare between the two British kingdoms consigned to history, and the cross-border tensions that had marred relations since the fall of Regent Morton in 1579 largely eliminated. For this reason, most text books or surveys of sixteenth-century English foreign policy (including my own) devote little or no space, to Anglo-Scottish relations after 1586 or at best 1587.[1] Events in Scotland seem largely to drop out of English foreign policy considerations, and the activities of James VI are assumed to have had little impact within England.

It might be argued that the close family relationship between Elizabeth I and James VI was of paramount importance in creating and maintaining this new state of peace and harmony. Was it not because James realised that his future lay with the English succession that he signed the treaty of Berwick and developed the entente? After all, he had wanted a clause recognising his title to be included in the treaty, and required at the very least a duchy in England as the price for his friendship.[2] Although guarantees about the succession were not in fact included within the terms of Berwick, James did secure a letter from the queen in which she promised not to do anything that might damage his claim. So did he not adhere to the amity in the hope that Elizabeth might recognise his title to the succession and that her subjects might find a close ally an acceptable monarch, even though he was a foreigner?[3] For her part, was not the usually tight-fisted Elizabeth prepared to buy James off with pensions and elusive promises concerning the succession in order to stop him from independently pursuing his dynastic ambitions?

The negotiations that led to Berwick in fact owed little to the family relationship between the two monarchs.[4] Elizabeth's motive was to ensure James's good will at a time when relations with Spain and the Guises in France appeared so threatening in order to prevent Scotland from being used as a base to launch an invasion of England. Furthermore, when the English government initiated discussions for an Anglo-Scottish alliance in 1584, it hoped and intended that the projected treaty should be just one chain in a broad international, defensive, Protestant league. In April 1585 Edward Wotton was sent to Scotland to propose an alliance which would include not only James but other Protestant princes, and to tell James that Elizabeth considered 'it very meet and expedient that both we ourselves as also the rest of the Princes that make profession of the religion we profess, should join and unite ourselves together for the common defence thereof'.[5] The Scottish supporters of the alliance also hoped it might be a step towards a wider Protestant league. When the then Scottish Secretary, Sir John Maitland of Thirlestane, expressed his wish in June 1585 to promote an amity with England against the 'ante Christian confederacy', believed to have been forged between France and Spain in the treaty of Joinville, he also recommended that Elizabeth call a meeting of continental Protestant rulers 'to concert common measures against the common enemy'. For this reason Francophile and Catholic Scots were hostile to the treaty no matter that it might advance their king's claims to the English throne. It was only because England's diplomatic drive in Scandinavia and North Germany failed at the first hurdle that the league was limited to the two powers. Neither monarch was entirely satisfied with this outcome, however, and in 1589 James with Elizabeth's approval and financial support tried to broaden the alliance so that it would comprehend his brother-in-law, the king of Denmark and a number of German Lutheran princes, but again with no success.[6]

Once the treaty of Berwick was signed, it is certainly true that both monarchs used the language of affection and kinship as a rhetorical device to emphasise obligations. James, in particular, exploited their family relationship in attempts to squeeze concessions from Elizabeth, while she and her ministers used every opportunity to remind James that he needed her affection and support if he were eventually to inherit the English throne. James drew attention to their blood tie and Elizabeth's role as his godparent by addressing her (at least until 1588) as 'my loving mother' or 'dearest mother' and referring to himself as 'your natural son' and 'most loving devoted brother and son'.[7] On her side, Elizabeth always preferred the more conventional address between monarchs, namely 'sister and cousin', sometimes prefixed by 'loving', sometimes affectionated', sometimes 'faithful' or 'assured'.[8] Nonetheless, in the main body of her letters, she did several times remind James that she had been his godmother and had acted as his surrogate mother in protecting and defending him during his minority and that he consequently owed her thanks, respect and obedience.[9] The tone of her letters has been described as 'curiously maternal and tutorial', as she frequently adopted the tone of a world-weary and exasperated parent forced to offer a wayward child advice and issue him reprimands.[10]

Rhetoric apart and despite their ties of kinship and religion, deep seams of mutual suspicion and acrimony lay just below the surface of the two monarchs' professions of loving friendship. Far from feeling it safe to put Scotland on the back burner of international concerns, Elizabeth had to expend money she could ill afford and invest diplomatic effort into keeping the alliance alive. Men well experienced in Border affairs – such as Thomas Randolph, Robert Bowes and George Nicolson – were based in Scotland as resident ambassadors or accredited agents, and the queen sometimes supplemented them with *ad hoc* embassies to James both to make specific demands of the king and, where possible, to smooth over difficulties between the two monarchs. In addition Elizabeth encouraged informal contacts between the two courts: the earl of Essex was permitted to replace the earl of Leicester (after his death in 1588) as a sympathetic intermediary; Lord Burghley, Francis Walsingham (till his death in 1590) and later Robert Cecil exchanged letters regularly with James's English friend Roger Aston, a gentlemen of James's privy chamber, while both James and the English government used James Hudson, the one-time servant of the Master of Gray, as their agent.[11]

In this essay, I look at the main reasons for the disputes that developed between Elizabeth and James after 1586 and show that, although a few new causes of conflict disturbed Anglo-Scottish relations, most of their disagreements and quarrels arose from the traditional points of friction between the two realms: Scotland's potential to operate as a military base for foreign powers hostile to England; the tendency of English monarchs to run roughshod over the honour of their Scottish counterparts; the inclination of the Scots to interfere in Ireland; and the perennial raids across the border. James's claims to the English succession emerged as a major problem only after 1596, but this issue too was hardly new as a cause of tension in Anglo-Scottish relations. At the same time, by examining the methods used by Elizabeth and James to contain or resolve their disputes, the essay is intended to throw light on the conduct of foreign policy, in particular the personal nature of diplomacy.

I

The first major flare-up between England and Scotland after Berwick concerned James's honour and arose over the execution of Mary Queen of Scots on 8 February 1587. In the months that followed Mary's trial and conviction for treason in October 1586, Elizabeth and her advisers failed to take sufficient notice of James's petitions to secure his mother's pardon and convinced themselves that James would 'wink at' his mother's execution. They were mistaken. According to Maitland, James took Mary's death 'deeply in heart as a matter greatly concerning him both in honour and other ways'.[12] The king believed that his personal honour was touched not only because he had failed as a son to protect his mother, but also because Elizabeth had treated him as a man of little account by ignoring his strong entreaties on Mary's behalf. Furthermore, Elizabeth's claim to have jurisdiction over the Scottish queen undermined James's rights and status as king of Scotland. James's subjects were equally outraged at Mary's death and loudly called for revenge, demanding an end to the English alliance and some form of military retaliation against Elizabeth. The result was an immediate diplomatic breach between the two realms, disturbances on the border, and international uncertainty about the future of the Anglo-Scottish league.[13] During the last week of February and throughout March 1588, reports reached the English government that the Scots were planning raids over the border as reprisals and that only the weather and time of the year were stopping them from launching a major incursion into England.[14] It was also heard in England that James 'giveth ear to foreign nations', a rumour that was not without foundation, as the king had indeed made overtures to France for an alliance against England.[15] For nearly a year diplomatic intercourse was suspended; James refused to admit Sir Robert Carey,

Elizabeth's special envoy, into Scotland or to communicate directly with either the queen or the English ministers whom he held responsible for the execution. The English government took these threats seriously. To protect the Borders and withstand an invasion, the wardens of the Marches were ordered to muster armed men and be in a state of alert.[16] On the political front, Elizabeth tried to pacify James and keep him in the league by totally disassociating herself from the final decision to execute Mary and by punishing Secretary William Davison severely for issuing the death warrant. She also sent James verbal and written assurances that his title to England would not be imperilled by his mother's treason.[17] The alliance just about held firm, although skirmishes on the border intensified and anxiety about James's intentions continued in England.

During the period of threat from the Spanish Armada the cracks in Anglo-Scottish relations were largely repaired, since James ignored pressure from pro-Spanish nobles in Scotland to provide Philip II with military aid. No doubt Philip's representation of the invasion as a Catholic crusade and his promotion of the Infanta Isabella's spurious claim to the English throne did nothing to warm James to the Spanish cause. Nonetheless, William Ashby, the English envoy dispatched to Edinburgh in June 1588, had been sufficiently alarmed at the presence of pro-Spanish earls at the Scottish court that he had taken the precaution of promising James a larger pension, an English dukedom and recognition of his claim to the succession, promises that were dismissed by Elizabeth as soon as the invasion scare had passed.[18] Although, or perhaps because, Spanish communications with some of the Scottish nobility continued during 1589, Elizabeth continued to look kindly on James, and during his six-month absence from Scotland (October 1589 to May 1590, while he was in Norway and Denmark in order to escort his new bride, Anne of Denmark, back to Scotland) Elizabeth ordered her Border officials to cooperate closely with their opposite numbers and be ready to help the king's council in an emergency, if necessary with arms. Her concern was to prevent the pro-Spanish earls taking advantage of what might be seen as a power vacuum to seize control.[19]

After James's return, however, the Anglo-Scottish entente became increasingly more fragile. In the first place, disputes continually arose between the two courts over issues related to the terms of the treaty and league of friendship. The most important of these concerned the amount and regularity of the pension to be paid to James by Elizabeth.[20] No mention of the pension had been made in the terms of the treaty itself but an

English subsidy had been promised in a separate letter from Elizabeth to James and was viewed in Scotland as an integral part of the league.[21] James believed that he was entitled to at least £4000 per annum, and grew exasperated when Elizabeth insisted that the annual payment should be no more than £3000, and also when she failed to pay up at fixed times. He considered, moreover, that other gifts to him should be treated as extras and not as part of the pension. Thus, he was not impressed when Elizabeth deducted from the pension the £2000 worth of plate sent to him as a wedding gift. He was equally irritated when Elizabeth withheld £500, the sum he had been given in 1590 to pay some of the expenses of a Scottish embassy which was intended to begin a process of mediation for peace between England and Spain.[22] In December 1591 James wrote a personal letter of complaint to Elizabeth which summed up his feelings: it was not only his need for the money that irked him,[23] he explained, but also the dishonour of constantly having to request his dues:

> I weary to be so long time suitor, as one who was not born to be a beggar but to be begged at ... remember, that as I am your kinsman, so am I a true prince. The disdaining of me can be no honour to you ... [24]

In June 1596, James protested that 'that annuity is proper ours', promised in exchange for the lands of his paternal grandparents in England which had not come to him on their death. If Elizabeth were to refuse it, he continued, 'we can think no less than one just point of the break of the league'.[25] Elizabeth, however, denied that James had any claim to English lands. She also thought that James should realise that she was strapped for cash because of the military help she was supplying to defend the Protestant cause in the Netherlands and France, a cause that should be as dear to him as it was to herself. Furthermore, from her perspective, the pension to James was recognition and reward for his good behaviour and not a right to be received regardless. Hence she declared herself unwilling to pay the sum when James appeared to be pursuing policies not in the English interest. When pressed about the pension in the spring of 1598, she justified not having paid it since September 1596 on the grounds of James's 'unkind using' of her, complaining specifically that he had allowed breaches of peace to occur on the Borders and received and sustained rebels against her rule in Ireland.[26] In the event Elizabeth usually paid up, but only after James sent embassies to petition her to meet her commitments. In total Elizabeth supplied him with the not inconsiderable sum of £58,000 between 1586 and 1603.

It was James's independence and refusal to follow the directives of the English government that did most to rock the entente and keep alive the traditional causes of Anglo-Scottish suspicion and discord. A large part of the purpose of the treaty of Berwick had been to lock the Scottish back-door to England, but to many English observers it seemed that the Scottish Catholic lords – principally the earls of Huntly, Crawford, Errol and Angus – and possibly James himself were ready to hand the door-key over to England's enemies. The Elizabethan intelligence gatherers were efficient in uncovering news of Jesuit activities in Scotland and intercepting communications between the Catholic earls and the Spanish governments in Madrid and Brussels. Thus, during 1589 various reports reached England that the earls were sending messages and 'certain instruments' to the Catholic powers, while in 1590 the crew of a Spanish bark which had been captured by the English confessed that they were expecting to carry treasure to the Scottish Catholic lords the following year. During 1592, moreover, rumours of Huntly's involvement in plots with Spain grew more regular if less imprecise.[27] All this information was passed on to James along with exhortations that he take action against these lords. Huntly, however, was a favourite of the king and the English accusations of his complicity in conspiracies with Spain were disregarded.

In the last week of 1592, however, a far more serious piece of evidence against Huntly and his friends came to light. A Catholic courier, named George Kerr, was arrested in Scotland before embarking for the continent, and suspicious looking papers were found in his possession. Amongst them were eight empty sheets of gilded paper (to be known as the 'Spanish blanks'), which had been signed by Huntly, Errol and Angus, together with the seals of arms of each of the three earls, which could be affixed at some future date to the empty sheets. The English government believed that William Crichton, a Scottish Jesuit then resident in Spain, intended to insert on these 'blanks' terms he would negotiate with Philip II for an invasion of Scotland, a belief which on the face of it was confirmed when Kerr admitted to a plot involving the Catholic earls and aimed at helping Spain land troops in Scotland as a preliminary for an invasion attempt on England.[28] This evidence was immediately passed on to James (who had anyway been kept well informed of events by sources in Scotland) in the expectation that he would now be forced to act. Yet, despite strong and persistent pressure from England and the Scottish Kirk, James appeared either too weak to take decisive action against the pro-Spanish forces in his realm or else unwilling to do so. A number of English observers, doubtless somewhat paranoid, suspected that he was allowing Catholics free reign in his realm to cover up his own pro-Spanish and pro-Catholic proclivities, but Elizabeth herself was inclined to think that James lacked the leadership qualities required for the task of strong kingship.

In letter after letter from 1589 until 1594 Elizabeth expostulated with James for not expelling the Jesuits or putting the Catholic earls under restraint.[29] She also dispatched high-level embassies, usually led by peers of the realm, to the Scottish court to make known her feelings. When the earl of Worcester was sent to Edinburgh in June 1590 to deliver to James the Order of the Garter, a ritual which would seal the closeness of their relationship and display to the outside world the amity between the two realms, Elizabeth had also instructed him to extract promises from the king that he would punish the Catholic earls who had participated in the Brig o'Dee revolt against him in 1589.[30] In February 1593 Elizabeth sent an embassy led by Lord Thomas Burgh to Scotland to bolster 'her sundry letters of princely and friendly advice' and to 'solicit and animate' James to arrest the Scottish Catholic earls of Huntly, Errol and Angus who had just been implicated in the 'Spanish blanks' affair, 'lest time bring the danger so far onward'.[31] In December the same year Lord Edward Zouche was sent as an extraordinary ambassador for similar purposes.

James usually promised much but delivered little. Until early 1593 he made no attempt to arrest the Catholic earls. Then, confronted with the 'Spanish blanks' and evidence of their conspiracy with Philip II and the pope, James marched into northern Scotland against Huntley, Errol and Angus, and seized some of their lands. But the earls were not arrested and brought to trial, as Elizabeth wanted. George Kerr, furthermore, somehow escaped from Edinburgh Castle and was never recaptured. In September 1593, it was reported from Berwick that Huntly and his friends still had influence at court and that James inclined himself to 'the papists' faction' too much 'for our good'.[32] In November, by the Act of Oblivion the earls were promised that if they converted to Protestantism they would be immune from prosecution over the 'Spanish blanks', a decision that Elizabeth found unacceptable. In fact, the earls did not take advantage of the act, yet they were still left unmolested.

Historians have offered a range of reasons for James's lack of co-operation. It has been surmised that he may have wanted to maintain the Catholic faction as a useful counterweight against the power of the Kirk and the Protestant earl of Bothwell.[33] Another suggestion has been that he showed 'flagrant leniency' towards the Scottish Catholics, because 'of course James did not want to alarm or offend English Catholics who ought to support his claim to the succession'.[34] More recently James has been credited with recognising that political unity in his realm would be put at risk if he launched an attack on powerful members of the Scottish nobility.[35] While most of these considerations probably influenced him to a greater or lesser extent, James's attempts to shield Huntly and his friends from the English queen and the Scottish Kirk also stemmed from his determination to maintain control over his own affairs. The explanations that he gave to Elizabeth for his non-action (when they were forthcoming) were inevitably somewhat different. In July 1590 he told the English resident ambassador, Robert Bowes, that he had no reason to arrest or punish Huntly and his friends, as he was not convinced that they had done anything wrong after he had pardoned them for their insurrection against him which ended at Brig o'Dee.[36] Although, later on, James accepted the complicity of the three Catholic earls in the affair of the 'Spanish blanks', he explained that he had no resources to march against them and asked Elizabeth to provide the necessary funds. But beyond sending him an instalment of his annuity and promising him two ships, no further English assistance was forthcoming so James came to use that as a justification for Huntly and the other earls remaining at large. By the end of 1593, James excused himself on the grounds that the earls had admitted their Catholicism but denied 'the great crime' of conspiring with Spain. Without confessions or witnesses (Kerr had by then disappeared), he continued, the earls would probably be cleared if the case went to trial.[37]

Until late 1592, Elizabeth had been inclined to be patient, if irritated, at James's non-compliance with her demands that he arrest the Catholic earls. Events on the Continent had been demanding her attention and she wanted to avoid a head to head confrontation with her formal ally. The affair of the 'Spanish blanks', however, convinced her that Huntly, Angus and Errol were directly endangering England's safety. Over the next year, James's failure to bend to Elizabeth's will and her consequent fear that he would turn Scotland into a Catholic base became a still greater problem because of events in Ireland. During 1593 the English government faced revolt from the Maguires of Fermanagh, and in 1594 it feared that a rebellion led by Hugh Roe O'Donnell of Tirconnell and Hugh O'Neill, the earl of Tyrone, was imminent. Elizabeth and Burghley were both alarmed that their policy of creating a Protestant British Isles was disintegrating and that England's security was consequently under threat. On an immediately practical note, moreover, they needed James's co-operation to stop supplies reaching the Ulster chieftains through the west of Scotland.

For these reasons during 1593, and especially 1594, Elizabeth effectively turned her back on the treaty of Berwick and returned to the pre-1586 policy of building up relationships directly with the 'well affected' in Scotland and dabbling in internal Scottish politics. In early 1593, her special ambassador Lord Burgh was instructed to make contact secretly with the 'well-affected' members of the nobility and to organise or encourage an association of Protestant lords and 'other men of good quality and valour' sworn to serve the king against his Catholic enemies. Burgh was chosen for this mission because his ancestral descent from the Scottish House of Atholl was thought to make him acceptable to the duke and earl of Atholl and their friends, who included the earl of Bothwell then in trouble with the Scottish king.[38] Burgh was told to be circumspect and secret in his dealings with the lords so that 'the King and that party may not know that it come from you or the ambassador'.[39] Later that year, Elizabeth instructed Lord Zouche in a similar vein; he was to confer with potential friends of England amongst the Scottish councillors and nobility, and was permitted to secretly 'promise them on our part' reasonable demands for money 'to make their party more strong, than their adversaries'.[40] As a second string to her bow, Elizabeth also allowed Essex to open up lines of communication with Huntly to see if behind-the-scenes diplomacy might possibly bring him into line, but throughout 1593 and 1594, her main diplomatic drive was directed towards the Protestant Anglophile lords.[41]

Part of the same strategy was Elizabeth's underground protection of the maverick earl of Bothwell, who was in James's eyes a 'vile man', a sorcerer and traitor.[42] Bothwell had escaped from prison in Scotland in 1591 and straight away offered his services to the queen. Although Elizabeth did not take him directly under her protection, she did little to stop her English borderers from giving refuge to the earl and his company of armed men, yet as fugitives from justice they should have been immediately arrested and handed over to the Scottish government in accordance with the treaty of Berwick. Once the affair of the 'Spanish blanks' erupted, Elizabeth tried to intercede with James on Bothwell's behalf on the grounds that the earl, who was a Protestant (even though he had been one of the Brig o'Dee faction), could do good service against the Catholic earls.[43] James, however, would not countenance any such idea and demanded Bothwell's arrest. At last in June 1593, in response to James's loud complaints and protests that Englishmen were aiding his rebel, Elizabeth ordered her officers on the Borders to 'give no countenance to the Earl Bothwell nor any of his' and to arrest any Englishman who was known to harbour or entertain him.[44]

By the end of the year, however, Elizabeth was prepared to do a more direct deal with Bothwell. Listening to advice from some of her officials in the north of England that he was the 'fittest instrument' to take up arms against the Catholic earls or to put pressure on James to take military action against them, Elizabeth allowed negotiations to be opened up between Robert Cecil and friends of Bothwell.[45] In these negotiations Elizabeth made it clear that she expected the earl to use his men only against the Catholic earls. Thus Cecil explained that Elizabeth would 'both allow and strengthen them [i.e. Bothwell's men] speedily and assuredly' after they had removed their adversaries, provided that they did nothing to harm James, but on the contrary 'preserving the king's person most preciously'.[46] To her relief, Elizabeth learned that Bothwell was of the same mind and only intended to attack Huntly and the other Catholic earls 'and see what they can do for the driving of them out of the country without ever looking towards the King'.[47] But in March 1594, news leaked to the English court that Bothwell had plans to march on the king's court in Edinburgh. Immediately Elizabeth and Cecil tried to warn the earl off, telling his intermediary that:

whatever you do, persuade these parties so disposed to be well advised of violating their duty by any such enterprise, and to employ themselves against the Earls and their favourers, being from the Court or presence of the king ... [48]

At the same time as Elizabeth was making secret overtures to Protestant Anglophiles in Scotland and duplicitously abetting Bothwell, she also moved away from a diplomacy that had relied on a mixture of blandishments and reprimands. Instead she adopted an altogether more confrontational stance. The velvet gloves were off during the mission of Lord Zouche in January 1594. The envoy's message from Elizabeth to James was uncompromisingly tough, even insulting in places, as when she referred to James as a 'seduced king' and his realm as 'wry-guided'. In no uncertain words, she told James: 'For your own sake play the king and let your subjects see you respect yourself, and neither hide nor suffer danger and dishonour.'[49] Zouche himself, moreover, was an unacceptable envoy to James, who complained that the baron had been one of the judges at the trial of Mary Queen of Scots and was an 'enemy to my title, being Burghley's dependar, who favours the house of Hertford', that is to say the sons of Lady Katherine Grey who had a rival claim to the throne.[50] At the same time, Burghley was ready to send a message to Chancellor

Maitland that in accordance with the 1585 'Act of Association' James's right to the succession would be imperilled if he threatened the queen's estate by conspiring with the Catholic earls; Maitland was to remind James that 'there are sundry competitors in title' who would benefit from his exclusion.[51]

· Despite his concerns about the succession, James did not take these threats lying down. On 13 April 1594 he composed a sharply critical letter to Elizabeth, in which he complained about Bothwell's presence and protection in the north of England.[52] Parodying the wording of her last message, sent via Lord Zouche, James called Elizabeth 'a seduced queen':

> For, to affirm that these things are by your direction or privity, it is so far against all princely honour as I protest I abhor the least thought thereof. And again that so wise and provident a prince having so long and happily governed, should be so sylid [deceived] and condemned by a number of her own subjects, it is hardly to be believed, if I knew it not to be a maxim in the state of princes that we see and hear all with the eyes and ears of others, and if these be deceivers we cannot shun deceit.

Towards the end of the letter James quoted a line from Virgil's *Aeneid* '*flectere si nequeo superos Acheronta movebo*' ('if I cannot prevail upon the gods, I will stir up hell'), an implied threat which was not lost on the recipient. The Scottish envoys charged with delivering this missive were also instructed to demand what amounted to a public apology from the queen for listening to false reports that he himself had intelligence and dealings with Spain.[53] Relations between England and Scotland at this time were so bad that James expressed doubts whether or not the league would survive and he began to make overtures to Henry IV of France, inviting him to the baptism of his new-born son and offering to renew 'that most ancient league'.[54] Elizabeth, too, had doubts as to whether the league could continue in the present adverse circumstances; as Cecil informed Lord Zouche, she holds 'nothing more precious than the keeping of the Amity, which if things be true as your lordship doth advertise, she must needs break'.[55]

In fact, the spring of 1594 proved to be the lowest point in Anglo-Scottish relations, as both monarchs decided to draw back from the brink of a rupture in the league. They each recognised that co-operation was ultimately in their best interests and that neither could afford to provoke the other too far; Elizabeth needed security along the English Borders, while James's hopes for the succession could be fatally damaged if he totally lost the good will of Elizabeth and her ministers. James understood, moreover, that in order to bring the Kirk on his side against Bothwell, he might have to sacrifice Huntly. Additionally, both monarchs began to question the value of their relationship with their respective *protégés*, Bothwell and Huntly, for they were proving unreliable friends as well as the main cause of conflict between the two realms. Elizabeth realised the danger of colluding with Bothwell, after he ignored her instructions and marched with some 600 footmen against the king just outside Leith in April 1594. Not long afterwards, James began to lose confidence in Huntly, suspecting that the earl was conspiring with Bothwell and planning to join with him in an armed rising, not unlike that of Brig o'Dee.

It was James who made the first move to repair relations. In early June 1594 he apologised for his offensive letter of 12 April, claiming – not very convincingly – that Elizabeth had misinterpreted its meaning.[56] Elizabeth immediately responded in a positive fashion: she accepted James's invitation to act as god-mother to his first-born son, Prince Henry, 'beholding my luck so fortunate as to be the baptizer of both father and son', and made arrangements for the earl of Cumberland to attend the boy's baptism at the end of August with a 'a cupboard richly wrought' as a 'liberal' gift.[57] She also agreed to a renewal of the pension, including arrears, and on 22 June released £4000 to be sent to James.[58] Shortly afterwards, James proclaimed the Catholic earls traitors, ordered the forfeiture of their lands and began to make moves to expel them from his realm.[59] At the baptism of his son, James treated Elizabeth's representatives with great honour; he delayed the ceremony to allow the 5th earl of Sussex (who had to replace the sick earl of Cumberland) to arrive in time at Stirling Castle, and gave him pride of place in the church service and festivities afterwards. Sussex carried the young prince in his arms from the royal chamber to the Chapel Royal, accompanied by Robert Bowes the resident ambassador, and he held the baby as it was named Frederick Henry. At the banquet which followed, the two Englishmen sat at the king's right hand, while the ambassador from Denmark sat on his left.[60]

Once the baptism celebrations were over, James kept his word and sent armies against Huntly and his friends. In early October 1594 the young earl of Argyle accepted the king's commission and marched against the earls in the north, while James set out towards Aberdeen with another force. By this time, James had little choice but to take military action because Huntley had flouted his authority in July by attacking Aberdeen in an attempt to free his Jesuit uncle who was then imprisoned in the town. Although the expeditions against the earls were not entirely successful and they were not captured and imprisoned, Elizabeth signalled her approval of James's new decisiveness by paying him another £2000 in November 1594, presumably in the hope that the money would encourage a further campaign against the earls which would result in their arrest and exile.[61] At last in the spring of 1595, Elizabeth obtained the goal she had so long worked for when Huntly and Errol, as well as Bothwell, were ordered into exile.

II

Over the next two years – 1595 until the end of 1597 – the Anglo-Scottish league was in better shape, although relations between the two monarchs remained difficult. During this period James seemed inclined to prove himself a good ally to the English queen. He was ready, for example, to assist the queen in her struggle against Irish rebels by issuing proclamations prohibiting the movement of Scots or munitions to Ulster.[62] He also intervened personally to accommodate Elizabeth when new conflicts on the Anglo-Scottish Borders threatened to cause a breach between the two realms. In June 1596 he proposed the establishment of an Anglo-Scottish commission to keep permanent peace on the Borders, after a series of high-profile raids. More significantly, he agreed to the arrest of Sir Walter Scott of Buccleuch, the keeper of Liddesdale, who had attacked Carlisle Castle the previous April in order to release a Scottish prisoner and notorious freebooter, known as 'Kinmont Willie' Armstrong. Buccleugh justified his unlawful action by claiming that 'Kinmont Willie' had been illegally captured on a day of truce by Lord Scrope, the English deputy warden of the West March. Elizabeth, however, refused to accept that Scrope was in the wrong and complained bitterly to James about Buccleugh's attack on one of her castles. Although James was sympathetic to his warden, he was also anxious to settle the dispute and conciliate the queen. Recognising that she saw the attack on her castle as a 'blemish' to her honour, James was prepared to have Buccleugh arrested so 'that it may be seen I will not allow of anything that ye might interpret to be an offence unto you'.[63] In November of the same year, again in defence of Elizabeth's honour (or so he claimed), James took proceedings against David Black, minister of St Andrews who had spoken in a sermon disparagingly of the queen and England's religion.[64] At the end of the same month James gave Elizabeth the singular honour of inviting her to be the sole witness at the baptism of his daughter and naming the baby 'Elizabeth' after the queen.

Yet despite James's apparent attempts to be helpful, Elizabeth remained cold and suspicious towards her cousin. She had little confidence in the sincerity of his professions of friendship, not least because in the autumn of 1596 she was receiving unconfirmed reports that Huntly had returned to Scotland, rumours which soon proved to be accurate.[65] Although Huntly had to be reconciled to the Kirk before being permitted to attend upon James at court and take over his estates, Elizabeth was dismayed at his restoration to favour and subsequent elevation to a marquisate. She was equally concerned at James's appointment of other Catholics to important positions in his government. Joining with the Kirk she issued strong warnings to the king about the dangers of tolerating and giving power to papists in his territories.[66]

At the same time, Elizabeth was growing increasingly annoyed by disturbances in the Borders which continued to fester despite James's attempts to mediate and promote her interests. When the Scots failed to meet their obligations of providing pledges, in accordance with the terms of a new treaty which had been negotiated in May 1597 with the aim of preventing further clashes on the border, Elizabeth could barely contain her rage. She complained that 'we see nought but fruitless promises' and warned:

> Seeing the King's own heart is so affected to these kind of servants as it cannot permit him to use the office of justice and honour toward us who hold him so dear. We will in the mean time advise our selves of a better course to comfort our oppressed subjects and to enable them to defend and revenge them selves of notable Injuries ... [67]

Nor was Elizabeth appeased by the honour that James had bestowed upon her in asking her to act as the sole witness at his daughter's christening. In all probability she realised that the king would exploit the occasion for his own ends; after all, he had asked her to declare him second person in the realm at the very same time as he had forwarded his invitation to the baptism.[68] Although Elizabeth was not to be flattered into agreeing to both, she had reason to suspect that James would take advantage of her representative's involvement in the ceremony and the name of the baby to proclaim to the world his close kinship with the royal house of Tudor and his consequent title to the English throne. At the christening of Prince Henry in 1594, her ambassadors had had to listen to the presiding bishop's oration which drew attention to the 'proximity and nearness of blood' between the royal houses of England and Scotland, and so it seemed likely that James might well try to do something similar at this second baptism.[69]

Elizabeth indicated her displeasure with James in, by now, familiar ways. As usual she withheld payment of the pension, causing him to send letters and messengers to England to seek it. No gratuity was delivered to him between September 1596 and April 1598.[70] For a time, she completely ignored James's letters addressed to her, and when she did eventually respond in January 1597, she did not mince her words in criticising his conduct and rehearsing her grievances against him. No wonder that James took strong exception to the 'uncouth style' of her reply.[71] Additionally, Elizabeth showed little honour or courtesy to the king at the baptism of his daughter; no grand embassy was sent to attend the ceremony in Scotland, but instead Robert Bowes, her resident ambassador, was instructed to act as the queen's proxy.[72] To Bowes's embarrassment, moreover, she supplied him with no christening gift for the princess:

> According to the usual customs it was generally expected that I should have presented the child with some gift from her Majesty. But for such as I had not any present to deliver nor knowledge of her Majesty's pleasure for the 'inplement' of any to be given at that time or afterward. Therefore I tho[ugh]t good to pass it over in the fairest and most indifferent terms. ...[73]

As late as March 1597, a gift had still not been dispatched despite reminders from Bowes; indeed there is no evidence that it was ever sent. Significantly, Elizabeth was not invited to the baptisms of Princess Margaret in April 1599 or Prince Charles in November 1600; the former event was an all-Scottish affair with Huntly and Hamilton acting as godparents; and although the king of Denmark and duke of Brunswick were initially invited to attend the prince's baptism, two French noblemen and several Scottish noble men and women ended up as the witnesses and godparents.[74]

III

It was during this period of Scottish co-operation and English frigidity that the succession first began to surface as an issue that might seriously disturb Anglo-Scottish relations. Initially there seemed to be little or no problem. Although Elizabeth consistently refused to name James her successor or give him the title of prince of Wales, she nonetheless effectively cleared his path to the succession by putting obstacles in the way of his rivals, Lady Arbella Stuart (James's first cousin) and the sons of Lady Katherine Grey (the claimants from the Suffolk line privileged in Henry VIII's will). As part of the negotiations leading to Berwick, she had written James a letter in June 1586 in which she promised to do nothing that might harm his right and title to the English succession, and she had repeated this assurance after the execution of Mary Stewart. She appeared to be as horrified as James when she learned of the publication and dissemination in 1595 of *A Conference about the Next Succession to the Crowne of England*, a work thought to have been written by the leader of the English Jesuits abroad, Robert Persons, and printed in Antwerp under the pseudonym of Doleman. The second part of this book examined the title of some fourteen potential claimants to the English throne and challenged James's title on legal as well as religious grounds, favouring instead those of Philip II's daughter, the Infanta Isabella.[75] Doleman also preferred to James the claim of two English candidates descended from the Suffolk line: Thomas Seymour, the younger son of Lady Katherine Grey (whom Doleman mistakenly called Henry) and William Stanley (who had just become the 6th earl of Derby). Either one, Doleman hoped, might be induced to marry a Catholic (preferably Isabella) in return for the throne.[76]

The *Conference* was not the first work to be published abroad on the succession, but James viewed it more seriously than the others.[77] Although he claimed to be unworried by its conclusions, he was said to be both 'highly offended' and unsettled by its appearance. No sooner had he heard of it than his ministers had 'mightily inveighed in pulpit' against its author, 'calling him thief and traitor to both sovereigns and countries'.[78] James's concern led him to have Elizabeth's letter of June 1586 formally registered in November 1596, and it was then too that he asked the queen to name him heir apparent or second person in England.[79]

James's sensitivity about the succession issue was expressed in other ways, all of which cumulatively alienated him from Elizabeth. In November 1596, he protested at the portrayal of his mother in Edmund Spencer's *Fairy Queen*, published in 1596, which threw the Scottish queen in a bad light (Book II, chapter 9) and thus implicitly questioned his own suitability to inherit the English throne. According to Robert Bowes, James considered the book dishonoured him personally, and blamed

Elizabeth for its publication since her commissioners were responsible
for approving all works in print. Fifteen months later James ordered
Walter Quinn, who had already written a Latin response to Dolman's
tract, to print an answer to Spencer.[80] Towards the end of the following
year, James became alarmed when he heard reports (which were in fact
untrue) that the queen and English parliament had acted disrespectfully
towards his mother and spoken out against his title to the succession.[81] In
reaction to this news, in December 1597 James made a speech in his own
parliament which berated Elizabeth for the execution of his mother, the
non-payment of the pension, and the attitude of the English parliament
towards his title. His oration, which according to one report railed
against Elizabeth's 'false and malicious envious dealing against his own
person and state', was greeted with approval by his audience. The parliament at once granted him 200,000 marks both to cover the cost of sending an ambassador to the queen 'to be plain in these behalfs and to know
what he may trust to anent the title, the gratuity and her Majesty's goodwill towards him' and to dispatch various other embassies to his allies
abroad to solicit them to 'stand his friends' and attain his rights.[82] At the
same time, partly in an effort to show his independence of the queen so
that she would not take him for granted, James accepted letters from the
rebellious earl of Tyrone and offered to mediate between him and the
queen. He also received in person at his court Sir James MacConnell
(also known as Sorley Boy), another Irish rebel, who was held responsible for slaughtering the Governor of Carrickfergus.[83]

In accordance with his commitment to the Scottish parliament in
December 1597, James dispatched an embassy to England the following
spring. Elizabeth had already conveyed to him her indignation and dismay at the tenor of his speech to that assembly. His words, she complained, were 'not more to my disgrace than to your dishonour'. 'I do
wonder', she continued, 'what evil spirits have possessed you, to set for
the so infamous devises, void of any show of truth.' Elizabeth adopted a
tone of hurt injury and she demanded amends: 'And be assured, that you
deal with such a king as will bear no wrongs and endure [no] infamy', she
told him.[84] Wrong-footed James retreated, for he had no intention of
causing a breach, but simply wanted to press Elizabeth into issuing a formal recognition of his title to the succession as well as granting a renewal
of the pension. Consequently, he wrote Elizabeth a grovelling reply in
which he denied the reports of his speech and pledged his commitment
to 'that old contention of honest amity.' His envoy to London, Edward
Bruce the titular abbot of Kinloss, who carried this message was also

instructed to reassure Elizabeth that James had provided no assistance to her rebels in Ireland and would do his utmost to keep peace on the Anglo-Scottish Borders.[85]

In his instructions, Bruce was additionally told to raise a new matter with the queen. This concerned the case of Valentine Thomas. Thomas had been recently arrested by officials in the north of England on suspicion of conspiring with recusants against the queen and planning to engineer the return to those parts of the 6th earl of Westmorland, a leader of the Northern Rebellion who had fled abroad in 1570. Thomas admitted the offence but also claimed that he had been suborned by James to assassinate Elizabeth. Disbelieving Thomas's account, Elizabeth did not immediately raise the issue with James, but he soon got wind of Thomas's accusation and took it very seriously indeed. Although the matter was actually of very little consequence, it was to obsess James for several years because of his belief that it impinged on his right to the succession. Bruce was therefore instructed in the spring of 1598 to demand that the king should be publicly exonerated.[86]

When Bruce arrived at the English court, Elizabeth was preoccupied with a full-scale rebellion confronting her in Ireland and she was therefore content to be conciliatory and buy off James with the annuity in return for his co-operation in cutting off men and supplies to the Irish rebels. For this reason Bruce, successfully and unusually, squeezed £6000 from Elizabeth, a sum which included arrears, although she initially only offered him £3000. He also received assurances that Elizabeth had neither abused Mary Stewart nor spoken against James's title, both of which were perfectly true. Despite these gains, James professed himself discontented with the outcome of the mission because the affair of Valentine Thomas had not been settled to his satisfaction.[87]

As far as the English government was concerned, the Thomas case was utterly trivial. Elizabeth entertained no doubts that James was completely innocent and she had no intention of taking Thomas's accusation seriously. James, however, not only insisted on a public acquittal, but demanded that Thomas should not be charged with attempted murder at his trial and that all mention of the assassination attempt be erased from the records. Otherwise, he felt, his reputation and hopes for the succession would be put at risk. James's fear was that, unless Thomas was publicly discredited, the accusation 'burieth his honour in the grave of oblivion and blemisheth his line and posterity for ever'.[88] He was equally worried that an accusation of seeking to murder the queen might place him within the scope of the 1585 Act of the Queen's Surety (which he

miscalled the 'Act of Association') and so provide his enemies with an
excuse for excluding him from the English throne. Doleman had already
argued that the 'Act of Association' debarred James from the succession
because of Mary Stewart's treason; James was determined to prevent the
Thomas case being used in this way against him as well.

Although Elizabeth and the English Privy Council did their best to put
the king's mind at rest, James was not convinced that he was safe. In
September 1598 he told his ambassador in London, David Foulis, to
obtain an authentic copy of the Act so that its terms could be scrutinised.[89]
He then requested from Elizabeth a public declaration that he was innocent of Thomas's accusation but, when Elizabeth issued a patent to that
effect, he quibbled with its wording and complained that she had written
it as if under duress and not because he deserved it.[90] The Thomas affair
grumbled away throughout 1598 and 1599, threatening to alienate James
from England. As James Hudson warned Cecil, if Elizabeth did not satisfy
the king with a public acquittal, 'it will make him not only careless to content [her] but studious to find means to better his conditions and make
him stray his actions and proceedings from her Majesty altogether'.[91]

Hudson's observation was perspicacious, for James was indeed looking
for other means to safeguard his claim to the succession. In May 1598 he
initiated a diplomatic campaign to whip up foreign support for his title
to the English throne after Elizabeth's death. In the hope that the German
Protestant princes of Germany and Scandinavia would feel uneasy at the
prospect of England falling prey to a Catholic candidate sponsored by the
Spanish king, James aimed to mobilise his brother-in-law, Christian IV of
Denmark, and his wife's German kinsmen to work together on his behalf.
All the Protestant princes were asked in 1598 to send their ambassadors
to the England to 'importune' Elizabeth to declare James her official successor and, if she refused, to provide him with military support 'in antic-
ipation of the crisis' that would occur on her death. Their replies,
however, were disappointing. Certainly they all declared approval of his
title but none would offer him military aid, at least not in the present circumstances. Nor would they provide individual diplomatic support, but
would only consider common action. Some of them agreed to help him
by sending a joint embassy to England to warn Elizabeth of the dangers
that would arise if James were not named heir; but the conservative duke
of Saxony doubted the wisdom of any diplomatic intervention and questioned 'whether their intercession may not make the mind of the Queen
again waver rather than promote your cause'. In any case, the Protestant
princes refused to take any final decision about a concerted diplomatic

effort until they had all met together and agreed upon their tactics.[92] James was thus left pretty high and dry.

James also sent agents abroad to neutralise or win over Catholic rulers who were likely to favour one of the Catholic candidates promoted by Persons. In 1598, Robert Lord Semple visited Philip III, who had recently succeeded to the throne of Spain, in the hope that he would depart from the policy of his father, abandon the claim of the Infanta Isabella to the English succession, and support James's title.[93] James, meanwhile, sent another nobleman to discuss the English succession with the French king, and engaged in a dialogue with the pope in order to ward off his excommunication and prevent papal recognition of Isabella's claim.[94] Given that James also maintained contacts with English Catholics, particularly those exiled abroad who had been supporters of his mother, some observers in England feared that to secure the throne he would promise to make concessions to Catholics and might even be tempted to abjure, following the example of Henry IV in 1593. Queen Anne's suspected conversion to Catholicism did nothing to allay these anxieties.[95]

What were Elizabeth's reactions to James's obsession with the Thomas case and his manoeuvrings to secure the succession? As far as Thomas was concerned, she appeared outwardly reasonable and patient, but she clearly thought the king was being unduly sensitive about the issue and 'hath conceived so many causeless apprehensions'.[96] There are also signs that she saw James's constant badgering her over Thomas as an irritating distraction from more important matters of state and that she simply could not understand why he kept returning to the case in his list of grievances. In her view, she had done her best to satisfy the king in every way that was consistent with her honour. Some of his demands, however, were impossible to meet (for example that the indictment against Thomas be cancelled), while others proposed lines of action he had previously rejected.[97] Elizabeth, consequently, suspected that James was either looking to provoke a major quarrel or else was trying to exploit the Thomas affair to extract concessions on other matters. Her eventual solution was to put an end to the matter by holding Thomas in the Tower without trial; in this way, she hoped, the accusation would not be aired in court and all publicity would soon die away. That was how the matter was left until James's accession when Thomas was tried and executed as a felon.

James's overtures to foreign princes abroad did not go unnoticed in England and unsurprisingly Elizabeth was annoyed that the succession issue was being discussed in this way while she was still alive.[98] As a general principle, she declared the succession was:

> a matter of so sour and distasteful nature to any Prince as the bespeaking
> aforehand by public embassy assistance for the recovering of that estate
> and fortune in which Almighty God hath placed us an absolute and free
> monarch without help or dependence of any but God's ordinance.[99]

In any case, she protested, the season was not right for James to send an
embassy to Denmark and the German princes, nor was there any need for
James to justify his claim to the throne in answer to Doleman's book,
which 'in these days touch you little'. The embassy to Denmark she found
particularly offensive as she had heard that James's ambassadors had
given Christian 'lewd reports of her valetudinary state, when we bless God
for it'.[100] Not only would such false reports do James's honour little good,
she complained, but they would also provide comfort to 'the enemies of
our common amity'. It is unlikely that she was mollified when James
reportedly justified his action in the following way:

> there was no other meant but that she is mortal ... and if she should by
> manifesting of the title to the right here him self, clear that point to the
> world and her people that she might leave them when it should please
> God to call her (as he for his part prays she may live long) in peace and
> out of the danger of the huge and great troubles that other ways will then
> come, her Majesty's life, reign and end would and ought to be memo-
> rably honoured and praised over all the princes yet ever written of.[101]

As for his communications with the Catholic powers, Elizabeth's main
anxiety was that James's search for Catholic friends abroad might result
in him giving power to Catholics within his own realm, providing sanctu-
ary for English Catholic exiles, and making closer contacts with recusants
in England. In fact James's uncertainty about the succession and his failure to obtain any guarantees from Elizabeth or help from foreign princes
did encourage him to build up closer relationships with English
Catholics. At the same time, though, he was also in secret contact with
English puritans who favoured his claim.[102] But beyond warning James
against putting his reliance on Catholics, Elizabeth was in no position to
influence the king and with full-scale rebellion in Ireland to suppress she
could not afford to alienate him further.

Whether or not because of his unease about the succession, James
seemed to be picking up on 'any wrongs how little so ever be done to his
subjects' and to his honour.[103] He complained bitterly when in August

1598 the English deputies of the Middle March chased a hunting party of Scots over the border, inflicting casualties on and capturing prisoners of the offending Scots.[104] In early 1599, he was upset and 'something angry in deed' that the queen had not thanked him for issuing a proclamation against the earl of Tyrone.[105] Later that year James was 'exceeding angry' when Edmund Ashfield, an English recusant visiting Scotland, was kidnapped and bundled back to England by servants of the Governor of Berwick under the very nose of Sir William Bowes, Elizabeth's special ambassador.[106] When in August 1599 James sent James Sempill of Beltries to seek redress, Elizabeth tried to appear conciliatory and keep the peace, even though James's protection of Ashfield was considered by some in England as a sign of the king's untrustworthiness in religion.[107] Elizabeth's main interest at this time was to stop James dabbling in the succession and to prevent Scottish military aid reaching Tyrone. Her principal diplomatic activity, therefore, was to calm James down and persuade him to wait patiently for her death.

By 1600, however, James was in a state of even greater fretfulness about the succession, because of political developments within England. During 1599, the earl of Essex fell from royal favour, leaving Robert Cecil and his friends as the pre-eminent men in government. As Paul Hammer has shown, James had been in regular contact with Essex over a number of years and trusted that the earl supported his title. Cecil, however, James thoroughly mistrusted for he knew of his earlier communications with Bothwell and believed that the principal secretary (like his father before him) supported the pretensions of the House of Suffolk. To make matters worse, James began to hear rumours in 1599 that Cecil might persuade Elizabeth to favour a candidate acceptable to Spain as a price for a peace settlement which would bring an end to the long and expensive wars. Late in that year, unfounded reports were circulating in Scotland that England had begun negotiations with Spain for a treaty, in which would be included a clause resolving the succession in the Habsburg interest. According to some news-mongers, the two sides intended to recognise the claim of the Infanta Isabella to the English throne; according to others, they planned to arrange a dynastic marriage between Lady Arbella Stuart and Matthias, the brother of the Holy Roman Emperor, as a preliminary to advancing her claim.[108] The collapse of the peace negotiations removed immediate perceptions of danger from that quarter, but James remained suspicious of Cecil's intentions, and feared that he might have to fight for the throne on Elizabeth's death. In November 1599 James swore his nobility in a General Band to help him pursue the throne of England, and the following December and June he tried unsuccessfully to raise taxation to pay for an army to be used for the same purpose.[109]

It is thought unlikely that James was privy to Essex's plans for a rising but we can never be certain, as the earl burned all his papers before his arrest. All that we know is that two of the conspirators confessed to a plan in which Lord Mountjoy would send troops from Ireland to support Essex's coup and James would gather an army on the border and send ambassadors to London to demand recognition of his title.[110] Mountjoy did not make any such move but James did in fact instruct two special ambassadors, the earl of Mar and Edward Bruce, to travel to London at the beginning of February 1601 to lay 'open all my griefs' before the queen and to make contact with Essex and his friends.[111] Before the embassy set out, however, James learned of Essex's abortive coup on 9 February and had to revise his plans. The ambassadors were now told to liaise secretly with other unnamed friends and listen to their advice. If these 'friends' wished him to 'lie still', then he would; if they wanted him to act as their head, 'assure them I shall be as willing and ready to supply that place as they can be to desire me only with that old reservation of the safety of the Queen's person, which ye maun [must] take them sworn t[o]'. But if his supporters were past saving, the ambassadors were to 'use then all the means ye can to get me a party there'. At the same time Mar and Bruce were told to confirm their acquaintance with the Lieutenant of the Tower and to 'obtain as great a certainty as ye can for the fleet'.[112] The embassy was intended to be impressive: Mar was one of the foremost noblemen in Scotland; both men were noted Anglophiles; and their retinue was very large.

The instructions concerning the public nature of the Mar and Bruce mission changed little after the Essex rising. In addition to laying out James's grievances before the queen and seeking the usual reassurances about the succession, the envoys were to request 'a plain declairaitoure' that James was 'untouched in any action of practice that ever hath been intended against her, especially in this last'; in other words to obtain a judicial declaration that James was innocent in both the Valentine Thomas case and the recent Essex rising. In fact James expected 'a flat and obstinate denial' of all his requests to the queen, and it is evident that the 'private negotiations with the country' were the main purpose of the embassy. The only demand the ambassadors were told to pursue 'earnestly' concerned the judicial declaration. Otherwise, they were simply to show the 'honour, respect, and love' due to the queen's person and bow out graciously. Cecil and 'his followers', however, were to be given a stark warning: 'since now when they are in their kingdom they will thus misknow me, when the chance shall turn I shall cast a deaf ear to their requests'.[113]

The Scottish embassy was received coldly at court, because Elizabeth was well aware of James's secret dealings with Essex and therefore naturally suspicious of the king. Besides, she had no wish to hear yet another recitation of James's grievances and demands. Her answer to him was therefore rather abrupt: she denied that James had any cause for complaint against her, and assured him that she had acted in his best interests in her dealings over Thomas. Nonetheless, at the last minute she offered to raise James's pension to £5000 provided that he was friendlier towards her and deserved it.[114]

The embassy was even more successful in achieving its main aim, that of building up a new group of friends who would work for the Scottish succession. Its great coup was in reaching an understanding with Cecil, who agreed to enter into a secret correspondence with the king. In the first of his letters to James, probably conveyed by Mar and Bruce on their return home, Cecil sought to set the record straight: he and the queen had never favoured a Spanish succession nor had any intention to 'cut off the natural branch and graft upon some wild stock'. He went on to make clear that he would not help James in any way that might harm his mistress, and urged the king to cease raising the succession with the queen, as it only provoked her into suspicions against him: 'you will find it in your case, that a choice election of a few in the present, will be of more use then any general acclamation of many', he advised.[115]

The new connection with Cecil made all the difference to James's relations with Elizabeth. From May 1601 until Elizabeth's death James followed Cecil's advice: he avoided further quarrels with the queen, kept her informed about his dealings with foreign powers, and penned affectionate letters to her that included no demands. When the Spanish landed troops at Kinsale, James even offered to supply troops to help dislodge them. Although he still feared he might have to use military force against a Catholic claimant from abroad, he was now confident that he could rely on the support of influential friends in England. For her part, Elizabeth swallowed her own suspicions about James, and ensured that his dealings with Essex were neither pursued in the trials of the conspirators nor written up in the semi-official narrative of the rebellion.[116] She had effectively (though not of course officially) chosen the king as her successor and would not jeopardise his exclusion by the Act of Queen's Surety. Until her death, she paid the increased pension in half-yearly instalments as thanks for his 'kindness' towards her. On the Borders, meanwhile, both monarchs played down any local incidents and the wardens and their deputies responded by co-operating more closely with their opposite numbers. This improvement in Anglo-Scottish arrangements meant that Elizabeth did not feel the need to send any special ambassadors to Scotland after August 1600, or replace her accredited agent George Nicolson with a resident ambassador as had been mooted earlier.

IV

Throughout the period examined here, the state of Scotland was of great importance to Elizabeth and she took care to be well informed about James's dealings at home and abroad as well as about the activities and sentiments of the Scottish lords. Her leading councillors were encouraged to gather intelligence from a wide range of sources: English ambassadors and spies of course but also Scottish Presbyterian ministers and James's own personal servants. In the 1590s most of this information was channelled through the Cecils and Essex on their way to the queen. Elizabeth's policy decisions were not therefore made from a position of ignorance, although some of the reports she received were unnecessarily alarmist.

From surviving English sources, historians can find little evidence of internal debates about how to handle problems related to Scotland. There is some indication that Cecil favoured a confrontational policy towards James during the affair of the 'Spanish blanks' as well as supported giving underhand assistance to Bothwell, whereas Essex preferred to reach some agreement with Huntly that would satisfy both James and Elizabeth. Otherwise, the sources are quiet about areas of disagreement over policy. If harmony did indeed prevail, the reason may have been that Essex was content to leave the Cecils to be the front men in Elizabeth's Scottish policy after 1595 while he secretly forged his own strong links with James through his agents.

At the heart of English diplomacy were Elizabeth's personal letters to the king and her negotiations with him through resident and special ambassadors although, as seen above, she sometimes also relied on indirect approaches to Scottish noblemen, especially when relations with James were at their worst. In her diplomacy Elizabeth generally proved adept at signalling to James her approval or annoyance and just how far he could go before risking serious offence and a possible breach: the tone of her letters, the flow or suspension of the annuity, and the generosity of her gift-giving were all devices she employed to convey her mood and concerns. James showed skill in reading the signs and responding appropriately. As a result the arguments between the two monarchs were contained and the league held together.

Elizabeth's policy towards Scotland after the treaty of Berwick was almost entirely reactive. Only in seeking to draft Scottish mercenaries from the Western Isles and Highlands into service in Ireland did she take the initiative.[117] Otherwise, as in her foreign policy elsewhere, Elizabeth's behaviour and diplomatic efforts were reactions to crises and problems as they arose. Her interests were: to preserve England's security by preventing Scotland operating as a base for Spanish troops or Catholic troublemakers, to prevent Scottish aid to her rebels in Ireland, and to maintain law and order on the Borders while protecting her sovereignty and defending her servants. Whenever these interests seemed to be threatened she dispatched letters or ambassadors to James. But she was also forced to respond to James's anxieties about the succession, a matter she would much rather forget. Between 1596 and 1601 she tried to reassure and placate the king while keeping to her decision not to name a successor, but here she proved unsuccessful. Only after James mended bridges with Cecil and listened to his advice, did the king cease his secret diplomacy abroad and repair relations with the queen. The succession question put to one side, Elizabeth could enjoy two years of friendship with her cousin and ally, perhaps unaware that a number of her subjects had already turned towards the rising sun.

NOTES

Thanks are due to the British Academy for a travel grant that allowed me to consult manuscripts in the National Library of Scotland and University of Edinburgh.

1. Anglo-Scottish tensions are played down, for example, in Pauline Croft, *King James* (Basingstoke, 2003), pp. 22–3 and T. I. Rae, *The Administration of the Scottish Frontier, 1513–1603* (Edinburgh, 1966), pp. 206–22. No attention is paid to post-1586 Anglo-Scottish relations in P. S. Crowson, *Tudor Foreign Policy* (1973) and Susan Doran, *England and Europe 1485–1603* (1996). On the other hand, Anglo-Scottish relations are the subject of Helen Georgia Stafford's *James VI of Scotland and The Throne of England* (NYC, 1940) while a chapter is devoted to Scotland in W. B. MacCaffrey, *Elizabeth I: War and Politics 1588–1603* (Princeton NJ, 1992), pp. 303–28. Although these are both important studies, the emphasis in their accounts differs from the approach of this chapter. For an older, yet still valuable, history of Scotland which throws considerable light on Anglo-Scottish relations, see Patrick Fraser Tytler, *History of Scotland [to 1603]* (4 vols, Edinburgh, 1864), iii.

2. 2 August 1585, Thomas Wright, *Queen Elizabeth and her Times* (2 vols, 1838), ii, p. 253; 16 May 1586, A. L. Cameron and R. S. Rait (eds), *The Warrender Papers* (2 vols, Edinburgh, 1931–32) ii, pp. 213–4.

3. M. Lee, *Great Britain's Solomon* (Urbana, IL, 1990), pp. 65, 98.

4. For a different view, see Simon Adams, 'The succession and foreign policy', *History Today* 53 (5) (2003), p. 47.

5. April 1585, PRO, SP 52/37 pp. 47–53.

6. *The Warrender Papers*, ii, pp. 127, 133–41; 29 July, 22 and 30 August 1590, *CSP. Scot.* x, pp. 366–8, 384–6, 388–90. See also, 8 July 1585, E. Lodge, *Illustrations of British History* (2nd edn 1838), i, pp. 264–8.

7. For example, James to Elizabeth, 27 June 1585, HMC *9 Salisbury*, xiii, pp. 268–9; 3, 13 and 19 August 1585, John Bruce, 'Letters of Queen Elizabeth and King James VI'. *Camden Society* 46 (1949), pp. 18–19, 21, 22; 9 November 1586, BL, Cotton MS Caligula C ix fo. 597; 1 August 1588, *CSP. Scot*, ix, p. 588. See also, Lena Cowen Orlin, 'The fictional families of Elizabeth I' in Carole Levin and Patricia A. Sullivan (eds), *Political Rhetoric, Power and Renaissance Women* (Albany, New York, 1995), pp. 85–110, esp. pp. 98–101

8. See Bruce, 'Letters', *passim.*

9. 21 January 1593, Bruce, 'Letters', pp. 71–3. Modern spelling in Leah S. Marcus, Janel Mueller and Mary Beth Rose (eds), *Elizabeth I: Collected Works* (Chicago, 2000), p. 366. See also, 11 September 1592 and 29 June 1596, Bruce, 'Letters', pp. 75–6, 115.

10. J. E. Neale, *Queen Elizabeth* (1934), p. 385. She labelled her words as 'plaine dealing' and 'sister-lyke counsell'; 16 March 1588 and May 1593, Bruce, 'Letters' pp. 82, 162.

11. Scottish Record Office [hereafter SRO], GD124/15/18/1 and 2. Essex told Maitland that there could be nothing more welcome to Elizabeth than a correspondence which would maintain 'the amity of the two crowns'.

12. Robert S. Rait and Anne I. Cameron, *King James' Secret* (1927), p. 56.

13. Susan Doran, 'Revenge her foul and most unnatural murder? The impact of Mary Stewart's execution on Anglo-Scottish relations', *History*, 85 (2000), pp. 589–612

14. J. Bain (ed.), *The Border Papers* (2 vols, Edinburgh, 1894–96), i, pp. 47, 252, 253.

15. Ibid. pp. 249–50. *Extract from the despatches of M. Courcelles, French ambassador at the court of Scotland 1586–7*, ed. Robert Bell Bannatyne Club (Edinburgh, 1828), pp. 44–5, 54

16. *Border Papers*, i, pp. 247, 249.

17. PRO, SP 52/ 42 nos 26 and 35; HMC 9 *Salisbury*, iii, p. 236.

18. *CSP. Scot.* ix, pp. 588–90, 599–600.

19. *CSP. Scot*, x, pp. 209–11; J. R. Dasent (ed.), *Acts of the Privy Council* (32 vols, 1890–1907), xviii, pp. 241–2, 250.

20. Other sources of conflict included the failure to extradite fugitives as laid down in the treaty.

21. Julian Goodare, 'James VI's English subsidy' in Julian Goodare and Michael Lynch (eds), *The Reign of James VI* (East Lothian, 2000), pp. 110–25.

22. 2 April 1590, BL, Additional MS 23241, fos 31–3v.

23. The subsidy of £3000 would amount to about one-sixth of his total income. Goodare, 'English subsidy', p. 121.

24. Bruce, 'Letters', pp. 68–9.

25. PRO, SP 52/58 no. 112.

26. 27 April 1598, *CSP. Scot.* xiii (i) pp. 196–7.

27. *CSP. Scot.* ix, p. 682, x, pp. 210, 263, 434, 682–3.

28. *CSP. Scot.* x, p. 828; *The Warrender Papers*, ii, pp. 192–202; F. De B. Medina, 'Intrigues of a Scottish Jesuit at the Spanish court: unpublished letters of William Crichton to Claudio Acquaviva (Madrid 1590–92)' in T. M. McCoog (ed.), *The Reckoned Expense: Edmund Campion and the Early English Jesuits* (Woodbridge, 1996), pp. 215–45.

29. SRO, GD 406/1/43; *The Warrender Papers*, ii, pp. 102–4, 181–2; Bruce, 'Letters', pp. 71–3, 95.

30. *CSP Scot*, x, pp. 351–3. The rebels were so called because they had confronted James at Brig o'Dee near Aberdeen in April 1589. In addition to the Catholic earls, they included the Protestant Francis Stewart, earl of Bothwell. For Huntly and Brig o'Dee see, Ruth Grant, 'The Brig o'Dee affair, the sixth earl of Huntly and the politics of the Counter-Reformation' in Goodare and Lynch (eds), *The Reign of James VI*, pp. 93–109.

31. BL, Harleian MS 4648, p. 110.

32. *Border Papers*, i, p. 502.

33. David Harris Wilson, *King James VI and I* (London, 1956), pp. 99, 100.

34. Michael Questier, 'The politics of religious conformity and the accession of James I', *Historical Research*, 71 (1998), p. 20.

35. Grant, 'The sixth earl of Huntly', pp. 93–109.

36. *CSP Scot.*, x, pp. 361–4.

37. December 1593, Bruce, 'Letters', p. 97. See also, 19 September 1593, G. P. V. Akrigg, *Letters of King James VI and I* (Berkeley, 1984).

38. The Atholl family in Scotland were said to be friends of the earl of Bothwell. *Border Papers*, i, p. 475.

39. Anderson's History of Scotland, National Library of Scotland [hereafter NLS], Advocates MS 35.5.3 (iii), fo. 257; *CSP. Scot.* xi, pp. 45–8, 69–70.

40. Instructions for Lord Zouche, 20 December 1593, PRO, SP 52/52 p. 17.

41. For Essex's separate diplomacy see Chapter 9 by Paul Hammer in this volume and Paul E. J. Hammer, *The Polarisation of Elizabethan Politics: The Political Career of Robert Devereux, 2nd Earl of Essex, 1585–1597* (Cambridge, 1999), pp. 165–7.

42. [late March 1593] SRO, GD1 371/3

43. 10 February 1593, *CSP. Scot.*, xi, p. 44.

44. *Border Papers*, i, pp. 418, 454, 465, 467, 476, 478.

45. 18 July 1593, *Border Papers*, i, p. 475.

46. 18 January 1594, PRO, SP 52/52 p. 24. See also, *Border Papers*, i, pp. 514, 522–3, 533. Henry Lok had been Cecil's intermediary with Bothwell from the summer of 1593.

47. Carey to Burghley, 17 April 1594, *Border Papers*, i, p. 530.

48. 4 March 1594, PRO, SP 52/52 p. 43.

49. *CSP. Scot.* xi, pp. 239–41, 241–2, 244, 248, 251–2, 258–9. Elizabeth to James, 22 December 1593, Bruce, 'Letters', pp. 98–100.

50. 17 April 1594, *The Warrender Papers*, ii, p. 43.

51. The misnamed Act of Association (properly called the Act for the Queen's Surety) excluded from the English throne any claimant who was involved in plots against the queen's life. For Cecil's draft letter, see *CSP. Scot.* xi, pp. 251–2. This was only to be imparted to Maitland (James's Lord Chancellor) 'if he shall see cause'.

52. *The Warrender Papers*, ii, pp. 226–8, also printed in Akrigg, *Letters*, pp. 128–30.

53. 20 April 1594, NLS, Adv. MS 33.7 (vol. 21) no. 2.

54. James to Essex, 13 April 1594, Akrigg, *Letters*, pp. 130–1; *The Warrender Papers*, ii, p. 238.

55. 25 January 1594, PRO, SP 52/52 p. 30.

56. James to Elizabeth, 5 June 1594, Akrigg, *Letters*, pp. 132–4. *Border Papers*, i, p. 537.

57. *CSP. Scot.* xi, p. 410; *The Warrender Papers*, ii, p. 266.

58. *Border Papers*, i, p. 550.

59. *The Warrender Papers*, ii, pp. 251–2.

60. J. Nichols, *Progresses and Public Processions of Queen Elizabeth* (1823), pp. 355–63. For the full contemporary description of the baptism, see *A True Reportarie of the Most Triumphant and Royal Accomplishment of the Baptism of ... Prince Frederik* (1594). STC 11214.6.

61. *CSP. Scot.* xii, p. 203.

62. Cambridge University Library, KK, 15; *CSP. Scot.* xiii, p. 121.

63. 17 August 1596, Akrigg, *Letters*, pp. 146–7; *CSP. Scot.* xii, p. 141. For fuller details of the events, see Rae, *Scottish Frontier*, pp. 216–7.

64. *CSP. Scot.* xii, pp. 453–4. Black had also attacked James and Queen Anne.

65. 23 October 1596, *CSP. Scot.* xii, p. 347.

66. Elizabeth to James, 5 January 1597, Edinburgh University Library, [hereafter EUL] Laing MS, iii, pp. 45–6.

67. 7 June 1597, BL, Harleian MS 4648, fos 172r–3r.

68. 4 October 1596, *CSP. Scot.* xii, p. 337.

69. *A True Reportarie*, sig C; *CSP. Scot.* xi, pp. 422, 431; Nicholas Tyacke, 'Puritan politicians and King James VI and I, 1587–1604' in Thomas Cogswell, Richard Cust and Peter Lake (eds), *Politics, Religion and Popularity in Early Stuart Britain*, (Cambridge, 2003), pp. 34–5.

70. *CSP Scot.* xii, p. 203.

71. 5 January 1597, Bruce, 'Letters', pp. 120–1; 12 and 24 December 1597 and 2 February 1598, *CSP. Scot*, xiii, pp. 131, 162. Akrigg, *Letters*, pp. 152–3. Instructions for Mr Robert Bruce 1598, NLS, Adv. MS 33.1.7 (vol. 1) no. 51.

72. *CSP. Scot*, xii, p. 347.

73. BL, Cotton MS Caligula D ii fo. 207.

74. For Margaret's baptism, *CSP. Scot.* xiii (i), p. 450; for Charles, xiii (ii), pp. 739–40, 748, 758.

75. R. Doleman, *Conference About the Next Succession to the Crown of England* (Antwerp, 1594) STC 19398. A modern facsimile was published in 1972, volume 104 of English Recusant Literature (Menston: Scolar Press, 1972). For the background to its publication, see Peter Holmes, 'The Authorship and Early Reception of "A Conference About the Next Succession to the Crown of England" ', *Historical Journal*, 23 (1980), pp. 415–29.

76. Doleman's recommendation concerning William Stanley came too late as he had already married a Protestant in June 1594.

77. In March 1594 the government learned of the *News from Spain and Holland* printed in Antwerp in 1593 which had identified sixteen claimants to the succession. HMC 9 *Salisbury*, iv, p. 498.

78. 7 and 18 January 1596, PRO, SP 52/58 nos 3 and 10.

79. *Register Privy Council Scotland*, v, pp. 324–5.

80. Nicolson to Cecil, 25 February 1598, *CSP. Scot.* xiii (i), p. 167.

81. *CSP. Scot,* xii, pp. 359–60, xiii (i), p. 136.
82. *The Warrender Papers,* ii, pp. 435; 16 and 17 December 1597, PRO, 52/61 nos 61 and 62.
83. *CSP. Scot.* xiii (i), pp. 35–6, 237–8, 317.
84. 4 January 1598, Bruce, 'Letters', pp. 121–3.
85. February 1598, Bruce, 'Letters', pp. 123–5; Instructions for Bruce, NLS, Adv. MS I (vol. 2) no. 51.
86. James to Elizabeth, 1 March 1598, HMC *6th Report,* p. 660; *CSP. Scot.* xiii (i), pp. 232–3.
87. 27 April, 2 and 22 May 1598, *CSP. Scot.* xiii (i), pp. 106–7, 203–5, 209–11.
88. [June] 1598, PRO, SP 52/62 no. 38.
89. 26 September 1598, *CSP. Scot.* xiii (i), pp. 298–9.
90. Stafford, *James VI,* pp. 194–5.
91. PRO, SP 52/63 no. 22.
92. *The Warrender Papers,* ii, pp. 362, 366–71, 377–80.
93. NLS, Adv. MS 33.1.10 nos 7, 9 and 10. Professor MacCaffrey claims that the overture to Spain was 'almost certainly not authorized by James', but the instructions for Lord Semple and his letter to James indicate otherwise. MacCaffrey, *War and Politics,* p. 318.
94. Intercepted letters from Spanish ambassador to Rome, 5 March 1596, NLS, Adv. MS 29.2.6. fo. 165v; 4/14 June 1598, *CSP Dom., 1598–1601,* p. 59; HMC 9th Report, *Elphinstone MSS,* pp. 196–7; Thomas Morgan to James VI, 4 and 13 December 1601, *CSP. Dom. 1595–7,* p. 419; 31 October 1597, *CSP. Scot.* xiii (i), p. 118.
95. *CSP. Dom. 1595–7,* p. 391.
96. 31 December 1598, PRO, SP 52/52 p. 233.
97. 25 April 1599, *CSP Scot.* xiii (i), pp. 455–61.
98. *CSP. Scot.* xiii (i), pp. 306, 439, 366.
99. 31 December 1598, PRO, SP 52/52 p. 234.
100. 25 April 1598, PRO, SP 52/62 no. 29; SP 52/52 p. 234.
101. 20 January 1599, PRO, SP 52/64 no. 11.
102. Akrigg, *Letters,* pp. 166–7; Tyacke 'Puritan Politicians and James VI', pp. 21–44.
103. October 1598, PRO, SP 52/63 no. 50.
104. *CSP. Scot.* xiii (ii), pp. 252–3, 378–9.
105. PRO, SP 52/64 no. 11.
106. *The Warrender Papers,* ii, pp. 435; 16 and 25 June 1599, *CSP. Scot.* xiii (i) pp. 498–501, 506–7, 524, 527, 536–8.
107. For some criticisms of James in the Ashfield affair, EUL, Laing MS iii 245, fos 59–60.
108. NLS, Adv. MS 34. 2. 10 fo. 79 r–v; *CSP. Scot.* xiii (i), p. 623, (ii), p. 631; A. Teulet, *Papiers d'Etat* (3 vols, Paris, 1852–60), iii, pp. 612–5.
109. *CSP. Scot.* xiii (i), pp. 576–8.
110. John Bruce (ed.), 'Correspondence of King James VI of Scotland and Sir Robert Cecil and others ...' *Camden Society,* 78 (London, 1861), pp. 80–110. For the Essex rising, see MacCaffrey, *War and Politics,* pp. 530–6 and Mervyn James, 'At a crossroad of the political culture: the Essex revolt, 1601' in his *Politics and Culture* (Cambridge, 1986), pp. 416–65.
111. Akrigg, *Letters,* pp. 168–70. Essex had asked for an embassy to arrive by 1 February, but James chose to send his envoys a week later.

112. Akrigg, *Letters*, pp. 170–1, 173–7.
113. Ibid.
114. 14 May 1601, HMC 9 *Salisbury*, xiv, pp. 175–8; 30 April 1601, Bruce, 'Letters', p. 137; 11 May 1601, *CSP. Scot.* xiii (ii), p. 822.
115. Bruce (ed.), 'Correspondence', pp. 3–8.
116. Stafford, *James VI*, p. 217.
117. For these initiatives, see MacCaffrey, *War and Politics*, pp. 324–6.

9

THE CRUCIBLE OF WAR: ENGLISH FOREIGN POLICY, 1589–1603

Paul E. J. Hammer

Elizabethan foreign policy has traditionally been studied through the surviving papers of the royal secretariat, headed by the principal secretary or secretary of state. Often paired with a junior colleague, the secretary drafted and received official documents on behalf of the queen, oversaw the work of lesser secretaries (such as the secretary of the Latin tongue, whose duties included maintaining correspondences with foreign states or individuals which were conducted in Latin), and exerted a considerable influence in the making of royal policy by his daily attendance upon the queen, membership of the Privy Council and control of the agenda for council meetings. Aided by his junior colleague and his own personal clerks, the secretary also acted as the sovereign's mouthpiece to her ambassadors abroad, sending out instructions and receiving their regular (often weekly) dispatches, which he reported to the queen in summary form. Because Elizabeth's aversion to tedious reports was almost as great as her hunger for foreign news, the latter task was especially important and permitted the secretary a degree of latitude in how certain points were presented for royal consideration.

Although the secretariat played a central role in royal government, many of the papers which it produced and received were retained in private hands by individual secretaries and their families, who treated the documents as their own personal property. Despite repeated efforts during the course of Elizabeth's reign to gather up papers from the studies of secretaries of state after their deaths, the crown never succeeded in recovering all the secretarial papers. As a result, many such documents now reside in 'private' collections such as the Cecil Papers at Hatfield House and the Lansdowne, Harleian and Cotton collections at the British Library. Nevertheless, by 1610 the crown's archive of secretarial papers had grown sufficiently large to warrant the formal appointment of two 'keepers and registers of the papers and records' to safeguard the documents and make them available for consultation by the king and approved royal councillors. The swelling size of this archive also demanded increasingly refined schemes to classify these 'State Papers'. By the late nineteenth century, this long and fitful process of 'digesting' and 'methodising' produced an elaborate series of 'State Papers' classes held in a purpose-built Public Record Office. So-called 'Domestic' State Papers were arranged into different series according to the relevant reign, while 'Foreign' State Papers (for the period 1577–1782) were broken into sub-classes according to which foreign country a document relates to. Each series of papers was bound into large volumes in strict chronological order, obliterating the original filing systems which had been used by previous secretaries of state. A numerical reference system was subsequently introduced, by which the main run of 'State Papers Domestic' for Elizabeth I's reign became SP 12, while 'State Papers, Foreign: France', for example, became SP 78 and 'State Papers, Foreign: Spain' became SP 94.[1]

The crucial point about the State Papers for the final decade or so of Elizabeth's reign is that they principally reflect the work of two principal secretaries: Lord Burghley, the Lord Treasurer, who added control of the secretariat to his other responsibilities after the death of Sir Francis Walsingham in April 1590, and his son, Sir Robert Cecil, who performed much of the secretary's work even before he was finally appointed as Walsingham's long over-due successor in July 1596. The overwhelmingly Cecilian provenance and content of the State Papers for the 1590s – which is especially striking for the foreign classes – has significant implications for our understanding of foreign policy during this period.[2] The 1590s witnessed an increasingly intense struggle over the direction of royal policy, in which the Cecils (despite their self-effacing image of being merely the queen's loyal servants) were active, indeed leading, participants. However, Burghley and Cecil represented only one of two competing strands of opinion among the English political élite. The rival perspective was championed by Robert Devereux, 2nd earl of Essex, the queen's favourite, who ultimately became master of the ordnance and earl marshal. Since Sir Robert Cecil finally emerged as the great victor of Elizabethan politics and the State Papers reflect Cecilian interests and priorities, there has been a strong tendency by historians to marginalise the strand of opinion represented by Essex. Scholars have also usually assumed that Elizabeth herself inherently favoured the policies advocated by the Cecils. To some degree, this is correct. Burghley's conservatism and desire (as Lord Treasurer) to limit military expenditure mirrored Elizabeth's own inclinations. Nevertheless, Elizabeth was genuinely open to persuasion on many matters, and perhaps especially on issues of real importance, when her sharp intellect allowed her to recognise a range of alternative courses of action and her deep-seated reluctance to make a quick decision created the opportunity for debate. During the mid-1590s, Essex's arguments often ultimately carried the day.

The Cecilian bias of the State Papers Foreign was well known to the late R. B. Wernham, whose work has thoroughly dominated our understanding of late-Elizabethan foreign policy. In addition to writing important essays and magisterial surveys,[3] Wernham spent a life–time – almost seventy years – editing the State Papers Foreign.[4] By any standard, this represents a truly monumental contribution to scholarship. Wernham recognised that Essex played a key role in foreign affairs in the 1590s and portrayed the earl's involvement in government in a far more positive light than most previous scholars, who had tended to dismiss him as a mere dilettante and royal toy-boy. Nevertheless, Wernham's overwhelming reliance upon the papers of the royal secretariat means that his account of foreign relations in the 1590s primarily reflects the contents of papers written and received by Burghley and Cecil. This is especially true of the second volume of his 'Armada' trilogy, which covers the years 1589–95. Although Wernham recognised that Essex created 'something very like a rival "foreign office" to that run' by the Cecils during these years,[5] the sheer bulk of Cecilian material and the remarkably infrequent references to Essex in most of the State Papers Foreign classes allowed him only limited insight into the earl's actions and motivation. By contrast, Wernham clearly made a major effort to reduce his dependence upon the State Papers Foreign for the final volume of the trilogy, in which Essex is a central figure.

This essay builds upon Wernham's foundations by utilising a wide range of materials of Essexian provenance to reconstruct a fuller – although, inevitably, still incomplete – portrait of the earl's involvement in foreign affairs. Essex had a broader and more profound commitment to international relations than Wernham and other scholars have recognised. This essay will explore Essex's vision of England taking a leading role in European affairs, why he felt so driven by this vision of the future that he even tried to coerce the queen into implementing it, and how circumstances in the mid-1590s gave him a brief period of significant – perhaps even predominant – influence in the shaping of Elizabeth's foreign policy, before becoming marginalised in the latter years of the decade. This essay also emphasises the interaction between foreign and domestic affairs and posits a revised version of the paradigm by which Wernham and other scholars have interpreted events in the 1590s. Instead of regarding the struggle over England's relations with foreign powers as a spill-over from competition between Essex and the Cecils for 'domestical greatness', this essay suggests that the connection between domestic politics and foreign policy effectively functioned the other way around. Believing that Burghley's dominance of domestic issues was almost unchallengeable but also likely to be short-lived (the Lord Treasurer was aged 70 in 1590), Essex put his energies into military and foreign affairs, which he judged to be the most important areas of government policy during war-time. Essex believed that success in this critical area would ensure his prompt succession as the queen's most influential councillor when Burghley died and that the 'domestical greatness' which his followers desired so fervently would follow as a by-product of his achievements in the sphere of foreign affairs. For Essex, if not for most of his patronage-hungry followers, foreign and military affairs consti- tuted the most urgent issues of the day and he repeatedly risked his 'domestical' standing for the sake of influencing England's relations with foreign powers.[6]

English foreign policy in the period between 1589 and 1603 was prin- cipally shaped by three major challenges: changing patterns of overseas trade, and especially the continuing perturbations in England's cloth trade with the Continent, which was continuing a long-term decline after its peak of the mid-sixteenth century; the unresolved question of the royal succession; and, above all, the great war against Spain. As a taboo subject in England, the succession had the least obvious impact upon the realm's foreign relations. Elizabeth forbade open discussion of the matter, even in parliament, and friendly foreign powers respected this conven- tion. This also applied to James VI of Scotland, who was the most obvious candidate to succeed Elizabeth following the execution of his mother, Mary Queen of Scots, in 1587. Nevertheless, unofficial speculation about what would happen when Elizabeth died was widespread, both within England and without. As seen in Chapter 8 by Susan Doran, James VI sometimes felt sufficiently insecure about his prospects to sound out Italian states, and even Spain, about the possibility of securing international support for his claim to the English throne if he moved towards Catholicism.[7] Such restlessness was, in part, a product of Elizabeth's resolute silence on the matter. However, James was also alarmed – like Elizabeth – when an English Catholic author using the pseudonym 'R. Doleman' openly aired the whole question in *A Conference about the Next Succession to the Crowne of Ingland* and argued strongly for the claim of the Infanta Isabella, the daughter of Philip II of Spain. Published in Antwerp in 1594, this book was smuggled into England and caused a huge storm when it finally came to the queen's attention in October 1595 – especially as it was mischievously dedicated to Essex, on the grounds that 'no man [is] like to have a greater part or sway in deciding of this great affaire'.[8] Although it was intended to rally English Catholics behind Philip II, the book ultimately had the reverse effect and helped to ensure that Spain could not promote Isabella as a viable alternative to James when Elizabeth finally went into terminal decline.[9]

Overseas trade had a far more direct impact on English foreign policy. The outbreak of war against Spain in 1585 finally confirmed the end of England's long commercial dependence upon the cloth market of Antwerp and forced the Merchant Adventurers, the English merchants who monopolised this trade, to find an alternative Continental outlet for their goods. The trade in woollen cloth was immensely important because it was England's biggest export industry and employed large numbers of English men and women as weavers, spinners, clothiers and related trades, as well as supporting sheep-owners. It also produced a healthy stream of income for the crown – money which Elizabeth desperately needed to prosecute the war. Serious efforts to find a new market to replace Antwerp had been underway since the 1560s, with the chief alternatives being the German cities of Emden (until 1587) and Hamburg. These towns, however, proved a poor substitute for Antwerp, and relations between English merchants and the Hanse towns of northern Germany (including Hamburg), which had already been deteriorating for at least a hundred years, became increasingly acrimonious. In 1589, the English cloth market was re-located to the small town of Stade, a few miles outside Hamburg. The English merchants of the Eastland Company, who traded into the Baltic, had similarly set up at Elbing, adjacent to the Hanse city of Danzig. Both locations put English interests outside Hansard jurisdiction, while enabling trade with Hamburg and Danzig to continue. Although some Merchant Adventurers preferred to trade at the Dutch town of Middleburg, the volume of cloth exported through northern Germany meant that England's chief economic life-line remained vulnerable to the political influence of the Hansards upon neighbouring towns and princes and, ultimately, upon the Holy Roman Emperor himself. The Hanse was by no means united in its opposition to the English (as the back-door trade at Hamburg and Danzig suggests), but the Hansards were especially angered by English ships seizing foreign vessels heading for Spain and Portugal, where the Hanse had strong commercial ties.[10]

These difficulties became especially acute after the outbreak of war because it was official English policy to intercept any shipments of food or other strategic goods bound for Spain and Portugal. Such cargoes constituted a significant element in Hansard trade. This policy also encouraged English privateering, which had been a problem for decades, but now reached new heights. The war terminated England's own peace-time trade with Spain and Portugal and encouraged those who had been involved in it to turn to privateering. After the defeat of Spain's *Gran Armada* in 1588 released English shipping which had previously been held back for national defence, perhaps 200 English ships put to sea in 1589 (and every year thereafter) to plunder 'enemy' shipping.[11] Privateers rarely showed much concern about distinguishing between 'enemy' ships and other foreign vessels – let alone between contraband goods and other forms of cargo – and their activities generated a steady chorus of complaints to the English government from foreign merchants and officials. One result of this new 'trade' was that privateering soon matched (or slightly exceeded) the value of England's former trade with Spain and Portugal.[12] However, the consequence of this steady flow of captured goods into the realm was a constant series of diplomatic brushfires which required regular dowsing to prevent a major outbreak of damaging retaliatory action against England's own merchants. Although there were endless complaints from the Dutch, French, Danes and others, the greatest likelihood of a major diplomatic and economic disaster rested with the Hanse, whose hostility still threatened the vital cloth exports into northern Germany. In 1589, Elizabeth's government freed more than 70 Hansard grain ships which had been seized by English vessels off the coast of Portugal, rather than risk retaliation against the Merchant Adventurers. Despite this, Spain tried to exploit Hansard anger towards England and regularly encouraged moves in Germany which would cripple English trade, while English merchants and diplomats sought to counter these initiatives. Although business continued (as it usually does, under almost any circumstances), it did so under the shadow of the war.[13]

The nature and changing fortunes of England's war with Spain had by far the greatest influence on its relations with foreign powers during the latter years of Elizabeth's reign. So great was the human and material commitment required by this war that English government and society became increasingly 'militarised' by the 1590s.[14] The nature of the war certainly changed in 1588. Although English troops were sent to defend the Low Countries in 1585 and aggressive maritime strikes were launched against Spain and its New World colonies, Elizabeth continued to believe that a negotiated peace with Spain was possible, indeed essential, until mid-1588. Fearing the cost and uncertain outcome of an all-out struggle with Spain, she was determined to secure a negotiated settlement and pushed hard for formal peace talks. Although most of the Privy Council had grave misgivings about these negotiations because they believed Spain's real goal was the conquest of England, the talks finally began near Ostend in March 1588. It gradually emerged that the Spanish were not serious about negotiating, and the Spanish governor of Flanders, the duke of Parma, lacked proper authority from Philip II to conclude any agreement. Instead, Parma's goal (on Philip's orders) was to ready his army for an invasion of England while diverting Elizabeth's attention by maintaining the pretence of negotiation as long as possible. The magnitude of this deception had barely become apparent to Elizabeth when the Spanish fleet, the *Gran Armada*, appeared off the south-west coast of England in mid-July.[15]

The arrival of the Armada transformed the conflict against Spain from a war which Elizabeth had never wanted and from which she was anxious to escape into a struggle of national survival. The deception which had accompanied the Armada's final preparations also created an enduring English belief in Spanish perfidy, further inflaming passions which had already been aroused in earlier years by Spanish involvement in plots to assassinate the queen. Elizabeth would never trust Philip again. To English minds, the thwarting and dispersal of the *Gran Armada* represented divine retribution for Spain's treachery. In the months which followed the Spanish defeat, a combination of relief, a new belief in the efficacy of English arms and extravagant hopes of material gain helped to launch a huge expedition against Spain and Portugal which embodied England's riposte to the Philip's 'enterprise of England'. This expedition, which finally sailed in April 1589 under the command of Sir John Norris and Sir Francis Drake, represented a unique opportunity to strike a major blow against Spain while its naval forces remained in disarray. The failure of this venture was a major setback, especially as it cost England almost as many lives as the Spanish had lost in their defeat of the previous year. The heady optimism which had arisen after the victory of 1588 now gave way to recriminations about the cost of the expedition and the failure of Norris and Drake to attack Spain's remaining warships while they were still under repair.[16]

The painful debacle of the Portugal expedition was compounded by news of the assassination of Henry III of France in late July. This brought the French crown to Henry of Navarre, a Protestant prince whose accession as Henry IV of France was bitterly opposed by the Catholic League, who had allied themselves with Spain. Henry's succession not only threw gasoline upon the fire of civil war in France, but also made his realm a new battlefield in the struggle between England and Spain; just as Philip II could not accept the prospect of France being ruled by a hostile Protestant king, so Elizabeth could not afford to see Henry toppled by his Catholic enemies or the French Channel ports made ready to welcome some future Spanish Armada. Despite the bitter disappointment of recent events at sea and ominous news from the Low Countries that Parma was almost ready to launch a major new offensive there,[17] England now found itself compelled to find extra men and money to aid the embattled king in France. Along with the failure of the Portugal expedition, the contested succession of Henry IV brought a new and ominous character to England's strategic outlook. If the triumph of 1588 had encouraged thoughts of a rapid end to the war, the events of mid-1589 dashed those hopes. Although it reduced pressure on the Dutch, especially after Parma led his army into France in July 1590, the emergence of France as the new prime area of conflict escalated and expanded England's war against Spain. Indeed, the latter half of 1589 marked the start of what might termed 'deep war', when no end to the fighting seemed in sight and Elizabeth's regime could only seek to endure, as new threats and commitments mounted up on all sides.

By early September 1589, the first of an initial 4000 English troops were being levied for service in France. Thousands more soldiers would follow in 1590 and each successive year until 1594. They were sent to fight – and died in large numbers – for the sake of a 'common cause' which temporarily united England and the French crown against Spain and the French Catholic League. However, this 'common cause' was a fragile alignment, especially in Elizabeth's mind. Although she recognised the necessity of sending ever more men and money to France, she deeply resented her lack of choice in the matter. She also grew increasingly mistrustful of Henry IV himself, fuming over the way he consistently ignored or bent the conditions which she set for each new tranche of aid. Time and again, she spoke of peremptorily withdrawing English forces from France or denying the king any more support, only to be convinced otherwise by her own second thoughts and the pleading of the Privy Council. Elizabeth's regular outbursts of frustration meant that the council – and especially its two most influential members, Burghley and Sir Christopher Hatton, the Lord Chancellor (until his death in November 1591) – had to manage the queen as well as the running of the war itself. By dint of perseverance and their long experience in dealing with her moods, Burghley and Hatton contrived to maintain Elizabeth's support for the 'common cause' even during the fiasco of the Normandy campaign of 1591.[18] This much-touted joint Anglo-French operation to capture Rouen proved a huge waste of lives and money and demonstrated conclusively that Henry would pursue his own political and military interests regardless of the promises which he had made to Elizabeth.[19] Nevertheless, the consequences of withdrawing support for the king seemed even more unpalatable. As Cecil observed, 'if this occasion overpass, half a million [pounds] next year will not so much help him'.[20] The support which Elizabeth and her council gave to the French king became even more grudging after the middle of 1593, when Henry abjured his Protestantism in order to win broader acceptance of his royal authority among his Catholic subjects.[21] Elizabeth was outraged and Burghley echoed his sovereign's fury, privately praying for 'some notable avenge upon the French king for his perfidy towards God and man'.[22] The mounting mistrust between the two allies was obvious to Thomas Wylkes, a clerk of the Privy Council: 'if the king of Spain be dead, we are like enough to care little for France'.[23] If the Spanish threat had not prevented it – especially the building of a fort in March 1594 to blockade the port of Brest, which required a major Anglo-French operation to capture it – Elizabeth may well have acted upon her threats to withdraw English troops from France. As it was, the queen was compelled to delay this action until after the Spanish fort near Brest was finally overrun on 7 November 1594.[24] By the end of February 1595, for the first time since 1589, there were no English soldiers fighting in France.[25]

In contrast to the growing scepticism, even hostility, which Elizabeth and Burghley expressed towards Henry IV, the earl of Essex was genuinely enthusiastic for the king's cause.[26] Essex's extended family, which included the earl of Leicester (his step-father), Sir Francis Walsingham (his father-in-law) and Sir Philip Sidney (his step-cousin), had long believed in the critical importance of English solidarity with European

Protestants.[27] This commitment to the 'Protestant cause' was not merely a matter of religion, but also reflected a deep-rooted desire to win military renown – to fight abroad in a godly cause and be rewarded for it, like the crusaders of old. This was the traditional dream of aristocrats, but remodelled for the new age of religious warfare. Unlike Leicester and Sidney, however, Essex was not prepared to see his hopes of martial glory repeatedly frustrated by Elizabeth's distaste for war. Although he established himself as a firm favourite of the queen after his return from fighting in the Low Countries in 1585–86, and especially after Leicester's death in September 1588, Essex was never very happy in the golden cage of court and craved the excitement and camaraderie of war. Profoundly disappointed by the failure of the Portugal expedition, which he joined in open defiance of the queen's wishes, he re-focused his hopes of winning military renown and advancing the 'Protestant cause' on France after the accession of Henry IV. Essex believed that a genuine Anglo-French understanding should be the core of a broad anti-Spanish alliance and saw himself as a loyal advocate, even friend, of the king. He lobbied passionately to win command of the English force in the Rouen campaign of 1591. Although it proved an inglorious and expensive failure (even costing the life of the earl's brother, Walter), the campaign cemented the personal bond between Essex and Henry. The two men met for the first time in late August, after Essex made a long and dangerous journey through enemy lines to confer with the French king.[28] This unauthorised excursion infuriated Elizabeth and raised suspicions in her mind about whether Essex would really prefer to serve a warrior king – even a foreigner like Henry – than a female sovereign like herself. These suspicions were well founded, but she ultimately forgave him for his lack of discretion.

In large measure, Essex earned this forgiveness by demonstrating to Elizabeth that his concern for events on the Continent served her interests. Following his return from Normandy in early 1592, Essex began to spend heavily on gathering foreign intelligence, thereby relieving the crown of the burden.[29] This was important because Elizabeth's failure to appoint a new principal secretary after Walsingham's death and Burghley's determination to prune royal expenditure meant that there was no longer either a secretary to co-ordinate intelligence-gathering for the queen or a dedicated budget to support it.[30] Essex's enthusiastic creation of an extensive system of intelligence networks helped to fill this vacuum. The earl was also valuable to the queen for his military experience and continuing patronage of army officers. His willingness to lavish his own time and money upon these soldiers helped to subsidise the war effort and unburden the crown's desperately over-stretched finances. From Essex's perspective, the queen's encouragement to indulge his passion for foreign and military affairs not only accorded with what he believed to be the chief priorities of a country at war, but also enabled him to showcase his qualifications to succeed Burghley as the queen's chief minister in a sphere which did not directly challenge Burghley's current pre-eminence. With Burghley more than 70 years old and increasingly infirm, Essex believed that he would not have long to wait.

Elizabeth finally formalised her recognition of Essex's capabilities by appointing him to the Privy Council in February 1593. As many scholars have recognised, this restored to the council something which had been missing since the time of Leicester and Walsingham – a truly effective advocate of waging aggressive war against Spain and a vocal and committed supporter of England's alliances with the Dutch and the French king. This stance was not simply a reflection of his martial ambitions. A generation or more younger than any of his conciliar colleagues except Sir Robert Cecil, Essex had lived his whole life under the shadow of Spanish hostility towards England and instinctively conceived of his country's future in international terms. Gabriel Montgomery, the son of a famous Huguenot leader, had been one of his childhood companions, and he had been raised 'to parle French'.[31] Many of Essex's contemporaries, who looked to him as their spokesman, shared his belief that England was genuinely part of Europe – what they called 'Christendom'. While Essex's large following of army officers tended to regard Europe primarily as an arena for their own future employment, the earl's more refined friends and followers shared his distinctly Europhile intellectual and cultural tastes. Many of his friends spent lengthy periods travelling in France and Italy, learned foreign languages (including Spanish), mixed with foreign visitors to England (many of whom were entertained lavishly by Essex) and adopted the new Continental vogue for applying insights learned from reading Tacitus and other classical Roman authors to contemporary affairs. Although such interests were by no means restricted to the earl's circle, it is striking how fully Essex and his closest friends embraced both political and cultural membership of 'Christendom'. Elizabeth and Burghley, with their memories of the 1540s and '50s, had a very different perspective and the queen, in particular, still hankered for some means to reverse the loss of Calais to France in 1558. Their long experience of the French menace heightened their anger over Henry's conversion to Catholicism: if its king proved perfidious even in matters of faith, who was to say what France might do in the future? By contrast, Essex's personal bond with Henry helped him to accept the political utility of the king's action. Indeed, Essex exhibited a similar practicality by complementing his own high-profile reputation as a Protestant leader with a more covert advocacy of toleration for English Catholics who disassociated themselves from Spain. He was a crusader against Spain and Spanish Catholicism (which he denigrated as cruel and involving the worship of 'gods of wood and paint'), but not against Catholicism more generally. This shadow reputation as a champion of toleration not only helped him to challenge Spanish attempts to establish Spain as the natural defender of English Catholics, but also eased his establishment of contacts with Catholic powers overseas.[32]

Essex's eagerness to cultivate anti-Spanish Catholics at home and abroad reflected his belief that the security and future prosperity of England could not be divorced from the fate of Europe as a whole. For him, as for many of his friends, the 'tyranny' of Spain threatened not merely England or even France and the Low Countries, but 'Christendom' itself. By contrast with Elizabeth or Burghley, who sought to restrict England's costly entanglement in European affairs and ultimately mistrusted foreigners, Essex firmly believed that England shared common interests with its Continental neighbours, even those distant from the Channel, such as the Italian states. Like Leicester and Walsingham before him, Essex combined devout Protestantism with a deep interest in the culture and politics of Catholic Italy. As he observed to one of his foreign agents, it was his personal misfortune that God had never allowed him to visit Italy, the 'garden of Christendom'.[33] Burghley, on the other hand, feared that travel beyond the Alps might contaminate young English gentlemen.[34] The gulf between Essex and Burghley gave them different perspectives on events abroad. Where Burghley (and Elizabeth) saw foreign duplicity and endless demands on England's inadequate resources, Essex saw opportunities to cultivate alliances against the arch-enemy, Spain. For Essex and his friends, the belief that the war against Spanish 'tyranny' was fought upon 'the stage of Christendom'[35] meant that this struggle could not be shirked, regardless of the cost. Not only did the war represent a God-given opportunity to win European-wide fame for England (and themselves), but the consequences of failing to subdue such a 'cruel', perfidious and endlessly expansive enemy would be terrible indeed. Moreover, by destroying Spanish power, England would be able to carve out an empire for itself from the wreckage of Spain's outposts in the Indies and the New World.

Such ambitions were very different from Elizabeth's war aims. Her goals were limited to securing her territories from invasion, solving the problem of the Low Countries by negotiating the removal of the Spanish army and protection for Dutch Protestants and, ultimately, restoring trade and diplomatic ties with Spain. Far from wanting to destroy the enemy, she counted upon a strong but safely distant Spain to counter-balance any future revival of French animosity towards England. Where Essex (and many other English men and women) looked to the future and envisaged a wide new world of opportunity, Elizabeth remembered how disastrously military adventurism had affected the realm in the 1540s and '50s and sought to avoid a repetition of those past calamities. Yet, despite their different objectives, Elizabeth believed that she could profit from the earl's desire to act upon 'the stage of Christendom'. With her encouragement, he stepped up his intelligence-gathering and foreign correspondence, and demanded (and received) copies of the regular dis-patches sent home by England's diplomatic agents in France and the Low Countries. Essex also took over responsibility from Burghley for main-taining indirect contact with the grand duke of Tuscany[36] and acted as host in England for Antonio Perez, the former secretary of Philip II who had fled to France and become a bitter enemy of Spain.[37] Burghley was probably glad to distance himself from such expensive and (in the case of Perez) distasteful activities, but the result was that Essex established a special expertise in Continental affairs. To a considerable degree, Essex and Burghley (who still controlled the royal secretariat in the absence of a secretary of state) began to manage separate, complementary and compartmentalised foreign policy initiatives for the queen.

The emerging pattern became clear in Elizabeth's dealings with James VI of Scotland during the latter half of 1593. Angry that James seemed unwilling to take action against three Catholic earls whose dealings with Spain had been revealed in the 'Spanish blanks' affair of late 1592, Elizabeth directed Burghley and Cecil to put pressure on the king by stir-ring up the maverick earl of Bothwell. At the same time, she also explored a more conciliatory option by encouraging Essex to open com-munications with the earl of Huntly, the leader of the pro-Spanish earls. Elizabeth alone co-ordinated these separate and contradictory initiatives. The queen's hostility meant that Essex's contact with Huntly soon proved abortive, but the Bothwell operation became a public fiasco. James was infuriated by this brazen intervention in Scottish affairs and a diplomatic mission to Scotland by Lord Zouche in early 1594 only hardened his resentment. Unable to criticise Elizabeth openly, the king instead focused his anger against the Cecils, who had implemented her policy. This helped to strengthen a budding covert partnership between James and Essex, by which Essex would support James' bid to succeed to the English throne upon Elizabeth's death and James would reward Essex accordingly.[38] Although it was conducted through third parties and explicit promises were carefully avoided (at least on paper), the alignment between Essex and James gradually became an open secret and gave added reason for European politicians to cultivate the earl's friendship. This potential trump card also undoubtedly helped to embolden Essex's actions at home and abroad.

With Elizabeth's encouragement, Essex rapidly began to develop contacts across Europe, including northern Italy, France, Germany and the Low Countries. He also sent spies into Spain, whose reports he passed to the queen, and quietly developed links in Scotland which he largely hid from her. Essex's connections with the French and Dutch were so strong that almost every English ambassador or *chargé d'affaires* in France or the Low Countries during the 1590s was either his friend or client before he was appointed, or became one during his term of service abroad. Dutch and French envoys to England also paid special attention to Essex because he was known to be their chief advocate on the English council. As the queen's senior adviser, who had been a councillor since the start of the reign, Burghley received similar compliments from allied diplomats, although they were perhaps less warmly meant than those paid to Essex. As acting secretary of state, Burghley (aided by his son, Cecil) also oversaw the queen's correspondence with her diplomats in France, Scotland and the Low Countries, but his investment in intelligence was considerably less than the earl's, even when supplemented by networks in France and Spain which were controlled by his friends, Lord Cobham and Lord Howard of Effingham, the Lord Admiral. Nevertheless, Burghley balanced Essex's specialisation in Continental affairs by having prime responsibility for the queen's policies in Scotland and totally dominating Irish affairs, in which Essex played a very limited role.

The growing bifurcation between Essex and Burghley underlines the extent to which the queen herself sought to control the making and execution of policy. Even if she was not prepared to pay for expensive intelligence or new quasi-diplomatic contacts abroad from her own depleted coffers, she was happy to see Essex spend his money on these activities so that she could benefit from them. In part, this reflected the crippling burden of the war on royal finances. More importantly, though, it encouraged a degree of competition between Essex and Burghley, which provided the queen with fresher and fuller intelligence, better-argued advice and the possibility of choosing between different policy options. For Elizabeth, the ability to choose was critical because it underpinned her own authority and self-image as a prince; as an unmarried queen, she had evolved an elaborate style of (literally) man-management which discouraged her male advisers and courtiers from forming a solid bloc and trying to dictate to her and, instead, forced them to compete with each other for her approval. War sharply limited the queen's ability to choose and this was one reason why she remained anxious to find a secure and honourable peace as soon as circumstances permitted. However, Elizabeth's desire for choice did not mean that she wanted unrestrained competition between Essex and Burghley. If anything, she sought to control and channel Essex's emerging rivalry with Burghley, while harnessing his enthusiasm for Continental and military affairs to her own advantage.

One consequence of this channelling can be seen in the patchy nature of the State Papers Foreign for the 1590s. The 'State Papers, Foreign: Venice', for example, is remarkably thread-bare in the mid-1590s: only one surviving document was written in 1594, two in 1595, four in 1596, five in 1597 and none in 1598. It was only in 1600–01 that reports from Venice again began to approach the frequency of 1587–92, when John Wroth had served as a resident English agent there.[39] However, this does not mean that England temporarily ceased to be interested in Venice, which remained a major hub of international trade, a key participant in Mediterranean politics and an Italian state which kept Spain and the papacy at arm's length. Although there was a hiatus following Wroth's departure, the main explanation for the dearth of information in the State Papers Venice is that Essex, rather than Burghley or Cecil, took charge of contacts with the republic. Despite suffering a series of setbacks in 1595, Essex's resident agent in Venice, Dr Henry Hawkyns, was sending back weekly reports by early 1596. Every Friday, Hawkyns sent off a gazette of Italian news, compiled by local assistants, and a covering letter of his own.[40] The London end of the operation was run for Essex by his friend Anthony Bacon, who tried to send Hawkyns news from England every Saturday.[41] Although many have been scattered or lost, scores of these documents still survive among Bacon's papers.[42]

The paperwork generated by Hawkyns' mission shows that Essex – and the queen, who received regular briefings on Hawkyns' dispatches – utilised Venice as a base for securing intelligence about Spain, the papacy, Italy and the broader region of southern Europe and the Mediterranean. However, despite Hawkyns' own pretensions to being an

English ambassador, neither Elizabeth nor Essex seem to have pursued larger diplomatic goals in Venice. By contrast, there are tantalising hints that Essex cultivated a much more ambitious relationship with Florence. Building upon his earlier contacts with the grand duke of Tuscany, Essex despatched Sir Thomas Chaloner to serve as his resident agent there in 1596 and even sent one of his own secretaries, Henry Cuffe, on a lengthy mission there over the winter of 1597–98. As he wrote in his letter of credence for Cuffe, 'I do favour and esteem him much and send him into those parts to make him more fit to be used in any negotiation that way.'[43] Essex's ultimate goal seems to have been the creation of an anti-Spanish alliance built around Henry IV of France (whose re-admission to the Catholic Church the grand duke helped to negotiate during 1593–94 and who married the grand duke's daughter, Marie de' Medici, in 1600) and embracing the Dutch, England and perhaps also Scotland. Such an alliance would have fulfilled Essex's dreams of grand action upon 'the stage of Christendom', but it would also have run entirely counter to Elizabeth's war aims. How far these designs progressed and how much Elizabeth knew about them remains uncertain because Essex's papers were later severely culled. In the hours before his final arrest at Essex House on the evening of 8 February 1601, many of the earl's papers were burned 'lest (as he said) they should tell tales'.[44] Anthony Bacon also apparently destroyed most of his papers relating to the period 1598–1600, presumably at about the same time and for the same reason. As a result, the extent of Essex's dealings with Florence must remain the subject of speculation, barring the discovery of unknown documents in an Italian archive. This is also true for his contacts in Germany and central Europe, which were apparently significant, but have left little trace. Although Henry Wotton served as Essex's secretary for 'Transylvania, Polonia, Italy [and] Germany', it seems that his files were destroyed almost in their entirety.[45] Given these yawning gaps, it is probable that no truly definitive assessment of the earl's impact upon England's relations with foreign powers can ever be offered.

Nevertheless, it is apparent that Essex's involvement in foreign affairs continued to escalate during 1594–95. He doubled the size of his personal secretariat, established the intelligence-gathering station at Venice, and sent new spies to France and Spain. He now required agents such as Dr Hawkyns not only to send regular intelligence reports, but also to compile elaborate dossiers on the intricacies of individual foreign states. Young gentlemen whom he sponsored during their Continental tours were encouraged to produce similar reports. Although he was anxious for information to help him better understand European politics, Essex also believed that such work had longer-term benefits: as he told Hawkyns, 'the chief end of my employing you be rather your enabling hereafter then your present service'.[46] Emboldened by his secret understanding with James VI and by Burghley's increasing ill health, Essex was already seeking to train men who could administer the more expansive foreign policy which he envisaged himself presiding over in the future. During 1596, he also overhauled his own visual image, abandoning the English neo-medieval style evident in earlier portraits of him by William Segar and Nicholas Hilliard in favour of the more sombre and distinctly Italianate style of Isaac Oliver and Marcus Gheeraerts.[47]

Essex's grand plans increasingly placed him at odds with Burghley and Elizabeth, but the tensions between them only became overt after the destruction of the Spanish fort at Brest in November 1594. This victory marked the end of the 'deep war' which England had entered in between 1589 and 1590 because it removed the immediate Spanish threat and presented Elizabeth and her government with a choice about the future conduct of the war. For the first time since the aftermath of the Armada campaign in 1588, England could either seize the military initiative from Spain by launching new offensive operations or scale back the national war effort. This possibility of choice broke down the previous consensus about the war. Elizabeth's decision to shed her Continental commitments by withdrawing troops from France and redeploying many of them to Ireland was heart-breaking for Essex.[48] Although the move reflected Burghley's entirely justified concern that events there were getting out of hand, the transfer of resources from France to Ireland distressed Essex because it meant that English troops would be locked into what he regarded as a 'miserable, beggarly'[49] war from which they could not easily be withdrawn for fresh service on the Continent. Even worse, in Essex's mind, was the timing of the queen's action and the disregard for her French allies which it suggested. Elizabeth withdrew her troops from France in February 1595, just a month after Henry had proved his commitment to the war against Spain by doing what she had always refused to do – formally declare war on Spain. Anxious to be free of the burden of maintaining troops in France, she brushed off the king's invitation to emulate him and to build a new Anglo-French alliance.[50] Instead, Elizabeth continued her practice of issuing a separate proclamation to justify each specific action which she took against Spain and its allies, as if the war were not really continuous, and hence could be stopped at any time. For Essex, who underestimated the magnitude of the danger in

Ireland and remained focused upon the fate of 'Christendom', the queen's decision not to join with France suggested that she still did not understand the full extent of the danger posed by Spain. Bolstered by the information and arguments of Antonio Perez, who had spent almost two years as his guest (until July 1595) and thereafter corresponded with him from France, Essex sought to change the queen's policy. Where she and Burghley had scaled back England's war effort, devoted new attention to Ireland and begun to pressure the Dutch for repayment of the money which England had spent on the war in the Low Countries, Essex sought to revitalise England's flagging ties with its allies and to escalate the war against Spain. The divergent visions of the war held by Essex and Elizabeth now became increasingly obvious.

Essex's advocacy of the French cause during 1595 was passionate, but unsuccessful. His support for the efforts of visiting French envoys and the idea of an Anglo-French conference to discuss joint operations against the common enemy proved unavailing. By December 1595, when his friend Sir Henry Unton, went to serve as ambassador in France, Essex was so frustrated by his lack of success that he secretly instructed Unton to exaggerate the difficulties faced by the French king in his reports home.[51] However, like the agitation for a conference, Unton's dispatches had little impact upon the queen. She would accept nothing less than the return of Calais as her price for further aid to France and this was a price which Henry was unwilling to pay. Essex had more success in defending the interests of the Dutch. He convinced Elizabeth not to reduce English forces in the Low Countries.[52] Despite the queen's bluster over the refusal of the Dutch to begin repaying her costs in fighting the war there, Essex also succeeded in forcing her to scotch wild rumours that she might abandon the Dutch in return for peace with Spain.[53]

Essex's main success in 1595 was to reverse the scaling-back of England's war effort, which he achieved by switching his emphasis from the war in France to the war at sea. Given Elizabeth's aversion to the French alliance, this represented a necessary change of tactics in pursuit of his larger goal of reviving the war against Spain, but it also reflected a changed assessment of the military situation. By the middle of 1595, Essex's intelligence sources had convinced him that Spain was preparing to try again what it had failed to do in 1588. At first, his claims about a new Spanish Armada made little impression on the queen. Other councillors, including Burghley and Cecil, argued (correctly) that this was an alarmist interpretation.[54] Nevertheless, opinions changed dramatically after four Spanish galleys from Brittany launched a minor raid against

Cornwall on 24 July.[55] Now it seemed that the realm was perilously vulnerable to Spanish attack and that Essex's fears were justified after all. This perception helped him to win the queen's approval for the long-delayed expedition of Sir John Hawkins and Sir Francis Drake, which was intended to interdict the flow of silver to Spain from the New World by seizing and garrisoning Panama.[56] The expedition ultimately proved to be a disaster (partly because the Spanish were forewarned about its objectives by Sir Walter Ralegh's loose lips[57]), but it ended the moratorium on major naval operations which had been in place since the end of 1591. Given the difficulties of defending England and Wales, let alone Ireland, the best option for resisting an invasion seemed to be a pre-emptive strike against the Spanish fleet before it could put to sea, the same strategy which had been attempted, but thwarted, in 1588. The initial planning for this operation was undertaken by the Lord Admiral, but Essex was appointed as co-commander in early 1596 and brought new drive to the venture. Essex poured his resources into the expedition because he not only intended to neutralise the Spanish fleet, but also secretly planned to seize a Spanish port and garrison it. He spelled out this intention – which ran directly contrary to the queen's orders – in a letter which he left behind to be delivered to the council only when the fleet was beyond recall.[58] In effect, he sought to defeat the policy of disengagement from the Continent by subverting the objectives of the strike against Spain and committing Elizabeth to a Continental war whether she wanted it or not. As he admitted to one of his secretaries, 'I know I shall never do her service but against her will.'[59]

Essex's effort to hijack what became the Cadiz expedition of 1596 proved a frustrating failure. Although the city was captured, the Lord Admiral and many of the other senior officers refused to accept Essex's plan to hold it. In the end, it was sacked and abandoned.[60] At court and among the council, there was outrage at Essex's actions, despite the victory. Almost certainly, Elizabeth's fury prompted her to appoint Cecil as secretary of state in early July, despite having promised Essex not to do so.[61] Fearing the consequences of the earl's victory at Cadiz and emboldened by Cecil's promotion, key members of the court and council began to form an anti-Essex coalition, centred around Burghley and Cecil. Some of the earl's own supporters also began to draw back and re-consider what political price they might be prepared to pay for endorsing his pursuit of a European vision which, however appealing, now seemed alarmingly out of step with the queen's wishes. Essex's commitment to the war against Spain therefore had a profound impact on domestic politics. It made him a marked man among his colleagues and raised the prospect of his political isolation if he could not win the queen to his point of view.[62]

In the short term, these dangers were obscured by the dictates of the war, which had entered a new and more threatening phase. This made Essex indispensable and gave his aggressive plans greater relevance, while encouraging a temporary suspension of political strife at court. In April 1596, Spanish troops besieged and captured Calais. Philip II also moved to sap English resources by sending aid to the earl of Tyrone's rebels in Ireland,[63] a decision which was reinforced by his desire to strike back for the humiliating occupation of Cadiz by English (and Dutch) forces. Nevertheless, the magnitude of the injury done to the king's honour at Cadiz also required that it be answered in kind.[64] As a result, the Cadiz expedition triggered the very threat which it was supposed to prevent. Despite the lateness of the season (and consequent autumnal gales), a Spanish fleet sailed north in mid-October – only to be shattered by a storm. News of the enemy fleet's departure triggered a massive and costly call-out of ships and soldiers in England.[65] In fact, the fleet's instructions demonstrate that this was not an attempted repeat of 1588, despite what was believed in England. Although it was originally aimed at southern Ireland or Milford Haven in Wales, where it might perhaps have been able to 'do a Cadiz' against Elizabeth, the Spanish fleet was re-directed at the last minute towards Brittany because the shortness of time and resources would have prevented it achieving anything worthwhile before winter set in.[66] As it was, the Spanish fleet did not make it even as far as Brittany. Yet the very fact it sailed showed that Philip II was bent on revenge and that a new round of naval engagements was likely in 1597. This made Essex, who had commanded the realm's defences in October and November, the man of the hour.

Faced with the prospect of attack by Spain, Elizabeth and her government adopted many of the actions advocated by Essex. In the wake of the fall of Calais, when Essex and the Lord Admiral were preparing to sail for Spain, Elizabeth reversed her policy towards France and accepted the sort of alliance which Essex had been urging for the last eighteen months. By the Treaty of Greenwich (signed on 14 May 1596), England and France concluded an offensive and defensive alliance against Spain, and England promised money and men to France. In reality, the treaty was less impressive than it appeared and lacked the substance which Essex had hoped for. Secret clauses limited the number of English troops to a mere 2000 men (because of the queen's increasingly burdensome commitments in Ireland) and restricted their service to the coast of Picardy. Although the treaty was later expanded into the so-called Triple Alliance, involving the Dutch, in late October, it was a hollow document. England offered little more than a token commitment to the war in France, less, in fact, than the Dutch provided.[67] From Elizabeth's perspective, the chief value of this alliance was that it prevented Henry from making peace with Spain without her approval, underlining her mistrust of the French king. For Essex, the Triple Alliance at least provided a basis for future co-operation. His disappointment was soothed by commissions from the queen to reform the ordnance office, overhaul the militia and lead a new expedition to Spain. For the latter, he was even permitted to establish a garrison on Spanish territory – a remarkable turn-around from Elizabeth's position of the previous year.[68] By the middle of 1597, Essex seemed poised to wage war in a manner which marked a distinct break with Elizabeth's usual policy of avoiding or restricting military commitments on the Continent. Essex's status as the realm's senior general and the certainty of a new Spanish naval assault gave the queen and the earl's colleagues on the council little choice but to accede to his demands.

Although the strategic situation ensured that Essex had a decisive influence on English policy over the winter and spring of 1596–97, the changing fortunes of war soon eroded his position. When Essex's new Anglo-Dutch expedition set sail to attack the Spanish fleet in its home port, hostile winds quickly battered it back to England. By the time Essex's fleet sailed again, in mid-August, most of his army had been demobilised. This destroyed Essex's plan to establish a garrison on Spanish territory and sharply reduced his ability even to attack the Spanish fleet at Ferrol.[69] In the end, attacking Ferrol proved impossible and the expedition was reduced to trying to intercept the annual Spanish treasure convoy as it arrived in the Azores. To Essex's dismay, the convoy escaped to safety by a mere three hours.[70] Worse was to come. The return home of Essex's fleet in October coincided with the arrival in English waters of Spain's fleet, which had not been lured to defend the Azores. This was an even more formidable force than that of the previous year and its appearance underlined the complete failure of Essex's operation as a means of national defence. Fortunately for the English, the Spanish fleet again suffered from a last-minute change of instructions. Reversing his actions of 1596, Philip II scrapped the plan to seize Brest as a base for invading England in the following spring and instead ordered his fleet to head directly for the English port of Falmouth.[71] The Spanish fleet also again tempted fate by setting sail late in the season, and suffered accordingly when it was hit by a storm and driven homewards. Although the losses were less severe than in 1596, this second successive failure was a shattering blow to Spanish morale.

The bitter disappointments suffered by England and Spain in their great naval offensives of 1597 helped to revive thoughts of peace. On the English side, Essex's failure ruined many of his followers and severely dented his reputation. His efforts to compensate for his weakened position by demanding that Elizabeth appoint him as earl marshal drove the political in-fighting at court to a new level of bitterness. Although he finally got his wish, the method which he employed – refusing to take part in council business and effectively blackmailing Elizabeth – angered the queen and provided fresh political ammunition for his rivals. It also raised the question of how much longer his participation would remain essential for the proper functioning of government, especially as new developments threatened to marginalise Essex's agenda of aggressive international co-operation against Spain. In mid-October, the death of the Lord Deputy in Ireland left the English position there in a precarious state. England also finally had to face the economic consequences of English merchants being banned from trading in the Holy Roman Empire. This action, which came into force at the end of September, marked a triumph for Spanish diplomacy and a victory for the Hanseatic merchants of northern Germany in their long-running struggle against their English counterparts of the Merchant Adventurers and the Eastland Company.[72] Although there was soon widespread evasion of the imperial order, its economic and political impact on England made the resumption of trade a key argument for peace in 1598. As the ban came into force, Elizabeth remained confident enough to reject a Danish offer of mediation between England and Spain.[73] However, news that the French king was already negotiating with the enemy meant that England's whole strategic environment was about to undergo a radical transformation.

The question of peace or war in 1598 created the biggest diplomatic and political crisis of the 1590s. Although the debate was ostensibly only about whether or not to enter negotiations with Spain, it seemed that there would be enormous pressure to agree a treaty if these peace talks ever took place. The stakes, therefore, were high. As Elizabeth herself told a visiting French envoy, the question placed her 'between Scylla and Charibdis and [she] had never seen a matter of such importance since she became Queen of England'.[74] Although it was not confirmed until the signing of the treaty of Vervins on 22 April, it was increasingly clear that Henry IV would make peace with Spain regardless of his commitments to England or the Dutch. Elizabeth could do little more than vent her fury at the French king when she heard the news. Vervins, however, also gave England a six-month period within which it could apply to join the settlement. The vital question was whether the queen should take up this offer. On the one hand, the material and human costs of the Spanish war were exacting a heavy toll upon the realm, especially as the harvests of 1595–98 were among the worst of the whole century.[75] The burden of open rebellion in Ireland and the new trade ban in Germany added to the appeal of peace. On the other hand, English concern about Spain's future intentions ran very deep and the problem of the Low Countries remained unresolved. England ould no more afford to see the Dutch overwhelmed in 1598 than in 1585, especially if the huge sums which had been spent on the war in the Low Countries were ever to be recovered.

The debate about these issues was intense. The chief advocate of peace was Burghley, who saw it as an economic and social necessity for the realm. In the old Lord Treasurer's eyes, this would also be the last and crowning achievement of his long political life.[76] Essex was equally passionate in his opposition to peace. If anything, the demise of the French alliance, on which he had built his career, made him even more determined to hold the line on behalf of the Dutch, who remained ardently opposed to Spain. He also feared that England would be gambling on the continued good will of an enemy which he believed was innately treacherous and still resented the humiliations which it had suffered at English hands. As he argued repeatedly, 'from Spain, there can be no true peace meant'.[77] Burghley became so infuriated with the earl's stance that, on one occasion, he pulled out a psalm book and quoted at him the verse that 'men of blood shall not live out half their days'.[78] Modern scholars have often criticised Essex's bellicosity and instinctively praised Burghley's desire for negotiation (which fits better with modern sensibilities), but the bitterness of their debate reflects the fact that they were both correct. The realm desperately needed a break from the war. Yet it was not obvious that peace would have provided real relief. Despite medieval notions of Christian harmony, the word 'peace' in early-modern Europe usually carried connotations which reflected the classical Roman concept of *pax*, which meant 'peace won by victory'. Peace without a victory – as was the case in 1598 – therefore seemed a problematical concept and immediately stirred visions of deception and of a short-lived truce intended only to gain advantage when the conflict was renewed. In this light, Spain's offer of peace was a strategic manoeuvre aimed at undermining England's military capacity, while re-building its own. Many contemporaries agreed with this analysis, and recent studies of Spanish policy support Essex's contentions.[79]

By the end of June 1598, when Elizabeth met with her council to discuss the appointment of a new Lord Deputy for Ireland, the tensions created by the debate about peace were so deep that they exploded into acrimony between Essex and Elizabeth herself.[80] The result was a 'great quarrel' between Essex and Elizabeth which permanently damaged the earl's standing and kept him from participating in council business until the middle of September. Essex's growing estrangement from his conciliar colleagues was further demonstrated by his authorship of an 'Apologie'.[81] This tract, which was circulated in manuscript form among his friends, countered criticisms from his rivals that he was a war-monger and reiterated his argument that peace, with an undefeated Spain, was impossible. Although Essex subsequently claimed that it had 'escaped' from his study,[82] the 'Apologie' was only one of series of tracts which he released (or tried to release) during the mid-1590s to influence political debate by appealing over the heads of the queen and his opponents to a broader public audience.[83] Like the growing factionalism at court, this phenomenon was a clear sign that debate about the war – or, more precisely, the prospect that it might be ended – was injecting a new extremism into English politics. For Essex, in particular, the collapse of the French alliance and the dangers of negotiating with Spain meant that his previous espousal of an alternative foreign policy increasingly gave way to fretful anxiety that he was being outmanoeuvred in a struggle for domestic political influence. Only by winning this domestic struggle, he believed, could he avert the dangers which would ensue if the 'peace-dreamers' (as he called them) won the queen over to their cause.

Despite her natural sympathy with calls for peace, Elizabeth soon realised that she could not abandon the Dutch – or the huge investment of English money which they represented. She was happy, however, to use the threat of peace to extract more concrete benefits from her relationship with them. This involved tough negotiations with Dutch envoys during July and August 1598.[84] Essex, who remained the chief Dutch advocate in England, took no part in these talks, which were led by Cecil. By a new agreement signed on 6 August, the Dutch promised to start repaying a £800,000 war debt at £30,000 per annum, to pay the wages of English troops in Flushing and Brill, and to provide support if England were invaded or sent new expeditions against Spain.[85] This agreement ensured that England would not join the Franco-Spanish peace and drastically cut the queen's costs in the Low Countries, freeing up resources for the war in

Ireland. In effect, Elizabeth's price for eschewing peace talks with Spain was the minimisation of her remaining Continental commitments.

Although he had helped to defeat the drive for peace, Essex was politically marginalised by the events of 1598. Essex's life-long Francophilia now seemed irrelevant and his prolonged absence from court meant that Cecil and his allies were the chief beneficiaries of Burghley's death in August. The earl's long-cherished hopes of filling the gap left by the old Lord Treasurer's demise had come to nought. News of a catastrophic defeat at Yellow Ford and the prospect of the total collapse of English control in Ireland also relegated events in Europe to secondary importance: England's strategic interests now became overwhelmingly centred on Ireland. In this transformed political and strategic environment, it seemed that Essex's only road back to political relevance – and to trumping his domestic rivals by winning fresh martial glory – lay in taking command of the large new army which Elizabeth sent to confront Tyrone in 1599. Although he finally secured this command, it was a sign of how much things had changed that Essex was forced to abandon his hopes of figuring on 'the stage of Christendom' (temporarily, at least) and stake his future on success in a theatre of war which he had always despised. His subsequent failure to confront Tyrone in Ulster destroyed forever his aura of military indispensability, while his decision to offer Tyrone a truce exposed him to the queen's fury and humiliation by his domestic rivals. Essex's penultimate effort to influence royal policy by military action resulted in his political and psychological melt-down over the winter of 1599–1600.

Essex's sojourn in Ireland during the spring and summer of 1599 meant that Cecil and his allies dominated Elizabeth's counsels when she again pondered the prospect of peace. Philip II died on 3 September 1598 and was succeeded by his son, Philip III. Philip II, however, bequeathed the sovereignty of Spanish Flanders to his daughter Isabella and her future husband Albert (the so-called 'archdukes'). For a while, Elizabeth hoped that Philip II's 'donation' of the sovereignty of Flanders might offer a solution to the vexed problem of the Low Countries, but the Dutch refused to compromise their hard-won national unity, and the new Philip III was determined to take a hard line against the Dutch and to secure the military victory against England which had eluded his father. Instead of a new opportunity for peace, the advent of the archdukes initiated a confusing and often contradictory interplay between the governments in Brussels and Spain.[86] While Albert sought an end to the conflict which ravaged his new dominions by despatching a private representative in January 1599 to invite Elizabeth into fresh peace negotiations, Philip pursued distinctly bellicose policies. By August 1599, the threat from Spain seemed sufficiently urgent to trigger another major invasion scare – the so-called 'invisible Armada'. In fact, the Spanish fleet sailed to defend the Azores against a marauding Dutch fleet, but faulty intelligence prompted a full-scale emergency in England. Yet, despite the bewilderment caused by Spanish actions and the alarm which it caused the Dutch, Elizabeth remained determined to pursue Albert's overtures to see where they might lead. This culminated in a meeting of English and Spanish envoys at Boulogne between May and July 1600, but the two sides could not even agree on the basic matters of protocol which were necessary for the real negotiations to begin.[87] Despite the fears of Essex and his friends in 1598, the opening of talks with the enemy certainly did not result in the pursuit of peace at any price. Nevertheless, these contacts with the enemy helped to encourage one final act of political desperation by Essex. Excluded from the council and believing that his opponents were engaged in treasonous negotiations with the Spanish to abandon the Dutch and exclude James VI from the English throne, Essex and his surviving supporters plotted a *coup d'état* to 'rescue' Elizabeth and take control of the government. These plans remained incomplete when Essex and his friends were panicked into a half-hearted insurrection in London in February 1601. Its failure finally cost Essex his head.

The Essex rising was the ultimate expression of an extremism which had been formed in the crucible of war and which strained Elizabethan politics almost to breaking point by the late 1590s. Thwarted in his hopes of succeeding Burghley as the queen's chief councillor and fearful that his domestic rivals intended to lead the queen into a reckless peace with Spain, Essex came to believe that military men such as himself had a right and a duty to 'save' the queen and realm from this prospect, if necessary by force: in order to wage the sort of all-out war against the Spanish which he believed was necessary for military success, he and his 'friends' must first deal with their political 'enemies' at home. Thanks largely to Essex's hesitations and lingering hopes that Elizabeth would recall him into her favour, this militarised approach to politics was never put into practice and virtually the only blood shed in the late Elizabethan power struggle was the earl's own.

Without the quelling of this extremism by the destruction of Essex's rump of die-hard Hispanophobes, it is hard to see how the war against Spain could ever have been ended by negotiation. Yet the fall of Essex and humbling of his supporters gave little immediate impetus towards peace. Although letters continued to be exchanged with Albert's officials and an envoy from the archduke visited England during the autumn of 1601, the prospect of further talks was dashed by news that Spanish troops had landed in Ireland at Kinsale in September 1601.[88] This underlined, once again, how vulnerable England remained to Spanish aggression while the rebellion continued in Ireland. By sheer good fortune, the Spanish landing occurred in the wrong place and forced Tyrone's army to concentrate far from its chief strongholds, exposing it to a crushing defeat on Christmas Eve. The English victory at Kinsale took much of the heart out of Tyrone's supporters (especially as the Spanish troops, who had not joined the battle, surrendered on 2 January 1602),[89] but it did not end the rebellion.

When the Privy Council met to discuss the future prospects of the war on 24 May 1602, Lord Buckhurst, Burghley's successor as Lord Treasurer, argued that the realm was being impoverished by its military exertions and that the best hope for the future lay in ending the 'lingering war' with Spain. If they discussed the present state of the war (the surviving notes of the meeting are distinctly abbreviated), he and his colleagues might have agreed on the current stalemate at sea and in the Low Countries, where even a dramatic Dutch victory at Nieupoort in June 1600 had not changed matters for long. Since July 1601, the rival forces there had been bogged down in the great siege of Ostend, which would ultimately continue until 1604. However, Cecil, the Lord Admiral and Sir William Knollys disagreed with Buckhurst's advice. In their assessment, peace with Spain was impossible while Ireland remained unsettled. Since England's security still depended upon the Low Countries being free from occupation by Spanish or French armies, the queen would have to continue providing secret military aid to the Dutch, who refused to make peace with Spain. This would inevitably provoke retaliation in kind by the Spanish, who 'have & will aid the rebels in Ireland', which would undermine the chief attractions of making peace in the first place – specially as everyone agreed that 'it was the Irish wars [which] had impoverished England, & not the wars of Spain or Low Countries'. In the opinion of the three councillors, peace had to be established in Ireland before any secure peace could be made with Spain itself; only in this way could Spanish meddling in Ireland 'in requital' of English support for the Dutch be averted. The road to peace therefore ran through Ireland, not Spain or the Low Countries.[90] Essex had made the same point to Cecil when opposing talk of peace more than four years earlier: 'a few crowns bestowed in Ireland & Scotland [by Spain] will presently vex us & in a short time beggar us'.[91]

It was only in the closing months of the reign, however, that circumstances finally moved towards a resolution of these problems. Although they could not discuss the succession openly, Cecil and his allies on the council were at last able to begin seeking favour with James VI after the fall of Essex in 1601. Once Essex was safely dead, his longstanding ties to the king were extinguished and his old rivals were finally able to take up the cause of ensuring a Scottish succession to the English throne, thereby ending the threat of war in the north and quietly safeguarding their own hold on power for the next reign.[92] In Ireland, where the rebellion smouldered on throughout 1602, the conflict was finally ended by granting a pardon to Tyrone and implicitly recognising his authority in Ulster.[93] Although peace required it, Elizabeth agreed to this compromise with profound reluctance. Indeed, many observers believed that the queen's concession to Tyrone raised painful doubts in her mind about the treatment of Essex in 1599 and the tragic events which had followed, plunging her into a bitter despair which gradually eroded her will to live.[94] Whether or not this contemporary interpretation of Elizabeth's gloomy final days is accurate, the final negotiations in Ireland coincided with her terminal decline. The most crucial precondition for peace with Spain – peace in Ireland – was therefore only fulfilled as Elizabeth herself lay dying. It would be the task of the new king, James VI & I, to turn the immediate cease-fire with Spain which greeted the old queen's death into a formal peace.

NOTES

1. *Guide to the Contents of the Public Record Office,* ii (1963), pp. 1–3; H. Hall, *Studies in English Official Historical Documents* (1908), pp. 30, 60, 133.
2. The extent to which the State Papers of this era are Cecilian is emphasised by the terms of the draft warrant appointing the two keepers of the secretarial archive in 1610. Both men were adherents of Sir Robert Cecil (by then earl of Salisbury) and, despite being granted the office for life, both could be dismissed by Cecil 'at any tyme by writing under his hand and seale'. The papers themselves are described as being those of Salisbury's predecessors as secretary of state 'as also some such other papers as he shall thinke fitt to depart with, being either such as he hath collected of his owne tyme or such as were left to him from his late father, the Lord Burghley' (Henry E. Huntington Library, Pasadena, CA, Ellesmere MS 2940).
3. Key works by R. B. Wernham include 'Elizabethan war aims and strategy' in S. T. Bindoff, J. Hurstfield *et al.* (eds), *Elizabethan Government and Society* (1961), pp. 340–68, a range of more narrowly focused essays, *The Making of Elizabethan Foreign Policy, 1558–1603* (Berkeley, 1980), *The Expedition of Sir John Norris and Sir Francis Drake to Spain and Portugal, 1589* (Navy Records Society, 127, 1988), and his 'Armada' trilogy: *Before the Armada: the Growth of English Foreign Policy 1485–1588*

(1966); *After the Armada: Elizabethan England and the Struggle for Western Europe, 1588–1595* (Oxford, 1984); and *The Return of the Armadas: the Last Years of the Elizabethan War Against Spain, 1595–1603* (Oxford, 1994).

4. Wernham joined the Public Record Office staff in 1930. and became an external editor for the *Calendar of State Papers Foreign* in 1932. He subsequently created and compiled the *List and Analysis of State Papers, Foreign Series*, covering the period from 1589 to December 1596. (1964–2000).

5. Wernham, *Return of the Armadas*, p. 37; idem, *After the Armada*, pp. 495–6.

6. P. E. J. Hammer, *The Polarisation of Elizabethan Politics: The Political Career of Robert Devereux, 2nd Earl of Essex, 1585–1597* (Cambridge, 1999), pp. 89–91, 324, 401. Cf. Wernham, *After the Armada*, pp. 419–20, 495–6.

7. H. G. Stafford, *James VI of Scotland and the Throne of England* (New York, 1940), passim; J. D. Mackie, 'The secret diplomacy of King James VI in Italy prior to his accession to the English throne', *Scottish Historical Review*, 21 (1923–24), pp. 267–82.

8. Doleman, *Conference*, sig. *2v-*3r. The author was almost certainly the Jesuit and ardent Hispanophile, Robert Persons: P. J. Holmes, 'The authorship and early reception of *A conference about the next succession to the crowne of England*', *HJ*, 23 (1980), pp. 415–29.

9. Ibid., pp. 426–7. See also A. J. Loomie, 'Philip III and the Stuart succession in England, 1600–1603', *Revue Belge de Philologie et d'Histoire*, 43 (1965), pp. 492–514.

10. Wernham, *Before the Armada*, pp. 346; idem, *After the Armada*, pp. 252–3, 256; G. D. Ramsay, 'The foreign policy of Elizabeth I' in C. Haigh (ed.), *The Reign of Elizabeth I* (1984), pp. 160–7; idem, *English Overseas Trade during the Centuries of Emergence* (1957), pp. 30–3, 108; T. H. Lloyd, *England and the German Hanse, 1157–1611: A Study of their Trade and Commercial Diplomacy* (Cambridge, 1991), ch. 6; W.-R. Baumann, *The Merchants Adventurers and the Continental Cloth Trade (1560s–1620s)* (New York, 1990), passim; J. K. Fedorowicz, *England's Baltic Trade in the Early Seventeenth Century* (Cambridge, 1980), esp. p. 35.

11. K. R. Andrews, *Elizabethan Privateering* (Cambridge, 1964), pp. 4–5. There was also a steadily growing illicit English trade with Spain in defiance of the official ban: P. Croft, 'Trading with the enemy, 1585–1604', *HJ*, 32 (1989), pp. 281–302.

12. Andrews, *Privateering*, p. 128.

13. Wernham, *After the Armada*, pp. 250–61; idem, *Expedition of Norris and Drake*, pp. lvii–lx.

14. J. S. Nolan, 'The militarisation of the Elizabethan state', *Journal of Military History*, 58. (1994), pp. 391–420.

15. G. Parker, *The Grand Strategy of Philip II* (New Haven, 1998), pp. 200–1, 212–13.

16. Wernham, *Expedition of Norris and Drake*, passim.

17. The attack was thwarted by Parma's illness, a mutiny by Spanish troops and news from France: Wernham, *After the Armada*, pp. 82–7.

18. This is best illustrated in letters from Sir Robert Cecil to Hatton, which are printed in P. E. J. Hammer (ed.), 'Letters from Sir Robert Cecil to Sir Christopher Hatton, 1590–91' in I. Archer (ed.), *Tudor Political Document. Camden Society* (2004).

19. H. A. Lloyd, *The Rouen Campaign 1590–1592: Politics, Warfare and the Early-Modern State* (Oxford, 1973); Wernham, *After the Armada*, chs 13–16.

20. Cecil to Hatton [13. September] 1591, University College, London, Ogden MS 7/41, fo. 31v.

21. A. G. Williams, 'The abjuration of Henry of Navarre', *Journal of Modern History*, 5 (1933), pp. 143–71; M. Wolfe, *The Conversion of Henri IV: Power, Politics and Religious*

Belief in Early Modern France (Cambridge, MA. 1993), esp. chs 6–8; Wernham, *After the Armada*, p. 488.

22. Burghley to Cecil, 4 September 1594, Cambridge University Library, MS Ee.iii.56, no. 26.

23. Wylkes to Thomas Edmondes, 20 September 1593, BL, Cotton MS Caligula E ix (i), fo. 181v.

24. Edward S. Tenace, 'Spanish intervention in Brittany and the failure of Philip II's bid for European hegemony, 1589–1598', Unpublished University of Illinois PhD dissertation, 1997, pp. 349–53; Wernham, *After the Armada*, pp. 550–2.

25. Ibid., pp. 552–4.

26. For Essex, see Hammer, *Polarisation*, passim.

27. S. L. Adams, 'The Protestant cause: religious alliance with the West European Calvinist communities as a political issue in England, 1585–1630'. Unpublished University of Oxford DPhil. dissertation, 1973, esp. chs 1–3; K. Duncan-Jones, *Sir Philip Sidney: Courtier Poet* (1991), passim; B. Worden, *The Sound of Virtue: Philip Sidney's Arcadia and Elizabethan politics* (New Haven, 1996), esp. chs 3–7.

28. J. G. Nichols (ed.), 'Journal of the siege of Rouen, 1591, by Sir Thomas Coningsby', *Camden Miscellany*, i (1847), pp. 13–22; E. M. Tenison, *Elizabethan England: Being the History of this Country 'in Relation to All Foreign Princes'* (12 vols in 13, pr. for subscribers, Leamington Spa, 1933–61), viii, pp. 401–13; M. Petitot (ed.), *Collection Complète des Mémoires Relatifs à l'Histoire de France* (52 vols, Paris, 1819–26), 40, p. 284.

29. Hammer, *Polarisation*, pp. 112, 153.

30. Ibid., pp. 154–5; idem, 'An Elizabethan spy who came in from the cold: the return of Anthony Standen to England in 1593', *Historical Research*, 65 (1992), pp. 280, 283.

31. Hammer, *Polarisation*, pp. 28–9.

32. Ibid., pp.175, 241, 309–10.

33. '... mon malheur a esté tel que Dieu n'aye jamais voulu permettre d'avoir veu l'Italie, le jardin de la Chrestienté, ...', P. E. J. Hammer, 'Essex and Europe: evidence from confidential instructions by the earl of Essex, 1595–6', *EHR*, 111 (1996), p. 381.

34. 'Suffer not thy sonnes to pass the Alpes', F. Peck, *Desiderata Curiosa: or, a Collection of Divers Scarce and Curious Pieces Relating Chiefly to Matters of English history* (2 vols, London, 1732–35), i, book i, p. 65.

35. Hammer, 'Essex and Europe', p. 369.

36. Hammer, *Polarisation*, pp. 178–80.

37. For Perez, see especially G. Ungerer, *A Spaniard in Elizabethan England: The Correspondence of Antonio Perez's Exile* (2 vols, 1974–76).

38. Hammer, *Polarisation*, pp. 165ff. See also, Chapter 8 by Doran in this volume, pp. 203–34.

39. For Wroth's reports, see PRO, SP 99/1, fos 23r–203v.

40. Hawkyns to Bacon, 17 [7] January 1596, Lambeth Palace Library (LPL), MS 655 fo. 237r.

41. Bacon to Hawkyns, 2 April 1596, ibid., MS 656, fo. 305r.

42. For Hawkyns and his work, see Hammer, *Polarisation*, pp. 181–4, 198, 253; idem, 'Essex and Europe', pp. 361–2; Ungerer, *Spaniard in Elizabethan England*, ii, p. 168.

43. Hatfield House, Cecil MS 140/70: undated draft in Essex's hand. This letter is enciphered in Cecil MS 140/71. I am grateful to the Marquess of Salisbury for permission to cite from the Cecil MSS.

44. William Camden, *The History of the most Renowned and Victorious Princess Elizabeth, late Queen of England* (4th edn, London, 1688: Wing no. C 363); Ungerer, *Spaniard in Elizabethan England,* ii, p. 234.

45. Edward Reynoldes to Anthony Bacon [December 1596], LPL, MS 660, fo. 214r: Wotton had left England before Essex's final fall and the destruction of his files may simply reflect the fact that they were neatly bundled up in Essex House, whereas other papers were still held in various offices and cabinets.

46. Hammer, 'Essex and Europe', 374.

47. Hammer, *Polarisation,* pp. 206–11.

48. H. Morgan, *Tyrone's Rebellion: The Outbreak of the Nine Years' War in Tudor Ireland* (Woodbridge, 1993), pp. 177–8, 180.

49. [Robert Devereux, 2nd earl of Essex], *An Apologie of the Earle of Essex, against those who Jealously, and Maliciously, Tax him to be the Hinderer of the Peace and Quiet of his Country* [1603]: *STC* 6788, sig. E1v.

50. Wernham, *After the Armada,* p. 557.

51. Instructions from Essex to Unton 23 December 1595, LPL, MS 652, fo. 264r–v.

52. Wernham, *Return of the Armadas,* p. 34.

53. J. L. Motley, *History of the United Netherlands from the Death of William the Silent to the Twelve Years' Truce* (4. vols, New York, 1900. edn.), pp. 377–9.

54. Hammer, *Polarisation,* pp. 187–9.

55. Tenace, 'Spanish intervention in Brittany', pp. 381–3; Wernham, *Return of the Armadas,* p. 32.

56. K. R. Andrews, *The Last Voyage of Drake & Hawkins,* Hakluyt Society, 2nd ser., 142 (1972), esp. pp. 15–17.

57. Wernham, *Return of the Armadas,* p. 25.

58. Hammer, *Polarisation,* pp. 250–1, 367–8.

59. Essex to Edward Reynoldes, 10 May 1596, LPL, MS 657, fo. 140r.

60. Wernham, *Return of the Armadas,* ch. 7; Hammer, *Polarisation,* pp. 250–5; J. S. Corbett, *The Successors of Drake* (1900), ch. 4.

61. Hammer, *Polarisation,* pp. 368–71.

62. Ibid., p. 362.

63. Morgan, *Tyrone's Rebellion,* pp. 206–13.

64. H. Kamen, *Philip of Spain* (New Haven, 1997), pp. 307–8; *CSPV* ix, p. 223.

65. Wernham, *Return of the Armadas,* ch. 9.

66. P. C. Allen, *Philip III and the Pax Hispanica, 1598–1621* (New Haven, 2000), p. 252, n. 13; Tenace, 'Spanish intervention in Brittany', p. 397. See also Chapter 7 by Pauline Croft, pp. 178–202.

67. Wernham, *Return of the Armadas,* ch. 5.

68. L. W. Henry, 'The earl of Essex as strategist and military organiser (1596–7)', *EHR,* 68. (1953), p. 372.

69. Ibid., p. 379; Hammer, *Polarisation,* pp. 264–6.

70. Corbett, *The Successors of Drake,* pp. 202–4; G. B. Harrison and R. A. Jones (eds), *A Journal of All that was Accomplished by Monsieur de Maisse, Ambassador in England from Henri IV to Queen Elizabeth, anno domini 1597* (1931), pp. 7–8.

71. Tenace, 'Spanish intervention in Brittany', pp. 414–24; Wernham, *Return of the Armadas,* pp. 184–5.

72. Ibid., pp. 198–201; Lloyd, *Rouen Campaign,* pp. 341; Baumann, *Merchant Adventurers,* pp. 16–17, 121.

73. Wernham, *Return of the Armadas*, pp. 200–1; N. G. Goodman, *Diplomatic Relations between England and Spain, with Special Reference to English Opinion, 1597–1603* (Philadelphia, 1925), pp. 7–8.

74. *De Maisse's Journal*, p. 62.

75. D. Palliser, *The Age of Elizabeth: England under the Later Tudors* (2nd edn, Harlow, 1992), pp. 43, 58–9, 220.

76. *De Maisse's Journal*, p. 113.

77. Essex to Cecil, 24 February 1598, BL, Lansdowne MS 86, fo. 55v.

78. Camden, *History*, p. 555.

79. Allen, *Philip III*, esp. pp. vii–xi.

80. Camden, *History*, p. 556.

81. This document survives in a large number of manuscript copies. A pirate printed edition appeared in 1600, but was suppressed. It was finally published in 1603 (see n. 46), quickly followed by an edition in Dutch.

82. HMC 9 *Salisbury*, viii, p. 545.

83. Other such partisan documents included his letter of travel advice to the earl of Rutland in early 1596, his abortive attempt to have a 'True relacion' of the victory at Cadiz published in late 1596 and his exchange of letters with Lord Keeper Egerton about a subject's duty of obedience in 1598.

84. J. C. Grayson, 'From protectorate to partnership: Anglo-Dutch relations, 1598–1644'. Unpublished University of London PhD dissertation, 1978, pp. 29; Wernham, *Return of the Armadas*, pp. 239.

85. Wernham, *Return of the Armadas*, p. 243.

86. Allen, *Philip III*, esp. p. 19; Loomie, 'Philip III and the Stuart succession', p. 494.

87. Wernham, *Return of the Armadas*, ch. 20; Goodman, *Diplomatic Relations*, ch. 5.

88. Wernham, *Return of the Armadas*, pp. 372, 413; Allen, *Philip III*, p. 72; J. J. Silke, *Kinsale: The Spanish Intervention in Ireland at the End of the Elizabethan Wars* (1970; Dublin, 2000 edn), esp. chs 7–8.

89. Ibid., chs. 9–11, C. Falls, *Elizabeth's Irish Wars* (1950), ch. 22; Wernham, *Return of the Armadas*, pp. 384–7.

90. H. S. Scott (ed.), 'The journal of Sir Roger Wilbraham, solicitor-general in Ireland and master of request, for the years 1593–1616', *Camden Miscellany*, x (1902), pp. 49–50.

91. BL, Lansdowne MS 86, fo. 55v.

92. J. Bruce (ed.), *Correspondence of King James VI of Scotland with Sir Robert Cecil and others during the Reign of Queen Elizabeth*, Camden Society, orig. series, 78 (1861).

93. N. Canny, 'The treaty of Mellifont and the re-organization of Ulster, 1603', *Irish Sword*, 9 (1969–70), p. 7.

94. Eg. *The Letters of John Chamberlain*, edited by N. E. McLure (2 vols, American Philosophical Society, Memoirs series, xii, 1939), i, p. 187; *CSPV*, ix, p. 557; PRO, SP 12/287, fos 50–2; T. Birch, *Memoirs of the Reign of Queen Elizabeth* (2 vols, 1754), ii, p. 506.

INDEX